SALLY SCULL AND TEXAS

BETTY NEWMAN WAUER

Copyright © 2023 Betty Newman Wauer.

All rights reserved. No part of this book may be reproduced, stored, or transmitted by any means—whether auditory, graphic, mechanical, or electronic—without written permission of both publisher and author, except in the case of brief excerpts used in critical articles and reviews. Unauthorized reproduction of any part of this work is illegal and is punishable by law.

ISBN: 979-8-89031-664-6 (sc)
ISBN: 979-8-89031-665-3 (hc)
ISBN: 979-8-89031-666-0 (e)

Because of the dynamic nature of the Internet, any web addresses or links contained in this book may have changed since publication and may no longer be valid. The views expressed in this work are solely those of the author and do not necessarily reflect the views of the publisher, and the publisher hereby disclaims any responsibility for them.

One Galleria Blvd., Suite 1900, Metairie, LA 70001
(504) 702-6708

ACKNOWLEDGEMENTS

Dozens of relatives and friends provided moral support for this undertaking. All of Betty's children and their families helped immeasurably. These included Bill and LeeAnn Nichols, Brad and Gina Nichols, Brent and Patricia Nichols, and Barry and Sharon Nichols. And several of Betty's grandchildren must also be thanked: Beau, Blake, Bradrick, Brandon, Clint, Dale, Elizabeth, Nathan, and Matt.

I am most grateful to Sharon for locating Betty's research materials, and to LeeAnn for providing several illustrations that are located within the various chapters.

ATTACHMENT 1:

Betty had admired her great great Aunt Sally Scull for all of her adult life, and had done considerable research into Sally's history. She discovered that most of what had already been written about Sally was inaccurate and had included many incidents that were incorrect and overly dramatic. Betty therefore wanted to present Sally as she actually was, a pioneer woman who lived an exciting life but also a life with losses and loves during a time when Texas was brand new. Sally's family and acquaintances included all of the ordinary people who eventually became extraordinary Texans. In a large sense, Sally Scull and Texas provides an insiders perspective of the beginning of Texas.

Betty's novel follows as closely as possible what is known of Sally's life. She touches on the major events of the time; although, telling the true story of Sally Scull was her intention. Betty's novel brings to life the story of a true Texas hero, a hero that also just happens to be a woman.

ATTACHMENT 2:

Betty's initial sketch of a cover is included, but she would have preferred a cover that might illustrate some of the early Texas history that was part of Sally's life. For instance, illustrations of the Alamo, the Fannin massacre, the Goliad canon, and the San Jacinto monument are pertinent. They might appear to be shaded in the background.

ATTACHMENT 3:

Betty Newman Wauer passed away in April 2013. She was a seventh generation Texan, and a member of both 'The Descendents of Austin's Old 300' and 'Daughters of the Republic of Texas.' She was extremely proud of her ancestors, especially the Texas Rabbs; she actually wrote a family newsletter titled 'The Texas Rabbs" for eight years with an average of 75 subscribers per year. She also wrote numerous articles and gave talks about those ancestors.

CHAPTER 1

Texas! It seemed it was in the air, all around, where you could almost touch it. That's what everyone talked about, all the time.

Sally was going to be six in a short time, and even though she thought she was pretty smart for her age, she couldn't really understand what was so important about this place called Texas.

She was sitting on the small front porch in front of their house, thinking about things. She'd like to go wandering around, but that wasn't allowed. There were too many Indians and unruly ruffians in the area. At least that's what Mama said. Besides, it was getting late and she'd soon have to go inside.

First, she thought she'd try to sort out this thing about Texas. Daddy said, 'We live just south of the Red River in Jonesborough. So we're in Spanish Texas.'

But Granddad had moved with Grandma, Uncle Tommy and Uncle Ulysses 'down into Texas' so Sally wasn't sure where Texas really was.

Everyone said it was big, and everyone seemed to want to go there. So she guessed she did too.

Granddad and Grandma had been gone for almost two years now. Mama said they left in 1821. It was hard for her to remember them. Daddy had been going back and forth to Granddad's place, staying gone for months at a time. Sally really missed him when he was gone, and was glad he was home now. She wished they'd decide to either move there or make this their permanent home. It wasn't so bad here. The river and the trees were pretty, and it was the only place she could remember living.

She was deep in thought when she heard Mama call her name. "Sally, pay attention. I've called you twice now. One more time and I'll get a switch."

"I'm sorry, Mama." she said. "I was thinking."

Sally went inside and started getting ready for bed. Daddy was out helping one of the neighbors and was going to be late. Sally knew that Mama was always restless until he got home, and hoped she could get her to talk awhile. She waited until the baby was asleep and then asked, "Mama, did you have to move around a lot? What was it like when you were six?"

For a minute she thought they'd all have to go to bed, but Mama looked at her and at the older children, and said, "I've told you these stories a hundred times, but I guess it won't hurt to talk awhile. At least until your daddy gets home."

Mama got the mending basket, pulled the rocker closer to the table and the lamp, and sat down. They all gathered around.

"What did you ask me? How in the world do you expect me to remember what it was like when I was your age." Then she laughed. Sally thought Mama looked pretty as she thought about that life.

"Pennsylvania is a beautiful part of the United States, and we had a nice home and everything we wanted." she said. "But more than anything else, the things that stand out the strongest in my childhood memories are of my Grandfather Rabb. He made a fortune from flourmills and whiskey distilleries.

"Mama." Mary said. "Would you start from the beginning tonight? It's not that late and you haven't told the whole story in a long time. Please."

"The whole story? You don't want me to start with when God was born do you?" And Mama laughed.

Sally loved the times when Mama was so happy. She thought it was probably because Daddy was back from Texas.

"Start with your Grandfather and Grandmother Rabb. Please." Mary said. And there were other "Please, Mama, Please."

"Oh, my word. That's a long time ago. I guess we can start but we may have to finish some other time. So, let's see. My grandfather's name was Andrew Rabb and he was born in eastern Pennsylvania in 1740. How many years ago is that, William?"

Sally was trying to subtract the years but that one was hard. It took William a few seconds but he said, "It was 83 years ago."

"Good." Mama said. "And my Grandmother Rabb, actually her name was Mary Scott before she married, was born in 1742, in the same area. She and Grandfather were married in Lancaster County, Pennsylvania. Soon after they married they moved to the western part of the state, which is Fayette County now."

At that point Minerva said, "Your daddy was their second child and his name is William Rabb and he married Mary Smalley, who is your mother." Sally and all the others frowned at her for interrupting.

Mama said, "That's right."

When she didn't say anything for a few minutes, Sally said. "Tell about the house. I like to hear about the house."

"Alright. That's a subject I like to talk about. Grandfather and Grandmother Rabb's home was a big brick house, two and a-half-stories tall, and the best thing about it was the view. It faced northeast toward a high cliff above Brown's Run. There were high hills on the south, east, and west sides. To stand on the porch and take in that beautiful scenery..."

She stopped in the middle of what she was saying and Sally thought, 'Mama is looking at that scenery right now. I wish I could see what she's seeing.'

Sally heard Mama sigh quietly then she started talking again. "Since my daddy was one of the oldest children, and I was his first born, I wasn't much younger than his youngest sisters. I spent so much time in that house. It was a wonderful time and place.

"I remember how sad it was for everyone though when Grandmother Rabb died. She died in 1798, when I was eight years old. Grandfather remarried about two years later to a young lady named Catherine Pentecost."

"That stuff just makes you sad. Tell us about him being in the Revolutionary War." William said.

"I bet your granddad has told you that a dozen times. Why don't you let me rest a few minutes and you tell us about that." Mama said.

Sally could tell that William was glad Mama had asked him to tell that part. She guessed a boy would rather talk about a war than people and houses.

"Granddad says that the Revolutionary War was a long time ago around 1776 and that's the war when we fought the British and won independence for America. Anyway, during that war his daddy recruited and equipped a company of mounted volunteers and served as Captain of the unit. They were known as the Westmoreland Rangers. Granddad also says that his daddy was a prominent distiller and played a significant part in the Whiskey Rebellion."

Sally listened as William carefully said, 'pro-mi-nent' and 'sig-nif-i-cant' and she thought, 'I wish I was as old as William.' But William was still talking so she started listening again.

"Grandfather Rabb was against the…"

"Excise law. It had to do with taxing the whiskey they made." Mama said.

"Yes, excise law. But Granddad says that after the first heated protest, his daddy thought it was wiser to oppose any violence that might cause him to lose any of his property. Granddad always smiles when he says that. He says Andrew Rabb was one shrewd man when it came to holding on to property. He says it's the Scotsman in him.

"Also great grandfather Rabb served as a judge in both Westmoreland and Fayette counties. Then he was murdered." William said the last with disgust.

"Oh, goodness." Mama said. "Let's don't go over that gruesome story again."

"But, you can't finish that part of the story if you don't tell what happened to him." Minerva said.

William started to say something but Mama butted in. "I'll tell this so we can make short work of it." She picked up another stocking to darn and said. "He was poisoned so that the house could be robbed while everyone was at the funeral. But the arsenic poison didn't work right away, and Grandfather didn't die for several months. He even went to Virginia to take some hot baths, hoping for a cure but nothing helped. He died there in 1804. Even though they knew who was guilty, they never caught him."

"I sure wish I could get my hands on him." said William. Then added, "Granddad says that's a terrible cowardly way to kill a man."

"I know. Daddy, your granddad, didn't hear about it in time to go see Grandfather Rabb before he died. Daddy had gotten his inheritance early, and we'd moved the year before. It's been so long ago, but it still makes me sad."

They were all quiet for a few minutes, then Mama said, "But, my childhood was mostly pleasant and I think it's time to get to bed now."

Very quickly Sally said, "Just a few more minutes, please. Tell us about your other grandparents."

All the other kids joined in, so Mama said, "Alright, but just for a few more minutes. Let's see. I know you all want me to tell about Grandfather Smalley being killed by Indians but I'm not going to start with that. Does anyone remember where Grandfather Benjamin and Grandmother Smalley were from?"

"I do." Louisa said. "They were born in a state named New Jersey that's right beside the Atlantic Ocean. Grandma Rabb says that her father and mother moved from New Jersey to near Fort Pitt, in western Pennsylvania, in 1764. That's sixty, uh fifty nine years ago."

William said, "Grandma says it was around 1772 or 1778, I forget, when her daddy was killed. She was just a little girl at the time. Her daddy and two other men were working in a field about a mile from the settlement. Her brother, William, was a boy at the time. He'd gone to take his father some water when a band of Indians attacked. The Indians killed the men and captured William and some other boys. Grandma says her brother William went through some awful things. They cut his ears, and…"

Mama said, "I think we can do without all the details tonight, William."

They were all quite for a few minutes and Sally thought, 'I'm thinking about those things anyway so I must not be doing without the details.'

Mama said, "Uncle William was held captive by the Indians for many years. My Mama said it was a terrible time for Grandmother

5

Smalley but then she eventually married again, to Archibald Henderson. Mama says it was a wonderful day when Uncle William escaped from the Indians and came home. It wasn't long after that when the Smalley and Henderson families moved to Columbia, near Fort Washington, Ohio.

"Of course, my mama was already married to my daddy by then, so she didn't go with the rest of her family. That was in 1797."

William said, "Grandma said that her brothers, William and Benjamin built a sawmill and a gristmill in Ohio. And William served as a hunter and a guide and he worked with the army as an interpreter in the expeditions against the Indians."

"That's right." Mama smiled. "Your daddy can be proud of how you always give the man's point of view on things."

Louisa asked, "How old were you when you moved from Pennsylvania?"

"Well, I was born in 1790, and we moved to Ohio in 1803, so how old was I, Sally?"

"You were 13!" Sally said.

Mama told them the years her brothers were born, Andrew in 1793, John in 1798, and Thomas in 1801, and had them tell her how old they'd been at that time. She was always using things like that to teach them.

"You didn't go to Ohio because your Grandmother Henderson went there, did you?" asked Louisa.

"No." Mama said. "My daddy and his brother, John, and others had made trips down the Ohio River and then on to the Mississippi River for years. That was the route the Rabb and Newman families used to take their flour and whiskey products to New Orleans to sell. They'd build flatboats with lumber cut in their sawmills, then use them to transport the flour and whiskey. When they reached New Orleans they'd not only sell the flour and whiskey, but also the lumber used to make the flatboats. Then they'd make their way back home.

"During those trips, they got to know the various areas they passed through and Daddy made up his mind to buy land in the Mississippi River valley. So, in 1803, our family along with some other families left Pennsylvania and started west.

"Grandmother Henderson and that side of the family already lived in Ohio. And some of my daddy's relatives lived there too, including his Uncle Samuel Rabb, so it was an ideal stop on the way west. Daddy stayed there a short time then he left us there and went on farther west to select the land for our home on the Mississippi River."

Mama's story was interrupted suddenly by Daddy's arrival outside. Sally could see that Mama was relieved to have him home.

After he put his horse up, he came in and appeared to be happy that some of them were still awake. He tousled each head, which didn't really make Mary and Louisa very happy, but Sally didn't mind any attention she got from him. Then he sat down to eat the stew and cornbread that Mama had heated.

"Daddy," Minerva said. "Mama was just telling us about her side of the family and about the families moving to Ohio. Will you tell us about it too?"

Mama said, "Now don't bother him, he's tired. It's time for you kids to get in bed."

"Let them stay up till I finish eating." said Daddy. "I was gone so long this year; I need to make up for lost time."

He ate a few bites then said, "Well, the Newmans and Rabbs have known each other for years, in Pennsylvania and other places. Some of both families were into milling, both sawmills and gristmills. My daddy was born about 1768, I think."

Minerva asked, "Did they know the Smalleys too?"

Daddy said, "I wouldn't be surprised if the Newmans and the Smalleys knew each other then. I know they knew each other in Ohio because they all lived in Warren County for a spell."

He didn't start talking again so Minerva got some hard looks from the other children. It was Louisa that said, "Tell us more about your family, Daddy."

"Well, I don't remember exactly when my mother and daddy were married. I guess it was before I was born." And he took a big bite and looked at Mama with a grin.

She said, "I guess that means it's my turn. My daddy was born in 1770 and mother in 1771, both in Pennsylvania. Mama and Daddy were married in 1789 in Fayette County."

"Tell us about when you left Pennsylvania, Mama." William said.

"Well, our particular Newman and Rabb families, along with some others, made our way from western Pennsylvania mostly by way of the rivers. We went by flatboats up the Monongahela River to the Ohio River and then along the Mississippi River. We stayed for a time with relatives in the Warren County, Ohio area."

Daddy never talked too much, and they liked hearing him, so they all waited patiently until he finished a few more bites of stew.

"I remember how much fun the trip was for me as a young man. I got to ride and hunt to my heart's content, and I loved seeing all that country. But I also remember how hard it was on my mother and the other women. The cold weather was really bad. We used packhorses and there were a number of times that we had to swim the horses across cold, swollen streams. My daddy and the other men made bark canoes to get the women and children across so they usually stayed dry. But each crossing was dangerous and terribly uncomfortable for them."

"Oh, I try to never think of any of that." Mama said to Daddy. "The worst time of that entire trip was when we had to wait so long to cross the Ohio River. I can't tell you how many times I cried and wished I were back at Grandmother Rabb's house under one of her big soft quilts. Or sitting in the great room in front of the fireplace smelling Grandfather Rabb's pipe."

"It was bad." Daddy said in answer to all the questioning looks he got. "The Ohio River was partially frozen and we had to wait a week before we could cross it. A number of times we had to wait for days at a time to cross some of the streams. We ran out of all kinds of things and it was a miserable time for the women but they were incredible; they just kept right on, and they made it through it all."

Daddy had stopped talking and Sally thought 'I bet he's thinking about his mother and daddy and missing them.' She hoped none of the others would say anything about that because if they did Mama would make them all go to bed so as not to make Daddy feel bad. She was glad to hear Mary ask about something different.

"Tell us about when you and Mama first fell in love." Mary said.

"You should ask your mama to tell you about that." Daddy answered, and he acted like he was really busy finishing his stew.

"I think it's a good idea for you to tell them about that." Mama said. "I believe I'd enjoy hearing your version."

Daddy said, "Well, after a short stay in Ohio, my daddy and your mama's daddy moved on. They left the families in Ohio to visit with relatives and rest some. They'd both chosen a piece of land on the east bank of the Mississippi River in Indiana Territory. That was in 1804, and they were two of the earliest pioneers in the Fort Russell area."

"Joseph." Mama said.

"I'm getting there." He said. "So while we were in Ohio I had time on my hands, and one day, I looked at your mama and was just thunder-struck. There she was the prettiest girl I'd ever seen. So, I asked her to marry me, and here we are."

Mama laughed and said, "I thought he'd never noticed I was alive, except to pester me. I'd been smitten with him for ages and he'd hang around helping my Daddy and not pay me any mind at all. And when he did take notice, he sure didn't just pop the question. He was shy and tongue-tied, and I thought I'd die of old age before he made a move."

They all looked back at Daddy and he said, "The day I fell in love with your mama was the best day of my life and every day just gets better." Then he shoved his chair back and said, "Ask your mama about the next few years and about us having all you little varmints."

Mama looked at him and smiled and he smiled back at her. They all knew this was his way of getting out of talking, and he liked to hear Mama tell the stories as much as they did.

William went over and pulled Daddy's boots off and Louisa went and got him his pipe and tobacco. The other children moved as close to him as they could.

As Mama picked up the dishes and cleaned the table, she said, "We got married in Warren County, Ohio, on June 12, 1806. There were so many Newman, Rabb, Smalley, and Henderson relatives living close by the church could just barely hold them all. Even though both our fathers were away at the time, it was a wonderful day.

"And our first child, Mary, was born in 1807." And she smiled at Mary. "Soon after that, our fathers returned, and our part of the Newman and Rabb families moved west. Now it's your turn again."

Daddy said, "Your Granddad Rabb bought land in St. Clair County, in Indiana Territory, in 1808, and more in 1809 about the time that area became Illinois Territory. Your two granddads were in a number of business ventures together and were both into milling. Your Granddad Rabb is a natural born miller."

"And your Granddad Newman, my daddy, can build just about anything from wood with almost no tools. He built a pole cabin when they first arrived there, then a real comfortable log house soon after that. He's a really good carpenter."

"You must take after him, Daddy." William said. Sally could tell that Daddy was pleased to hear that.

"Just a year or so ago, around 1819, he built a turning lathe. He's got a knack for building all kinds of things. But that's getting too many years past what we were talking about. So now it's your turn again." He said to Mama.

Mama nodded and said, "We had our first son, William Rabb Newman, in Illinois, in 1810, and my mama had my brother, Ulysses, that same year. And soon after that 1812 came along, and that was a big year. The Territorial Governor appointed my daddy Judge of the Court of Common Pleas for the county."

"That was about the time the area where we lived was changed to Madison County, Illinois." Daddy said.

Sally didn't know why the places changed names so much, but for some reason it seemed important to the grownups when they were telling stories. She asked, "That's why he's called a judge now, isn't it? And that was the year you were in the war too, isn't it?"

Daddy smiled at her and said, "Yes and yes."

"Why did they have that war, Daddy?" William asked.

"Well, the United States and Great Britain still had a lot of disputes so in June of 1812, the United States declared war on them. The war lasted for over two years, ended in a stalemate, but when it was over it assured our independence from Great Britain. It was just known as The War of 1812. I served in the Illinois Militia in Captain Samuel Judy's Company of Mounted spies and served for a short time with Captain James B. Moore's Mounted Company, then with Colonel Ferguson, and Major Stephenson. And my voice box is getting tired. It must be your mama's turn again."

"Well guess what else happened in 1812?" Mama asked.

Louisa looked happy and said, "I was born, and you named me Louisa."

Mama said yes, and it was probably time for bed now.

"No, no, not yet." said Minerva. "Sally and I haven't been born yet."

Everyone laughed, and Daddy told Mama, "You better hurry up before the three little ones wake up and we have to tell them about when they were born. We'll never get to bed."

William said, "Before Minerva was born Granddad built the biggest gristmill ever built, right? Tell us about that first."

"Good gracious! Alright. But its going to be the short version." said Mama. Then she turned to Daddy and said, "You know, you encouraged this so you tell them about the gristmill."

Daddy said, "Your Granddad Rabb got approval to erect a dam and gristmill on his land and in 1813 built a large four-story mill on Cahokia Creek. The mill had four burrs. A burr is a grinding stone. Anyway, it probably wasn't the biggest gristmill ever built, but it was huge and people from all over came to see it. Next time your Uncle John is around ask him about that mill. He can talk for hours and tell you everything about it.

"The next year, 1814, he was elected to represent Madison County in the Legislative Assembly of Illinois Territory and he attended sessions of the legislature during both 1814 and 1815."

"And that's where he met the Austins, right?" William asked.

"Yes it was. Your granddad's property was located a short distance away, across the river from where Moses Austin had a lead mining and smelting operation. Moses' son, Stephen, helped manage Moses' business interests and also served in the legislature of the Missouri Territory. Their home was close to St. Louis, in Missouri Territory, only a few miles from Kaskaskia, where the Illinois legislature met. Your granddad had an interest in lead ore leasing, so occasionally, when he went to the Illinois legislative sessions, he'd visit with the Austins."

William said, "And that's why we're here, because Granddad met Mr. Austin. Right?"

"Well, not totally." Daddy said. "Your granddad had already started looking for the next place with not so many people. So when Moses Austin started talking about the Spanish territory to the south, a number of people, including your granddad, starting thinking of the opportunities.

"Your grandma says she wished your granddad had never met another man with the same need to find the next wilderness to tame. But she also says it really wouldn't have mattered, William Rabb would've just kept going anyway. And as you know, we were here long before the Austin's had everything arranged."

Daddy stopped for a minute then continued, "But, we need to get these last two girls born so we can go to bed. And I believe that's your mama's job."

"Where were we?" Mama asked. Sally knew she was just teasing them and that she hadn't forgotten at all.

"It was in 1814, that the next blessed event occurred. Our little Minerva was born." Mama said. She looked at Sally and said, "And in 1817, you were almost a Christmas present. Both of you girls were born while we were still in Madison County, in Illinois Territory."

Mama added a bit more about when Minerva and Sally were born then said, "Now. No more. Shoo. Off to bed with the lot of you." And they could tell she meant it.

Sally always hated for the talk to stop, but she was sleepy. So she was glad to crawl in bed with the other girls. She thought about the three younger than her, Elizabeth, Thomas, and Ali. They'd all been born since they'd moved to Jonesborough.

Then she thought about Mama telling about when she was born. 'When we had Minerva, it made it three girls and only one boy. Your daddy told me that instead of all the pretty little dishwashers, he needed some more boys to help him with his chores. I told him I was going to teach these three girls to help me, so the next child, whether a girl or boy, would have to be the one to help him.'

Sally especially liked to hear Mama tell that story. Because, even though she was a girl Daddy called her his little helper.

Cause Mama and Daddy's next child had been her, Sarah Jane Newman, and they called her Sally!

CHAPTER 2

It was September and the weather had been very pleasant. But when they got up the next morning the sky was overcast and everything looked gray. Sally didn't like days like this; she liked the sun, and she liked warm weather.

Daddy had left early that morning to go help the neighbor again. Sally heard him tell Mama they needed to get the roof on the man's house before the weather turned bad. He'd probably be late again tonight.

Sally hurried through her household chores so she could go help William outside.

"Mama, can I go now?" she asked.

"Yes, but go straight to the barn." Mama told her. Then she stood at the door and watched until William waved from the barn to let her know that he had Sally with him.

Sally started gathering eggs while William finished milking.

She enjoyed being with him and the barn was one of her favorite places in the morning. She liked the smells and the sounds of the animals, especially the horses; she loved horses more than anything, other than her family.

She and William worked quietly for awhile, and then they heard the rain falling on the barn. William looked out, then said, "Come on, it looks like it's fixing to come down real hard. We need to get the milk in the house."

Sally ran toward the house, making sure she didn't break the few eggs she'd gathered.

William closed the barn and was right behind her. They got under the porch overhang just as the clouds turned loose.

"Mama, you want me to build up the fire?" William asked.

Mama said, "That's a good idea. It's really gotten colder."

The rain slowed down, but didn't seem as though it was going to quit. Mama got out the reader and the chalkboard, and started on their lessons.

As much as Sally loved horses, she hated schooling. She wished reading and writing had never been invented.

All of a sudden there was noise outside, and Daddy, Uncle John, Aunt Mary, and little Gum were making their way inside. "Since no work is going to get done in this downpour, I decided it was time for a visit." Daddy said.

He also said that Uncle Andrew and Aunt Margaret would be over soon. All three families lived close together and Mama loved it when her brothers and their families were around, so it would be a good day. Sally was very pleased when they were allowed to put the schoolwork away and join in the visiting.

After the older girls helped Mama get Daddy, Uncle John, and Aunt Mary a cup of coffee, and set out some bread and jam, they all found a place to sit. The house had two large rooms with a lean-to on the side. One room was for sleeping and the other for everything else.

Sally got Elizabeth, Thomas, and Gum, and put them on a quilt next to the door to the main room so she could play with them but still hear what the grownups talked about. Ali was almost a newborn, so was in a crib.

The grownups were talking and laughing when Uncle Andrew and Aunt Margaret arrived. Uncle Andrew let Margaret, who was expecting their first child, off right at the porch, and then took their horses to the barn. By the time he got back to the house he was soaked.

The six grownups talked about all kinds of things and then started talking about the people that lived in their area. Sally wasn't too interested in most of the people they talked about. But she listened when Aunt Mary and Aunt Margaret talked about their families, even though she already knew most of it

Sally knew that Aunt Mary's parents were John and Elizabeth Crownover and they were from North Carolina and had moved here just a couple of years ago. Aunt Mary said she was the fifth child of a family of eleven children and that she was born in 1805, in Buncombe County, North Carolina.

Aunt Margaret said, "Mary and I have a lot in common. We're almost the same age; I was born in 1805, in Warren County, Kentucky. And there are eleven children in my family too and I'm number three."

Sally knew about Aunt Margaret too. Her parents were William and Sarah Ragsdale. They came to the Red River area in May 1818, and settled in Jonesborough. Sally was half listening and playing with the little ones at the same time, when she thought, 'Both of the aunts said they were born in 1805 and my sister, Mary, was born in 1807. Mama is a lot older than them.'

She decided she'd ask Mama about ages someday, but Aunt Margaret had just said, "Mary and I've been talking about our families long enough. We want to hear more about this family we've married into, especially more about your mama and daddy."

Sally liked to hear about Granddad and Grandma so she started paying attention again. Mama, Uncle Andrew, and Uncle John, with Daddy adding a few details, went over some of the same things Mama and Daddy had talked about the night before.

Then Aunt Mary said, "Tell us again about when your daddy decided to move south toward Texas and sold that mill John liked so well."

"Yeah, Uncle John. Tell us about the mill, please." William said.

Uncle Andrew answered quickly before Uncle John had a chance, "Well, young William. You came close to never getting to know your Uncle John. Cause poor old John was so upset about leaving that four-story mill that I thought he was just going to stay there with it."

"Let me tell you, that was a real work of art. I'm still not sure Daddy made the right decision when he sold it." Uncle John said.

"Sure he did. Daddy sold that first property in Illinois in 1817 and the rest of it along with the gristmill the next year and made a sizable amount of money from it. You can't say he didn't make the right decision; you just wanted to keep that big mill." Uncle Andrew said.

Uncle John described the mill for William then turned to Uncle Andrew and ended with, "I'm going to have a big mill like that one of these days and if you're somewhat agreeable I might grind some flour for you."

Uncle Andrew grinned at him then looked at Aunt Margaret and continued, "It was the summer of 1818, about the same time your family got here, that our entire family moved to this area, to Clear Creek. But, Daddy already had his sights set on the next move. This was just a stopover."

Sally knew that Clear Creek was the name of the settlement on the other side of the Red River, in Arkansas Territory.

Mama joined in the conversation. "My mama and I tried to make our homes as comfortable as possible under the circumstances, but we knew we'd be moving again. It's been a part of life for so many years. We should be used to it, but it's a hard way to live. Just as you get to know your surroundings, make friends with your neighbors, and get a garden in, the men are ready to make the next move. The only thing that kept us from being unhappy was that most of the family was still together. But it didn't stay that way."

Daddy said, "That's right, and after we got to Arkansas, your mama started worrying about her boys. She knew Andrew and John were getting sweet on two pretty girls in the area, and she was afraid when they got married they might not stay with the family."

Mama said, "She told me real often how thankful she was that you joined us, and hadn't kept me from moving with her and daddy."

Daddy looked at Uncle Andrew and winked and said, "She shouldn't have worried. I'd leave Rachel before I'd leave William Rabb and all these adventures and new places." Then he laughed and dodged the dishcloth that Mama threw at him.

"Well," said Uncle Andrew "Mama doesn't have to worry. I think the whole community is going to head south sooner or later."

"Daddy sure wasn't going to wait around for someone to tell him where or when he could move." Uncle John said.

"No he wasn't." Uncle Andrew agreed. "He was certain the United States and Spain were going to agree on the Colorado River in Texas as the dividing boundary between the two countries, and he wanted his land on that River."

He turned to Aunt Margaret and continued, "You know the United States and Spain had been negotiating on the boundary since 1817. But at the beginning of 1819, the United States agreed to give up its claim to the territory south of the Red River. So that treaty meant Texas was still Spanish property."

Uncle John added, "That didn't sit at all well with Daddy. He had some choice words for the United States government."

Uncle Andrew stood up, shook his fist in the air, and with an intense look on his face and with a slight Scottish accent said, "I'm going to have that piece of land on the Colorado River. Hang the government, both of them."

They all laughed and Mama said, "You sounded exactly like him."

Daddy said, "He doesn't mince words, does he? I guess no one was surprised when he started making trips south."

Sally listened as the men talked for awhile about Granddad, Daddy, and her uncles making a number of what they called "exploratory trips" in both 1819 and 1820, into the south-central part of the province of Texas.

Then they got on the subject of how bad things had gotten across the river. Uncle Andrew said, "Things are even worse now than they were three years ago when we lived there. If a family is away from home for even a short time, the Indians or some unsavory characters will break in and take everything they have."

Uncle John said, "That's one of the reasons Daddy had us all move here to this side of the river. And it is a little better here, especially with us all living so close together."

"It's still practically lawless though and getting worse all the time. But we all know that the main reason your Daddy wanted to be on this side of the Red River is that he knew we'd for sure be in Spanish Texas." Daddy said.

They were all nodding in agreement when Uncle John said, "Speaking of unsavory characters, I remember when Joseph decided to take a hand against that one no-account."

Sally had heard the story before, about when Daddy had gotten into trouble. It was hard for her to believe that her daddy could have beaten a man up, but that was the story. She wasn't sure what it meant, but Daddy had been indicted in the court for assault and battery.

Uncle John and Uncle Andrew had gotten up and were going round-and-round; acting like they were throwing punches at each other. Everyone was laughing.

Mama finally told them, "Alright, you two. Stop it. You'll make the children think that's the way to solve problems, and fighting never settled anything."

Uncle Andrew said, "Well, it sure settled that problem!"

Mama changed the subject. "There were good things that happened in 1820. That's when we had Elizabeth, and when John and Mary were married."

Sally had already begun to notice that when the subject of babies being born, and marriages and such were discussed, the men soon lost interest. The three women, and Mary and Louisa remained in front of the fireplace, and the men and William moved closer together near the end of the table.

Minerva had come over and was playing with the little children, so Sally went and sat on the stool behind Daddy, trying not to be noticed. But Daddy looked around, grinned at her, and motioned her to bring the stool up next to his chair.

Uncle Andrew was talking about the people living on the south side of the Red River instead of across the river in Arkansas Territory. "I figure when the Arkansas Territorial government made everyone mad by trying to collect taxes from this side of the river, that worked right into Daddy's plans."

"I'm sure you're right." Daddy said. "Since they didn't provide any security or any services to us, your daddy told them they could just forget collecting taxes. I've told them the same thing."

Uncle John said, "And because he thought that tax was totally unfair, he figured he had his reason to go ahead with his move to the Colorado River."

The mention of the move to the Colorado River changed the direction of the conversation. Now they were talking about the Austins.

Sally didn't understand much of what they were talking about, but she'd noticed that William listened carefully, so she decided she would too.

William asked, "Do you think if Moses Austin had known about all these problems he'd still have wanted to come to Texas?"

Daddy said, "Well, Moses had major financial trouble in St. Louis. His lead mining interests were way down and his banking venture had failed. So he developed this plan to establish an Anglo-American colony in the Spanish province of Texas, with himself as empressario. He planned on charging each colonist a land settlement fee. So yes, I believe he'd have come to Texas, problems and all."

Sally said, "Daddy, can I ask a question?"

"Sure, Honey." He said.

"Did Moses Austin ever get to come all the way to Texas?" She asked.

It was Uncle Andrew that answered. "He sure did, Sally. Moses rode 800 miles to the town of San Antonio. That's a long way from here even. He got there in December 1820. That's when he asked for permission from the Spanish government to settle colonists in the province. He didn't have any luck with the Spanish governor though until he met an acquaintance, Baron de Bastrop. With the Baron acting as his agent, he managed to get the Governor's endorsement of his plan. Then the plan was sent on to the higher-up authorities and he headed back home."

Daddy continued the story. "The trip home to Missouri took about four weeks. For pretty much the whole trip he was in cold, wet weather and without enough food. He contracted pneumonia. Even though he was sick, he must've felt like he'd accomplished what he'd set out to. Because he learned that on January 17, 1821, permission had been granted for the colony."

Uncle John added, "Moses Austin spent his last strength on this Texas venture. He lived only a few months more. We heard he died around the middle of June. I guess one of his last requests was to his son, Stephen. He asked him to finish what he'd started in Texas."

"After hearing the news about Moses' death, everyone in the settlement was sad about it. Daddy said it was hard for him not to feel guilty about Moses. He said he felt the loss of a friend, but was also worried about what was going to happen to our chances for land." Uncle Andrew said.

"He sure was pleased when he heard that Stephen had promised his father he'd carry on the settlement of the colony." Daddy said.

"It's easy to admire Stephen." Uncle John said. "You know he settled in the Arkansas Territory in 1819, and right away became a representative in the Arkansas legislature. I don't know what he wanted to do with his life, but he dropped everything and went about doing what his father had requested of him."

"Granddad got to go with him to pick out the land, didn't he?" William asked.

Uncle Andrew said, "He sure did. But before that Stephen went to San Antonio and got the authorization to carry on the colonization under his father's grant. That was in August '21. He was given the terms and restrictions and permitted to survey the land between the San Antonio and Brazos rivers; so he could select the site for his colony. Stephen and a small group of Americans, including your granddad, explored the area and decided that the most impressive region was between the Colorado and the Brazos rivers. Then Stephen returned to New Orleans, published the terms, and invited colonists to apply. The settlements would be located on the Colorado and Brazos rivers."

Daddy said, "I thought it was interesting how much respect your daddy had for Stephen after the exploration trip. He sounded like he thought Stephen might be able to accomplish even more than Moses could, and that's high praise coming from him."

"I never saw Daddy as excited as he was when he got back from that trip with Stephen." Uncle John said. "He'd marked off the exact site he wanted, and he went to work to get it."

Uncle Andrew said. "And nothing short of death is going to keep him from getting it either. I hope those Mexicans know what they're up against when they take the old man on. It was the summer of '21 that he wrote the letter to the Spanish Governor of Texas, wasn't it?"

"Yes it was." Daddy said. "You know his intent was to let the Governor know that he planned on moving to a location on the Colorado River with Stephen Austin. He told the Governor that he expected to move his family and goods there that autumn. And that's exactly what he did. But when I carried that letter to San Antonio I thought we'd all relocate with him. I know he was right about the children being safer here until the land grants are guaranteed. But, he can sure be a stubborn old codger."

The women had been listening to the men for the last few minutes, and at this point Mama got up and asked if anyone would like another cup of coffee. Most all the grownups said yes, so she put on a fresh pot.

Sally had heard most of all that had been said, especially the stories about the time when her grandparents left. It had been in the fall of 1821. Granddad loaded as much as he could on horses, gathered some of their stock and headed toward the Colorado River. Grandma and their two youngest, Uncle Thomas and Uncle Ulysses, went with him, leaving the rest of them to wait until a later time.

Mama said, "The day they left us was one of the hardest days of my life. I could barely see them through my tears, but I watched until I could no longer see even a speck. The last view I had of my mama was her sitting on the horse with her body bent over almost on the horse's neck."

"I was at a loss as to how to comfort you." Daddy said.

They were all quiet a few minutes then he continued, "One of those times I was down there, your daddy and I got to talking about when they'd left here. He said it was the first time in years that he thought he'd maybe gone too far for your mama. He said he almost turned everything around and went back. But of course he didn't. And, being the woman she is, your mama cried her tears, wiped them away, and got on with taking care of things. She's as strong a person as he is."

"Yes she is." Mama said. "I don't know how long I cried when they left, but with all these children to care for you have to get past it. We've sure stayed busy since then. John and Mary were married around the same time they left, and then Andrew and Margaret married the next year. Both of you were pretty smart I might add."

Uncle Andrew and Uncle John both made a mock bow.

Mama continued, "And our Thomas was born in 1821. I finally had another boy for Joseph."

"Yes, that was great." Daddy said. "William was eleven when Thomas was born and he was so happy to finally have a brother. I had to watch him because he wanted to put Thomas on a horse before he could even sit up on the floor."

Mama looked at Uncle John and added, "And everyone got to celebrate with John and Mary when they had Gum."

"Zebulon Montgomery Pike Rabb, I'll have you know." Uncle John added.

Sally had been thinking about Gum's real name when she realized that the grownups had moved away from talking about babies. They were now talking about how they'd worried about Granddad, Grandma, and the two boys after they' d first moved away.

"I was so relieved when we got the first message from them." Mama said.

"How long was it before you heard anything?" Aunt Margaret asked.

Uncle Andrew said, "It was just a few months. A man in the settlement brought a very welcome letter from Daddy. The news was mostly good as far as their health. But they were having constant troubles with Indians and the bad rumors about the land situation was worrying Daddy. At the time he wrote the letter, he didn't know anything further than that.

"The next letter we got from him was quite a while after that. He said that Stephen had arrived at the Colorado sites in January a year ago, and learned of the rumors of a change in government in Mexico City. Daddy and some of the other settlers went with Stephen as far as San Antonio to find out what was happening. They learned that the Spanish government had been overthrown, and the area was now in the hands of the Mexicans. So Stephen left immediately for Mexico City."

Daddy said, "At first the Mexican government refused to honor the Spanish grant to Moses. It wasn't until January '23, this year, that the authorization was granted. Then there was another change in the Mexican leadership and that authorization was annulled. It's been one of the most frustrating times I've ever gone through. I can't imagine how Stephen feels. He's surely wanted to quit this whole thing more than once."

"I'd think so too, but there'd sure be some disappointed people if he did." Uncle Andrew said.

"We got the letter just last week from daddy saying that finally, in April, Stephen succeeded in getting a contract to settle three hundred families in Texas." Uncle John said.

"So here we wait, but not for long I'll wager." Uncle Andrew said. "Knowing Daddy he's more than impatient about when he's going to get all his family settled on the Colorado River."

The conversation was broken up when baby Ali started crying and woke Gum, so that Mama and Aunt Mary had to nurse them.

Uncle John got up and walked over to Aunt Mary and gazing down at his wife and son, said, "Well, we could finish all our reminiscing by just concluding that this year was just about babies, babies, everywhere."

Uncle Andrew put his arm around Aunt Margaret and Sally wondered if they were thinking about their baby too.

Daddy said, "Well, Rachel and I are old hands at this, so we can sit back and enjoy the obvious pride of John and the anticipation of Andrew."

Mama said, "Yes, and it sure is funny watching my husband and my brother strut around and brag about their sons. You'd think they did it all by themselves."

Aunt Mary and Aunt Margaret both agreed with her, and the three men just grinned.

Sally really loved her new little brother, but she couldn't figure out what was so great about boys.

It was warm and cozy in the house and Mama and Aunt Mary soon had the two little ones back to sleep. The other small children were napping, so Sally got up quietly and went and stood by Daddy. He pulled her up to sit on his knee, and the timing was perfect cause that's when Uncle John got Daddy in trouble with Mama.

They'd been talking about Texas as usual and especially about the things going on where Granddad had located. Uncle John had just said, "Were the Indians that nearly killed you that time different than the tribes we see around here?"

There was total silence in the house, and everyone was looking from Mama to Daddy. Sally didn't know what was going on, but saw Mama's face change to that look she got when one of them had done something that displeased her.

Uncle Andrew looked at Uncle John like he'd made a big mistake, and Uncle John started stammering and trying to change what he'd said, but it was too late.

Mama said, "Joseph Newman, what's John talking about, and don't you try to get around the subject. What haven't you told me? What happened?"

Daddy said, "Aw, Rachel, it wasn't anything. John's got the story mixed up."

By then, Mama was standing in front of him with her hands on her hips.

Uncle Andrew laughed and said, "You might as well tell her the truth, Joseph, cause she's not going to leave you alone until you do. Besides, she'll hear it sooner or later. You might as well tell it like it really was."

"I guess you're right." Daddy said. "Sit down, Rachel, and just remember that I'm here and I'm safe and sound. You know I don't like to worry you. I truly was going to tell you about it one of these days."

Mama sat down and said, "Then go on and tell me. And tell it like it happened!"

"Well, you know it wasn't long after Christmas, just at the start of this year when you were so worried about your folks. I'll admit that I probably took advantage of your feelings because I wanted to make another trip to find out what was happening about the land. But I was worried about your folks too.

"Leaving you and the kids again was hard to do, but with Andrew and John nearby I didn't have to worry about you staying safe. And a few of the other men in the settlement were going with me, so I didn't think I was in much danger either.

"It was a great trip and when I got there and your folks were doing so well, it seemed like a good idea to stay awhile. That's when we sent word back with those men from across the river. Anyway, I stayed with your folks awhile, helped them clear some land and do some building. But the Indians had gotten much worse; they were stealing everything they could get their hands on.

"Two of the settlers in the area, John Tumlinson and Robert Kuykendall, got permission from the Mexican governor to raise a small company of men to range between the houses and settlements. The idea was to try to protect the settlers and their property from the Indians and the bandits.

"I joined the company and we were staying at an area called Camp Rascal. All of us were getting low on ammunition, so one day in July the company captain, Morrison, asked John and me to go to San Antonio for some powder and lead.

"We saw signs of Indians all along, even saw a few, but nothing threatening until we were nearing the Guadalupe River. There were three Waco Indians by the river and they were acting real friendly. I'd heard about them doing this and then taking advantage of the situation, so I didn't trust them at all. I warned John to keep his distance and keep riding, but he didn't."

He hesitated for a long moment then continued. "One of those savages offered his hand to John. As John reached out to shake his hand, the Indian jerked him from his horse and killed him. I could tell he was dead before he hit the ground.

"The next few minutes seemed real long. I had to fight to keep on my horse. He was trying to get away from the Indians and almost succeeded in getting away from me too. The Indians chased me maybe six miles before they gave up. I believe the only thing that saved me was that I was already on my horse, and they had to get on theirs. It was that close."

Daddy finished the story by saying, "I had to tell his kin that John was dead. That was a hard thing to do. There are a mess of those Tumlinson men and boys, and I tell you true, that's one settler those Indians are going to regret killing."

Everyone was quiet. Then Mama let out a long held breath, got up and said, "Well, I think it's time to think about fixing some supper."

Daddy gave Sally a kiss on the head, put her down, and went and gave Mama a hug. She hugged him too, then hit him hard on the upper arm.

It was still raining, and Sally hoped the other families would just spend the night. That way they could all visit and listen to the grownups tell some more stories. She watched the little children again, while her two aunts and the three older girls helped Mama cook some bacon, gravy, and cornbread. After supper Sally stayed awake as long as she could, but finally fell asleep to the sounds of happy voices.

Not long after that visit, the day they'd all been looking forward to finally arrived. Early one afternoon, Granddad and Uncle Tommy came riding into the yard.

Sally was surprised to see Mama act almost like a little girl. She cried and laughed and held on to Granddad and asked a dozen questions at once. "How's Mama? How's Ulysses? Are you all right? Are you hungry? How are you, Tommy? Are you hungry?"

Granddad laughed too and said, "We're fine, Rachel. We left your mama and Ulysses in good health. They sent their love. And I'm not very hungry, but your brother can eat a horse nearly anytime."

"Where's Joseph and the boys?" asked Uncle Tommy.

"Oh my word. I'm not thinking at all." Mama said.

And then she started issuing orders right and left. She told William to go tell Daddy, Uncle Andrew, and Uncle John that Daddy and Uncle Tommy were here. Then she started telling Mary and Louisa to get supper started.

"Wait a minute, Rachel. At least let me say hello to my grandchildren before you send them off doing things." said Granddad.

Sally watched him closely as he talked for a few minutes with William and then the older girls before they went to do what Mama had told them to do.

When he turned to her he looked right in her eyes and said, "You've got to be Sally."

"I don't know if I've got to be Sally, but I am." she answered.

Granddad gave her a big smile and said, "Well, you were just a bit of a girl when I left, but even then you looked directly at a person. Just like you do now. I'm glad to see you again, Sally." And he gave her a hug and then went to see the younger children.

Sally watched him for a few minutes then looked around and saw Uncle Tommy looking at her. She felt kind of shy all of a sudden.

He grinned and came over. He put his hand out and she took it. He shook her hand and said, "I'm glad to see you, Sally. I've heard a lot about you."

"Who would tell you about me?" she asked.

"Well, your Daddy talks about you a lot. Seems they use some of the same words to describe you that they use on me. You seem awful young to already be thought of as strong-headed and tough. Guess you and I'll have to get better acquainted. We may need to sympathize with each other once-in-a-while."

He patted her on the head and walked over to where Granddad and Mama were talking.

Sally knew she was going to like Uncle Tommy, but she wasn't sure what to think about him calling her tough. That's what Mama always said about the times and the old rooster. Oh well, she'd have to think about that later, because William, Daddy, and the others were hurrying into the yard.

There were hugs all around and lots of questions again and Sally thought she saw tears in Granddad's eyes. Then she thought she saw tears on most of the other faces too, even Daddy's. She guessed they were really glad to see each other.

It was a noisy, exciting evening. At times, it seemed to Sally that all the grownups were talking at once. Poor Granddad didn't get a minute's peace until they all finally went to bed.

By the next morning, all the grownups could talk about was getting everyone and everything ready for the move to Granddad and Grandma's place on the Colorado River. They were all worried about Grandma and Uncle Ulysses but they were still real excited too.

By late afternoon the next day, many of the neighbors, and some people they didn't even know, had stopped by to ask Granddad about what was happening in Texas. After being interrupted a number of times the men finally quit working and just started visiting.

Granddad sat on the front porch and people just sat on whatever they could find, all as close to him as they could get. Sally thought it was strange that so many people could be so quiet. Even the children seemed to know that this was a special time as Granddad told them about the situation in Texas.

"Well, some of you already know all I know." Granddad began. "And most of you know parts of it. But I've been asked so many questions last night and today that I can't keep up with who knows what, so I'll just start from when Stephen Austin got back from Mexico City.

"That was in August. Stephen went to Castleman's house, and Sylvanus got word around that Stephen was there. Sylvanus Castleman is a neighbor of ours, on the Colorado. Stephen spent a little more than a year of delay and frustration in Mexico City and from hearing him tell about it I knew he had a rougher time of it than we did.

"But it was almighty hard on us settlers not knowing what was going on with Stephen or what was happening with the land situation. Finally the Mexican government approved the contract in April and the fact is that the new contract is even more favorable than the old one. Each family will get a league of land; that's over 4,400 acres and single men will get at least a quarter of that."

Granddad had to stop talking because at least half the men were asking if they'd heard right.

"You heard right." Granddad said with a big smile. "A league of land."

Uncle John said, "All this sounds like the stories Cousin Freeman Smalley, the preacher, tells about the children of Israel going into the promised land, '…a good and spacious land flowing with milk and honey…'"

There were murmurs of agreement and Sally heard a number of people say 'Amen.'

In answer to a question, Granddad said, "I think the trip will take almost three months for a large group that includes women and children. There aren't any roads, only trails. Most families will have a small herd of cattle and that'll slow you down some. We plan to use our horses to transport the family members and our belongings. I'd suggest anyone traveling do the same.

"Along the way, you'll be able to gather honey, and there ought to be some wild grapes still around. There are pecan trees along the creeks. Deer, turkey, ducks, and other wildlife are plentiful, just like around here. No one should go hungry."

Granddad told them more about the land and the settlers that were already in Texas and the talk and questions went on for hours. Finally with his voice hoarse and looking obviously tired he said, "It was right after the visit with Stephen, that we got everything set as good as possible for my wife, Mary, and youngest son, Ulysses. Then Tommy and me headed out to get the rest of my family.

"I can tell you I'm anxious to get back to my home. I'll be glad to talk some more later, but for now, I've talked myself out." And he got up and walked into the house.

Sally had enjoying hearing Granddad talk, but she was tired too. She was surprised that Mama had let her stay up this late. As she crawled into bed with the other girls she could still hear the excited, but quiet voices of the people in the yard. She fell asleep thinking about all Granddad had told about the beautiful area that was now his home, and soon to be her home too.

They were ready to go; ready to leave Jonesborough for the Rabb home on the Colorado River. Sally looked around and counted all her family to make sure they were all there. She thought, 'There's Granddad and Uncle Tommy. Daddy and Mama are here with Mary, William, Louisa, Minerva, me, Elizabeth, Thomas, and Ali. Over there Uncle Andrew and Aunt Margaret are on their horses, and Uncle John, Aunt Mary, and little Gum are right beside them. So all my family is ready.'

A man named James Gilleland and his family, a young man named John Ingram, and a few other people were also traveling with them. But Sally decided that she had enough family members to worry about so those other people would just have to worry about themselves.

Sally looked at her mama and daddy and her uncles and could see how excited they were. Then she looked at Granddad.

He had the most satisfied look on his face and she thought, 'I think my Granddad Rabb is taking his family exactly where he wants us all to be. Texas!'

CHAPTER 3

Sally thought the trip would never end. At first it had been fun, like going out on a hunting trip or something, but she'd hated not having a real home at night.

As the weeks passed it had gotten harder. The grownups were tired and worried about Indians and weather and food and everything else it seemed to her. She and the other children tried their best to not displease any of the grownups so as not to get one of those tired grumpy looks.

The only fun times were when something unusual happened. Like the day they found some wild grapes. There were vines all over the place and they stayed an entire day there and nearly all of them gathered and ate grapes. They kind of made your mouth pucker, but they still tasted good.

On another day, Uncle Andrew discovered a tree with bees bussing around it and they all stopped and the men built a fire and smoked the bees away and gathered the honey. Everyone had all the honey they could eat and it was wonderful.

Those times didn't last very long though and it was just ride and ride some more. It was at the end of one of those long days that Sally heard Daddy talking with the other men about the cattle. Some of them had started getting sick. She hoped that wouldn't mean they had to stop, because as much as she hated riding every day, she wanted to keep going. She was ready to get to where they were going.

Uncle Tommy and another man volunteered to stay with the cattle drive them slowly and let them rest more often. No one wanted to do it that way, but that was what was finally decided. As they drew further away from them that next day, Sally kept looking back and wondering about Uncle Tommy. She hoped he'd be all right.

Then one evening, a night or two after leaving Uncle Tommy, Granddad said, "You know what?"

And a number of people said, "No, what?"

With a big smile on his face, Granddad answered, "We're only three days from home."

Everything changed. Sally couldn't believe the difference. The grownups laughed and teased each other and she must've gotten her head patted a dozen times. No one was grumpy at all. She kept count of the days and sure enough three days later they arrived at the Colorado River.

They all got off the horses and everyone went to the edge of the river and just stood there for the longest time. It was really pretty but the water looked swift and scary. She hoped they wouldn't have to cross it. She looked all around for Grandma and the house and didn't see anything but trees and the River.

As she looked at Granddad he turned and saw her. "Come here, Sally girl."

She went to him and said, "We're at the Colorado River now, but where's your house, Granddad?"

"Well, the house is a little less than a mile from here, on the other side of the River. And even though the old Colorado looks high and fast, we aren't going to have any trouble getting across."

He asked all the others to gather around and said, "We left Jonesborough on the first of October and it's now the fifteen of December. Our journey took two and a half months. I'm real proud of the whole bunch of you. Now why don't you boys let your mama and brother know we're here." And Uncle Andrew and Uncle John aimed their rifles skyward and fired in a prearranged sequence.

Sally thought Mama would just walk across that river; she was that excited about Grandma being so close. With Daddy carrying baby Ali and riding on one side of Mama, and Granddad with little Thomas, and riding on the other side of her, they made it across. Mama waited on the other side with Ali and Thomas while Daddy and Granddad came back across to help the other children.

Uncle John carried Gum and rode beside Aunt Mary; and Uncle Andrew rode close to Aunt Margaret. It didn't take too long and all the family and the horses and their belongings were safely across the river. Sally was watching the last horse come up out of the river when she heard Mama cry out. She turned around in time to see Mama running toward the two horses coming down the hill toward them.

Granddad started to walk that way too, then stopped. He took out his kerchief and blew his nose and acted like he had to check something on his saddle. But Sally knew he was trying not to show what he was feeling. When she saw his face she knew how worried he'd been about Grandma and Uncle Ulysses. She guessed the trip had been a lot longer for him than it had been for her.

Mama was walking along beside the horse, holding onto Grandma's hand and they were both laughing and crying. It was Granddad that helped Grandma off her horse. The two of them stood and looked at each other for a long moment then everyone was hugging each other and laughing and talking all at once. Other than the concern Grandma showed when she discovered that Uncle Tommy wasn't with them, it was a wonderful time.

They just kept visiting and talking and Sally thought they'd just stay here beside the river until it got dark. And she really wanted to see where they'd live. Finally Granddad said, "Well, I think we'd better be getting on to the house before the Indians decide we built it for them."

Sally was kind of shy around Grandma at first, but she'd never gotten so many hugs. Each time any of them got within arms length of Grandma they got a hug. She'd laugh and say, "I'll quit all this pretty soon, but I'm just so relieved to see you." Then she might just hug you again. The hugs were full of love, so Sally didn't mind them at all and soon forgot about being shy.

Grandma and Granddad's house was very snug and comfortable for four people, but it was too small for the entire family. So all the men went to work immediately and within a week they'd built another room on the house. This was a big room and would be used by Sally's family. The men planned on building smaller rooms for Uncle Andrew and his family, and Uncle John and his. All the families shared the common space.

Sally thought the place Granddad had chosen was really pretty, but mostly all she saw were trees. The area was called Indian Hills, which everyone thought was appropriate. The Indians were so bad that one to two men had to be on watch at all times. William was thirteen, and so was Ulysses, so most often they were the daytime lookouts. Uncle Tommy got home with the rest of the cattle about a week after the family had arrived and he and the other men took turns at night guarding the area.

Daddy warned them to always be watchful. "The Indians probably won't take us on when we're together and ready for them, but they're always on the lookout for catching one or two individuals away from the group. So under no circumstances are any of you to be by yourself. You hear me, William?"

"Yes, sir. I hear you." William answered.

"You girls can go out in the little yard area in front of the house, but only if there are grownups that know you're there. And Rachel, even when you're just out for a few minutes you keep a close watch. You hear?"

"Yes, Joseph. I know to be careful."

The only time Sally could stay out and watch Daddy work on something was when he was working close to the house. She wasn't allowed to get but a few feet from him and at the slightest sound he'd grab his rifle and tell her to go to the house. And that's where she and all the children spent most of their time, in the house.

At first Sally enjoyed doing some little chore or other and listening to the women talk. Mama said she and Grandma had two years to catch up on. And Grandma had to get acquainted with her two new daughters-in-law and her new grandchildren, and reacquainted with the older grandchildren.

It didn't take long until Sally was spending lots of time looking out the door at William and Ulysses and wishing she could be outside with them.

The evenings were the most pleasant times because that was when all except the men on guard would sit and visit. The talk was mostly about when they'd get their land grants and what they'd do on their land.

Granddad talked mostly about getting started on building his gristmill. "You know I've got an agreement with Stephen that I'll supply the colonists around here with flour and lumber. And it's almighty important to me to keep my word. I think that site on the river is perfect for the mill and I've got everything in mind for how we'll build it. Now if we can just keep the pesky Indians at bay long enough, we can get it done."

It was a special evening when they heard Grandma say; "Now that the family is together again I think its time to get ready to celebrate. We need to make this our best Christmas yet. We'll not only celebrate what Christmas is all about, but we'll also celebrate the fact we're together again; and where these men seem to want to be."

The next day was just three days before Christmas. Mama asked Daddy, "Can you send William and Ulysses out for a deer or a couple of turkeys?"

Daddy said, "Sure, but I don't want them going by themselves. I'll ask Tommy to go with them."

As they were getting ready to go Uncle Tommy told the boys, "With any luck we'll run into some Indians too, at least I hope we do."

Sally was standing close enough to hear and she thought the two boys weren't sure if they wanted to run into any Indians or not. She sure didn't want them to.

She wanted to go with William and her uncles and asked, "Can I go, Mama? Can I go?"

Mama put a fast halt to that idea so Sally decided she'd just be in a huff all that day. She sat down just outside the front door and watched the three as they went into the woods. She saw Uncle Tommy and William both look back at her. Sally really loved William, but she hated being just six years old while he was already thirteen.

She heard Mama walk to the door and knew she was looking out occasionally to make sure Sally was still sitting by the door. She also knew that Mama wasn't worried at all about her being in a huff. Mama didn't have much sympathy for people that felt sorry for themselves. And Sally knew that was what she was doing.

She was sitting very still watching a squirrel, but she was thinking about Uncle Tommy. On the trip south she'd watched him all the time. She decided he could out-ride and out-shoot all the men and he wasn't afraid of anything. She'd heard the women talking about that and knew that Grandma and Granddad worried that he took too many chances. He'd always been patient with her and taught her all about the horses. He'd even let her hold and try to aim the rifle. It was too big for her, but she liked to try.

He told her, "I can't let you shoot it because we have to make every shot count. Besides your mama would say you're too young."

He started calling her 'Tagtail', and although Sally pretended she didn't like it, she did. He always made sure none of the women were around when he let her touch the gun. He'd said, "I'm not afraid of your daddy, but I sure don't want to get crosswise with your mama. I know my sister's temper well enough to not get it aroused."

Uncle Tommy didn't seem to mind that anytime she wasn't doing chores for Mama, or hanging around her daddy, she was very quietly watching everything he did. She sure hoped he wouldn't marry someone else before she got old enough, but he probably would. He was pretty old. He was already twenty-two.

The squirrel ran up a tree out of sight and she started to get up. Then she became aware that her name had been mentioned in the conversation going on between Mama, Grandma, Aunt Mary, and Aunt Margaret. She guessed it wasn't nice to listen unless they knew she was listening, but she wondered what they were saying about her.

Aunt Margaret said, "I sure don't understand why she'd rather watch the trimming of a horse's hoof or how to fix a wagon wheel. She'll never need to do all that kind of work."

Aunt Mary added, "One day, before we came here, I was using my mama's spinning wheel. Sally and the girls were over at my house and they were watching. I was real pleased to see that Sally was so interested until I realized she was mostly interested in how it worked, not necessarily in making the cloth."

"Well, you might be surprised at all the chores I've had to help with." Grandma said. Then she directed a comment toward Mama. "Our Sally is a bit of a tomboy, isn't she?"

"Well, she's certainly not like her sisters. She'd much rather be working with Joseph and William." Mama answered. "She's full of energy and she learns everything real fast. Except for her letters. You know, she picked up arithmetic earlier than all the others but dear goodness that child nearly drives me crazy when I try to teach her to read and write."

"She sure will wish she'd learned her letters when she gets older." Aunt Mary said.

And that was when Sally got totally tired of that conversation. She looked around and saw Daddy working not too far away. She walked over beside him and said, "Can I stay here with you until they get back from hunting?"

Daddy said, "Sure. Just stay close."

It wasn't long before they heard guns fired and not long after that until the three hunters came into the yard. Uncle Tommy was leading the horse they'd taken with them and over its back hung a deer. Both William and Ulysses were carrying turkeys, so all three had shot something.

Everyone crowded around and all the grownups bragged on the two boys for each getting a turkey and it was a fun time. Sally decided she was just too happy to stay in a huff, so she helped pluck turkey feathers.

She was almost asleep that night when she heard Mama talking to Daddy, telling him what the women had said about her. Mama said, "Do you think we need to worry about Sally being such a tomboy? Should I make her stay away from you men while you're working?"

When Sally heard her Daddy's answer, she knew why she loved him so much. "Does she always do the chores you ask her to do?"

"Yes, that's no problem." Mama said.

"Then don't worry about her." After a few minutes he added, "She has a real natural talent with the animals, especially the horses. She's quiet and doesn't get in the way. And she's a quick learner. Sometimes she'll hand me a tool or something before I even ask for it. I don't see anything wrong with letting her learn all she's able to."

Then he made a suggestion to Mama that nearly made Sally cry. "And now that we're talking about it, why don't you make over a pair of William's outgrown pants for her to wear under her dress."

Mama was quiet for a few minutes, and Sally held her breath. Then Mama said, "Well, we've got plenty of help with all us women and the older girls around. If Sally's going to be your other helper, then I guess that's probably the thing to do. But I better never see her without the dress covering the pants."

Sally was so happy she thought she'd just die, but she decided sleep was better and would make the time pass faster until she got those pants.

Finally, it was Christmas Eve; Sally thought it'd never get there. Even the grownups were excited and happy. Everyone had been staying up late and being secretive about what they were doing, and there were lots of looks between the grownups and more hugs for everyone, especially the little ones. The men decided not to work that day, except for tending the stock and watching for Indians.

They got the fires built for cooking and hauled some extra water for cleaning, but that didn't keep them busy enough. Soon Daddy and the uncles started jostling around and teasing each other and as Grandma said, 'Just generally getting in the way.' She finally told Granddad, "Alright, Judge. Quit enjoying all that tomfoolery so much and take those overgrown boys and go cut a Christmas tree."

The men immediately got their guns and an ax and started off. All the children were used to not being able to go past the small yard, so they just stood and watched them leave. The men walked off real slow, then looked at each other and grinned, and turned around and said, "Well, what're you waiting for? Come on."

It was like a stampede.

Daddy went back and got Thomas, and Uncle John went to get Gum. Aunt Mary wasn't sure she wanted to let him go. But Uncle John gave her a kiss on the cheek, eased Gum out of her arms, put him up on his shoulders, and took off to catch up. Gum was giggling and holding on to his daddy's hair and everyone started laughing.

It took an hour to pick out a tree because there was always a better one "over there." Just the right tree was finally spotted, cut, and dragged back to the house. It was set up in the front yard and everyone got to put something on it for an ornament.

Grandma and Mama had a few tree ornaments they had put away, and Aunt Mary and Aunt Margaret had made a few. Daddy was a good carver and had made a few wooden ornaments to hang on the tree. He'd also carved pieces of oak into egg shapes and carved an image into each. On the ones for the boys he'd carved an outline of a horse. For the girls he'd carved an outline of an angel, all except for Sally. Sally's had the outline of a pony.

They took their time decorating the tree. Aunt Mary even loaned them some of her pretty yarn. Granddad used it to help them tie shiny rocks to put on the tree. When they finished Sally thought it was the most beautiful tree in the whole world.

The women had cooked all day and there were wonderful smells. The big meal was scheduled for the next day but they had a good supper. As evening came on a large fire was built close to the tree and the family gathered around and told stories and sang songs. Except for Uncle Tommy. All the men had offered to take turns standing watch, but Uncle Tommy said, "I'm the single one. You need to be with your wives and children." The men slapped him on the shoulder, told him thank you, and didn't protest too much.

Sally thought this was the most wonderful night of her life, but at the same time she wondered how anyone would ever go to sleep with all this excitement. And if they didn't go to sleep then how could Christmas ever come. But when she looked around at the other children on the old quilt, she noticed that some of them were already asleep. And it wasn't long until she realized that Mama was carrying her and Daddy was carrying Minerva, and they put them in bed with Mary and Louisa.

The next thing she heard was the sound of whispering voices. She kept her eyes shut and listened. She hoped it was that Saint Nicholas fellow Granddad talked about. But she thought he was probably just a story. She sneaked a peek and saw Daddy give Mama a kiss and a hug, and she decided she'd rather it was them than that Mr. Nicholas.

She raised up and could see that everyone was awake. All her brothers and sisters also had their heads out of the covers. Mama and Daddy just stood there with their arms around each other for the longest time, looking at them. Sally knew it was a special moment, but she just wanted to get up and start the day moving.

It took forever but finally everyone was up, had washed and done the other things necessary, and were gathered around the tree. It was a little cold but she hardly noticed.

Grandma had a large pot of coffee for the grownups, and had brewed a tea for the children. Sally asked, "What's that, Grandma? It sure smells good."

"Its tea made from blackberry leaves and I've sweetened it with honey. It's really good and it'll make you feel warm inside." And Grandma was right. It was wonderful.

"Now while you enjoy your drinks, I'm going to read the Christmas story out of the Bible." Grandma said. They all enjoyed hearing that.

Then at last everyone had their gift, each wrapped in a piece of cloth, and they were waiting to open them. The gifts were always opened one at a time starting with the youngest first. The mothers helped the younger children open theirs.

The only girl younger then Sally was her little sister, Elizabeth, so she was watching her closely as she opened her gift. Usually all the girls got the same girl thing and all the boys got the same boy thing. Elizabeth opened hers and it was what Sally expected, another doll.

Now it was her turn. She hated it when everyone was watching her. She wanted to tell them to let Minerva open her gift first, but she knew she couldn't do that. She took a deep breath opened her gift and looked at the doll.

Everyone was staring at her as she held it up and looked right at its face. Grandma had made a head by stuffing a piece of muslin and painting a face on it. Aunt Margaret had used some old yarn for it's hair, a brown almost the color of Sally's. Mama had used some old scraps to make the body and sewed it to the head, and Aunt Mary had finished it with a pretty little dress.

Grandma had made the face really pretty and Sally was so busy wondering what she'd used to put the rosy looking color on the doll's cheeks that it took a minute to hear Minerva saying, "Is it my turn, is it?" Sally looked up and thought that all the grownups were looking relieved.

She guessed they thought she liked the doll. She wished she could just act like she felt. But it was a good day and she didn't want anyone to be unhappy. So she said thank you very much and watched Minerva and then Louisa open their gifts. They both got beautiful dolls just like she and Elizabeth.

Then it was William's turn and Ulysses too. They were so close in age that everyone said they should open them at the same time. Both boys looked around and didn't see anything. Then Daddy and Granddad walked over to them and brought out the rifles they'd hidden behind their backs.

William's gun was the one he always borrowed from Daddy, and now it was his. Sally was watching him and she knew he was having a hard time with his feelings. And so was Daddy. He said a few things to William about being responsible and taking care of the gun. Then he cleared his throat and said, "Son, if anything ever happens to me you'll need to take care of your mama and your sisters and brothers."

And William said, "I'll always take care of them, Daddy."

Sally had been so caught up in watching Daddy and William that she didn't even notice how Ulysses had reacted to his rifle, and she almost missed seeing Mary's face when she opened her gift. Mary was sixteen and when she put the cape around her shoulders everyone said "ahhh" or something like that. Aunt Mary had woven a beautiful light colored cloth and Mama had made a cape for Mary. She looked pretty and grownup in it.

Mary ran and hugged Mama and Aunt Mary. Then everyone was laughing and hugging each other.

All the grownups got some kind of practical gift and it was finally time to put out the food. Sally had never seen so much. There was deer meat and the two big roasted turkeys, and cornbread dressing and gravy, and a dish of some kind made with wild onions and pecans. At first Sally didn't want to try that, but she did and it was good.

And on the end of the table Grandma set out her biggest pan and in it was a berry cobbler. That was what Sally had smelled all morning and it made her mouth water. "Grandma, what's that?" She asked.

"Well, you just wait and see. But you'll like it."

Ulysses whispered to Sally. "It's made from dewberries that Ma and I picked. She dried them and saved them just for today."

"What's a dewberry?" Sally whispered back.

"Mrs. Castleman said most people around here call them dewberries but they called them blackberries where she came from. So I guess they can be whatever you want them to be, dewberries or blackberries. But, whatever, they sure are good." He said.

Everyone ate until they couldn't eat anymore. Then not only the kids took an afternoon nap, but most of the grownups napped as well.

Sally had liked the turkey and dressing, but she was sure the blackberry cobbler was the best dessert she'd ever had. She ate two helpings. And now she couldn't take a nap because she was afraid she was going to be sick. She didn't want Mama to know, because Mama had asked her if she was sure she needed a second helping.

She wandered out to the porch and noticed the stick horse leaning against the steps. Ali was only a few months old so Mama had made him a nightshirt that he could grow into. And Daddy had made the stick horse for little Thomas. Sally picked it up and looked around to see if anyone could see her. She was just getting ready to try it out when she heard William. He was keeping watch on one side of the house and Ulysses on the other.

She quickly put the stick horse down and started to go in the house, but William motioned her to come over. She guessed he wanted a drink or something and he was close enough to the house so she walked over and asked what he wanted.

He said, "Nothing. I just saw you there by yourself and I guess I'm kind of lonesome. This sure gets tiring."

"Really?" she said. She thought it must be exciting getting to stand watch with a gun. Sally sat down on a log and looked at her brother. He'd gotten almost as tall as Daddy this last year. He was watching her too.

She said, "What are you looking at?"

And he grinned at her and said, "What are you looking at?" And they both laughed.

They talked for awhile about the night before, the Christmas tree, the gifts, and all the food. "You didn't want a doll again, did you?" he asked.

"No. I never play with the one I got last Christmas or the year before so I don't know why they keep giving me another one."

Then before she even knew what was happening, she was crying. She started to run to the house, but William caught her arm. He looked around carefully then sat down against the tree and pulled Sally into his lap. He put his rifle down where he could get it quickly.

She tried to get up or at least get mad at him, but she didn't really want to. "Sally, why are you always mad at me?"

"I'm not mad at you. I want to be you or at least like you. I don't want to be a silly ole girl. And I don't like stupid dolls at all. You get to do all the things I don't get to do."

"I'm sorry." Then he added. "Do you want me to treat you like a brother, instead of a sister?"

Sally quit crying and looked at him to see if he was serious. "Would you?" she asked him.

"I'll give it a try. But that means you'll have to help me clean my rifle pretty often."

She gave him a smile like she usually saved for Uncle Tommy and then relaxed. She was almost asleep when she felt William kiss her on the head and heard him whisper, "I wish I knew how to make you happy; you're so different from the other girls. I guess it's worth a try to treat you like a brother."

Sally roused up a few minutes later when Uncle John walked up. He was startled to find her there and quietly asked William if he wanted him to take Sally to the house. William shook his head no but when he tried to get up while holding her Uncle John had to give him a hand. Sally had roused up enough to get up but was just too sleepy.

She heard William tell Uncle John. "I was a little worried about my watch, but it was almost time for someone to come relieve me when she fell asleep. I listened carefully and I didn't hear anything."

Uncle John answered, "It's alright. Maybe the Indians will leave us alone a few days."

William carried Sally to the house and was inside before Mama noticed. Before she could wonder why he was carrying her he shook his head and grinned so Mama wouldn't worry. All the other kids were through with their naps so Mama had him lay Sally in the middle of the girl's bed.

Sally kept her eyes closed and snuggled against the warmth of the bed. William stood over her a minute and she heard him whisper to Mama. "I don't understand girls at all and especially this one. If she's already this difficult at six years old, what'll it be like when she's older?"

Sally wanted to ask him what he meant but just couldn't stay awake. And there was too much going on and too much talking for her to sleep long either. She stayed in bed for a minute more enjoying having it all to herself instead of being crowded in like the middle piece of wood in a stack of firewood.

She turned over to get up and felt something rough on the bed cover. She raised up to look and saw Mama standing in the doorway wiping a tear away with the corner of her apron.

"This world is awfully hard on women, Sally. And in spite of what you have in your hands, you're still a girl." Mama said.

She didn't understand that at all. Of course she was still a girl. But all she said was, "I know, Mama."

Sally sat there holding the best present ever and wondered why any girl would want a doll when she could have a pair of pants!

CHAPTER 4

The days right after Christmas were fun but then the next few months were just long. To Sally nothing was worse than having to stay in doors most of the time.

It was finally spring time and the children were allowed to get outside some. But then a band of Indians stole most of Daddy and Granddad's horses. A group of men helped get most of the horses back, but the same tribe of Indians were being seen around the housing area every day.

Uncle John, Aunt Mary, and Gum had moved a short distance away, but the rest of the family had remained at Granddad's place. The family temporarily included John Ingram, the young man that had traveled here with them.

Daddy and Uncle Andrew had decided to move to a place called Egypt, farther down the Colorado River. They said there were fewer problems with the Indians in that area. Sally didn't want to move, but she didn't like being scared all the time either. Sometimes she thought about how Mama had grown up, in a big comfortable safe house. She wished that all little children could grow up that way. She didn't remember a time that she didn't have to be careful and always afraid.

It had been difficult for Granddad to give in, but this time the rest of the family wouldn't let him make the final decision. No one would agree that he could stay and take care of the place by himself. They would either all stay or all go. It was finally his concern for the safety of the children that won him over. He agreed to go with them for now, but would return when the Indian problems eased up here.

Sally hated the thought of the trip until she asked if it was going to be like when they traveled here. Daddy said, "Oh no. It's only about fifty or so miles from here to Egypt. It'll take us less than a week."

Even a week seemed long to Sally but she wanted to hurry so they could get away from all the Indians. Finally everyone was ready; the horses were all loaded and most of the family was out in the yard. Sally saw that Grandma was standing at the door of her house having one last look around. It was just at that moment that Sally heard Daddy.

"Rachel! Get the children back in the house." He said it in a quiet voice, but the one he used when he expected you to obey immediately.

It scared Sally and she tried to see what was happening, but Mama had baby Ali in one arm, Thomas in the other, and was shoving the girls in the door. Mama, Aunt Margaret, and Grandma got inside quickly and all Sally could see were Daddy and the other men walking slowly backward, staying between the women and the Indians walking into the clearing. A lot of Indians.

When the men were at the door Granddad said, "Get inside."

The four men backed inside and Granddad said, "Shut the door easy and put the bar across."

"No sir." said Uncle Andrew. "If you stay out there we're staying with you."

The other three men were saying the same thing.

Granddad said, "You boys listen to me. You can protect us all better if you stay inside. And if I stay out here maybe they won't try to break in. Those children inside are the most important thing."

Uncle Tommy and John Ingram were still protesting but Sally saw Daddy and Uncle Andrew look around at the families.

Grandma said, "I think he's right. So far he's been able to talk the Indians into just taking something to eat, and leaving us alone. Besides, the decision's made." And she pushed the men aside and shut the door. Then she put the bar across.

It was deadly quiet in the house, but Sally could hear the Indians outside. They were calling and saying things; she didn't know what.

Uncle Andrew stayed right by the door; there was a gun slit that he could see through. Grandma was standing beside him. There were two small shuttered window openings on either side of the door, one on each side of the house and one at the back, all with gun slits in them. They were all tightly shut in preparation for the journey.

Daddy moved to the front right side opening and Uncle Tommy took the left. William and Ulysses were watching the sides of the house and John Ingram went to the back.

Mama handed the two little boys to Mary and Louisa and moved up to stand behind Daddy and looked out. "Dear God. I've never seen so many Indians. They just keep coming out of the trees. The whole clearing is full of them."

Sally was standing close to Elizabeth and the other children and she saw Mama and Daddy turn and look at them. She wondered if you could feel the fear in other people. It seemed like it right now.

She'd heard the grownups talk about things she wasn't supposed to hear; knew that they worried more because Mama and Daddy had so many young girls, and that made her even more afraid. She was glad when Mama walked back over to stand with them.

One of the Indians said something and it got quiet outside. Then he said something else and Granddad said, "You're welcome to something to eat."

The Indian didn't answer.

From inside the house Daddy said the same thing in Spanish. "You are welcome to something to eat."

The Indian answered in Spanish and Daddy translated both sides of the conversation so that everyone knew what was being said. "The Chief says they'll eat later. They're just here to be friendly. They don't want us to leave our homes."

Granddad didn't say anything and in a minute the Chief said something else to him.

"He wants you to have the one doing the talking come outside." Daddy told Granddad.

"Tell him the one talking is of no importance. He only says what I tell him to. I'm in charge." Then he added, "Sorry, Joseph."

Daddy said, "That's a good answer." Then he told the Chief what Granddad had said.

The other Indians started grumbling and the Chief demanded a beef.

Granddad told him they were welcome to a beef.

They immediately killed one, ate part of it raw, then a few of them built a fire in the pit and threw large pieces of the cow on it. As it cooked more of them started talking to Granddad in Spanish.

"You are kind man. Let me shake your hand." One said.

Another said, "You have a fine gun. I would just touch it."

Then worst of all for the ones inside the house to hear. "Let us inside so we can kiss the women and children. We will be friends."

That brought out a chorus of requests to be allowed to just kiss the women and children.

Granddad quickly said, "Joseph, keep your voice calm. Don't show any anger. Just tell them, 'No, our women and children are resting and that wouldn't be a good thing right now. And I don't want to shake hands right now either.' Then ask them if they'd like something more to eat or anything that might distract them."

Uncle Andrew said, "I don't know how you can stand there looking so calm, Daddy."

"I don't have any choice." was the answer.

Uncle Tommy said, "The Chief has started striding around looking agitated. He's waving his arms in the air and talking real loud. What'd you say?"

Daddy said, "I asked him where they're headed and he said they're on the warpath against another tribe. Right now I think he's trying to stir up his men. I hope to hell it doesn't backfire on us."

At that time some of the Indians started making treats. One said, "Old man, we are many. We can break down the door and get what we want." Others joined him.

Before Granddad had finished what he was saying, Daddy was already talking.

Granddad said, "Whatever you said last is working. The Chief and his lieutenants have backed up a step or two and they've quieted the others down."

Daddy said, "I told him, 'Yes, you can easily kill me and get in the house. But there are many guns inside and the men in the house will kill many of you. All in the front will die first.'"

The Indians were talking among themselves and Sally thought everyone in the house was standing as still as a rock. No one made a sound.

After a few minutes the Chief said something to Granddad.

Daddy said, "The Chief says since he and his tribe are on the warpath they don't have any warriors to spare. So they'll just wait until a better time."

"Tell him they're welcome to go to hell!" Granddad said.

Daddy said, "I just told him 'Good fortune against the other tribe.' But I'd much rather have told him what you said."

"Looks like they're going to finish off the cow and maybe settle down and leave us alone awhile." Granddad said, and he sounded relieved.

Mama got a chair and took it over to the door for Grandma. Grandma said, "Thank you, Honey." And she nearly fell into the chair.

"We've never had more than a dozen or so Indians before. And I thought that was too many." Grandma said to no one in particular.

A few hours went by with only a little back and forth talk between the Indians and Granddad. There was still a few that kept trying to get him to let them look at his gun or in the house to kiss the women. Most of the time he didn't even answer them and they'd drift off and eat some more of the cow.

Uncle Tommy said, "That one surly looking bastard, the one with the bad leg is the one to watch out for. He's the most persistent about getting inside. I'd like to put a hole in him so he'd shutup."

"I've been watching him too. Looks mean as a snake. Sure glad he's not the Chief." Daddy said.

"I don't know how much more of this I can stand." Uncle Ulysses said. "I just want to go outside and tell them to go the hell away or I'll help them."

Uncle Andrew said, "I'd guess we all feel just about that same way. But you know our course of action has already been chosen. There's just too many of them, little brother."

Granddad said, "That's right. We got to keep our heads. Staying calm is probably the only way we might have a chance to live through this."

"I can imagine how all you men feel. But please don't let your feelings get the better of your senses." Grandma said. Then she continued, "Right now I'm so tired that I could almost forget how scared I am. It's hard to believe that just this morning I was fretting about having to leave my home again. Now I wished we'd left yesterday."

Sally thought 'That's just what I've been thinking.'

Uncle Andrew said, "I've got an idea." And he looked at John Ingram. "John, I want to ask something of you. And it isn't a little thing to ask."

John hesitated a minute then said, "Well, I won't know what it is until you ask it."

"You're kind of small-built and young enough to look almost like a boy. I think the Indians will let you go unmolested if they think you're going for corn to feed them and us. But instead of that you could go to Captain Burnham's place and bring some help. Burnham's is fifteen miles away, so you'll be taking a big risk. Are you willing to try it?"

Daddy said, "Andrew, one of us should do it. I'll go."

And Uncle Tommy said, "No sir. You and Andrew both have wives and children. I'm going to go."

Uncle Andrew said, "Tommy, you're too big to look like a young boy and on top of that you'd end up trying to kill a few of them and get yourself and us killed in the mean time."

"He's right, Tommy." John said, "They'd kill either one of you right away, and Mr. Rabb too. Then all the rest of us would be next. Andrew's right. I can act like a scared boy and maybe get away with it. Fact is it won't take much acting. Anyway, I'm willing to try."

When Uncle Tommy started to argue with him John said, "Tommy, if I don't make it through and things don't go well here, I'd think you'd want to be with your family."

Uncle Tommy looked all around the room then nodded at John.

All the grownups talked for a few minutes then decided that was the only thing that might work.

With Daddy translating, Granddad made the proposal to the Chief. He told him that his family was in need of some corn and if the Chief would guarantee safe passage he'd send one of the boys to get some. At the same time the boy would get plenty for the Chief and his tribe too. It didn't take long and the Indians agreed.

All the grownups told John good-bye and he got a fierce hug from Grandma. Sally knew they were all afraid for him. Uncle Andrew squeezed John's shoulder as he let him out through the door. When he shut the door behind John he leaned his head against it and Sally heard him mumble something.

Grandma reached over and patted him on the arm and said, "Son. Don't blame yourself. God willing, John will get back here safe and with help for us."

There was more talk between the Indians and Granddad but finally Sally heard a horse moving away from the house and knew John Ingram had left. She thought he must be really scared; she sure was.

Daddy said, "There's just too many Indians to be able to tell if any of them went after John. Maybe they won't. I think this Chief has them under control; even that surly one."

Uncle Andrew agreed. "I think he's pretty interested in getting his tribe all fattened up for the warpath, so maybe they let John go."

Mama went over and handed Grandma a cup of coffee. They hadn't wanted any cooking smells coming from the house but she'd made a small fire to make coffee.

Mama said through the door, "Daddy, are you doing alright? Do you want some coffee or something to eat?"

Granddad said, "That coffee smells almighty good, but I'm okay for now. I don't want anything to upset the standoff. Maybe the Indians will decide to get some sleep after awhile and then I'll let you get me some coffee and food."

"Alright, Daddy." she said. "Rachel?"

"Yes, Daddy?"

"Is your mother doing alright?"

And Grandma answered for herself. "I'm doing well, William. How are you holding up?"

"Well, I'm tired. But mostly I've just been kicking myself for not getting all of you out of here before today."

Grandma said, "We've never had more than a dozen or so Indians before. I thought that was too many, but you men could've handled that number. There was no way you could've known such a large bunch would come all at the same time."

The grownups talked quietly. Mama, Aunt Margaret, and the older girls got everyone, except Granddad, some cold cornbread and dried meat. All the grownups had coffee. Even Sally got to sip some coffee. She didn't really like the taste much, but she always liked how it smelled.

Suddenly Uncle Tommy asked, "What's going on, Judge?"

"I'm not sure yet. It's so close to dark that I can't see all of them, just the ones around the fire. But they don't seem hostile."

Sally heard the Chief talking and she whispered, "Daddy, what's he saying? Is he talking to Granddad?"

"No. It sounds like he's giving a speech but he's using his own language. I don't know what he's saying." he answered.

The Chief went on talking and talking and talking. Sally had never heard anyone talk for so long. She dozed off for a time but woke up when she heard Uncle Andrew say something.

"What's happening now, Daddy?" he asked Granddad.

Granddad was talking so quietly that Sally could just barely hear him. "Looks like he finally finished the speech and the whole tribe is stacking their bows and laying out all over the place, but mostly they're bedding down over by the trees."

"Can you believe they're stacking their bows like that?" Uncle Tommy said.

Uncle Andrew answered, "You'd think they didn't have a care in the world."

"I guess when there's so many of them and so few of us they don't a care in the world." Daddy said.

After a few more minutes Granddad said, "I could sure use a cup of coffee and a bite to eat about now. But make sure no light from the fire shows when you open the door. Open it just wide enough to get a mug of coffee through."

Uncle Tommy said, "Now come on, Daddy. I'll come and stay out there and let you in to rest awhile. No one will notice and you need the rest."

"Son. I'd feel the same way if it was the other way around, but I'm not willing to take even one small chance that someone will notice something and get all excited. I'll rest when this is over."

Granddad stayed just outside the door, and Grandma, Daddy, Uncle Andrew, and Uncle Tommy stayed awake inside the house. Everyone else slept off and on. Sally tried to stay awake but she couldn't. Once in awhile when she'd hear a noise she'd look around and everything looked about the same.

Something woke her and she was really scared. She lay real still and listened hard.

Then she heard Granddad say, "There's horses coming. Look sharp. Don't know how the Indians will behave."

"They've heard them too." Daddy said. "Looks like they're running into the trees."

In just a few minutes some men came riding into the yard and Daddy, Uncle Andrew, Uncle Tommy, Uncle Ulysses, and William went outside to join Granddad.

They left the door open and Sally could see that it was almost daylight. She could also see only four men and four horses. She was glad they were here but she wished there were as many of them as there were Indians.

She heard Granddad say, "Welcome, gentlemen. I can tell you that we're almighty glad to see you!"

"Hello, Judge Rabb." One of them said. Then two of them rode to one side of the porch and the other two went to the opposite side. With those four on horseback and the four men and two almost grown men standing on the porch, all with rifles, they faced the Indians.

The Chief walked to the middle of the yard beside the stack of bows and stopped. He looked at Granddad and said something.

"He said 'You win this one.'" Daddy told Granddad.

The Chief made a motion to his men and they each collected their bows and went over to the side of the yard. The chief stood motionless until the last man had his bow and then he said something to Granddad.

"He said, 'You are not so many but too many for this day. There will be another time.'" Daddy said.

The Chief pointed at Granddad and said something else. "Your family can be proud. You are a brave man."

He waited until Daddy had told Granddad what he'd said, then he walked proudly over in front of his men and they followed him out of the yard.

There was absolutely no noise as the Indians walked away, until Uncle Ulysses broke the silence. "Would you look at them. They're marching off like they planned it this way all along."

Granddad said, "You men get down and we'll heat some coffee and get something to eat."

They shook hands all around and Granddad said, "I think you all know my wife, Mary. And most of you know our daughter, Rachel, and Margaret, our daughter-in-law. But I want my grandchildren to meet the men that rode all night, right into certain danger, to help us. You children come on out here."

Sally had been watching through one of the openings in the wall and had seen the Indians leave. It was the first time all night that she didn't think she was going to die at any moment. She went outside with the others. The fresh air felt almost as good as not having any Indians around.

"Children, this is John Henry Moore and Jesse Robinson. You all met James Gilleland on the trip from the Red River to here. And I don't imagine we'll ever forget you, John Ingram."

Uncle Andrew walked over to John and gave him a hug that lifted him off the ground. "I sure won't." He said. "John, I've not been so glad to see someone in a long time. All night long I've regretted asking you to go. I'm very grateful."

John was just embarrassed and told him, "It was just something that had to be done."

"Hell's fire, Ingram." John Moore said. "I thought you were exaggerating about how many Indians there were. A rough guess would make it around 175 to 200. Soon as we can, we need to get word around about them."

With great relief at the departure of the Indians, the family hurriedly packed again, loaded the horses, and with the additional three men accompanying them, started along the river on the opposite side taken by the Indians. Sally had been more afraid than she'd ever been. It wasn't until it was over that she found out that the grownups had all felt like they would probably never see the light of another day.

Daddy, Uncle Andrew, and Uncle John had known for a number of weeks that they might have to look elsewhere for land for themselves. They all liked the Indian Hills area, but the constant Indian problems had taken a toll on everyone. With young families to worry about, they'd already been talking about settling farther down the Colorado River where there were more settlers and less Indian trouble.

The settlement of Egypt, about fifty miles from Granddad's place, was called that because a man named Eli Mercer had a business there and always had some seed corn for sale. People all around talked about going down to Egypt to get food, just like the brothers of the Joseph in the Bible.

After escaping from such a large group of Indians they thought any area would look good. But it turned out not to be just any area and the men were excited about the land. By that summer Daddy had decided he wanted to have his land near Egypt and had selected the place he wanted. Sally thought that maybe they were finally at home, on Newman land.

Daddy, Granddad, William, and all her uncles very quickly had a house built. The first one was for the Newmans, because they had the largest family. It had two rooms, a small one for Mama, Daddy, and the smallest children, and a big room for everyone and everything else.

Then they all camped at Uncle Andrew's place, a few miles away, to help build his house. Uncle Andrew and Aunt Margaret had their first son, William, a few months earlier so were glad to get in their home.

Uncle Tommy got his land just the other side of Andrew's land. He wasn't married and didn't want to be tied down to a house yet so he just put up a small shelter. Uncle John had chosen land on the Brazos River, farther away to the south.

Sally loved the land and the river. And she liked that there didn't seem to be as many trees as there were at Granddad's place. She decided she loved everything about her new home, until Granddad told them it was time for him and his family to go back to their home.

None of them liked to be separated from each other, but the horses were loaded and with Uncle Tommy along to help, Granddad, Grandma, and Uncle Ulysses left to go back up the Colorado. After they'd seen them off, Uncle Andrew and Uncle John and their families left for their homes.

Mama cried. And the girls cried. And Sally cried.

Daddy reminded them that at least this time they weren't so far away from each other. And Sally didn't cry very long. She was so excited about so much to do and see and learn. And she noticed that Mama wasn't sad for long either.

Mama was giving orders right and left about what to do to get their new home as comfortable as possible, get the garden started, and a dozen other things all at once. Sally really wanted to be working with Daddy and William, but Mama was treating her like one of the girls. She knew it was best to work real hard and do just what Mama wanted and then maybe she'd let her go help Daddy and William.

Every evening Daddy talked about the land and what he wanted to do with it. Once Sally heard him tell Mama, "We've built a house, a barn, and other structures, put all kinds of work in the place, and don't even own the land yet. It sure is getting the cart before the horse."

Sally thought that sounded kind of ridiculous, cause it just wouldn't work at all. The horse would have to be in front of the cart. But she didn't ask him about it because she liked to listen to him when he talked about the land. He sounded different, like it was something really special.

More than once she heard him say, "I sure will be relieved when we get the grant for the land. It's probably foolish to build all this before we own the land, but that's how everyone does it. You know we'll get an entire league and an additional labor of land."

He'd explained to them that a league was about 4,428 acres and a labor was about 177 acres. But Sally didn't really know how much land a league or an acre was. She just knew Daddy and Mama were happy and that's all that mattered.

Then the big day finally arrived and Sally thought she'd never forget that day. It was early one morning when Mr. Austin, Mr. Bastrop, and a number of other men, acting as witnesses, came to the house. Uncle Andrew was there too.

Sally heard Mr. Austin tell Daddy. "Joseph, there are requirements here that are somewhat different, some things the Mexican government considers the customary things to do. You'll be told what to do at the appropriate time." And he smiled.

"Stephen, I'm so pleased to get the land and get this done that I don't care what the requirements are." Daddy answered.

Mr. Austin led Daddy a little way from the house and all the men followed. Mama, Aunt Margaret, and all the children followed the men. Then the men did some strange things.

They took Daddy by the hand, led him around and told him in loud voices, "By the power vested in us by the Mexican government, we're putting you in possession of this land."

Then Mr. Austin and Mr. Bastrop told Daddy what he was expected to do and he did them. He shouted out loud and pulled grass. He threw stones and set some stakes in the ground. And he did a few other strange things.

Sally was totally amazed to see Daddy do all those things. She looked at all the men and instead of laughing they were looking serious. They looked like they were playing some sort of game but she knew it wasn't. She guessed children just weren't supposed to understand grownups.

After finishing what they were doing around and near the house and barn, they left to go all around the league of land that was to belong to Daddy. Mr. Austin told Mama that it would take all day because they had to do the same ritual in a number of places. Mama told Daddy and Mr. Austin that she'd have supper ready when they got back and they were all invited to eat.

William got to go with Daddy and the men. Sally would've been angry about being left out, but she'd seen what they had to do and she didn't really want to see it done over and over.

The men came riding back early that evening. Mama, Aunt Margaret, and the older girls had worked most of the day and had a supper of chicken and dumplings ready. After the meal Daddy brought out the old crock jug and offered all the men a swallow. That seemed to be appreciated as much as the food. Then even though they were invited to stay over night, the men left.

Everyone was still excited by the unusual activity of the day, so Mama allowed the children to stay up later than usual.

Daddy said, "Rachel, you need to see all this land. We didn't actually cover the entire league, of course, that would've taken too long. But we did see an almighty lot of it, and I can tell you it's…"

He stopped talking and just looked at her for a minute. Then he went over picked her up and twirled her around and then danced a little jig with her. Mama was telling him to stop it and laughing at the same time.

Sally said, "Daddy. You didn't finish. It's what?"

"It's the best land I ever saw. That's what." And he gave Mama a kiss right on the mouth.

"I tell you," he continued, "I felt a little foolish doing all those things, especially pulling grass and shouting all over the place. But to get this land I'd consider doing even more."

All of a sudden Uncle Andrew laughed.

Mama asked, "What?"

Uncle Andrew said one word. "Daddy."

And Mama, Daddy, and Uncle Andrew laughed for a long time.

William started laughing too so Sally asked him, "What's funny?"

"Can you see Granddad doing all those things Daddy had to do today?" William asked her.

Sally had been surprised to see her Daddy do all those things and she couldn't even imagine Granddad behaving that way. But he wanted his land as much as Daddy did so he probably would.

Sally heard Daddy say that Granddad, Uncle Andrew, Uncle John, and Uncle Tommy would all get their land grants this summer too. She was happy about that. Maybe now they could all settle down here in Texas and never have to move again.

CHAPTER 5

The first few months at their new home had been wonderful. But then there were problems with Indians again. Some men came by one morning and told them that some settlers that lived up the river a ways had been murdered by Indians. They were heading that way to see if they could help.

Mama asked, "Do you know the names of the people killed? Where they were located?"

One of the men said, "I don't remember the names, cause I'm not that familiar with the people in that area, but I'm pretty sure it wasn't too close to your folks. I met Judge Rabb, your daddy, when they were here with you folks, and it wasn't his name I heard."

Mama looked relieved and said, "If you get close to my folks house would you please stop by?"

Daddy reached and caught her arm and asked her to come in the house. He turned to the men and said, "Would you fellows wait a bit? Why don't you get down and rest your horses. You girls get them a drink of water."

When they got inside Sally heard him say, "Rachel, I don't want to leave you and the children but I need to go help."

Mama agreed, "I can't stand the thought of you being gone and in danger but I know you're right. I'm so worried about Mama. You know Daddy will stay too long before he'll give up. Go see about them,

Joseph, as soon as you get close enough. And try to talk Daddy into coming here until things settle down."

By then all the family was in the house and William said, "I want to go too, Daddy."

"I need you to stay with your mama and the children." Daddy said.

William started to protest and Daddy put his hand on his shoulder and told him, "Son, I have to be the one going this time and we can't both be gone."

Sally could tell William was really disappointed but he didn't say anything more.

When Daddy left with the other men, the family stood in the yard and watched them leave. Sally was surprised when she noticed that Mama didn't cry. She just looked really worried. Daddy told her he'd get word to her about the folks as soon as he could. Then he was gone.

That first night was awful without Daddy there. Mama and William both stopped and listened to every sound and Mama was fussy and made everyone do all kinds of chores. Sally was glad when William asked if Sally could go help him with the animals. Mama didn't want any of them outside but knew they had to take care of the animals, so she said yes.

"William, you be careful." she'd say each time. And he'd always reply, "I'll be real careful, Mama." It seemed to Sally that every time she looked toward the house Mama was standing in the door watching them.

As the days went by Mama relaxed some and a routine was established. Then one afternoon Preston Gilbert and his brother, Jasper, came to the house. Everyone was glad to see someone different.

"Howdy, Miz. Newman. My ma wanted to make sure you and your bunch was alright, so we rode over." Preston said. He was sweet on Mary, and everyone knew he was just making up an excuse to see her. Mama invited them to get down and visit.

Preston stumbled around like a silly boy and couldn't keep his eyes off Mary. Sally noticed that Mama wasn't displeased by him and was trying not to smile about it all. Sally thought it was fun to watch Preston and Mary. But she didn't like his brother, Jasper. He liked to pester too much.

Mama invited them to stay for supper and afterward said, "You boys will need to sleep here tonight; I'll make a place for you where the boys sleep. It's too dangerous to go back home this late. Your mama won't worry too much if you do that, will she?"

They accepted real fast. "Oh, no ma'am. She'll figure that's what we done. Thank you." said Preston.

Everyone sat around after supper and the two Gilbert boys told the most recent news they'd heard. They said Stephen Austin had organized a militia and had appointed Uncle Tommy as First Lieutenant.

"Really." Mama said. "I'm pleased Stephen is organizing some protection for us and very pleased that he made Tommy a Lieutenant. I can't think of anyone better. Did you hear any more about the Indian problems up river where my folks live? Or anything about Joseph or the men he left with?"

"No, ma'am. I asked about them but no one I talked to seemed to have heard much about that area. They're saying there's been lots more Indian activity around here lately so you need to be on the lookout all the time." Preston said. And he looked worriedly at Mary.

Mama said, "Yes, I know about that. William and I've been noticing things missing and signs here and there. We've been extra cautious lately."

Sally was surprised at that. She hadn't known that it was different. She decided she had to pay more attention.

Two days after the Gilbert boy's visit, just as William was putting the two horses and the cow in the barn the first daytime visit by Indians occurred. William saw them at the edge of the clearing. He shut the barn door and hurried to the house. Mama saw him and she grabbed Ali, had Thomas by the arm and told the girls. "Get in the house!"

Daddy and Mama had made everyone practice what to do, and they did what they'd been told. Mary, Louisa, and Minerva were closing the heavy shutters on the front and side window openings. The other openings were just gun holes. Mama was at the door waiting for William to get in, and Sally got Elizabeth, Thomas, and Ali to crawl under Mama and Daddy's bed.

She was supposed to get under with them, but she stayed right at the edge to make sure William got in. The minute he was in Mama shut the door and put the bar across. Then Mama and William had the rifles at two of the gun openings.

Mama said, "Ask them what they want, William. The rest of you stay quiet."

The Indians were in the middle of the yard and were talking but William couldn't understand what they were saying. He said, "I don't think they want anything to eat. They always make enough signs to indicate that. I think they're here for more than that."

Two of the Indians came close and started pulling on the door while another one was at the barn. William shot just over the head of the Indian at the barn and the two at the door of the house retreated to the edge of the yard. "They don't seem to care much about getting in the barn." He said. "They're staying away from it now."

Mama said, "Don't shoot that way again. I'd rather they got the cow and horses than get in here. Maybe getting the animals would satisfy them."

Sally knew Mama was worried that the Indians knew there were a number of young girls here. She and Daddy cautioned them all the time to be careful. But Sally thought it had to be easy for an Indian to hide in the trees and see them in the yard.

"They're squatted down under a tree at the edge of the yard. Probably trying to decide what they're going to do. There seems to be only a half dozen or so." William said.

Mama said, "There's plenty of water in the house and we have cornbread left from breakfast, so that'll be our meal for the evening. Louisa, you and Minerva build a fire and make some coffee. If the Indians stay around all night we'll need the coffee to stay awake."

It was quiet for awhile and both little boys had fallen asleep. Just sitting around made even Sally sleepy. But she came fully awake when they heard an Indian on the roof. They could hear him making his way to the fireplace.

William whispered, "Mama, I can probably shoot him through the roof. At least scare him off."

"No, not yet at least, I don't want holes in the roof if we can help it." she said.

Then Sally heard the Indian at the top of the fireplace. He was trying to climb down the chimney. She heard one of the girls suck in her breath. Sally was so scared she wasn't even sure she was breathing.

Mama suddenly handed her rifle to Mary and grabbed one of the feather pillows off a bed. She went to the fireplace, moved the coffeepot out of the way, and threw the pillow on the fire. Then she picked up the old rag rug and as she put it against the opening in the fireplace she said, "Louisa, hold one corner and Minerva, you hold the other."

Then as she took the rifle back from Mary she told her, "Wet some dishcloths and hand them to Louisa and Minerva. Girls, hold the cloths over your face with one hand and the rug with the other. Hold it as tight as you can to the wall."

Mama stood in the middle of the room with her rifle aimed at the rug over the fireplace. They smelled the worst smell possible from the burning feathers and heard awful coughing at the top of the chimney. Louisa and Minerva were beginning to cough too as smoke began to seep into the room.

Getting up from the edge of the bed Sally said, "Mary, let me help with the wet cloths." And the two of them rewet the pieces of cloth and Mary handed one to Louisa and Sally handed the other to Minerva. They wet cloths for all the rest and it did make it easier to breathe but the smell was bad and their eyes burned.

They could hear the Indian moving away and then heard him fall off the roof. Mama handed the gun back to Mary and said, "I'm going to pour a little water on the rug to keep it from catching on fire."

She took one corner of the rug from Louisa, moved it back a little and added, "Never mind. The pillow burned real fast and the rug didn't get hot enough to catch on fire. Put it down. Mary help me with the girls."

Louisa and Minerva were choking and crying from the smoke so Mama and Mary guided them to a gun opening in the back wall so they could get some fresh air. The smoke was clearing pretty fast but the smell still lingered.

William said, "Mama, come look."

And looking out through the gun openings they watched the strangest thing. Instead of helping the Indian who was black from the fireplace, coughing and choking from the smoke, and limping from the fall from the roof, the other Indians were laughing so hard they could barely stand. After what seemed a long time two of them helped the choking one and they walked away, still laughing.

Mama sat down in a chair and Sally noticed that her hands were shaking. She sat there for a few minutes then kind of shrugged and got up. All the children were looking at Mama and Sally thought, 'We're all proud of what she just did.' William stayed on watch and the girls helped Mama clean up the mess around the fireplace.

After some time had gone by and they hadn't heard anything William said, "It's going to be dark in another hour. I think this is a good time to go see about the animals."

Mama said, "I agree, but only the cow and horses. The others can just make it or not."

She stood at the door with the rifle and watched while William ran to the barn. He put out some feed for the horses and the milk cow and made sure there was some water for them, then ran back to the house. Everyone was relieved when he was back inside.

Even though it was hot Mama closed and bolted the door and kept a small fire in the fireplace. "We'll keep the fire lit, but I don't think they'll try that again for awhile."

Everyone laughed. Mama laughed too then said, "We need to be quiet so we can hear." She heated the coffee and she, William, and the three older girls had a cup.

"We'll have to take turns watching through the night." Mama said. "I want two awake all the time. I wish you could go for help but we need you here too much, William."

Mary said, "I've been hoping the Gilbert boys might come back by. That would help."

William said, "That'd be nice but we can't expect anyone to come. We're going to have to rely on ourselves."

"Mama, can I help stand watch?" Sally asked.

Mama told her, "I need you to stay with the three little ones so the other girls can get some sleep until it's their turn to stand watch."

Sally looked at William and said, "It'll be uneven then. I can help you stay awake."

William looked at her a minute then said, "Mama, Sally can probably outlast all of us. If I have her standing watch with me that'll let you and Minerva, and Mary and Louisa stand watch. That way one person won't have to double-up."

Sally thought Mama wouldn't agree but she did. She said, "Alright, that's not such a bad idea and we're all tired. Why don't you decide on who watches when."

William said, "I think the first of the night might be more active so Sally and I'll take it. Then around midnight I'll wake Mary and Louisa for the second watch. They can wake you and Minerva three or four hours later. Is that alright?"

Mama was so tired she just nodded her head. She nursed Ali, then got on her bed with him, Thomas, and Elizabeth. She told all of them to just stay in their clothes for the night and keep their shoes close. It was about nine o'clock and everyone was asleep almost at once.

Sally looked at Mama and her sisters and brothers and got a lump in her throat.

"I'm scared too." William said quietly. "We all are."

She said, "I wish Daddy was home."

William was looking outside through one of the gun openings and didn't say anything. He walked from one opening to the other every so often. Finally he sat down at the opening to the right side of the door, the one farthest away from the sleepers.

Sally was sitting by the table and William got up and motioned her to stand up so he could move her chair over next to his. "We can talk real quiet, and that'll make the time go faster. From what I hear, these Indians almost never go after people at night. They're smart enough to get a good night's sleep. Wish we could."

They talked quietly for the next two hours with William checking the other openings regularly. He started talking about having a place of his own and told Sally all about what he wanted to do when he got his land grant.

She asked him, "When I'm grown will I get a grant of land?"

And he said, "No."

"Why not?" And he told her what she hated hearing the most.

"Sally, only men with families or single men get land grants, although a couple of women have gotten grants too. The Gilbert boy's mama, Sarah Gilbert, got land but that's because her husband died."

Sally was looking really intense now and said, "But, that's not fair. Mary and the other girls and I came into Texas the same time you did."

William was too tired to argue with her about what's fair and not fair so he just let it go.

And by then Sally was having a hard time staying awake, so she couldn't keep her mind on what she thought was unfair anyway. Besides she knew that everyone just figured a woman would marry a man and he'd have land and that was that.

Just as she thought she couldn't stay awake another minute and would disappoint William and embarrass herself, William got up, stretched, and took another look outside. He checked all the openings then went and shook Mary and Louisa and told them it was time. He gave them a minute to wake up then tousled Sally's hair and told her he'd see her in the morning.

She crawled onto the bed where Louisa had been and was asleep when her head hit the pillow. It didn't seem like a minute had passed when she smelled coffee and heard the pot being put back on the fire. She raised her head and saw Mama and William standing at two of the gun openings drinking coffee. Minerva was just crawling back in bed. Sally decided she'd just stay there another minute then get up and join Mama and William.

But next thing she knew Ali was fussing and it was that time just before daylight. Mary was also up now. Mama came over and said, "Sally, you need to get up. I just fed Ali so I'll change him and then you need to keep him quiet."

Sally got up and was watching Ali. Mama was at the door saying to Mary, "You take the rifle and stand here with the door open just enough for you to see us. If anything happens you shut and bolt the door."

Then Mama took William's rifle and went and stood watch in the yard about halfway between the barn and the house. William had Daddy's old pistol as he went quickly to the barn. He checked the horses, milked the cow, and then hurried back inside the house with the milk.

While Mama and Mary stood watch the same way again William went back out and filled two buckets at the water barrel that was next to the barn. He brought them to the door and Louisa and Minerva each took one and poured the water in the barrel that was kept inside the house, then quickly returned the buckets to William.

Sally stood behind Mary and watched them. She'd put a cord with a wooden toy on it around her neck and she was holding Ali where he couldn't see Mama. Ali had a thumb in his mouth and was trying to get the toy off Sally's neck with the other hand.

When the inside water barrel was full William, Mama, and Mary came in the house and William shut and bolted the door.

Mama took Ali and sat down. Sally thought her own legs wouldn't hold her up so she went and sat down on the edge of the bed. She wished again that Daddy were here.

Sally looked at William and said, "They're out there aren't they?"

He said, "Yes."

Mary said, "William, don't scare her."

He didn't even look at Mary; he was looking through the gun opening. "She knows." He said. "You can feel them out there."

Mama looked at William and then put Ali down in his crib. She said, "We need to get as ready as we can. Mary, make some corn mush; make double what we would. Sally, get the old quilt let's fix the corner for some privacy. I don't want any of you out of my sight today, not even in the other room. And no one is going outside again today for any reason." Mama said the last part to William.

Sally got the quilt and took it over to Mama and she hung it by the corners on two nails in the ceiling logs. It was hung up that way each night and when the need arose the girls could go behind the quilt to use the chamber pot. But it was almost never hung up during the day. It was summer time and with the house closed up the smell would get bad. Sally was glad when Mama lifted up the small section that Daddy had cut in the floor for just that reason.

"Good. Now we can relieve ourselves when we have to and no one need go out of the room. Girls, it's time to get up." She said to Louisa and Minerva. They'd stayed up for the last watch and were still tired.

Elizabeth and Thomas woke up also as the older ones were getting up. Mama went and gave them both a hug then told Sally to help them while she helped Mary finish getting the food ready.

Sally listened as Mama was talking quietly to Mary and William, "We can make it a few days with what we have but not much longer. We have to hope someone will come help us."

"I wish Daddy would get here." Mary said.

Mama said, "No, I don't dare wish he would come. He might be alone and ride into the middle of the Indians before he knew they were here. I've said so many prayers. I just hope they're answered. For us and your daddy too, wherever he is."

"Whoop!!!"

They all jumped. It had gone from almost dead quiet one moment to noise coming from every direction the next. William, Mama, and Mary were instantly at the gun openings and Louisa and Minerva had the younger four under Mama's bed.

Sally didn't want to be under the bed and Minerva gave up and let her crawl to the edge. Minerva stayed with the younger three and Louisa went to stand behind Mama. There was nothing more they could do. There were only the two rifles and the pistol Mary was holding.

It was much worse this morning. "There's more this time and they look more determined than those yesterday." William said.

With that he fired his rifle. The sound was almost deafening in the room. He yelled at Mary, "Watch your side they may move that way."

Then Mama's gun fired and she said, "Damn, I missed."

Sally thought, 'I've never heard Mama say a bad word before and I wish she hadn't missed that shot.'

As William reloaded his rifle he told Mama, "You didn't miss and neither did I. They're moving back and helping the two we shot. One of them looks pretty bad."

Then the noise and motion was on them again. The Indians were trying to get to the door. Mama and William both shot again and it was impossible to miss.

As two more Indians fell William yelled, "We hit two more but four or five have reached the door. We've got to keep them from breaking the door in."

The Indians were yelling and banging on the door. William was reloading his rifle as fast as he could. Mama and Mary were trying to reload the other one. One of the girls screamed.

The house smelled like gunpowder and her eyes stung. Sally wondered who had screamed. It seemed important that she know but she couldn't tell.

Mama and Mary and William were all tight-faced and only paying attention to the guns and the Indians. Sally felt Elizabeth put her little hand on her arm and she pulled her close to her. They held on to each other. She thought to look for Thomas and Ali and saw that Minerva had crawled under the bed and had them both between her and the wall.

Louisa had the pistol now and was watching the side of the house. William fired again, started reloading his gun, and then yelled, "Mama!"

He was pointing at the bottom of the door.

The door didn't come all the way to the floor. An Indian had his foot under it and was trying to lift the door off its hinges. Mama ran to the corner, grabbed the ax and ran back to the door. She waited until the Indian put his foot down before he lifted again then she said, "Please, help us." And she struck his foot with the ax. Blood and several toes were all that remained.

There was a terrible wail outside the door followed by scrambling around and a thump, then another, like one Indian had fallen and knocked another down. No one in the house could see directly in front of the door so they weren't sure what was happening.

Mama put the ax down and got the broom. She swept the Indian's toes under the door and back outside. They could hear talking outside now and it sounded like arguing. Then with two of them supporting and half dragging the injured one the Indians ran from the yard.

It would've been easy for Mama and William to each shoot one but they didn't. They just watched them go toward the crossing at the river.

Mama looked around to check on the children. Everyone was scared but safe. She sat down in a chair and put her head down for a minute. Again it was eerily quiet. Sally thought the room almost looked like a painted picture. Nothing seemed to be moving.

Then Thomas asked, "What's happening?" And everyone moved.

Minerva said, "I'm getting out." and backed out from under the bed pulling the two little boys with her. They were all wet with sweat.

Minerva said, "It's getting too hot under the bed. And I can't stand not knowing what's going on."

"I know." Mama reached for Thomas and Ali pulling them both up on her lap.

Sally and Elizabeth got up and went and stood on both sides of Mama's chair as close to her as they could get.

Then Mama told the older four, "Come here, please."

They all walked over and stood around her and the four younger ones. Mama had her head down and said, "Thank you, God. Please protect us. Please take care of my children."

She then looked at them and said, "I'm proud of each one of you."

William motioned to Mary and Louisa and they went back to watch the outside.

Minerva said, "You know, Mama, even Ali didn't make a sound during all that. He had a thumb in his mouth and with his other hand was holding on to one of my fingers. He watched my face with his eyes as big as saucers. Thomas just lay there stiff as a board and never made a sound either."

Mama didn't say anything about that but asked, "Who screamed earlier? I thought maybe someone was hurt."

They all looked at each other. No one remembered screaming.

They took turns watching and listening as it got hotter and hotter. By noon it was miserable in the house.

William said, "Mama, I haven't seen or heard anything since they took off. I'm going to open the door a minute and let some fresh air in."

"No!" She said. Then, "I'm sorry, William. Do you think we should yet?"

He said, "Yes. We have to have some air. I'll only open it a minute or so."

Mama moved everyone to the side of the room then she took one of the rifles and went and stood beside William. He lifted the bar and pulled the door open. The fresh air felt wonderful.

There was no movement anywhere except a slight breeze. They could see blood on the step and a small trail of blood for a short distance then the dragging marks across the yard. Mama had the children all come to the door and get a breath of air. Then she told William she wanted the door shut again. Sally could tell William didn't feel there was that much danger now, but he didn't object. They'd all been through too much the last two days.

The day dragged on very slowly. About once an hour they'd open the door again for a minute or so. Mama ran out of chores to do in the house and told them to get out the writing slate and practice their letters.

'Oh no.' Sally thought. Mama made them sit down at least once a week to learn their letters and numbers. Sally liked numbers; they seemed to make perfect sense. But letters! She knew her ABC's. But to read the primer was pure torture. She just didn't like it at all.

She tried to pay attention but the more she tried the more miserable she got. And everyone else was getting even more miserable. After Mary tutored her for a few minutes Louisa took over, then Minerva took a turn. By that time everyone was about at the end of being able to listen to the stumbling over almost every word. Mama finally said that was probably enough for the day.

Mama then got out some pieces of cloth and taught the girls some different stitches. Then she read some but nothing seemed to keep their attention for very long. Everything was still too unsettled and they were all too uneasy.

Before dark William talked quietly to Mama trying to get her to let him go to the barn to tend the horses and cow. But she absolutely refused to let him go. She told him the stock would just have to make it through the night.

They stood watch again the same way they had the night before. It was much cooler so wasn't too bad, except it seemed like the watch times were twice as long as they were the previous night. Sally knew she was dozing off and William was letting her. Finally it was time for them to get to sleep and then morning was there again.

Mama had them do the same routine that they'd done the morning before. But this time, there was less milk from the cow and William was worried about it and the horses.

When they had the water containers refilled and were in the house again William told Mama. "We have to turn the stock out. We have enough feed for a day or two more but we should save that. And the water will last through today and then I'll have to fill the barrel from the river and that'll take time."

Then he said, "I think they're gone, Mama. We shot at least four of them. I know we killed two and possibly another one. I think when you chopped off the toes of that one it was unexpected and his sudden yelp unsettled them all. They just decided it wasn't worth it."

He waited a moment then said, "This bunch obviously didn't have any guns or they'd have used them. And they know that we've got more than one gun and made them pay for it. I think they're gone."

"I think you're probably right." Mama said. "But I don't want you farther from the house then you can run if you hear something."

He said, "Don't worry. I'll be real careful."

Sally remembered Daddy asking William to take care of Mama and the children if anything happened to him. She looked at William and thought he looked as tired as Mama did.

The next few days were a real strain. They all stayed extra watchful and very close to the house. The horses and cow came back by themselves every evening and William was able to shut them in the barn each night. They had enough feed left to give them a little every evening and that would keep them coming back. That was a relief to Mama and William. Mama had told him that if they didn't come back she wasn't going to let him go out to get them.

A week after the Indians had left, Mama was washing clothes beside the house. Sally was playing with the three younger ones nearby and William and Mary were hauling buckets of water from the river.

Suddenly, with a bucket in one hand and the rifle in the other, William came running from the river. Mary, carrying a second bucket, was just behind and running as fast as she could. William was yelling, "Horses, coming fast. Get in the house."

Sally saw Mary stumble and then saw William knock the bucket out of her hand, grab her arm and run toward them.

Then Louisa had her by the arm, Minerva had Elizabeth, and Mama had practically dragged Thomas and Ali into the house. William and Mary reached the house seconds later, all out of breath. They immediately put the bar in the door, grabbed the guns, and Louisa and Minerva were getting the little kids under the bed.

The horses were ridden into the yard and almost right up to the door. The next thing they heard was this loud voice.

"RACHEL!"

All at once everyone was saying, "It's Daddy! It's Daddy!"

William opened the door and they all poured outside.

It was not only Daddy but also Uncle Tommy and four other men. Almost everyone was talking at the same time. After Mama and all the children had gotten a hug from Daddy and Uncle Tommy things calmed down some.

Daddy told Mama they'd stayed with Grandma, Granddad, and Uncle Ulysses two nights ago and they were fine. But he thought they'd be coming back this way before long. Mama had the girls get the men a drink of water and they listened as Mama and William told about the Indian attacks.

Two of the men were married and they became very anxious to get to their homes. The other two were single men so were going to go with Uncle Tommy to check on Uncle Andrew and his family.

After the two married men left, Uncle Tommy wanted more of a description of the Indians; maybe they could find them later. Sally could tell Uncle Tommy was really pleased with how well they'd done.

He said, "You know, Sis, I'm real proud of you and the children. Would you like to join my militia group?"

She laughed and said "Never!" Then she held him very tight for a few minutes and told him, "Please be careful, Tommy." After a few more good-byes and messages for the other family Uncle Tommy and the two men were gone.

Daddy walked off toward the river and was just standing there looking at it. Mama walked over to him and they all watched as he pulled her close. After standing that way for a few minutes they walked back to where the children were waiting.

Mama and the girls went back to doing the laundry and Daddy went with William to check the animals. After eating supper and talking awhile they went to bed, but not before they each got an extra hard hug from Daddy. As Sally yawned sleepily she wished it'd always be like this, with all her family together.

And she hoped she never saw or heard another Indian!

CHAPTER 6

It was the end of the year already. With all the vegetables from the summer garden and with the wild game Daddy and William had killed they'd been well supplied with good things to eat. Christmas time arrived and none of the other families could join them.

Uncle John and his family couldn't go anywhere because early in December Aunt Mary had their second little boy, George Washington. Granddad, Grandma, and Uncle Ulysses had sent word that they couldn't leave their place because of the Indians. And Uncle Andrew, Aunt Margaret, Little William, and Uncle Tommy had decided to go stay with the grandparents for a week or so.

They missed the other families but Christmas was a happy time anyway. And soon the cold and blustery winter was gone too.

One day around the first of April they were all outside busy with chores. Sally was doing what she usually had to do in the mornings, taking care of Elizabeth, Thomas, and Ali. William was working with Daddy on a fence, and the three older girls were helping Mama in the garden. Sally and the young ones were playing under an oak tree close enough to the garden so Mama could see them.

William suddenly broke the calmness of the morning. He yelled from the fence-line, "Rider coming from the north, coming fast!"

Sally immediately picked up Ali and with the two younger ones, went running for the house. She made the other three go inside and she stood at the door to wait for Mama, Daddy, and the others.

Mama and the girls were at the porch when Sally noticed that Daddy and William had stopped at the edge of the yard.

Mama yelled to them, "What is it? Come on!"

They started walking toward the house, but were still watching the rider.

"He's white, and he's waving his hat over his head." William said. Then he let out a yell and started running out of the yard.

Mama was yelling at him and he turned finally and yelled back. Sally wasn't sure what he'd said.

Daddy told Mama, "It's Ulysses."

Sally climbed on the water barrel that sat at the corner of the house. It had a half-lid on it and they weren't supposed to get on it, but she wanted to be able to see. She watched William run toward the rider. When they met, the rider slowed down just enough to reach his arm down, grab onto William's outstretched arm, and then William was up behind him.

Both Ulysses and William rode into the yard waving their hats over their heads.

William jumped down. Then Uncle Ulysses was down and he grabbed Mama and twirled her around and around.

Mama was laughing and telling him to put her down. When he stopped and put her down she gave him a hug and a kiss and then started in.

"What are you doing here? Where's Mama and Daddy? Are they okay? What's going on?"

Uncle Ulysses was laughing. With one arm still around Mama's waist, he reached and shook Joseph's hand. As he turned Mama loose he said, "They're coming."

He grabbed each girl in turn and twirled her around like he'd done Mama. Sally was glad when it was her turn but she'd forgotten she was on the water barrel. She was kind of embarrassed. But she didn't really care; she was just pleased to see Uncle Ulysses.

William got him a drink of water and they all sat around him on the porch as he told them the news.

"The Indians are real bad again. They're not just stealing a few things but are dangerous enough that Daddy finally thought we'd better leave. Course I don't think he'd have given in yet, but Tommy came by to see us a few days ago and convinced Daddy to get out of there."

At a questioning look from Mama he continued, "Tommy comes by every time he gets close enough. He's seems to be doing real well. He's kind of thin Ma always says, but to me he's always been thin. Anyway he told Daddy we ought to come to your house awhile. We stopped by Andrew's place on the way and all of them should be here tomorrow."

Uncle Ulysses stopped talking and got up and stretched. He told Mama, "Rachel, you should've seen Ma. She nearly had a fit when I asked if I could come on down. She didn't want me coming by myself but Andrew told Daddy they hadn't seen any sign of Indians yet this spring. So Daddy told me I could go. When I left, Ma was still giving him dirty looks." He laughed as he walked off with William.

Mama asked, "Did Andrew send someone to tell John and Mary you're here?"

Uncle Ulysses said, "Yes he did." And he and William continued on to the barn.

The next day everyone was excited, trying to get things done and staying out of Mama's way at the same time. Finally about mid-afternoon Granddad, Grandma, Aunt Margaret, Little William, and Uncle Andrew came riding into the yard. After the greetings were over Mama was happy and everyone could relax.

By the next evening Uncle John, Aunt Mary, Gum, and baby Wash arrived. Now the only one missing was Uncle Tommy and they expected him to show up any day. He did get to come by for a few days but couldn't stay long. There were so many problems with the Indians here and there that the militia stayed on the move a good part of the time.

They'd all been together so much until the last few years and they'd missed the closeness. So they made the most of this time that they had together. They worked hard during the days. Then the evenings were spent in story telling, laughter, and the men teasing each other about one thing or another.

The children were allowed to stay up later when the families were visiting. Sally loved the little ones and was always willing to sit with them on a quilt on the floor. When they'd fall asleep she'd try to stay awake to hear the grownups talk. She'd wake up in the mornings wondering when she'd fallen asleep, but feeling good and wishing it could always be like this.

One day in late April the men were getting ready to leave for the Matagorda Bay area. Granddad was going to sell and exchange some of his land there. He also planned to get the two grinding stones that he'd sent to Scotland for. He'd ordered them over a year ago and they'd arrived in a ship just recently and been off-loaded at Matagorda. He was anxious to get the stones so that he could complete the mill and get it working.

Just before they left, little Thomas pulled on Granddad's coat and asked, "Granddad, how you going to get those cucka burrs to the house?"

Everyone laughed and Mama said, "He'll tell you all about it when they get back."

But Granddad took Thomas by the hand and led him over to the porch with the rest of the children following. He sat down and told them, "Well now. I'm going to have to do some tall thinking to figure out how to get them from Matagorda back home. That's going to be roughly one hundred miles.

"You know, Thomas, most people around here call them millstones or grinding stones because they're what we use in the mill to grind up the corn and such. But they're really burrs and the best ones come from Scotland. I wouldn't want any other kind. There are two of them and they're round and heavy as can be. Why it would take all of us men to just lift the smaller one."

Granddad started to get up but almost every child had a question about the stones. He answered a few of them then said, "Alright, follow me."

He didn't even look at Daddy, Uncle Andrew, and Uncle John waiting by their horses. But they looked at each other.

Uncle Andrew said quietly, "Might as well relax. We'll go when the Judge is ready and not a minute before."

By then Granddad had all the children, big and small, following him. So all the grownups were following along too.

When they got fairly close to the river Granddad told them, "We've got to find us a good spot. I'll do that while each one of you get some rocks about the size of your hand. Bring them to me and we'll build us a ring the size of the burrs."

Granddad found a spot he liked beside a big pecan tree. He drew a round mark on the ground and drew a small round mark in the center. Even the grownups helped gather rocks and pretty soon they had the ring finished. Then Granddad got out his knife and marked a spot on the pecan tree to show them how thick the big stone would be.

"The small burr will be the same size around but it'll be only about half as thick as the big one. Now you children keep this ring all nice and neat and when we get back with those burrs we'll see how good your granddad is at estimating sizes."

As he walked back toward the horses all his grandchildren were following along. Sally was thinking he had to be the smartest, best granddad ever.

Sally watched the men and William and Uncle Ulysses leave and as usual wished she could go with them. But she was happy to have all the little cousins to play with, so she thought it wasn't so bad to stay home this time.

Each day they carefully checked the stone ring to make sure it was nice and neat like Granddad wanted. Then one day, a few weeks later, they heard a strange racket in the distance. It wasn't long until William and Uncle Ulysses came riding into the yard.

"We got the burrs." They both said at once. "Just wait till you see them." When the men and the burrs finally arrived in the yard in front of the Newman house it was like Christmas time. There was so much excitement that Mama, Aunt Mary, and Aunt Margaret were having a hard time keeping all the little ones from getting too close to the oxen. Everyone wanted to see and touch the burrs.

Granddad told them, "Alright, everyone quiet down. Let's not all run over here at once cause you might spook the oxen." As he said that he laughed and so did the men.

Sally heard Uncle John say, "Yeah, they might move faster than a mile a day."

The oxen were unhitched and led away to graze and then all the children got to sit on the stones. After they had supper they all sat around and listened to the stories about the trip. It was magical sounding to Sally. She'd never seen the big gulf of water they talked about, or a beach, or a ship, or a town with lots of lights and stores and all kinds of other things. She thought William and Uncle Ulysses were really lucky to be so old that they got to go on the trip to get the burrs.

Mama waited for a break in the stories then asked, "What about the burrs?"

"When we first got there I couldn't believe the size of them." Daddy said. "They weighed about a ton each. We stood and looked at those two burrs for a long time. I looked around and there were a lot of men standing around enjoying the show. Some of them were making wagers on whether those stones were going to stay right where they were until judgment day."

Uncle Andrew interrupted. "But Daddy didn't pay anyone any attention and in short order he'd decided what to do."

And Uncle John interrupted him. "You should've seen it. It was so perfect." And he looked proudly at Granddad.

Granddad was pleased with all the praise but said, "I don't know why you boys are making so much of it. It was the only way to get them from there to here. And as soon as we can, I'm going to take them on home and get that mill going."

Uncle Andrew laughed and said, "Well, you can be humble about it if you want but I wouldn't take anything for the looks on the faces of those men."

Uncle Ulysses said to Grandma, "You should've been there. Daddy had two trees cut down, made an axle out of one and a tongue out of another. It took an almighty amount of effort, but we got those burrs, one on each end of the axle, to serve as wheels. Then Daddy had the tongue attached to the axle, hitched the oxen to it, and pulled the burrs just like it was a wagon."

Uncle Andrew laughed again and said, "It truly was something to see."

Granddad said, "The roadway wasn't always possible to use so often as not we just followed the river and made our own road. It wasn't easy but here we are with the burrs."

It was such a fun evening that Sally fell asleep with the men still talking and laughing about the burrs and their trip. She couldn't wait to see what Granddad actually did with those big stones. She had no idea how they could be used to grind something up.

The next morning, as soon as all the children were up and about Granddad said, "I think it's time to check on how good we were with our ring of rocks. No. Don't run off to the river yet. We have to take some measurements."

Granddad got a piece of rope and told William and Uncle Ulysses to go measure the burrs and tie a knot in the rope to show how wide across they were. Then he had them tie a knot to show how thick each burr was and he said, "Alright, follow me."

And once more Granddad led the way to the river and all the children followed, and so did the grownups. When they got to the ring of rocks Granddad told them, "Well, let me tell you. I'm mighty proud of you children. Because I can't see where even one rock is out of place. You've done a good job."

Then as everyone watched he had William and Uncle Ulysses take the rope and see how close the ring was to the actual size of the burrs.

Sally heard Uncle Andrew say, "Well, I'll be damned."

Uncle Andrew and Uncle John both walked over and Uncle John said, "Here, William, let me have that rope." And he and Uncle Andrew took the rope and measured the ring of rocks again.

Uncle Andrew looked at Granddad and said, "You know, Judge. That couldn't get any closer."

Granddad was standing off to the side with his arm around Grandma, and with a definite twinkle in his eyes.

For a few more weeks everyone was together, working hard during the days, and visiting in the evenings. Then before Sally was ready Granddad said it was time for them to go back home, take the burrs to his place, and try again to finish the mill.

Aunt Margaret was expecting another baby and Sally knew Mama had hoped they'd all stay until the baby was born. But by early summer Grandma, Granddad, Uncle Andrew and his family were gone.

They were all pleased that Uncle John, Aunt Mary, and their children planned on staying through the summer at the Newman house. There were now two small rooms and the one big one. The house was crowded but it didn't matter. They stayed outside most of the daytime and they enjoyed being together.

One morning Mama and Aunt Mary were working in the garden and Sally heard them talking about how dark the sky was to the northwest. Sally kept watching the sky. It was dark blue and pretty and once-in-a-while she could see lightning. She didn't hear any thunder though so she guessed it was too far away. At least that's what Daddy said that meant.

About noontime, Daddy, Uncle John, and William took a break from working and came to the porch for something to eat.

"Joseph, what do you think of the weather?" Mama asked.

"John and I've been watching the sky and it looks like it's raining pretty heavy somewhere north of us. You might want to finish whatever you're doing outside because it's probably going to rain after a while. We'll just have to keep an eye on it." he said.

Off and on for the rest of the day, one or the other of the grownups was talking about the weather or how the sky looked or all that lightning. It was making Sally feel uneasy. When it started to rain it was real hard and they had to run into the house. Usually they were glad to see rain, but this time the grownups were acting like they weren't sure. Daddy and Uncle John stood at the door for a long time talking about the river.

"How much rain do you think can fall in a day and part of a night?" Daddy asked.

Uncle John said, "I don't have any idea. A fair amount I guess. And it looked like it rained all day up north."

"More than enough to make the river rise." Daddy said.

"Yeah, it'll rise some for sure." Uncle John agreed.

The conversation went like that all evening. Sally thought worrying about the weather was a little like worrying that Indians were sneaking up on the house. You couldn't see either one in the dark. After Mama made her and the other children go to bed Sally stayed awake awhile and listened to the grownups talk.

Uncle John said, "Joseph, how high do you think the river could rise?"

And Daddy had answered, "Well, I've seen signs in a few places where it's got up real high at one time or the other. But I don't think there's any way it could get high enough to get in the house."

"I don't either." Uncle John said. "Just think how much water it would take to do that."

Mama said, "This has been an awful day. All we've done all day is worry about the weather and you two have done nothing all evening but worry Mary and me to death. Do you think we're going to be alright?"

"I'm sorry, Rachel. I think we've both just been borrowing troubles." was Daddy's answer.

Uncle John said, "I do too. Let's go to bed."

"Wake up! Wake up! The river has flooded! It's in the house!"

Sally woke up scared to death wondering what was going on. Aunt Mary was in the little room she and Uncle John were staying in and she was yelling about the river being in the house.

Sally shared a small bed with Elizabeth and she got off on the floor and was standing in the river. She couldn't understand that at all and jumped back on the bed and held on to Elizabeth. Daddy had a lantern and when he got close enough Sally could see that the water was just below the bottom of the bed.

She and Elizabeth started crying and Daddy said, "It's going to be alright. Come here, Elizabeth." And he picked her up. "Sally, I'm going to take Elizabeth over to the girls bed and then I'm going to come get you. Just stay on the bed."

Sally nodded and closely watched Daddy and the lantern until he was back to get her. He took her over to the bed where the three other girls were.

"Keep these two calmed down if you can. Real soon we'll all be safe on the hill at the back of the house." He said. Minerva was holding Elizabeth and Louisa pulled Sally close.

"Where's Mary?" Sally asked.

Louisa said, "She went to Mama and Daddy's room to help with Ali and Thomas."

"Where's William?"

"I don't know. It's dark. I don't see him." Louisa told her.

Sally yelled, "William?"

"I'm right here, Sally. I'm alright."

"Come over here with us." she told him.

Daddy said, "Go over and let her see you, son. Then come back over here. We need to make some fast decisions."

By then everyone was in the big room and Daddy and Uncle John both had lanterns and were talking about how to get them all out.

Daddy said, "We have to go up the hillside behind the house but that means we have to go out the front. If it's this high in the house that means it's six or eight inches higher outside. And there's that one low spot at the back of the house."

"Yes, and I've heard things hitting the house, something big once, so the river's carrying stuff with it." Uncle John said.

"Help me tie these two ropes together." Daddy said, "Then we'll tie one end to the corner porch post and I'll take the other end and tie it to that oak straight out back. I'm sure it'll reach that far. That tree will still be in the water but it won't be as deep as here. So once we're there the rest of the way will be fairly easy."

"And we can use the rope to hang on to in case the water's too swift. Good idea, but I want to do it." Uncle John said.

"I'm older than you, John, so I get to make this decision. Besides I'm the one that said we were just borrowing trouble."

"I'll take one of the lanterns. After you tie the rope to the tree give it a tug and I'll bring the lantern over and we can hang it in the tree. That'll help us when we start out with the family." Uncle John said.

"Good. That'll be good." Then Daddy turned to Mama and said, "Rachel, this will take awhile. After John gets to the tree with the lantern he and I'll make sure it's not washed out anywhere between the tree and the hillside behind it. While you're waiting for us, gather up as much food and things as you can and wrap it in the bedding so we can carry it. We'll come back for it later."

Daddy kissed Mama and Uncle John kissed Aunt Mary then they went to the front window. They opened the shutters and climbed through. Sally heard them both draw in their breaths and heard Uncle John say, "Wow. That's cold! How can it be this cold in the summer?"

"At least its stopped raining." Daddy said.

Then William pulled the shutters closed and she couldn't hear anything else from them.

Mama came over to the bed they were on and said, "All of you get dressed. Even if your clothes are wet put them on. And you older girls try to find all the shoes; you're going to need them. They'll be wet and hard to put on so help Sally and Elizabeth. And do it fast, real fast."

Mary had joined them on the bed and she was holding Thomas. Mama handed Ali to Mary too and said, "Sally, you and Elizabeth help Mary with Thomas and Ali. William can help me."

Then she turned to Aunt Mary and said, "Are you alright, Mary? Do you want one of the girls to hold Montgomery?"

Aunt Mary, holding her two little boys, had also joined the girls on the bed. "I'm alright now, Rachel. But I don't want to turn loose of either Gum or Wash. John already got my shoes and clothes for me, but if the girls can get some more of the boy's things I'd appreciate it."

Louisa and Minerva had both gotten up to get the clothes and shoes. "Hurry girls." Mama told them. She put a quilt on the table and was putting things on it.

William pulled Sally and Elizabeth's small bed over right next to the bigger bed. Then went across the room and pulled his bed over next to that. He said, "Part of you get on the smaller beds or that bed may give out." Then he went to help Mama.

Aunt Mary immediately crawled across to one of the small beds with her two boys. That left Mary and the four youngest in the middle of the big bed.

Louisa and Minerva had brought all the clothes and shoes to the bed and all the children were finally dressed. Mama and William were still gathering things together when they heard a loud thump on the wall.

Both Mama and Aunt Mary said "Oh, my goodness." at the same time.

Then Mama said, "William?"

"It was a tree or something and it sounded like it went by on the front side of the house." he said.

Sally heard Aunt Mary say something real low. It sounded like, 'Oh, John.' And then Sally realized why William had told them it had gone on the front side of the house. If it had gone at the back of the house it might have hit Daddy or Uncle John. And it might break the rope and they couldn't get back to the house. Louisa was holding her so tight that she could barely breath, but she didn't care.

It wasn't too much later that they heard Daddy and Uncle John on the porch. William opened the shutters and they climbed back in through the window.

Daddy started talking as soon as he was inside. "Alright, John and I have decided what we think is the best way to get us all to safety. And I don't want any discussion about it. Just move when we tell you to.

"John's going to take Gum and go first, and Mary will follow him with Wash. Then our Mary will go with Ali."

Mama interrupted, "No, I'll take the baby."

"Ali's lighter than Thomas and will be easier for Mary to carry so she'll take Ali." Daddy said.

Mama just nodded and didn't make any more objections.

"Rachel, you'll take Thomas and follow our Mary, then Louisa and Minerva will follow you. William you'll go next, with Elizabeth, she'll be a little lighter, and I'll bring Sally with me.

"As soon as John has Mary and his two boys to safe ground, he'll be able to help the rest of you if you need help."

Mama asked, "Why don't you and John take Mary and their two over there and then come back for our little ones? Wouldn't it be safer to make two or three trips?"

"We can't take that chance, Rachel. The river has already come up a few more inches, and a big tree hitting the house just right could possibly cause it to move. We have to get us all out as soon as we can."

Sally noticed Mama looking at Uncle John and Aunt Mary. Uncle John had Gum in one of the cloth baby carriers strapped to his chest and Aunt Mary had Wash strapped to her. And Uncle John was tying himself and Aunt Mary together with a piece of rope.

"Are we going to do that, Joseph? Don't you want to tie all of us together?" Mama asked.

"No, I don't want to do that." he said.

"But why not?" She was almost pleading.

Daddy lowered his voice but they could all hear him. "Rachel, if they lose their footing or something hits them they'll all be washed down the river together. That's John and Mary's choice for their family and I respect them for it.

"But there's so many of us that we'll be spread out for a ways. We've got some almost grown children that could make it by themselves. So if something happens to one of us, at least most of the others could still make it to the hillside."

"Oh, dear God." Mama said. And to Sally it sounded like a prayer.

Uncle John and Aunt Mary went to the front of the line where the rope was tied to the post at the corner of the porch. Daddy tied one end of a rope around Sally, then tied a loop in the other end and put it over his head and under his left arm. He walked to where Uncle John was standing and said, "Good luck, John, Mary."

Then Daddy walked back down the line checking each one and giving each a kiss. The first in line was Mary and Ali. "Honey," he said to her, "I've given you the hardest job. The baby's going to get real heavy by the time you get to the tree. The baby carrier is good, and he's strapped in good and tight, so use both hands on the rope." And he kissed her and Ali.

Mary didn't say anything she just nodded.

Mama had Thomas strapped to her and was next in line. Daddy kissed them both then moved down the line to the others. Because she was with Daddy, Sally had been able to kiss and be kissed by Mama and each of her sisters and brothers.

Daddy said, "The water is swift, so watch your footing. And there are things floating by that may bump you. Just hang on to the rope and get across as soon as you can. If one of you falls, no one else is to turn loose of the rope. Grab them with one hand if you can, but don't turn loose of the rope! Do you hear?"

Sally heard a chorus of "Yes sir." Daddy was at the back of the line so Sally could see them all lined up on the porch.

"Alright, John." Daddy said. And Uncle John stepped off the porch into the river.

It was only a few minutes until it was their turn. Daddy stepped off the porch with Sally and she could see the lantern hanging in the tree.

It looked so far away. She could see water around the tree where the lantern was hanging, but she couldn't see her family.

"It's okay, honey." Daddy said. "Just hang on tight."

She heard Minerva yell and heard Mama say, "What's wrong. Are you alright?"

"Something hit me and I almost lost my grip on the rope."

"Be careful. All of you. Be careful." Mama said.

"Keep moving, now." Daddy said. "John is almost at the tree."

Sally was trying to see Uncle John when Daddy said, "Sally, I'm getting tired of this position. See if you can get around to my back and lets try it that way awhile. Then you can see what's happening in the front easier too."

Sally was more pleased with that position because she could see the rest of the family better, but she didn't feel as secure as when Daddy was holding her in front of him. She held on extra tight.

William slipped and Elizabeth squealed. All kinds of questions were called out and William said, "It's alright, Elizabeth. We're alright." Then he added. "There's a slick place right here, Daddy. We're alright, Mama."

Then finally they were at the tree. Uncle John had taken Elizabeth from William and carried her to Rachel. Daddy was still standing there leaning against the tree.

"We made it, Daddy. No one drowned." Sally said.

He patted her on the arm but didn't say anything.

John had gotten back to them by then and reached for Sally. "Come on, Honey. Your mama is waiting for you." As he took her he said, "Joseph?"

"I'm alright. I'm tired. And there were just too many emotions there for a minute."

"I'm sorry I was so heavy to carry, Daddy." Sally said.

"You'll never get too heavy for me to carry, Sally. None of you will."

Mama and Aunt Mary were sitting beside a tree with all the little ones around them.

Uncle John put Sally down by Mama and Sally got a terrific hug. Then Daddy was there, leaned over and gave Mama a kiss, then gave each child a hug. He kissed Aunt Mary on the cheek then he grabbed Uncle John and gave him a hug too.

Daddy went over and sat beside Mama. She put her head on his shoulder and said, "My whole life was in that river. I've never been so scared. Even with the Indians."

"I know. It was the same for me too, Honey."

The two men sat and rested for a short time then returned to the house and brought as many of their belongings as they could. They made a number of trips, even managing to float the big water barrel across.

"That's all I've got in me, John." Daddy said.

Sally heard him and woke up. She'd meant to stay up until Daddy and Uncle John were back and she knew they were safe. But she'd fallen asleep.

Mama got up from between a number of little bodies and asked, "Did you get some dry wood?"

"Yes. We tore some out of the house. The upper inside wall of the house is the only thing in this world that's still dry. We brought the table too."

"Oh, thank you. I love that table. It's the first thing you made for this house." Mama said.

"Well, to be truthful, it made a good raft. We turned it upside down and loaded it with other things. But we knew it would be useful too." Daddy said.

"It sure will be. But I'm thinking slowly. What I was going to ask is do you want me to make some coffee?"

"No. No coffee. Just some sleep." Daddy said. And he stretched out on the ground beside William.

"Amen." added Uncle John. And he too lay down.

"You should at least get those wet shoes off." Mama said. But it was already too late.

Sally watched Mama as she went around and checked all the children, tucking a quilt in here and there. When she got to Sally she stopped gave her a kiss and whispered, "It was all scary but we're all safe now, so go back to sleep."

"I was just worried about all of you, Mama." she whispered back. "I knew I was alright. I was with Daddy."

Mama kissed her again then went and lay down close to Daddy. Sally looked at her family in the lantern light for a few minutes then turned and looked toward the Colorado River. She loved that river. It usually had such a quiet, calm sound, almost musical as it ran over and around rocks or tree limbs.

But now it sounded furious and dangerous as it roared its way along carrying things that bumped and ground together. It was making strange, awful noises. And when you could only hear it and not see what was happening it was really scary. Sally wished they were even farther away.

She woke up with the sun already way up in the sky. She raised up and looked around. Most of the children were still asleep, but she saw that Mary was awake. The four grownups and William were standing together a little way off watching something. The river!

She got up. Mary came over and the two of them went to look. The sounds got louder and louder as they walked. Sally reached and caught Mary's hand.

"Oh, my word." Mary said. Sally cringed behind her sister.

No one had heard them coming, but they all turned around when they heard Mary. Mama picked Sally up and Daddy pulled Mary over next to him and put his arm around her.

"I can't believe this. It's like an enormous lake all around the house." Mary said. "Where did all this water come from?"

Uncle John said, "From God. And our safe passage came from God too."

They watched the river for a little longer then Mama said, "I'm hungry and I know everyone else is too. Let's see what we can find to eat."

The food for the morning ended up being a little left over cornbread made into fried patties and some dried meat. After they'd eaten, Daddy got the coffeepot, and went around and refilled the cups.

"I don't know about the rest of you but I'm about as tired as I've ever been." He said. "We can't do much until that river goes down some so I think this is a good day to take it easy and count our blessings."

"I sure agree. With all of that." Uncle John said. "I was in a good spot to count all those blessings, one by one, as they safely crossed that water last night. And if no one minds, I'd like to say a prayer of thanksgiving."

Mama said, "I'd like that very much, John."

"Almighty God. We thank you for the safe deliverance of our families. We thank you for all your rich blessings even including this rain and this river. We ask that you bless and keep safe the members of our family that aren't with us now. We do pray mightily for their safety..."

Sally heard his voice break at that point and she realized that all the grownups were worried about the other families. She hadn't even thought of them and they all lived on the river too. She sure hoped God would answer that prayer.

"...We ask for your continued blessings and thank you with all our heart. In Jesus name we pray. Amen."

Uncle John finished his prayer and all the grownups added "Amen." This time Sally whispered Amen too.

Daddy asked Aunt Mary, "What woke you up last night, Mary? I didn't hear a thing."

Aunt Mary said, "I was asleep for a little while, but restless and thought I could hear the river. But we'd been talking about the weather and the river all day, so I thought I was just letting my fears make me imagine things. I decided to try to go back to sleep and I turned over to get more comfortable.

"For some reason I put my hand down over the side of the bed and I felt water! I couldn't believe it at first. Then all I could think of was that my babies were going to drown. That's when I started yelling."

Mama told her, "Well, I'm glad your fear of the river had you sleeping light. The rest of us were dead to the world." She looked kind of strange then added, "Well, I guess that's about as poor a choice of words as I could've thought of. Anyway, thanks to you we're all safe."

Even though the river went down slowly, it was only a few days before Daddy, Uncle John, and William were able to start hauling the house logs up on the hillside. It took a few more days to get everything moved.

Mama and Daddy talked about where to put the house and how nice it would be to have it bigger than it had been. Daddy said, "Well, its kind of stretching it to call this a hill, but it's a good bit higher than where we were. And far enough away not to be so dangerous, at least I hope so. This could have been a real disaster. I'll never be so ignorant of the power of a river again, or how fast they can rise."

A little over a week after the flood, Uncle Tommy came riding up to the camp. As everyone ganged around him he was looking all around as if trying to see if everyone had made it though the flood.

Mama grabbed him as soon as he was off the horse and said, "I'm so glad to see you. We're all accounted for. How's the rest of the family?"

Uncle Tommy answered, "Thank goodness! Everyone else is alive and well too. We're all really fortunate." He told them all about the other families, neither Granddad's house or Uncle Andrew's house had been flooded. But the areas where they lived had a lot of flood damage so they had lots of hard work to do.

Uncle Tommy stayed only a few hours and then said, "I have to go."

Mama said, "Oh, I wish you could stay at least one night. But I understand."

"You know them, Rachel. Both Mama and Daddy are walking the floor worrying about everyone in the family. The sooner I can get back and tell them that we're all alive the better it will be. I think Daddy frets about the family more than Mama does."

Sally knew it was hard for Mama and Uncle John to watch their brother ride away. They were both standing beside each other, waving at Uncle Tommy. He turned in the saddle and waved at them and Mama took a deep breath. Sally watched as Uncle John put his arm around her shoulder.

Sally looked over to where William was standing as he too was watching Uncle Tommy leave. She walked over beside him and he just kind of glanced at her. Then she hit him as hard as she could on the upper arm. And ran.

He yelled, "Ouch." And ran after her.

Sally was fast and was darting through the trees, but she knew William was faster and would catch her. They weren't allowed to hit each other and she wasn't sure why she'd done it. She had time to think that she might be in trouble, but then she heard people laughing.

She started laughing too just about the time William grabbed her from behind. He yanked her off her feet and stood holding her for a moment like he was trying to decide what to do with her. Then he carried her over to a tree close to their camp, climbed up on a stump, and stretching up draped her across a limb of the tree. He then moved the stump so that she couldn't get down from the limb, looked at her with a wicked smile, brushed his hands together, and walked a few feet away.

Sally got herself into a position so that she could sit on the limb while leaning against the tree trunk. She looked down and saw that it was too far from the ground to make jumping her first choice. So she was stuck in the tree for now. And everyone was standing there looking up at her.

Mama had her hands on her hips and looked like she was trying not to laugh. "So, young lady. Looks like you're in a spot! William isn't supposed to take punishment matters into his own hands, but I think this works just fine. I believe you can just stay up there a while until you learn that it isn't right to hit."

"Yes, ma'am." Sally answered and she had to try with all her might not to smile.

Mama said, "Alright. Let's all get back to our chores."

Daddy looked up at Sally and grinned. She wondered what he was thinking. He didn't seem mad at her at all.

She could see the river between the trees. And she could see the entire camp and the place they were getting ready to put their house. It was a good view. She didn't know how long it would be before she'd want to be down, but for now it was really nice to be in a spot.

Just when her backsides were beginning to get tired of the limb, she saw Daddy talking to Mama and saw them look her way. Sally tried to look like she was sorry for what she'd done. Daddy motioned to William and the two of them came over to Sally's tree. They stood there looking at her and both of them were grinning. Sally tried not to grin too, but it was impossible.

Finally Daddy said, "I don't know why you two did what you did, but the timing was good. It took everyone's mind off of worrying about and missing the other families. But that doesn't mean you can hit your brother, Sally. And it doesn't mean you can mete out punishment to the other children, William."

They both said, "Yes, Sir."

"Get your sister out of the tree, William. Then the two of you can go on a walk and apologize to each other for your actions." As Daddy walked away he said, "Make it a short walk. There's a lot of work to do."

William rolled the stump over stood it on its end under the limb and stepped up on it. He reached up and Sally let him help her down. They walked toward the river without saying anything. William picked up a small handful of rocks and started skipping them across the river. Sally did the same although she wasn't as good at skipping them.

"Don't think you're some kind of big hero." William said.

"What're you talking about?" Sally asked him.

"You hitting me didn't have anything to do with trying to get everyone's mind off our troubles."

"I never said it did." Sally said.

"I know why you hit me. You saw Mama watching her brother leave and you thought about how you'd feel to see me leave and you came over and hit me."

She didn't say anything, just looked at him.

William stood and looked at her too then just said, "Come on, Squirt. It's time to get back to work."

Within a month the house was completely rebuilt, but much bigger. It was now a four-room house. It was in a better location and they noticed there were fewer mosquitoes and they got more of a breeze.

Mama said, "You know I've decided the river did us a favor. This is wonderful." And she gave Daddy a big hug.

Uncle John told her, "Hey, William and I worked nearly as hard and long on this house as Joseph did."

Mama laughed and gave Uncle John and then William just as big a hug and said, "Thank you so much. And I know everyone helped. Thank you all. Our home is beautiful."

In the early part of August, Aunt Margaret had another boy, and they named him John. As soon as Sally got to see this new little Rabb, she decided he looked like Granddad and she loved him instantly.

She turned eight years old in December and felt like she was getting pretty close to being a grownup. Then before long it was another year, 1826.

Early in the new year, Granddad, Grandma, and Uncle Ulysses again had to leave their place because of the Indians. And in March, Granddad sold and exchanged some more of his land in the Matagorda area.

Uncle Andrew, Uncle John, and Daddy tried to talk him into keeping the Matagorda land and exchanging his land in the Indian Hills area for more land close to them. Uncle Tommy told them they were just wasting their breath that he'd talked to him about it over and over and it was hopeless. He just wouldn't give an inch. Granddad was determined to build his mill and keep his word to Stephen Austin, so after staying a few months they'd gone back home.

Then later that year, they got the worst news that Sally had ever heard. Uncle Ulysses had died! Uncle Tommy brought the news and he cried the whole time he was telling Mama. He said Ulysses had an accident while he was riding his horse, and that he'd died instantly.

He was only William's age, sixteen years old. He'd grown to be the biggest of the men and was so strong. Sally couldn't imagine him dead. How could they be the same without his happy self?

All the families loaded up and went to Granddad and Grandma's place. Uncle Ulysses had already been buried, but they had the funeral after all the family got there. Sally had never seen people change as much as Grandma and Granddad had changed. They both looked real old, and they almost never said anything. It was like all the spirit had gone out of them.

Sally knew William was really grieving too, but she didn't know how to help him.

Soon the men and the older children went back home, but Mama, Aunt Mary, Aunt Margaret and all the younger children stayed with the grandparents. Sally thought it was strange that the best and happiest Christmas and the worst and saddest Christmas she'd known so far had both been here at Grandma and Granddad's place on the Colorado River.

Daddy and all the uncles came back in January to take everyone back home. This time it was Mama that talked to Granddad about coming back with them.

"Daddy, there hasn't been a day since we got here that there hasn't been one problem or another with the Indians. Mama needs some time to recuperate and so do you. You need to come home with us for awhile." she told him. And they were all surprised at his answer.

"Alright, Rachel. I think you're right. Maybe being away from these blasted nuisances for awhile will be good for us all."

But leaving was terrible for everyone. When they were packed and ready to go the family went one last time to stand beside Uncle Ulysses's grave.

Uncle Andrew and Daddy walked beside Granddad as he went to his horse, and Mama and Uncle John helped Grandma to the wagon. Sally saw Uncle Tommy get on his horse and ride a little way away from the wagon to wait on the family. She guessed he needed a few minutes to himself.

Then she saw William. He stood for another minute with his hand on the cross, then turned around. Sally went over to him and said, "I'm sorry, William."

He reached and caught her hand and said, "I'm sorry too, Sally. Come on. Let's go home."

Granddad and Grandma stayed only a few weeks and then went back home.

Uncle John bought a hundred acres from Uncle Andrew and he and Aunt Mary built a house there. It was just a mile from Uncle Andrew's house, close to the town of Egypt, and much closer to the Newman house. In May of that year, Aunt Mary had a baby girl they named Melissa.

And Mama was expecting again too. Sally hoped it would be another girl for them, since the youngest two were boys. But that didn't happen and in October 1827, Mama had a boy that she and Daddy decided to name Joseph Austin, after Daddy.

The next year Uncle Andrew and Aunt Margaret had their first girl and named her Sarah. Mama, Aunt Margaret, or Aunt Mary was always expecting it seemed and there were babies all over the place when the families got together.

Once again Granddad and Grandma were forced to leave their place because of Indians. They stayed a time with each of the three families but mostly with Mama. Granddad seemed to be thinking of his place, his mill, and other things again, but Sally didn't think Grandma was over losing Uncle Ulysses. She seemed to stare off into space a lot.

When they were all together the men were always giving Uncle Tommy a hard time about wasting so much time being single. They'd tell him he could have his pick of the women and then he could be stepping over babies and little children just like they were.

Uncle Tommy always took the teasing well and would tell them not to be in a hurry, that someone had to be out there protecting them from the Indians. Then in early 1829, when the families were visiting together at the Newman place, Uncle Tommy left for awhile and brought a young woman back with him. Her name was Serena Gilbert, Preston and Jasper Gilbert's sister. Serena was shy and nice and everyone liked her.

Except Sally. Sally decided she didn't like her. And she was angry with Uncle Tommy and she thought everyone was disgusting the way they were all taking on about the two of them. The women had Serena with them and all you could hear was laughing and happy talk. And the men were together, slapping Uncle Tommy on the shoulders and making wise cracks and such. Sally just couldn't stand it.

She waited until she thought no one would notice and she went out to the corral. She found a corner in the shade and sat down. Daddy's big gray horse walked over and tried to nuzzle her. It gave up when she hit at him with her hand.

She didn't know how long she'd sat there, but when she heard someone coming into the corral she looked up hoping it was Uncle Tommy. But it wasn't. She was surprised because the last person she'd have expected to come find her was Granddad. But there he was.

He walked over beside her, leaned against the fence and said, "Did you get a chance to see the horse I'm riding now?"

Sally didn't have time to answer before he continued, "I bought him from John Ingram. He'd gentled him pretty well but the first time I got on him he just nearly threw me. I didn't tell your grandma that because she would've really gotten upset. Cause I was in a terrible spot. I've always told all the boys to make sure they're in a place with a soft spot to land when they try out a fresh-broke horse. And I neglected to heed my own advice.

"You know that rocky area just to the side of my corral?"

By this time Sally was standing beside him at the fence and she said, "Yes, Sir."

"Well," continued Granddad, "I was inside the corral with the horse saddled and was just fixing to climb on. Then something shiny caught my eye. It was in that rocky area and seemed real unusual. So I led the horse out to get a better look at it. I picked it up and it was a real pretty, strange colored rock. I put it in my pocket and then just absently-mindedly climbed on that horse.

"Well, he gave me a ride for my money. Not so much that I couldn't stay with him, but enough that I was beginning to wonder how long it takes for old bones to knit. I tell you true, I was a little worried for a few minutes."

Sally didn't remember Granddad talking to her quite like this before. He was talking to her like he'd talk to a grownup. She knew he was doing it on purpose, and she felt a great love for him. He wouldn't know how to console her any other way and she decided he didn't have to.

She said, "Granddad, did you keep that rock?"

He smiled, got it out of his pocket and said, "I sure did. Would you like to have it?"

Sally admired the rock for a minute then said, "No, Granddad. I don't need it. Thank you very much."

They both knew what she was thanking him for. She reached and caught his hand and they walked back to join the family.

When they got closer Sally saw both Mama and Daddy look toward Granddad and her and then look away, like they were relieved.

But when she looked to see if Uncle Tommy was glad that she was rejoining them, she knew he hadn't even known she was gone. He could only see Serena.

'Uncle Tommy is happy for the first time since Uncle Ulysses died.' Sally thought. 'And he's my uncle. I've sure been silly today and I guess its high time I quite thinking like a little girl. I am eleven after all.'

Sally looked at Granddad, gave his hand a squeeze and went to see if Grandma had made a blackberry cobbler.

CHAPTER 7

Daddy is sick.
Late last evening Mama had sent William to get Uncle Tommy. But neither one of them was here yet.

Sally knew she should get up but she also knew the floor was going to be cold. And the blasted outhouse wasn't going to be a treat either.

She thought about Daddy. They hadn't seen much of Mama the evening before because she'd spent most all the time with Daddy. And the few times she'd been around them she seemed worried. Sally didn't want to think worried thoughts.

She decided to burrow just a little deeper in the warm bed and let her thoughts wander. But not think about Daddy. She thought instead about Uncle Tommy coming over. That would be nice. She always enjoyed seeing him and Aunt Serena.

She thought about how silly she'd acted when she first met Aunt Serena, and was embarrassed. The day of the marriage had been so much fun. It was at the Gilbert home and it seemed to Sally that the whole community had been there.

It wasn't long after the wedding that Uncle Andrew, Aunt Margaret and their children had moved to Granddad and Grandma's place. They'd waited until the fall of 1829, after Aunt Margaret had given birth to their daughter, Adeline, then they'd moved. Uncle John had to wait until the end of the year for the birth of their baby, Marion. Then in early 1830, they too had moved.

Uncle Andrew and Uncle John had both decided to move there and help Granddad get his mill built. Not being able to keep his word to Stephen Austin was bothering Granddad more all the time. So the families had all agreed that this was the time to help get the mill built and running.

It was a terribly sad time for Mama. And Daddy too. Now they not only missed Grandma and Granddad, but also Uncle Andrew, Uncle John and their families. Sally knew Mama still missed them. She probably especially wished they were here now.

And Sally's thoughts went right back to what she didn't want to think about yet. Daddy.

She intentionally made herself think back to when the other families had left and she remembered that it was around that same time that she'd gotten her horse. That was on her 12th birthday, in December of 1829, and was one of her favorite things to think about.

She couldn't believe it when she got a horse. She found out later that Daddy had discussed it with Mama who wasn't much for it, but had been persuaded. Daddy had reminded Mama that it was Sally that filled in as another hand when he and William needed help. It just made good sense to get her a horse of her own so that she could help them until Thomas and Ali got a little older.

Daddy had asked Granddad and the uncles to keep an eye out for a horse for Sally. And Uncle Andrew had found this one. The horse was a small built three-year-old. Because it was small it wasn't valued very highly, so Uncle Andrew had gotten him for a good price. Sally had been really surprised to get a horse of her own and she valued him very highly.

Then it was Christmas time and right after that was when Uncle John and his family had moved. That was also the time when Mary married Preston Gilbert and they moved to a small house of their own. Mary was the first of the children to move away. Sally still missed her and wished things could've just stayed the same. But she knew it wouldn't be long before William, Louisa, and Minerva got married and moved away too. She just hoped no one would move too far away.

She let her thoughts drift through the rest of last year. Remembering the time in August that they got word that Aunt Serena and Uncle Tommy had their first baby, a boy. And they'd named him Ulysses. When Mama heard that she cried. She said it was happiness for Tommy and Serena, and sadness for the short life of Uncle Ulysses.

Then Mama and Mary both had babies later in the year. Mary had a girl, Amanda, making Mama a grandma for the first time. And in November, Mama had her tenth child, another boy. He was named Andrew Rabb Newman and they called him Andy.

Then it was December again and her thirteenth birthday. Christmas had come and gone, and the first month of the new year was almost past. It wouldn't be long until spring; they should all be happy. But something felt wrong. There was a shadow, just out of sight, and at first Sally hadn't known what it was.

'Oh no. I'm back to here and now and I don't want to be here.' she thought. But there was no going back.

Daddy had been in bed for a few days, which was very unusual. Most of the children were led to believe it was just a winter fever of some kind. Even Sally thought that until a few days before. She heard Mama talking to William about the thorn Daddy had gotten in his thigh. It happened when he and William were driving some cattle to the pen. Mama was worried that it had gotten infected.

The doctor came out from town and spent a lot of time with Daddy. So each day Sally thought that would be the day that Daddy would walk into the kitchen with a grin and say something like, "Alright. Which one of you little varmints aren't working yet." But he hadn't.

Then last evening she, William, and the three older girls had been in the kitchen when Mama walked in. "I need to talk to you," she'd said. "I've asked Elizabeth to keep all the younger children in the boy's bedroom so we won't be interrupted. As soon as we're through talking one or two of you need to go in with her. She's upset to be left out.

"William, I want you to go to Tommy's house and ask him to come over. Tell him it's Joseph and to come right away. I don't know whether to send for Mama and Daddy, and Andrew and John or not. I don't want to get them out in this cold weather, but they'd be upset if we needed help and they weren't here."

"Uncle Andrew and Uncle John both live close to Grandma and Granddad. They'll go get them and they'll all come together, Mama." William said.

"I think it'd be good to send them a message." Mary added.

Mama just stood there for a few minutes and no one said anything. Then finally she said, "William, you decide whether to ask Tommy to send someone on to get the others." She'd told William to be real careful and then she'd gone back to Daddy's room.

Sally was surprised that Mama was leaving a decision like that to someone else.

William had left right away and Sally and her sisters had gone and joined the other children in the boy's room. Louisa had talked quietly to Elizabeth for a few minutes and Sally knew she hadn't told her how much they were worried. Because Elizabeth hadn't seemed too upset.

Sally still didn't want to think all these thoughts. She shook her head and knew that wouldn't make them go away. She got out of bed as quietly as she could so she wouldn't wake Elizabeth; might as well let her sleep. She dressed as quickly as she could.

Louisa and Minerva were already up. The four of them shared the same room so Sally knew they'd gotten up a little earlier. It wasn't daylight yet, but Sally could smell coffee and hear sounds in the kitchen.

Amanda, Mary's baby, started making some noise and Sally heard Mary go get her. Mary and Amanda were staying in William's room for now. They'd been staying with the family since Daddy got sick. Mary was already expecting another baby, so Preston had been coming over from their place every few days to see how things were going.

Preston may have already told Aunt Serena about Daddy being sick. That would mean that Uncle Tommy knew too. But he would've already been here if he'd known how bad it was.

Sally heard talking in Mama and Daddy's room, but she couldn't tell what they were saying. Probably talking about hearing the baby and the other sounds of the morning. 'He isn't really old yet.' She thought. 'He's forty-four and Mama's forty-one, not nearly as old as Grandma or Granddad.'

She shook her head again but already knew that didn't do a thing with scary thoughts. She listened for another minute to the murmur of low voices coming from the kitchen and thought, 'Mary is probably telling Louisa and Minerva what to do; but I'm so glad she's here. And I hope William gets back soon.'

Sally knew Mama always felt better when all her children were at home. And right now Sally wished all the families were here. But enough of this; it was time to get moving.

The outhouse was just as miserable as she knew it would be. There was some ice here and there, but she knew it wasn't as bad as it could've been. At least the wind wasn't blowing.

She was hungry but eating could wait. The best way for her to take her mind off Daddy was to get going on the chores. She went to the barn, stopped at the door before going in, and looked back at the house. 'We've been living here for seven years now.'

'Why did I think of that?' She wondered. 'All kinds of thoughts and memories have been rumbling around in my mind the last day or so. I know why of course. It's because of Daddy.'

Sally put some feed out for the two cows then she started milking Bitchy first; to get that over with. After that she'd milk Sugar. The cow's name's came about because of their personalities. Mama hadn't liked the name Bitchy, but even Daddy called the cow that.

Bitchy began stomping around and Sally realized that she'd gotten slower and slower till she'd almost stopped milking. "Cut it out, you dumb pain in the butt." She yelled at the cow. "Any more trouble from you and I'll tie you up by your tail."

Sally aimed a few squirts of the warm milk into her mouth and that made her feel better. "Thank you, Bitchy. I appreciate the drink."

The other cow turned her head around and looked at her. "So what do you think, Sugar? That I've gone batty? Well, I've known lots of people that talk to animals. I talk to the horses. Just because I've never talked this much with you two before doesn't mean a thing. And if I'm yammering like some daffy old lady then I won't be able to think about Daddy."

She felt silly and was glad no one was around to hear her. Bitchy stomped and moved away from her. "So I quit talking and you get bitchy, huh?" The cow settled down and chewed contentedly. "So, you like to be talked to do you? I'll have to ask William what he tells you when he's doing the milking. Right now everything I can think to talk about makes me think of Daddy. And I don't want to do that."

But she couldn't think of anything else but Daddy and this land and place he'd worked so hard on and was so proud of. She'd shut the door to keep out the cold but it didn't keep out the thoughts in her mind. She thought of the cows, horses, and other stock they'd accumulated, all the land they'd cleared, and structures they'd built.

They'd lived in the four-room house, built after the flood, until just a few years ago. Then another house about the same size was built in front, but with a space in between. A covered porch that people called a 'dogtrot' connected the two. Mama and Daddy moved into the room that had been the kitchen in the old part of the house and the girls got their old room. The two smaller rooms at the back went to the boys.

William kept the room on the left back because he liked the outside exit and the younger boys got the room that had belonged to the girls. They still had to shift around when visitors come but the extra space was great.

The new addition was divided; a little more than half of it was the new kitchen and the other part was a parlor. There was a water-well right beside the end of the back porch. Daddy said it was in a great place and one day soon he was going to pipe water into the kitchen for Mama.

Thinking about Daddy's plans for the house made Sally feel like crying and she realized that Bitchy was behaving like her name again. "Alright. I'm through with you anyway, Bitchy. Now if I could just be through with all these thoughts running around in my head."

Sally got up from the milking stool and put the pail aside. She slapped the cow on the rump and had to dodge a hoof. "You nasty old bitch. If you were mine I might just make beef jerky. No wonder William named you Bitchy."

"It's your turn, Sugar." As she started the milking the cow turned her head around as if to see what she was doing. Sally wondered what it would be like to be a dumb ole cow and not have to worry about things like your daddy being sick.

'So think of something else.' She made herself think of their house and how comfortable it was and what it looked like now. Connecting the two houses with the dogtrot changed the whole look to the house. Now what was once the sides of the house had become the front and the back and there was a porch along the entire front and back and also a small porch at the side entrance to the kitchen. The lean-to that had been against the old part of the house had been removed.

The barn, milk shed, and corrals were on the kitchen side of the house and the hog pen a full quarter-mile straight out behind the barn. When you had to slop the hogs you hated the distance, but it sure made good sense when the wind was from that direction. The outhouse was in the same direction but not as far away.

Sally's thoughts went wondered back to Daddy so she intentionally made herself think about the place again. 'So what haven't I thought about? Oh. Stinking chickens.' The chicken coop was attached to the barn on the opposite side of the house. It wasn't safe to have the animals too far from the house, but both the hogs and chickens were kept as far away as possible to cut down on the smell. The one smell worse than a hog was a chicken.

At the left front side of the house, a little way up from the river was the garden. The family could sit on the front porch and see the beautiful Colorado River running right down beside the garden and buildings. Sally realized that she was seeing the River in her mind and she thought of the big flood and seeing the river from the tree on the hill that William had put her in.

"No. I don't want to think about that tree." She said aloud. She finished the milking and headed for the house with the two pails of milk. But as hard as she tried she couldn't keep the thoughts about that tree on the hill from running through her head. 'That's also where the family cemetery is located; about a mile behind the house on that small hill with the big beautiful oak tree in the middle.'

The pails of milk were heavy but she'd been doing hard work for as long as she could remember. She opened the door just wide enough to set the pails inside and said, "Here's the milk."

Minerva smiled and said, "Thank you, Sally."

She could tell Minerva had been crying. She just gave her a smile in return, took a deep breath to keep from choking up, and headed for the chicken coop.

The cows were acting up. She'd forgotten to turn them out and they'd ruin everything in there. She went back over to the shed and let them out into the inner pasture. Then she let their calves in with them so they could get the rest of the milk.

One of the calves was so pretty. She'd be glad when she could have her own place with her own stock. She loved that little calf. Maybe she could work extra hard and talk Daddy into... She stopped. It seemed like everything got back around to Daddy. 'I just have to keep my mind on the chores.' she thought.

She walked back to feed the chickens and gather the eggs. With William gone she had an awful lot to get done. She should've gotten Thomas and Ali up to help, but she hadn't wanted to wake them. No one but Little Joseph and Andy had slept much last night.

Before she'd gone to sleep she'd heard Daddy moan. She knew he'd try not to upset any of them, so he must really be hurting. Later on she heard Mama crying. It took a long time to go to sleep after that.

Maybe next time I go to the house I'll go give the little boys a hug, cause I'd like one myself about now. A hug like Daddy gives; not very often, but when he does he nearly hugs the wind out of you. Like he wants to show you how much he loves you.

Thinking of Daddy again made her think of the family. 'I hope you get here soon, Uncle Tommy.' William had left late last evening so must have spent the night with Uncle Tommy and Aunt Serena. 'It will be good to see them, and I hope Uncle Tommy sent someone to tell the others.'

She thought of Granddad and Grandma and her uncles. It would be especially good to have Uncle Andrew here. Sally had always felt that Daddy was kind of partial to him. It would take a few days for them to get here. Then she remembered that Aunt Margaret was expecting a baby at anytime now. 'Oh, I hope that won't keep Uncle Andrew from coming.'

She felt guilty for the selfish thought. 'Even if Uncle Andrew can't come, Uncle John and Aunt Mary will come.' Uncle John was so good and kind, and Mama would be glad to have Aunt Mary here with her. Mama was probably closer to both of them.

'Even though she's worried about them making the trip, Mama needs Grandma and Granddad to be here. And so do I.' she thought. Then she thought of Uncle Ulysses and wondered why. She didn't want to think about people that were dead. Not now.

But a thought about a funeral she'd gone to when she was a very little girl came into her mind. She didn't even remember who's funeral it was. She just remembered Mama's cousin, Freeman Smalley, was there. He was a primitive Baptist preacher; really fierce seeming and Sally had been afraid of him. Uncle John talked about him once-in-a-while and said he could say prayers like no one you've ever heard before. 'I sure wish you were here now, Cousin Freeman. Maybe you could say one of your prayers and get God to help Daddy.'

She'd gathered all the eggs but the ones the old hen was setting on. She knew they'd have a lot of people to feed. Maybe she should kill that old rooster.

Daddy would say, 'That old boy's as tough as an old boot and not fit to eat.' But he loved chicken and dumplings. Mary or Louisa could cook it and maybe Daddy could eat some. She'd talk to the girls about it.

Sally dreaded going back to the house even though she was cold and hungry; she was afraid she wouldn't be able to keep from crying. But she took the eggs and went into the kitchen. The room was warm and smelled good; like coffee and hot bread and sausage. She stood in the door a minute, then realized they were all three looking at her.

"Well, don't just stand there shivering cold." Mary said. And she folded her apron up at the waist, came over and pulled her close and hugged her. Sally hadn't expected that and would've dropped the eggs but Louisa grabbed the basket and she and Minerva put them in the cooler box.

Mary stepped back and told her, "Sit down and eat."

Sally said, "I should go check on the horses first but I'm so hungry. It smells wonderful in here." She sat down at the table, looked at Daddy's empty chair then looked away. She didn't dare ask how he was doing yet.

Louisa brought her a plate and said, "Two fried eggs just as you like them; hard in the middle and kind of lacy around the edges."

There was a sudden silence. Sally thought, 'We're all thinking that's how Daddy likes his eggs.'

Minerva quickly said, "Here's a piece of bread and some sausage. The butters on the table."

Mary was making some pies but she stopped and got a cup, filled it with coffee and then added some cream. She brought it to Sally. She got herself some coffee and sat down in the chair beside Sally. Louisa sat down on the other side of the table.

Sally was so glad to get the steaming hot coffee. She'd finished her eggs when Minerva came over to the table and grinned at her. Then she put a spoonful of blackberry preserves on her plate. Blackberry preserves. One of her favorite foods. It always reminded her of Grandma's house, Christmas time, and joy. They could use a little joy right now.

Sally looked suspiciously at all three of them, "Why are you waiting on me? And why are we eating like this?" Usually they had coffee and a piece of bread and sometimes a piece of dried meat. There was always too much work to do to take so much time on breakfast.

Mary said, "I know we only eat this way for special occasions. It may seem a little wasteful but we thought it would make us all feel better to have a good breakfast."

Minerva had joined them at the table and they talked for a few minutes about anything and everything except what was on their minds. Sally was usually too restless to dawdle over anything but she was tired, so she made that spoonful of blackberry preserves last as long as possible.

Minerva got the coffeepot and was refilling their mugs when they heard a loud groan from the bedroom. They heard Mama say something but couldn't hear the words. No one moved for a full minute. Then Minerva sat the coffeepot on the stove and came back to the table.

"It has to be awful for him to make a noise." Louisa said. Sally looked at her and saw that her eyes were full of tears. Mine are too, she thought.

She remembered a number of times when Daddy was hurt and he just clinched his teeth and never made a sound. Of course she'd heard him swear a time or two when they were building the new barn, but that was different.

She nearly burned her mouth finishing her coffee so she could get back outside. She couldn't stand to hear him and know he was hurting so she didn't want to be in the house. She got up and took her plate, fork, and mug to the wash bucket, cleaned them and put them up.

"Do you think Daddy would eat some dumplings? I could kill that old rooster." She asked.

Minerva answered, "That's a good idea. And the sooner the better so we can cook him long enough that maybe we can eat him."

"What's Elizabeth doing? Is she alright?"

Mary answered her. "She's being her usual wonderful self and taking care of all the little ones, including mine. She's just like you. She loves the babies."

Sally asked, "Are the bigger boys up? I could use their help."

Louisa said, "Mama fed Andy before we got up, so when he was fussy a few minutes ago I got him a little sugar water and he went back to sleep. Elizabeth is watching him, and last time I looked in the boys room she was dressing Little Joseph. Thomas and Ali were up but they're being slow."

Minerva added, "We'll get those two in here and make them eat, then send them out to you. They'll have too hard a time staying in the house and being quiet anyway. And working with you will make the time go faster for them."

"Thank you." Sally said. "And thanks for breakfast and all."

She was surprised when Mary said, "We're the ones that should be thanking you. I know we give you a hard time for preferring the horses to us, but we're sure thankful for you today. None of us care all that much about the outside chores."

Minerva kind of snorted and said, "It's more like we'd just rather be in a nice warm kitchen. But Mary's right. We do appreciate you."

Louisa added, "We've always appreciated how hard you work, Sally. Don't stay out too long today. It's cold. Come in once-in-a-while for some coffee."

'Well, hell.' Sally thought. 'I made it through this whole hour and now just as I'm leaving they turn soft on me and make me feel like crying again. And I can't leave until I ask.'

"How is he really?" She hadn't said it very loud.

"What?" Mary asked.

Sally turned toward her and said again, "How is he?"

Mary looked to Minerva, and Minerva said, "I took Mama a cup of coffee just before you came in and she said he's about the same."

Sally took a deep breath, then asked, "How's Mama?" She got three sets of shrugged shoulders. There wasn't anything to say to that so she went on outside.

She loved those three sisters, especially Louisa. But around them she always felt like the odd stray, the daughter that would rather be doing the work of a son. 'I may be a stray that way but they can't claim I don't belong.' She thought. 'According to Grandma I got my looks and temperament from my mama and my eyes and quietness from my daddy.'

"Wish I could make all these thoughts be quiet." she said aloud.

As she neared the corral she looked up at the sky. It was not terribly cold for early February, but there was kind of a heavy feeling to the air. She hoped a norther wasn't coming. All Mama needed to worry her to death was bad weather catching William and the families out in it.

The four horses they had in the pen all stamped and whinnied at her. They wanted some hay and a little attention too. Sally always spent as much time with the horses as she could and she loved them all, especially her own.

They called him 'Sapo.' She knew the name was silly. But when she got him last year Little Joseph was about three years old, and that's what he called him. Mama had figured out he was trying to say 'Sally's pony.' So, the horse was Sapo.

The horses nudged and pushed her as she got them some hay. She talked to each one in turn. William had turned Daddy's horse out last week because he wouldn't be needed for awhile. She kind of wished he were here, too. Oh, well.

She saved Sapo until last. She patted him and put her arms around him. He was more interested in the hay but he stood patiently and let her scratch his ears. She put her head on his neck and suddenly was crying.

"Hells, bells." she said out loud. The horse turned his head and looked at her. The quizzical look and the timing made her think of

Mama telling her she was going to get her mouth washed out with soap next time a curse word came out of it. That thought brought a sad little smile.

She looked up just as Thomas and Ali came running though the gate. She stepped back and made a quick wipe of her eyes with her coat sleeve. She was glad they hadn't seen her crying. They didn't need that right now.

She went in the barn with them and gave them a job to do then went back to her chores. She thought, 'I've learned all the things a woman has to do, such as cooking, sewing, and helping with the children. But what I like to do is take care of horses and cows, especially horses. I hate gardening. It's grueling, backbreaking work. I almost wish I was another brother instead of a sister.'

Uncle Tommy was always telling her she was a natural with a horse and she should've been a man. Then he'd laugh and say, 'But, that would be a waste, cause you're too damn pretty for a man.'

The first time he said that, she felt a little irritated because she didn't see what pretty had to do with anything. She just wanted to do everything William got to do and be appreciated as much. But the last year or so, she noticed how the boys and even some men looked at her. Maybe she liked that and no longer wanted to be a brother.

"What are you boys doing?" she yelled at Thomas and Ali. She'd gone into the barn and caught them scuffling around. They'd turned over a bag of chicken feed. Sally realized that instead of paying attention she'd been daydreaming again, or woolgathering, as Granddad would say. She should've given them more to do.

"There's all kinds of chores that need done. But instead of that the two of you are going around competing to see who can get into what first." She told them. "Not much feed spilled out, but I want you to pick up every last speck of it. You've been told all your life how scarce things are and how important it is to make every little bit count."

She stopped and looked at them. She realized that she'd been giving them the same lecture Mama would have. And worse than that, she could tell they were listening to her just about like they did to Mama.

She knew that look well too. You look right at the person, nod your head and look sorrowful, but you aren't really paying very close attention. You just don't want to get smacked. And you want to hurry and get back to what you were doing.

She told them to get it picked up, gave them another job when they were finished, and heard them giggling as she went back to work. She grinned to herself and wondered if that's what Mama did sometimes.

It was mid-morning by the time she finished feeding the hogs. Now she needed to catch and kill that old rooster and she was really tired. She hoped they could all get a good night's sleep tonight. But if some of the relatives got here it'd be crowded and there'd probably be another night without much sleep.

She got Thomas and Ali to help her with the rooster. They thought that was great fun. "Mary will smack you for chasing that bird around. She'll say you made him tough," she told them.

"This old bird was tough as a boot long before today." Thomas said. And Sally grabbed the rooster as they chased it past her.

"You boys take it to the kitchen. They'll have hot water ready to dunk it in. Maybe they'll let you pluck it." she said.

As they ran toward the kitchen she heard them both saying. "I get to first." She hoped the girls appreciated how well she'd managed that.

Sally heard the horses coming before she saw them. She picked up her rifle and walked toward the house. She got only a quick hug from Uncle Tommy before he went inside. William asked, "What's happening with Daddy?"

"No change, last I heard. But the girls will know more than me." And she followed him into the house.

Uncle Tommy had made quick work of greeting the ones in the kitchen and had already gone to Mama and Daddy's room. William got himself a cup of coffee and said, "I'll take Uncle Tommy a cup."

After he'd gone Mary asked Sally, "Did either one of them say anything? Did they send for the others?"

"There wasn't time for any of that." Sally said.

They waited for awhile then Mama and Uncle Tommy came into the kitchen.

"William's going to stay with your daddy for a few minutes." Mama said. "One of you get him a piece of bread or something and take it to him. He's hungry."

111

Sally thought, 'We all want to see Daddy, but we don't want to see him either.' And about that time Louisa said, "I'll take it."

"When was the doctor here?" Uncle Tommy asked.

"Just two days ago." Mama said.

"What did he tell you to do? When's he coming back?" he asked.

"He gave me some medicine to keep him comfortable." Mama said.

"Comfortable! Hell's fire! I'll go get him back out here. He ought to be here."

"Tommy, please." Mama reached and caught his hand.

He quit pacing and sat down in the chair next to her. "The doctor said…" Mama started then had to start again. "The doctor said there wasn't anything else he could do."

Uncle Tommy got up from the chair so fast it fell over. He looked around the room then turned and walked out the door.

"Should one of us go out with him?" Minerva asked.

Mama just shook her head no.

Sally hadn't known that the doctor had said that. She couldn't stop the tears from running down her face.

It wasn't but a few minutes until he came back in the room. He picked the chair up, turned it towards Mama and sat down. Then he reached and caught her hands. "I'm sorry, Rachel. I'd never intentionally make things harder than they are."

"I know that, Tommy." Mama replied.

"I sent someone to Andrew's place. I thought it'd be better if he and John go get Mama and Daddy. I'm going to head back home, get things set there, then bring Serena and the baby back with me. I'll be back sometime tomorrow afternoon."

"I hoped you'd spend the night." Mama said.

"I'd like to. But it'll be better this way. It'll take the others a few days to get here, and until Andrew's here I'll do whatever's needed so you or the kids don't have to worry about it."

Mama looked at him in a strange way. And Sally wondered what he meant about 'whatever's needed'.

Mama said, "Come tell Joseph goodbye before you leave." And she turned to Sally and said, "Come with us. You're the only one that hasn't been in to see him yet today."

Daddy was talking to William when they went in the room. But when he saw Sally he said, "Hello there. I hear that you can give a lecture and sound just like Mama."

She was so relieved. He sounded almost like he always did.

"Thomas and Ali told on you. Come over here and sit on the bed. Let me tell Tommy goodbye so he can get on his way, then you can tell me about the animals."

The two men talked for a few minutes then Mama and Uncle Tommy left the room.

It was a strange conversation for Sally. Other than gritting his teeth once- in-a-while, and the fact that he was in bed, Daddy talked like he would've at any other time. After she'd told him about the animals, he told her and William what they needed to do for the next few days. But pretty soon she noticed that he looked awfully tired.

"I tell you what, honey." He said. "You go see if those girls have those dumplings cooking. I'm going to talk to William a few more minutes, then I think I'll take a nap."

Sally said, "Alright, Daddy." She kissed him on the cheek, raised up a little and looked into his eyes. Did he know how sick he was? Did he know what the others were saying? He lifted his hand and touched her on the face. His hand felt hot.

"I love you." She said.

"I love you too." He answered. She looked at him another moment then left the room.

Uncle Tommy, Aunt Serena, and Little Ulysses made it over the next afternoon. And by the day after that friends and neighbors were beginning to drop by to check on Daddy and offer their help. The doctor came back for a visit and Sally wondered if Uncle Tommy had something to do with that.

She stayed outside and worked with William and Uncle Tommy most of the time. Each time they heard horses coming all three would pick up a gun and wait to see who it was.

Then finally around the tenth of February, Uncle Andrew and Uncle John rode into the yard. Sally was so glad to see them. They got off their horses, gave her and William a hug, then greeted their brother.

"How is he?" Uncle Andrew asked.

Uncle Tommy said, "Not good."

Sally knew that was true but she didn't want him to say it that way.

Uncle John said, "How's Rachel?"

Uncle Tommy shrugged and said, "Not good either."

Some of the children had come out on the little kitchen porch, so the five of them started toward the house and they all went into the kitchen. Uncle Andrew and Uncle John were giving everyone a hug when Mama came in through the other door. They both moved toward her and she nearly fell in their arms.

Uncle Andrew and Uncle John awkwardly held their sister, because she wanted to hold on to both of them. And she cried. Sally thought she couldn't stand it. They were all crying now.

Just a minute or two passed, and Mama straightened up and wiped her eyes. She asked, "Where are the others? Mama and Daddy?"

Uncle John told her. "Daddy thought Andrew and I should get on down here to help, so we came on as soon as we got word. Daddy, Mama, Mary and our children are coming by wagon and should be here in a couple of days."

Mama asked Uncle Andrew. "How's Margaret and the children? Oh, dear goodness. She has to have had the baby by now. With all this…" and she stopped.

He said, "They're all well, Rachel. We have a new baby boy that we named Thomas. Margaret's doing just fine and she said to give you her love. She would like to have come with us."

Then Mama took her three brothers across to the bedroom to see Daddy.

Sally went back outside by herself. She went around the house and was standing at the end of the back porch when she heard someone come out of Mama and Daddy's bedroom. Instead of going across to the kitchen he came out to the back porch. Something inside Sally gave up when she saw her Uncle Andrew's face. Tears were running down his cheeks. He put both hands on the porch post and leaned his head against it.

Before he saw her, Sally very quietly stepped around to the side of the house. As she walked to the corral, she heard Uncle Andrew clear his throat. Then she heard the kitchen door open and close.

There were so many people around. Granddad, Grandma, Aunt Mary, and her children had all arrived. And so many neighbors were in and out. Some of the men had set up some shelters outside. Beds were made in the barn, and there were fires going here and there to keep people warm.

All the women that came by brought food so that the girls wouldn't have to worry about the cooking. And the men wanted to do all the chores so that the family didn't have to do anything. Sally hated that. It was better when she had work to do.

She loved her big family. But she hated having all these other people here. Every time she turned around someone was looking at her with sorrowful eyes.

She was in the kitchen when Granddad came in and said, "Your mama would like for you children to come see your daddy."

After they were all in the room Mama said, "Joseph, the children are here now."

Daddy didn't open his eyes.

"Joseph, they're all in here now."

He just seemed asleep, except that his breathing was louder than it had been.

Finally Uncle John said, "Come on children. You can come back later when he wakes up."

Sally was in the corral with her horse, trying to avoid everyone when Gail Borden and Eli Mercer rode into the yard. Mr. Borden was the surveyor for the Austin Colony and Mr. Mercer owned the store in Egypt. She watched as Uncle Andrew came out to the porch to greet them. Then the three of them went into Daddy's room. Sally knew that Mama, Grandma, and Granddad were already in there. It was only a minute until she saw William, Uncle John, and Uncle Tommy walk across to the room too.

Sally went and sat on a tree stump at the back side of the corral. She only half watched the dozen or so people that were standing around in little groups, talking quietly. She knew she should appreciate them being here. They were all good people and were here to help. But she just wanted it to all go away.

'They've sure been in there a long time.' she thought. And not long after that she saw men walking out to the front porch. She got up and walked over to the front side of the corral just in time to hear a man say, "Well, they must of finished doin' the will."

Sally thought she couldn't breathe. She ran into the barn and leaned against the old cart. She heard someone come in and hoped it would be a family member, not someone else. She turned around and looked to see who it was, but couldn't see through her tears.

Then the one that was always there for her was holding her. She held on tight and said, "Oh, William. It hurts."

"I know." he said. And they both cried.

"We need to get back to the house, Sally."

"Alright." she answered. And they went to the house.

As they entered the kitchen Aunt Mary said, "I was just coming to get you. Your mama wants you to come to the bedroom."

Sally didn't know if it just worked out that way or not, but except for the youngest ones, they entered the room as they'd been born. Mary had her baby in her arms and went in first with William behind her. Then Louisa carrying baby Andy and Minerva with little Joseph followed William.

Sally looked and saw that Elizabeth, Thomas, and Ali were all standing close to her. She caught Elizabeth's hand, and Thomas reached for Ali's hand, and the four of them went into the bedroom.

Grandma and Mama were sitting in chairs pulled up close on one side of the bed. Grandma was sitting on one side of Mama and Granddad was standing at her other side. The uncles were lined up around the other side of the bed.

Sally watched as Granddad moved to the other side of Grandma and motioned to William. William went to stand beside Mama where Granddad had been. Sally didn't think Mama even knew they were there, she was just looking at Daddy.

The older girls stood at the bottom of the bed and the uncles backed up and got the other children in front of them. More people came in until the room was full. People were crying and she was too. But she was trying hard to stop so that she could see her daddy. Then

Uncle John said a short prayer. Sally didn't really know what words he said, because her heart couldn't hear right then.

She felt like the whole world got quiet, like everyone was listening. Then the next few sounds echoed round and round in her head.

She heard a gasp and then a sigh of air from her daddy, and then heard Mama.

"NO! JOSEPH!" Then Mama leaned over and lay her head on Daddy's chest.

One at a time, they each kissed their daddy good-bye and the aunts and friends got them out of the room.

The next day, on February 16, 1831, Sally stood and watched the box lowered into the ground and saw and heard the dirt shoveled in on it. And she felt the worst hurt she'd ever known.

Daddy was dead.

SECTION II

CHAPTER 8

The days dragged slowly by. Grandma stayed with Mama, but everyone else returned to their homes. Various neighbors stopped by occasionally but the sad atmosphere didn't make anyone want to stay long.

To Sally the empty spot left by Daddy was too big to fill. She wished the time would hurry by; that's what so many people said would heal the grief. Time.

Grandma got a letter from Granddad with news of him and the families there. He told about the progress on the mill and how close they were to completing it. He said everyone there was well and he hoped they were also. The letter ended with Granddad saying, 'Be sure to take good care of each other. Your husband, William Rabb.'

The day after that, Grandma told Mama she thought she ought to go back home. Mama waited until Grandma was resting and then got the older children together for a talk. "I'm worried about your grandma. She doesn't look well. She tells me that Daddy needs her, and I'm sure he wants her home, but she's the one that needs to be in her own home. And with him."

Mama looked toward the family cemetery for a minute then continued, "I don't want to leave right now but I need to be with Mama. William, you, Louisa, and Minerva can take care of everything here. There've been few Indian troubles recently so I don't think that's a big worry. I'll need Sally and Elizabeth to help me with the boys. We'll take Mama home and stay with her and Daddy awhile."

Sally thought the older three would protest, but they didn't. They didn't want Mama to go without them, but they all had sweethearts so that meant they didn't want to be gone from home. As for her, she was thinking it would be kind of nice to be at her grandparent's house.

They'd heard earlier that two of the neighbors were going to Gonzales to join the militia, so William got word to them of Mama's plans. The two men offered to travel with the family. The timing was fortunate but not terribly unusual. There was quite a bit of travel back and forth to the Gonzales area. If these men hadn't been going at this time the family would've just had to wait until someone else was going.

Sally thought 'better sooner than later.' She'd decided it'd be good not only for Grandma but for Mama too. There hadn't been a morning or an evening that Sally hadn't seen Mama at Daddy's grave.

Mama hurried her preparations, everyone helped, and the wagon was soon loaded. They were ready to go the morning the two neighbors came riding into the yard. There was a third man with them, Jesse Robinson, one of the men who'd come to their rescue at Granddad's house. They had known him a long time. He lived close to Gonzales and was headed back that way.

The family gathered at Daddy's grave. It'd only been a few weeks since he'd died, so the dirt still showed. By the time they returned home his grave would be covered with grass and wildflowers.

Sally tried to not cry, but couldn't help it. She silently told Daddy good-bye then followed William as he walked Grandma to the wagon. Sally was taking Sapo along so had him tied to the back of the wagon, along with the extra horse they were taking. She'd ride Sapo occasionally but would mostly help Mama drive the wagon.

Mary had come over to stay with them until they left, so she, Louisa, Minerva, and William helped Mama, Grandma, and the other children up into the wagon. Tears and good-byes were flowing back and forth.

Leaving was horrible! Sally looked back just before they lost sight of the house and could see the girls still waving good-bye. She looked over at Mama and saw that she was looking back too. She probably couldn't see a thing because a flood of tears was rolling down her cheeks. It was as if they were really leaving Daddy for the first time and the feeling was like being under a very heavy, very dark cloud.

Sally looked in the back of the wagon and saw that Elizabeth was holding both Andy and Joseph, with Thomas and Ali sitting nearby. They all looked miserable and sad. She turned back to the front, picked up Daddy's whip and flicked it just above the head of the horses and said, "Move faster, damn you."

Grandma's eyebrows went up and Sally realized she'd said it too loud. But Mama was leaning against Grandma and hadn't noticed.

They proceeded along with one man always in front, one to the rear, and the third usually close to the wagon. The three kept a constant watch for Indians and Mexicans. At the time Sally had urged the horses on with a curse, Jesse Robinson was riding alongside the wagon. She'd never paid any particular attention to him before. But, she noticed him looking at her and couldn't tell if it was a look of disapproval or if he was just noticing her for the first time. She blushed and decided to watch her tongue. She knew she shouldn't use curse words, but sometimes they just fit.

"Have you ever been to Gonzales?" he asked.

Sally was so surprised that she just looked at him and then away. It was the first time he'd talked directly to her. From the corner of her eye she could see that he was smiling.

She mumbled something that she hoped sounded like. 'No, I haven't.'

He started by saying that it wasn't a lot different than it was where Granddad and Grandma's place was. Then he was telling them about the Guadalupe River and was describing the area in glowing terms. By then everyone was listening to him and Thomas was leaning out of the side of the wagon asking him questions.

They camped the first evening in an open area near the Colorado River. The family was exhausted from the travel and their emotions. The three men took care of everything, even the cooking. That was embarrassing to Mama and Grandma, so by the next morning it was evident that they weren't going to let that happen again.

Before they got on the way that morning, Mama told Jesse. "Thank you for what you did yesterday. It was a lifesaver, not only for the children but also for Mama and me too. I really appreciate it."

"Well, I don't think I ever talked that much before in my life. Don't know that anyone would ever want me to again either. But I thought you could all use a little distracting and the Gonzales area is easy for me to talk about. It's my favorite part of the country, at least so far." Jesse replied.

The following two days went by without incident. Sally took turns with Mama in driving the wagon and also rode Sapo occasionally. Any time she rode, it was Jesse who rode beside her. He also asked Mama for permission to take Thomas and Ali for a ride. She agreed. So every so often the two boys rode the extra horse and joined Jesse as lookouts. Sally thought it was funny to watch them. Both boys hung on every word he said. She wondered if Jesse Robinson knew he'd elevated himself almost up to the level of their Uncle Tommy.

When they arrived at Indian Hills, the pleasure of seeing Granddad and Grandma together again made them all feel better. There was laughter and lighthearted talking for the first time in many weeks.

Granddad practically ordered the three men to stay the night and eat with them. He gave Jesse an especially warm greeting and told them all how much he appreciated them bringing his family safely to him. It was a good evening; Sally was happy to see all the family. When she helped Mama put the two littlest boys to bed, Mama said, "I thought I couldn't stand leaving home. It hurt so much. But this is a good thing. It's so good to be with Daddy, Mama, and the others."

They'd arrived in time to see the mill actually at work. It was a big building; very impressive to children that were unfamiliar with large structures. They all got a grand tour and got to watch as it ground corn into meal, just as it was designed to do.

Granddad thoroughly enjoyed giving the family a tour of the mill. But Sally thought he was either tired or not feeling well. She noticed that Uncle John was almost always at Granddad's side and didn't let him do any hard work. 'Uncle John is the one that seems to be managing the mill and Granddad is letting him. Something's not exactly right.' She thought.

They had a wonderful few weeks and all shared the relief Granddad felt in finally getting the mill built. Everyone was so proud of him. But Sally noticed that now all the grownups were watching him and trying to anticipate anything he needed or wanted. She wanted to ask Mama what was wrong with him, but didn't want to upset her. And then she didn't have to ask.

One afternoon, Granddad, Uncle Andrew, and Uncle John came riding into the yard. It was unusual for them to come home before dark, so something was wrong. Mama and Grandma immediately went outdoors when they heard them ride up.

Granddad told them he was all right, but he looked the color of the chalk they used to practice writing their letters. Over his protests, Grandma and Mama got him to go inside and insisted he sit down and put his feet up on a box. He wouldn't go to bed.

He said. "It's sinful for a body to go to bed in the middle of the day, unless it's to die or have a baby. And I don't plan to do either one at the moment. So leave me be and don't fuss so."

Grandma didn't let that bother her a bit and kept at him to rest. She got him a cup of coffee and went and sat beside him.

Sally followed along as Mama went out on the porch with her brothers. "What happened?" Mama asked.

Uncle John said, "He turned pale and put his hand on his chest. Then he would've fallen, but I held him up until he got his balance. He tried to pretend he was all right, but I could tell he wasn't. He didn't have any strength. So I yelled at Andrew and we decided to make him come home."

Uncle Andrew added, "He doesn't look good now, but you should've seen him right after it happened. He looked awful."

He waited a minute, but Mama didn't say anything so he continued. "I sent one of the workers to Burnam's place, to see if Burnam would send some men to find Tommy. Last I heard he was around Gonzales."

At that, Mama leaned her head against Uncle Andrew's chest and said, "This is too much." He just held her.

Sally asked Uncle John, "Can't we get a doctor?"

"Andrew told the worker he sent to Burnam's place to ask about one." he replied.

Sally thought 'Uncle John's voice has no hope in it.'

They tried to make Granddad comfortable, but he wouldn't lie down.

"If I lie down I won't get up. Andrew, did you send for Tommy?"

"Yes sir. I sent someone right away." Uncle Andrew told him.

Aunt Margaret and Aunt Mary and their children had gotten to the house, so it was full of people and noise. They were both trying to keep the children quiet and still, but Granddad told them, "Let them be. I want to hear them talking and laughing and having a good time."

He asked that a chair be placed next to his and one by one he asked each child to come over and sit beside him. He'd call them over, talk a few minutes, and end by telling them he loved them.

Sally knew he was telling them good-bye, but he was doing it in such a way that there wasn't much crying. She looked at Granddad and he looked so pale. He was having trouble breathing and was resting for a moment. Then he saw her looking at him and motioned her to come over. She walked to the chair and sat down.

He reached for her hand and as she put her hand in his she felt something in it. She started to look, but Granddad told her to wait. He talked to her very quietly and said, "Sally, you have a strong spirit. It's probably going to cause you some misery. Just always be true to yourself."

She didn't know what he meant. He took a few breaths then added, "When you see what's in your hand, don't cry. You can cry later, alright?" She wasn't at all sure she could keep from crying, but she nodded.

He said, "I love you, Sally girl."

"I love you too, Granddad." Then she got up and walked away. She hadn't noticed Granddad give any of the other kids anything, so she waited to look at it until she'd walked outside. She knew what it was, but didn't want to look just yet.

She sat down on the edge of the porch, put her hands in her lap, and sat there thinking about all the wonderful things she remembered about her granddad. Finally she opened her hand and looked at the rock. The same shiny rock Granddad had used to get her to quit feeling sorry for herself when Uncle Tommy announced his marriage.

She thought, 'I can keep from crying now, but not for long.' Holding tight to the rock, she went back in the house.

Supper had been cooked and some of it had been eaten; only the little kids were very hungry. Mama said she'd eat something later. Sally worried that Mama was too thin and not eating enough. She got some biscuits, bacon, and coffee and talked Mama into going out on the porch with her.

Mama finally ate a biscuit with her coffee, but nothing else. "I'd like to send someone to get William and the girls, but I don't think they'd have time to get here."

As Sally watched Mama fight back tears she wondered if it always hurt so much for your parents to die, even after they were old. She didn't know what to do to help Mama but she had to try.

"Mama, let's go see Elizabeth and the boys for a few minutes. They need to see you and maybe it'll make you feel better to see them."

"That's a good idea." Mama said. And they went into the side room where their family was staying.

Sally hugged Elizabeth and said, "I'm sorry I'm not helping you with the boys."

And Elizabeth said, "Don't be. You need to watch out for Mama. I'd rather be taking care of the boys than dealing with everything in there. We all talked to Granddad and that's all I want."

Then Elizabeth saw that Mama had been listening and said, "Oh, Mama I didn't mean that in a bad way."

Mama wrapped her arms around her and said, "My dear child, I don't think you could think anything in a bad way. Thank you for taking care of your brothers. Because of you I don't worry about them. And that's such a relief right now."

Mama kissed Elizabeth again, then hugged and kissed each of the four boys about a dozen times. Thomas and Ali probably would've just as soon not had all the kisses, Sally thought, but they were old enough to know what was happening. So they returned Mama's hugs.

Later in the evening, Sally was sitting in the big room dividing her time with watching Granddad and Mama. She'd just looked in on her family and all except Elizabeth were sleeping. Elizabeth was sitting by the lantern doing some embroidery. Sally thought what a wonderful sister she is. They smiled at each other and Sally went back to sit in an out of the way spot to watch Mama.

All the other children were asleep in other rooms, and other than Sally it was just the grownups in this room. They were sitting around the fireplace talking quietly. Granddad was having a harder time now, but no one was trying to get him to do anything other than what he wanted to. He seemed to be thoroughly enjoying the talking and reminiscing.

All of a sudden he held up his hand and everyone was silent. He cocked his head and listened, then said, "Well, there's nothing wrong with my hearing. There's a horse coming. And if God be with me, it'll be Tommy."

Sally was thinking, please, please let it be Uncle Tommy. And it was.

His horse had just barely stopped and he was coming through the door.

He looked around quickly, touched Grandma on the shoulder as he passed, and went and stopped in front of Granddad. He stood for the longest time looking down at Granddad then said, "Hey, Judge. You caught me camped just a few hours away. You trying to make me miss a fight or two?"

Granddad had a big smile on his face and his eyes were bright as he reached out both hands. Uncle Tommy pulled the extra chair close and caught Granddad's hands. He leaned his head over until his head was against Granddad's head. They stayed that way a minute then Uncle Tommy sat back and Granddad said, "I've been waiting on you, son."

Someone got Uncle Tommy something to eat and Grandma asked about Aunt Serena and little Ulysses. He said they were both doing real well and were staying with Serena's family while he was away this time.

They talked about many things and Granddad told a number of his favorite stories. But he didn't have much energy. After a quiet time he said, "I got my mill built, thanks to you boys. I've done most all I've wanted to do; and had a good time doing it."

He had to quit for a minute then continued, "I only have two major regrets and that's losing Ulysses and Joseph too soon. But today I've had the best gift of all. I've got my wife and my four children here with me."

He reached out to Grandma and she sat beside him and held his hand. Sally noticed that none of the grownups told Granddad not to talk like he was dying. They were just sitting around him, listening and nodding agreement.

She wanted to stay awake, but was nodding off more and more. Mama touched her on the shoulder and whispered, "Sally, you should go to bed. I'll wake you early in the morning."

Sally went and told each grownup goodnight, getting an extra nice hug from Uncle Tommy. She saved Granddad until last. He smiled as she kissed him on the cheek and raised his hand to pat her on the arm. But his hand was shaking and he put it back in his lap.

Sally traded "I love you." with him. After a long look she turned and walked into the room where her family was sleeping. Mama followed her and gave her a long hug. Sally needed the hug, but decided that Mama needed it even more. Mama told her good night and said, "I don't know what I'd do without you, Sally." Then she left the room.

Sally felt like she'd just fallen asleep when Mama was shaking her and calling her softly. "Sally, you need to get up."

She looked at Mama and could tell that she hadn't been asleep at all. She looked awful.

"I'll go to the outhouse with you." Mama said.

Sally had slept in her clothes so just had to put her shoes on. As they walked out the back door Mama put her arm through Sally's arm. They walked that way to the outhouse. When they got back to the porch Mama poured some water in the wash basin and they both washed their face and hands.

Sally started to go back in the house but Mama said, "Lets walk out to the garden."

Again they walked arm-in-arm. Finally Sally asked, "Granddad's gone, isn't he, Mama?"

"Yes." It came out with a little sob in it, but Mama got control and continued. "He was in pain, but he went relatively easy. His heart just gave out. He'd begun dozing off in the chair. We were all just sitting around him talking quietly. All of a sudden he woke up, looked around at all of us, then smiled a beautiful smile at Mama. And he was gone."

Sally was crying and Mama cried with her.

Mama said, "I don't know how a body can make so many tears. But this time I have to be strong for Mama. And I need you to be strong for your sister and brothers. Mama is going to need me, so I'll leave the children to you."

Sally wiped her eyes and replied, "I'll take care of them, Mama. Don't worry about us. You just please take care of yourself."

Within the space of just a few months they had to go through another sad funeral. Afterwards, Uncle Andrew and Uncle John and their families went back to their homes, but they came over often for visits. Even Uncle Tommy made it by about once a month. And Mama spent almost all her time with Grandma.

Sally, Elizabeth, and the boys stayed together most of the time. Throughout the next few months they were almost like a separate family. Sally and Elizabeth would take turns carrying baby Andy and all six of them would go and spend time with Aunt Mary and her children or Aunt Margaret and hers. And once-in-a-while the uncles would take them somewhere.

It was a special time for Sally. Because she'd always spent most of her time outdoors with William and the younger boys, she didn't really know Elizabeth well. She was discovering what a sweet, smart person she was. But even better than that she was fun to be with.

Sally knew she wasn't fun to be with; she was too serious. She'd always admired people that were happy and fun to be around, like Uncle Ulysses had been. And now she'd discovered that Elizabeth was like that and could even bring out the fun side of Sally. So even though they had a few chores each day, and were expected to take care of each other, they had a good summer.

Thomas and Ali had always been inseparable and Sally thought little Joseph and Andy would probably grow up the same way. And now Sally and Elizabeth had found out how much they liked each other. All six of them got very close and were enjoying the time together.

But Sally started noticing that Grandma was spending more and more time in the chair on the porch. They'd all worried so much about Grandma, and then Granddad had gone first. But by the end of the summer they knew Grandma's health was failing too.

Sally asked Mama about grandma and was told, "She just doesn't have the will to go on. I can't believe I can even say this, but I think it's just a matter of time for Mama."

Sally was worried even more about Mama's health. Mama was working so hard to take care of Grandma that she wasn't taking care of herself. She was thin as a rail and haggard looking. Sally and Elizabeth agreed that they'd divide the duties again. Elizabeth would take care of the little boys, with Thomas and Ali's help, and Sally would try to take care of Mama.

A number of times during the summer, kind of on a regular basis, Jesse Robinson had stopped by to see how things were going. Sally thought of that now and knew it'd been a few weeks since he'd been by. So maybe it wouldn't be long until he'd come by again.

And it wasn't but a few days after that when he rode into the clearing. Sally barely waited until he got off his horse to approach him. He looked surprised and pleased when she walked over to him.

Sally started right in, "Mr. Robinson, I'd like to ask a favor of you, please."

Jesse replied, "Well, Miss Newman, I believe you could ask almost anything of me. But first off you're going to have to call me Jesse."

Sally just looked at him for a minute. She thought, 'I think he's flirting with me. But I don't want to think about that right now.' She was too worried about Mama to spend the time and attention required for that.

So this time it was Jesse who was a little embarrassed. He quickly added, "What can I do for you, Sally?"

She asked, "In the next week or so are you going to be anywhere close to Egypt or San Felipe?"

"I'll probably be going that way before long. What do you need?" he asked.

And Sally blurted it all out. "I need you to stop by my home and tell William that Grandma isn't doing at all well, and I don't think she's going to make it much longer." She took a deep breath then continued, "I'm afraid for Mama. This is too much grief for her. Tell William to get some neighbors to watch the place and for him and the girls to come as soon as they can. Tell him it's going to take us all to keep from losing Mama too."

For a minute she thought Jesse was going to reach for her and she didn't know what to do. But he didn't. He climbed on his horse and said, "Alright."

"Alright, what?" she asked.

"Alright. I'm going to get William for you." Jesse answered.

"But you didn't eat or rest or anything. You mean you're going right this minute?"

"Yes ma'am." And he touched his hat and rode away without looking back.

Before a week was gone, William and the girls rode into the yard. Mary had left her two children with the Gilbert family and had come along with William, Minerva, and Louisa. Sally hadn't told Mama she'd asked Jesse to get word to them, so she was surprised and very pleased to have all her children with her.

After supper that evening Sally and Elizabeth joined William and the three older girls as they sat on the porch to talk. They talked about how bad Grandma looked, but the main concern was their mama. They all wanted to take her home but knew that wasn't going to happen yet.

The next day Uncle Andrew and Uncle John and their families all came over to visit with the new arrivals. As soon as she could Mama told Uncle Andrew, "William said Tommy had been at home for over a month, but he's back out here somewhere with the militia. I'm sure he's planning to come see Mama, but it may not be soon enough."

Uncle Andrew just looked very sad for a minute then said, "I'll ride over to the mill and send someone to find him. I won't be gone long."

Uncle Tommy got there two days later. To Sally it was like going through almost the same thing they'd gone through just a few weeks ago. But this time she didn't have to carry such a heavy load. It was a good feeling to have William and her older sisters here. This time there were more than enough arms to support Mama.

Grandma was in her bed with a few people sitting here and there around her bedroom. Mama was almost always at her side watching over her. Grandma didn't do as Granddad had done when he told each person goodbye. She was just letting each one do whatever they needed to do.

Sally looked in the room fairly often throughout the day, but she was waiting for a moment when no one else was talking to Grandma. Once when she looked in Grandma was propped up on pillows and appeared to be asleep. She walked quietly to the end of the bed and Mama gave her a tired smile. Just as she was thinking it wasn't a good time, Grandma opened her eyes.

She smiled sweetly at Sally and said, "Come, sit."

Sally sat and held her hand. She couldn't think of anything to say except how much she'd miss her. So she didn't say anything.

Grandma gave her a minute or two then said, "What will you remember about me, Sally?"

"Your strength." Sally said. "And your blackberry cobbler."

Grandma chuckled lightly and everyone in the room turned and looked.

Mama said. "Blackberry cobbler!" And there were lots of smiles and a few chuckles.

Grandma was smiling too, but had shut her eyes; she was so tiny and frail looking. Sally looked at her and knew she was going to cry if she stayed. So she leaned over and whispered in her ear, "I'll never eat or smell a blackberry that I won't think of you, Grandma. I love you very much."

And Grandma whispered back, "I'm glad you'll think of me in such a sweet way. I love you too, Child."

Something close to that was repeated throughout the day with children and grandchildren. And once again Grandma's children sat up through the night, all around her bed.

Sally woke up early and sneaked out of the bed. When she got to the kitchen door she heard something and looked behind her. It was Elizabeth. They went to the outhouse together and then came back and washed up.

They went into Grandma's room and moved over to the side, out of the doorway. William came over and stood with them. Their three older sisters were all standing not too far from Mama.

Mama and Uncle Andrew were sitting on one side of the bed and Uncle John and Uncle Thomas were sitting on the other. Sally could see Grandma in the middle of the bed, but couldn't see her face very well. She wasn't propped up like she'd been the day before.

Sally wondered if Grandma was dead. Then she saw her head move. And she wondered if death was close and that's what seemed to be in the room with them. Or was it that you could see how old and sick Grandma looked and knew she probably couldn't live much longer. Or did you think you felt death in the room because you'd just been around it too much lately.

She heard Grandma say, "I love you."

Grandma's daughter and three sons each said, "I love you too, Mama."

Sally wondered. Who was she saying I love you to? Her eyes were shut. Then she thought, 'It doesn't matter because every heart in this room answered her with an 'I love you too.'

It stayed kind of unnaturally quiet for a long number of minutes. To Sally it was like one of those pictures that some circumstances seem to paint in your mind.

Grandma lay there barely breathing, but hanging on. Then Uncle John reached over and gently moved a strand of her hair. Sally saw him look at Mama and his brothers, then he looked back at Grandma and said, "Mama, we've got each other and we're going to be fine. When you're ready, you go on and join Daddy."

Sally didn't hear anything from Grandma. Then she realized that the reason for that was that Grandma was gone now.

She watched as Mama bent over and kissed Grandma on the cheek and then each uncle did the same and they turned and walked out of the room. William got her and Elizabeth out of the room too. The last thing Sally saw when she looked back was her two aunts standing beside the bed, gently covering Grandma with the coverlet. Then they came out and shut the door to the bedroom.

Sally knew that before too long the two aunts and Mama would go back in and get Grandma's body ready for burial. Before that happened Sally wanted to see her Mama and she could tell Elizabeth and William felt the same way. They made their way to the porch where the grownups had gone.

Sally was surprised because Mama was just standing there talking to her brothers. Occasionally one or the other of them would wipe a tear away, but there was no heavy crying. Sally thought, 'I think everyone is numb.' When Mama saw them looking at her she just smiled tiredly but didn't come over. So the three of them went and joined Mary, Louisa, Minerva and the little boys.

They buried Grandma between Granddad and Uncle Ulysses, on the hill overlooking Rabb's prairie, not too far from the Colorado River; the place Granddad had chosen for their home.

Both Uncle Andrew and Uncle John wanted Mama and the children to move closer to them. But Mama said no and a few days after the funeral and after tearful good-byes, their family headed home.

Mama seemed to be handling everything all right. But day by day she slept more and got quieter and quieter until finally she was responding only when one of the girls put Andy in her arms to nurse. They all tried talking to her with no success. None of them knew what to do.

When they got home she didn't even go to the cemetery with them; just went in her bedroom and lay down on the bed. They got the doctor to come out and all he could say was, "These things just take time."

Through the fall they'd take her out to sit in her rocking chair on the porch and one of them would sit and read to her or talk to her about cheerful things. They'd cover her with a soft shawl, bring her tea, and treat her as if she were a beloved child.

Nothing worked. Until one morning. Little Andy had turned one year old in November and was always trying to keep up with four-year old Joseph. On this day, Andy stumbled, scratched his leg on a rough board on the porch, and cried.

Mama put out her arms and said, 'Come here, honey' just as Louisa came outside to see what had happened. Andy went to Louisa, instead of Mama.

Sally had started toward the porch when she heard Andy cry and had seen what had taken place on the porch. She stopped a little way off and watched. Mama stood up and looked around. Louisa was holding Andy, and Joseph was standing close to Louisa. Mama walked over, picked Joseph up and then hugged Louisa and Andy.

At last she began to ask for her sewing and something to do, and began to show an interest in other things. She began to eat better and gained some weight back and got a little color in her cheeks. They could see life in her eyes again and signs of that strong spirit.

"Today's my birthday, Daddy. I'm fourteen. It's my first birthday since you've been gone and I miss you." Sally was standing in the cemetery.

Then she laughed. "Listen to her, Daddy. You can hear her all the way up here. Uncle Thomas and his family and maybe some of the others are coming for a before-Christmas visit and she's giving orders like old times.

"And she's just gotten around to 'Where's Sally? Just because it's her birthday doesn't mean there's not plenty of work to do.' That means I gotta go.

"Tell Granddad and Grandma hello. I love you, Daddy."

"I'm coming, Mama!" And Sally laughed again as she ran down the hill to the house.

CHAPTER 9

Unease was growing all across their area. Every time someone came to visit the talk centered on the problems with the Mexican government. There was another revolt going on in Mexico and this time the favorite seemed to be a man called Santa Anna. It was widely thought that it'd be good if he took over control of Mexico.

Sally heard all the talk but also understood that most people were struggling more with crops and things than they were with what was happening in Mexico. She just wished that was all she had to think about. She and her sisters and brothers were struggling with the situation Mama found herself in.

It'd been a year since Daddy died, so Mama was considered available for courting. And Mama was an attractive widow. She was not only nice to look at, but even more attractive because of the land she got when her husband died. Add to that a very sizable inheritance due from her daddy's holdings and she'd become the most popular woman around.

Sally had learned to hate Sundays! By mid-morning each Sunday the single men in the area would begin arriving. There were days that four at a time would be trying to outdo each other to impress Mama.

Sally wished you could just shoot them like you would a randy old coyote trying to get to one of the dogs. She decided she'd take that job on if it weren't against the law. So far she didn't like any of Mama's suitors, and she was pleased that it didn't seem like Mama liked any of them either.

But that didn't last! By the middle of the summer, Mama was kind of smitten by the attention paid her by one Samuel J. Rose. He was a bit younger than Mama, a fair looking man, and extremely persistent. He began making an appearance more than just on Sundays and most of the other men seemed to have given up.

Sally and the other kids knew how lonely Mama was, and how hard it was for her to take care of the family without a man to help. So because Mr. Rose was seemingly the least objectionable of the men, they all gave their reluctant approval to a marriage.

Sally didn't tell Mama, but as far as she was concerned she was never going to have another daddy. Mr. Rose would be Mama's husband, not Sally's daddy! But she did hope the little boys would be able to accept Mr. Rose. They needed a daddy in their lives.

Probably due to their needs more than hers, Mama married Samuel Rose by marriage bond in the early fall of 1832. She wrote and told her family about her marriage and got a letter back from Uncle John. He started it out by wishing her God's blessings on her marriage and then told all about the mill and the happenings with the families there and the other news around La Grange.

Mama said that Uncle John was the best of letter writers and she loved hearing from him. Sally still missed having all of Mama's family close enough for frequent visits. And now her immediate family was beginning to leave home. Louisa was very shy but interested in a young man, and Minerva was getting very serious about David Silcriggs. Sally knew it wouldn't be long before all the older children were married and gone, and she felt like things were changing too much.

One day she was in the corral doctoring one of the horses. She didn't know how, but the horse had cut a small but deep gash on its left hind leg. She'd gotten the wound cleaned and had smeared some salve on it, and then realized someone was leaning on the fence watching her.

It was Jesse Robinson. He touched his hat and said, "Hello, Sally."

She said, "Hello." But she blushed and looked away. She got a rag to wipe her hands to give herself time to settle down. She watched him walk over to the horse and inspect the wound.

"You did a good job." He said. Then he stood and rubbed the horse's ear and looked at Sally.

She'd backed up nearly against the fence and was just standing there. He didn't say anything and she was getting uncomfortable. She didn't know how to read the look on his face.

He slowly took two long steps and was standing in front of her. She looked down and wondered why it was so hard to face him. Her heart was beating terribly fast and she felt strange. For a moment she thought he was going to turn and walk off. But he put his hand under her chin, tilted her head back, and leaned down and kissed her. She felt his lips on hers and felt or sensed him trembling.

He took a step back, turned and walked out of the corral. Sally's legs felt weak. She walked to the fence and was in time to see him ride out of view. She wished she knew if he'd looked back. She suspected he hadn't.

Then she heard Mama's voice. "Sally!"

She realized it was at least the third time she'd called, but the first two times hadn't completely gotten through. This time the voice was louder and it was Mama's 'you're going to get it if you don't answer me call.'

Sally answered, "Coming." As she started toward the house she saw that Mama had started her way, and they met about halfway between.

Mama didn't waste any time. "What did he want? Why did he stay so long?"

"He just said hello." Sally said. "And he looked at the cut on the horse's leg." She couldn't quite look right at Mama, but she felt Mama had relaxed a little.

"Alright." She said. "Go back to work."

Then before Sally started back for the barn Mama added. "Sally. Jesse Robinson is a good man. He's helped our family a number of times. But he hardly knows anything but fighting and killing. And the company he keeps is mostly rough men, just like him. Not only that, he's as old or older than your Uncle Tommy. He's too old for you, Child."

Sally didn't know what to say, so she said what Mama wanted to hear. "I know, Mama, don't worry." Then she went back to work. She wanted to be alone, to think about that kiss and the sensations she'd felt. She wanted to explore her thoughts, because she didn't know whether Mama should worry or not.

Her next encounter with Jesse occurred on one of those rare cool dry beautiful days. Sally was enjoying the relief from the hot humid summer they'd been going through. She knew this weather wouldn't last. They'd still have more hot and muggy days to go through before wintertime cooled it off.

She and William had been checking on the cattle for the last few days and had decided to drive a dozen head closer to the house. Being the cantankerous animals they were, one cow had decided she didn't want to go where they wanted her to go. When it broke and ran, four other cows went along.

William helped Sally calm the remaining seven cows, then told her he'd go collect the five runaways and meet her at the house. Sally was pushing the cows along watching them closely to be ready if one bolted. Her horse neighed and she saw a man sitting on a horse. He was under a large live oak about a quarter of a mile from the river. She started to reach for her gun, but then saw that it was Jesse.

She hesitated a moment then turned the cows toward the horseman. He never took his eyes off her as she rode his way. She knew she was blushing and felt nervous. She'd seen him only once since he'd kissed her. And that time he mostly visited with William and left soon. Mama had always been with Sally.

When she got close to the tree she pointed the cows toward the river and stopped in front of Jesse.

"Hello, Sally." She liked to hear him talk and wondered if he was from Kentucky like Aunt Margaret and her family. He had an accent like theirs. She had a moment's wonder of what she sounded like to him.

"Hello, Jesse."

He asked if she'd like a drink and she said yes. They rode to the river a little away from where the cows were drinking.

Sally jumped down, looped the reins on the saddle and let her horse get a drink. She leaned down and got a drink for herself and splashed the cool water on her face. She got her handkerchief and dried her face and hands. Jesse had gotten off his horse, tied the reins to a bush and was leaning against a tree watching her.

She looked at him. He was standing there with one boot up behind him against the tree and he had a grass stem in his mouth. He was tall and almost too slim. He wasn't a good-looking man but he had a strong nice face.

She took her horse's reins, led him over and tied him to a lower branch of the tree.

Jesse asked, "Where's William?"

"He's rounding up some strays." She said.

"How's your mama and the family?" he asked.

"They're fine, I guess." Sally said.

"I saw your Uncle Tommy recently. He was doing well."

Sally knew it was a one-sided conversation and she didn't want it to end. She tried to think of something to say and decided to ask him about his horse. But he was looking at her in such a way that she lost her line of thought.

She didn't know if he moved or they both did, but all of a sudden he was very close. He touched her cheek and then ran his fingers across her lips. Then he reached behind her head and untied the ribbon holding her hair off her neck.

She just stood there.

He put his hands on her upper arms and partly lifting her off the ground gently kissed her. He turned her loose and she might have fallen, but he had her in his arms and kissed her again. Sally could feel his body against hers, and knew she was responding to his kiss. They were both trembling this time.

Sally leaned her head against his shoulder and he put his hand on her hair and held her that way for a few minutes. In a raspy voice he said, "I'll help you get the cows home."

He turned her loose and was in the saddle before Sally could collect her thoughts. And he was already bunching the cows by the time Sally was mounted. She couldn't think clearly, and had all kinds of mixed up emotions tumbling all around. Did she do something wrong? Did he not like kissing her? Why was he just leaving? How could he just stop?

She didn't know the answer to any of this and was just confused. She joined him as they drove the cows toward home. Neither one of them said anything until they were still just out of sight of the house. She stopped and so did he.

She said, "You shouldn't ride in with me. Mama doesn't want me to be alone with you. She says you're too…" She stopped.

And he finished the statement. "…old. I know. She talked to me last time I came by." He was quiet for a minute then said. "Sally, I never backed off from anything in my life and I'm not going to start now. Although to be honest I'd rather face a dozen Indians or Mexicans."

They started the cows moving along again and drove them close to the corral where the two milk cows were kept. Mama had heard the cows and was standing in front of the house looking their direction. Sally saw her smile turn to a hard look when she saw Jesse.

As Sally got off her horse and threw the reins over the hitch, Jesse just sat on his horse a short distance in front of Mama. He tipped his hat and said. "Hello, Mrs. Newman."

Mama answered him a little curtly, but invited him to get down.

He said, "No thank you. I got to be getting on." Then added, "Mrs. Newman. Excuse me, Mrs. Rose, I'll wait awhile. But meaning no disrespect to you, only one person is going to keep me from Sally. And that's Sally."

Then he tipped his hat again and said, "Ma'am." He looked at Sally, nodded and then rode out of the yard. Sally watched him until he was out of sight and he never turned around. She always wanted him too.

Mama was standing there looking at her, and it was very obvious that she was angry. She said only one thing. "Has he touched you?"

"No!" Sally lied.

Then feeling guilty, she went and put her horse up and started on some other chores. The guilt went away very quickly because it couldn't stand in front of the onrushing thoughts and feelings that had taken over her mind and body.

She had a warm tingling feeling inside and blushed again. She wondered how people lived through these emotions. Is this what it's like to be in love? If so, she guessed Mama had a reason to worry.

Emotions were running high everywhere! It was 1833, and the Mexican government didn't trust the Texians, the old-time Texians didn't trust the Mexican government, and the new emigrants had come to Texas with the assumption that they were going to remain citizens of the United States.

Sally's emotions were as high and mixed as possible. On one hand she stayed in a state of excitement. On the other she and her family were in a state of turmoil, and none too happy.

To begin with, Mama was pregnant and none of the children were happy about that. Maybe if Mr. Rose had been different it would've been all right. But none of them cared for Mr. Rose. William would barely speak to him and had begun traveling with Uncle Tommy and the militia more all the time. Sally missed William terribly.

Early in the year Minerva married David Silcriggs. Sally knew Minerva didn't get married so that she could get away from home, because David had been courting her for a long time. But Sally was beginning to wish she could get away. Not that she wanted to leave Mama or the younger children, but she didn't like home as much with Mr. Rose acting like everything belonged to him.

One cold blustery morning in March, Sally was so mad she couldn't stay still. She'd gone outside to tend to the horses and Mr. Rose had come out and told her she should leave the horses to the men-folk, and stay inside and help her Mama like a decent young woman was supposed to do.

Sally just looked at him and didn't answer.

That really made him angry and he started in on her. "You listen here. You're about as disrespectful a girl as I've ever seen. And I don't like the way you look at me. It's about time you were taught a lesson in manners."

As he started toward her Sally quietly told him, "Mr. Rose, if you touch me you won't ever touch another human being."

She was as surprised as he was at what she'd said, but for some reason he stopped. Then he was not only angry but embarrassed that he'd let a woman get the better of him. The next hour was awful. Mr. Rose went immediately to the house. He yelled at Mama, telling her what a poor job she'd done raising her children and how he regretted ever marrying her.

Sally had followed him into the house and was standing by the door wondering what in the world she was supposed to do. Louisa and Elizabeth were standing against the wall on the other side of the room just as immobile as she was. She could also see the younger boys standing just outside the other door and she knew that eleven-year old Thomas was wondering what he should do too.

Mama tried to calm him down, but he turned from her and yelled at Sally. "See the trouble you cause? All because you're so disrespectful to your elders."

That was too much for Mama. She said, "Mr. Rose. I've heard all I want to about that. You said you needed to pick up some supplies at San Felipe. Why don't I help you get ready to go."

He just stood there a minute then stormed past Sally out the door. Mama went into her bedroom. The two other girls had already left and joined the boys. Sally knew Elizabeth would be doing her magic to calm them down, and she knew that later on Louisa would take care of Mama. So she just needed to get somewhere and cool off.

She went out on the front porch and stepped off on the side away from the barn. She'd never been so mad. Then she realized that Mama must be terribly embarrassed and maybe mad at her. She hadn't thought of that.

She heard Mama come out of her bedroom and go out through the kitchen door. Then a few minutes after that she heard Mr. Rose ride out of the yard. He was riding really fast. Sally thought, 'Poor horse.'

She went back into the kitchen. Mama and Louisa were quietly working just like nothing had happened. She wished she could handle things like that, but she couldn't. She took a deep breath and said, "I'm sorry, Mama."

"Did you do something wrong?" Mama asked.

Sally looked at her, not quite understanding what she meant.

Mama said, "Sally, you don't owe an apology when you didn't do anything wrong. I'll try to work this out and maybe it'll help if you stay out of his way for awhile."

Sally said, "Yes, Ma'am." And she went back to the barn. As was her usual habit when she was feeling strong emotions, she started working on the hardest chore she could find. She was busily cleaning out the worst part of the barn when she heard a horse come into the yard.

She had the pitchfork in her hand, started to put it down then really looked at it. She thought, 'I think I'm just about angry enough to use it on him.' She was standing in the middle of the barn with the pitchfork clutched in her hand, with a look of absolute hatred on her face when the side door opened and a man stepped in.

It wasn't Mr. Rose! It was Jesse!

Sally didn't know who was more surprised, Jesse or her. She was still so angry, but happy to see him. Jesse was watching her face in wonder as she struggled with her emotions.

Finally he said, "Sally, what's going on? I met Samuel on my way here and he was madder than a hornet. He said you're trying to break your mama and him up. What's been happening?"

Before she could answer she heard Mama call from the house. Sally said, "Lets go have a cup of coffee with Mama, then I'll tell you what's been happening." She knew that would relieve Mama and also give her time to calm down inside. At least she hoped it would.

She and Jesse went in the kitchen. Louisa and Elizabeth were glad to see him and the boys were almost jumping with joy. Sally thought maybe Jesse reminds them of William, or better yet, doesn't remind them of Mr. Rose. Mama tried to act like she wasn't pleased to have him here, but as she got him some coffee Sally could tell that wasn't true.

Jesse roughhoused with Joseph and Andy for a few minutes and talked briefly to Thomas and Ali about hunting and such. He talked to Louisa, always so shy and quiet, and she smiled with pleasure. Elizabeth was almost thirteen and Jesse made her blush when he told her what a beauty she was becoming.

Sally thought, 'We've all become so unhappy in our own home, just look at us. You'd think Jesse Robinson just brought Christmas.'

Mama let them have a few minutes then said, "Alright, sit down and be quiet now because I want to hear from Jesse about the latest news."

Jesse said, "Well, I know you're interested first of all in your family. So let's see. I was with both William and Tommy just last week; they're both doing well as far as I could tell. They told me to tell you hello, and William said he'd probably be coming back home in a week or so."

"Good." Mama said. Then waited on him to continue.

"I haven't seen Andrew or John recently, but Tommy has. He told me to tell you that everyone was doing fine. Tommy said there're so many children now that he can't keep them straight. But he said John writes to you pretty often and probably keeps you up on all that."

Mama smiled and said, "Yes. John writes regularly. Bless him."

Jesse told them all he knew about the latest Indian problems. It was still very dangerous in the sparsely settled areas. Then he talked a while about the growing tensions with the Mexicans. "Best I can tell it's mostly that neither side understands the other. I like most of the Mexicans that have their homes here; they work at making a living just like we do. But I shore don't like the Mexicans that are sent up from Mexico City or one of those places. They're sent up here to run things, and usually the first thing they do is get our dander up over things we consider of no importance."

Jesse was quiet a few minutes then continued, "All most of us settlers wanted was to work our land and be allowed to take care of our own problems. But the Mexicans get nervous every time we get together to discuss things. Course I admit that us asking for separate statehood is probably a scary thing to the Mexicans. You know about the convention at San Felipe in October last year when the men from the various districts of Texas met. They chose Stephen Austin as the convention president and drafted a number of resolutions to the Mexican government. That was most likely way too big a bite for the Mexicans.

"Well, now another convention has just been proposed to take place this coming April. I don't think the Mexicans are going to go along with anything proposed. Cause I bet by now they wish they'd never let us on the land."

He hesitated a minute then ended with, "I reckon we're going to fight them for Texas. And I reckon we'll win." Everyone was quiet thinking about fighting the Mexicans.

Jesse finished his coffee and stood up and stretched. He said to Sally, "I think with Thomas and Ali helping we can finish cleaning the barn."

She blushed and said, "No. Thank you. I can do it later."

"Now come on. We can help with moving the heavy things." And he got up and motioned to Thomas and Ali. They hopped up and followed Jesse out to the porch.

Sally looked at Mama and the girls and blushed again. She hated that but didn't know how to stop. Mama didn't say anything, so Sally went out to join Jesse and the boys. The four of them trouped out to the barn and started in.

Sally couldn't keep from looking at Jesse and every time she looked he was watching her. She'd forgotten all about Mr. Rose.

Thomas and Ali worked hard for awhile then rapidly lost interest. For once Sally was glad. She didn't want to get after them in front of Jesse so she didn't say anything.

Jesse stopped what he was doing, looked at the two of them and said, "Pretty tiring, huh?"

They both agreed and taking his question to mean he sympathized with them, made excuses for not wanting to stay and help. It wasn't but a few more minutes before they both wandered out into the yard. Sally didn't look at Jesse, but she could feel him watching her. They were alone in the barn.

After another hour they'd finished the work and it'd started to rain. Sally went to the side door and looked out. The boys were just going in the house and Elizabeth waved at her before she shut the door behind them. Sally knew Mama wouldn't expect her to come to the house while it was raining so hard.

The rain was blowing in the doorway and she backed up to keep from getting wet. It was cool, but she didn't dare close the door or Mama would send one of the boys out. She left the door open and turned toward Jesse. He was sitting on the end of the wagon watching her. Her heart was beating so fast she could hardly breath. She hesitated another minute, then walked over to him.

He stood up reached for the saddle blanket hanging on a nail and spread it on the wagon. Then he caught her by the waist, lifted her and sat her on the end of the wagon. Sally thought he was going to get up and sit beside her, but instead he leaned toward her and gently kissed her.

She returned the kiss, put her arms around him and pulled him closer. The kissing became very urgent and all of a sudden she was on her back in the wagon with him on top of her. She could feel his body against hers and she was both terrified and excited. He was touching her all over and kissing her on the neck and she wanted him to do more. Then he stopped and got off the wagon.

She felt like she'd fallen off a cliff. She opened her eyes, tried to calm her breathing and get control of her feelings. This was the second time he'd stopped and walked away from her. He was standing in front of the door looking out into the yard.

She felt angry and hurt and embarrassed. She got up, straightened her clothes, hung the blanket back on the nail, then jumped back up and sat on the edge of the wagon. During all this time neither one of them had said a word. Now as she sat watching him she thought to herself, 'I don't understand him at all and I'll be damned if I'll ask him what's wrong.'

Jesse walked back toward her but stopped when he was a few feet away. He broke the silence. "Sally, I'm sorry about what just happened. I can tell you're mad at me and I'm not at all sure what you're thinking. I'm not too good at understanding women-folk anyway and you're so quiet and different from most all of the women I've ever known. I never understand what you're about."

He waited a few more minutes then continued, "If I'm speaking out of turn I'm sorry, but I've been waiting a long time to say this. I know I'm twice your age, but you're fifteen now. And what just happened between us tells me you're ready.

"I love you as much as a man can love a woman, Sally. And I want you to be my wife."

He had such a look of love and hope on his face. She just sat there a minute, then jumped off the wagon and ran to him. He was twirling her around and the two of them were laughing and crying at the same time.

"Jesse, you have to put me down. I'm getting dizzy."

They stood and held each other and Sally had never felt so happy. But that feeling changed some when Jesse said, "Let's go talk to your mama about us getting married."

Sally wanted to put it off a few days, but Jesse insisted. It was raining only lightly now, so they headed for the house. About halfway across the yard Jesse reached and caught her hand. They walked that way into the house.

Louisa and Elizabeth were putting food on the table and Sally noticed there was an extra plate set out. Mama looked at them as they walked in the door and gave them a sad smile. She said, "Let's eat a bite, then the children can play in the bedroom and we can talk."

Jesse answered, "Yes, Ma'am."

And they shared the strangest meal Sally could remember. She was so nervous and excited she couldn't eat. Mama didn't eat much either and Jesse tried to eat some without looking at either Sally or Mama. The girls knew some of what was happening so were just dying to say something to Sally, but were afraid to because of Mama. The boys could also tell that something was going on so they were watching Jesse and Mama.

After they'd eaten Mama said, "Sally, you get the three of us some coffee. Louisa, you and Elizabeth take the boys to the bedroom and get them interested in something. I need to talk to Jesse and Sally."

There was a collective moan from them, but they all left the kitchen. Mama moved over to sit in her rocking chair and Jesse and Sally sat at the end of the table.

No one said anything for a few minutes. Sally believed it'd be easier to break a horse than go through this. She sneaked a peek at Mama and noticed that the look on Mama's face was sadness, not anger. All of a sudden Sally realized that other people were involved here, not just her. She felt a deep love for Mama.

Jesse said, "Mrs. Newman, I'd like to ask your permission to marry Sally."

Mama didn't correct him for calling her Newman instead of Rose. She just said, "I don't have to ask you if you love Sally. I've seen that for a long time. But I have to ask Sally."

She looked at her and said, "Sally, come over here and sit beside me." Sally went over, got the stool and sat down in front of Mama.

"Child. I'm sorry, let me start over." Mama began.

Sally said, "It's okay, Mama. You always call us that."

"No." Mama said. "Calling you 'Child' doesn't seem appropriate right now. Anyway, I want you to tell me. Do you love Jesse?"

Sally turned and looked at Jesse and for the first time said. "Yes, I love Jesse!"

Jesse got tears in his eyes and ducked his head.

Mama said, "Would you have to get married right now? Can't you wait awhile?"

Sally said, "We love each other, Mama. And we want to be together."

Mama leaned over and kissed Sally on the cheek. That was when the baby decided to kick, and Sally felt it. She jerked back and said, "Was that the baby?"

Mama actually laughed. She caught Sally's hand and held it on her stomach. The baby gave a strong kick, and Sally wondered how in the world she'd resented this baby. It didn't matter if its daddy was Mr. Rose or not. It would belong to her family. Feeling mama's stomach wasn't something they were invited to do, so Sally was filled with wonder at what she'd just participated in.

The tension was past. The three of them talked for awhile then Jesse said, "I better be getting on my way. I'll be out again tomorrow."

Mama said, "Why don't you just bed down in the barn. That way you won't have to make a trip for nothing." She called for Thomas and as soon as he came in the kitchen she told him to make sure Jesse could find everything he needed for the night.

Sally knew not to go outside with them so asked Thomas to see to the horses. She gave Jesse a shy smile and in return got a beautiful one from him.

Sleep didn't come very easy for Sally and she wondered if Mama or Jesse were sleeping any better. She woke up with the sound of someone chopping wood. It was already daylight and she jumped up and threw her clothes on as fast as she could. Louisa and Elizabeth were already up and out of the room. By the time she got to the kitchen everyone was waiting on her. They all sat down to breakfast and Sally thought there was no way her face could turn a brighter red. It seemed to her that everyone in the room was watching her.

As soon as they were through eating Mama told the four boys to go outside and get started on the chores. She then told the other two girls to start doing the dishes while she, Jesse and Sally made some plans. Then she started right in. "Where will you live, Jesse?"

Jesse said, "Well, I reckon we'll live somewhere in the Gonzales area where I've been living."

Mama gave a small sigh and said, "I'd hoped you wouldn't move her so far away at first. She's still young. And I worry that the Gonzales area is a dangerous place for women. I hear terrible stories about the Indians around there."

"Well." Jesse said. "There's still problems there. But I can build us a house close to town and I don't know a woman that can look out for herself any better than Sally. Besides, I'll be close most of the time. I don't look for the problems with the Mexicans to get serious for years to come."

Sally didn't like them talking about her like she wasn't there, but she was so excited and scared too that she didn't know what to think anyway. Things were going so fast. Before she knew what was happening, Jesse and Mama had decided that Sally and Jesse would go to San Felipe the next day and sign a marriage contract. Because of her pregnancy Mama couldn't go with them. Sally thought that Jesse seemed happy that they'd be going by themselves.

They spent the day getting the things together that she'd take to Gonzales. Sally had what her family called a hope chest, which every girl worked on from the time she was old enough to sew and make things. Sally didn't have a lot of things, so after looking at her meager collection, Mama gave her some things of hers and a few things that had belonged to Grandma. Then Louisa came into the bedroom and brought Sally some beautiful things she'd made.

Sally said, "Oh, Louisa, I can't take these. You should keep them for your hope chest."

And Louisa answered, "I can make more." And she gave Sally a hug.

Sally had never had so many pretty things and she was overwhelmed. She sat on the side of Mama's bed and buried her face in her hands. She had such mixed feelings. She wanted to marry and move in with Jesse, but she also wanted to stay with Mama and the other children. Both feelings seemed almost equally strong and that was scary.

Mama said, "Louisa, you and Elizabeth let me have a few minutes to talk to Sally."

Sally had thought that she couldn't be more uncomfortable. But she was wrong! Mama asked, "Sally, I know how you're feeling; sad, happy, and scared all at the same time. But you're a strong person and you'll be all right. But I do need to talk to you about other things.

And in a quieter voice Mama said, "Sally, how much do you know about what men and women do after they get married?"

Sally uncovered her face, looked up very briefly at Mama and thought, 'Oh no! I've died and gone to hell and this is my punishment for all the sins I've committed.' She didn't know if she mumbled an answer or not.

Mama was telling her very personal things without ever looking directly at her. Sally sneaked a look at Mama and thought that Mama was probably as uncomfortable with this conversation as she was.

Mama folded the new linens and things, then she refolded them, and then thankfully just when Sally thought she'd refold them all for the third time, she seemed to reach the end of what she thought it was necessary to tell her.

Sally had grown up in small houses, sometimes where everyone slept in the same room. Even though parents were careful, children were not always asleep all the time. She'd also seen all the farm animals mate, so even though she didn't know exactly what went on with people she wasn't ignorant.

And she now knew one other thing for certain. It wasn't fun to have your mama tell you about it. So the second Mama reached a stopping place Sally jumped up from the bed. "Thank you, Mama. Can we join Louisa and Elizabeth now?"

Mama gave her a quick hug and said. "Yes, let's do that."

Jesse wanted to get back to Gonzales as soon as they could. So by that evening the things they'd take with them were packed and ready to go. They'd be married first, then return for their belongings and leave for Gonzales

The next morning, Sally in her best dress and Jesse in a new shirt rode off toward San Felipe. Sally looked back and waved at her family standing in the yard. She wanted to cry and was happy at the same time. That seemed to be her new way of feeling about life.

They'd barely gotten out of sight of the house when Jesse stopped the horses. He quickly dismounted and helped her off her horse. And he kissed her so hard that her chin felt chapped. Then just as quickly he said, "Let's go. I want to get to town soon as we can."

Sally hadn't been to town in a long time and she was surprised at all the people and buildings. There were over thirty log cabins strung along the west bank of the Brazos River. All the buildings were made with logs and covered with clapboard roofs. Stephen Austin's house was about a half mile from the river and served as his headquarters.

Jesse and Sally went straight to the building where they could get married. The Mexican government required that both the man and woman sign a marriage bond in the presence of witnesses and the alcalde, the woman signing her maiden name. One requirement of the bond was that at the first opportunity they'd have a Catholic priest perform a sacramental ceremony. Until then the bond was a civil contract that secured the right of property to both parties and legitimized their children. Neither Jesse nor Sally were Catholic, so they didn't care if they were ever married by a priest.

It wasn't much of a ceremony. They just had to wait for the Clerk to write the marriage bond and they signed it. Then the alcalde said. "Alright, Jesse. I reckon you're married now."

They walked around the town for a time. They bought a few things in one of the stores and walked through some of the other shops. Jesse talked to some people he knew. All most of them wanted to know was what was happening around Gonzales. When they ran into Gail Borden he said hello to Jesse and Sally and with a big smile on his face asked what they were doing in town.

Jesse said, "Well, I suspect you've already heard. Sally and I got married and we're heading back to Gonzales tomorrow."

Mr. Borden gave her a kiss on the cheek and wished them a long and happy marriage. She was mostly thinking about Jesse saying they were 'heading back to Gonzales tomorrow.'

They got something to eat at the boarding house, which was a treat for Sally. The food wasn't as good as Mama's, but she'd never eaten in a public eating-place. Then once they were through eating it was as if Jesse felt like he'd done all he was supposed to do or maybe all he could stand and was now in a big hurry.

He hurried her to the horses, and hurried her past the stores and houses, and hurried her away from San Felipe.

As they rode back toward home she found it hard to look at him. They hadn't ridden far when Jesse turned toward the river and said, "There's a real pretty place close to the Brazos just over there a ways."

She knew where it was. It was a camping place where her family stayed the few times they came to San Felipe. And she knew what he wanted to do.

They rode to the river and instead of the usual place most people camped, Jesse went a little farther along until they came to a thick grove of oaks. He told her to get off her horse and follow him. They had to lead the horses and weave their way through some heavy brush until they came to a small clearing. There was a recognizable campsite but it didn't look as well used as the larger camp.

Jesse took her horse's reins and tied both horses to a tree. He unrolled his bedroll and spread it on the ground over a thick pile of leaves and he turned and looked at her. She'd seen that look on his face before.

Suddenly he was kissing her and at first she was returning the kisses. Then everything was out of her control. Jesse was still kissing her, helping her take off her clothes, and trying to get out of his at the same time. And it was over!

Sally just lay there for a few minutes. She didn't know how she was supposed to feel. She'd thought it would be wonderful and had wanted it to happen for over a year, and it hadn't been good at all. It'd hurt too and now she was afraid she'd cry.

Jesse just lay there beside her.

After a few more minutes she said, "Mama told me I should clean myself afterward." She thought, 'I sound like a damn simpleton.'

Jesse said, "Oh, I'm sorry Sally. I forget how young you are. I'll get my rifle and go to the river with you. No, don't take your clothes. It's close to dark and besides we're the only people around."

She grabbed her shawl and got the soap Mama had given her. She walked down to the river with him behind her. She'd wrapped the shawl around her but was still very self-conscious.

When she got to the river she was going to keep the shawl on, but Jesse reached out and took it from her. She hurried into the river until she was about waist deep. The water felt nice and with her back to him she cleaned herself. Then after she'd stalled as long as she could she turned around.

He was standing right at the water's edge with only his boots on, watching her. He had the rifle in the crook of his arm, but she thought it wouldn't be much protection because she doubted if he remembered he had it.

She'd helped take care of her little brothers for years so wasn't unfamiliar with body parts, but she was kind of surprised this time. It was almost dark now but she thought, 'If I can see him this well then he can still see me too.' She almost ducked down in the water, but decided she didn't want too.

Jesse picked up the shawl and held it out to her. She walked slowly to him, and he draped it around her back and pulled her to him. He kissed her again long and gently. Then he held her at arm's length and looked at her.

She'd never been nude in front of anyone before and she blushed and looked away. Jesse caught her chin in his hand, turned her head until she faced him, and said, "You have a beautiful body, Sally."

He handed her the rifle, picked her up and carried her back to the bedroll. Before he put her down he whispered in her ear, "It may not be the best thing you ever had, but it'll be close."

Much later she lay there thinking that Jesse was wrong. It wasn't close. It was the best thing she'd ever had, even better than blackberry cobbler.

As she was dozing off Jesse kissed her on the nose and whispered. "You're finally mine, Sally Robinson."

"Good." She said and fell asleep in his arms.

CHAPTER 10

Sally smelled coffee. She opened her eyes and saw that the sky was just beginning to lighten. Jesse was squatted down beside a small fire with a cup of coffee in his hand. How had he gotten up, made a fire, got the coffee on and all without waking her?

She needed to relieve herself in a desperate way, and how was she supposed to do that and still have a little dignity left? And there Jesse was, looking at her with a look she probably would've liked at another time.

With the cover held high up under her chin, and the knowledge that underneath that cover she had no clothes on, she looked back at Jesse and thought, 'Damnation! How the hell do I handle this situation? Oh, I don't have time to think about it any more.'

"Jesse, will you please turn the other way. I need to get up and go behind a tree." She didn't wait to see what he did; she jumped up and ran behind the closest tree. Then when she no longer had to face that problem she thought, 'Now how in hell do I get back to my clothes without looking like a foolish little girl?'

Sally stood there a long moment and then did what she always did. She went the direct route. She walked right around the tree to the bedding and her clothes.

Jesse was standing by the river with his back to her and she was grateful for that consideration. But he gave her only a few minutes then walked back to the fire. He poured her a cup of coffee, sat both cups on a stump, and just stood and watched her. When she'd finished dressing she walked over to him and he took her in his arms.

He kissed her long and gently and said, "I'd sure like to have a repeat of last night, but we need to get going."

Then with a big grin he continued, "And besides, we have some really close neighbors."

Sally looked around and was shocked to see two bedrolls in the next little clearing not very far from them. "Oh, no! Did anyone see me go behind the tree?"

Jesse laughed and said, "They came in around midnight and were so drunk they had a hard time finding the ground. They're still snoring."

As she started to turn and reach for her coffee Jesse reached for her and gave her another kiss. Before he could decide that he didn't care how many close neighbors there were she pulled away, got her coffee and moved to the other side of the fire. He uttered a quiet oath, groaned, then picked up his own coffee.

They made fast work of the coffee and some cold biscuits, then quickly got ready to go. Before she got on her horse, Sally looked at the spot where she'd become a woman. She wasn't quite sure how she was supposed to feel.

Then she thought about all the noise the two drunks must've made, and Jesse's coffee making noises and the fact that she'd slept through it all. She'd always been a light sleeper. She wondered if sleeping so soundly had something to do with the activities of the early part of the night. She'd been really nervous all day and the evening had been wonderfully tiring.

Jesse was sitting on his horse watching her. When she looked at him he said, "I'd sure like to hear about what you were just thinking. But it'll have to wait till we're on our way. Our neighbors are beginning to stir so let's get out of here before they want to visit."

They rode at a pretty good pace for an hour and chewed up the miles. Each time Sally looked at Jesse he was either looking at her or would turn to look. He even reached over and held her hand for awhile. The time passed and suddenly they were just a mile from the house. Sally slowed to a stop.

"Something wrong?" Jesse asked.

"No. I just need a minute."

For the last hour Sally had thought of nothing but riding into the yard and seeing her family. Now she was having a terrible time facing the thought that in two days she'd have to ride out of that same yard and leave her family.

She hated the feeling of being happy and sad at the same time. But she took only a little more than a minute then took a deep breath and said, "I'm ready."

Jesse waited and let her go first.

As she rode toward the house she thought, 'I'm ready to start this new life, but not ready to leave this old one.'

"I need some time here by myself." Sally said. "Is that alright?"

"Sure. Take all the time you need." Jesse said. He kissed her and walked down the hill leaving her alone in the cemetery.

"I'm so happy, Daddy. And yet I'm so sad too. How can that be? And I admit I'm kind of scared to be going off to a place like Gonzales."

Sally looked at the house and could see the wagon out front. It was loaded and ready to go. She could see that all the family was gathered around Jesse and the wagon.

"I like the fence we put around your grave. And the bench William built is a beautiful piece of carpentry work. You'd be proud of it.

"I gave Sapo to Joseph. Thomas and Ali already have horses and it just seemed right to give Joseph the horse that he named. Jesse got me a good, fast horse. He said I might need it in Gonzales. We'll have our two horses tied to the back of the wagon in case of trouble on the way. Of course we don't expect any problems and by this evening we'll join some men that are going toward Gonzales from San Felipe.

"I'm just putting off going now, I guess. It's so hard to say goodbye. I know Jesse wanted to leave yesterday morning when we got back to the house, but he gave me the rest of the day to visit with the family. Everyone was here except William. I hope I get to see him when we get to Gonzales.

"It's strange when I think about leaving. Here I stand talking to you and you're always with me now and I get to talk to you anytime I want to. It's Mama and my sisters and brothers that I'll miss so terribly, so it's them I need to go say goodbye to.

"I love you, Daddy." Sally touched the marker then walked out of the fenced area and closed the gate.

When she got a short distance away she turned and looked back at the small cemetery and big oak tree and thought. 'What a beautiful place this is.'

An hour later Sally climbed up into the wagon beside Jesse and through teary eyes looked at her family. Mama was leaning against Samuel; Sally still thought of him as Mr. Rose. She'd even managed to be civil to him and say a polite goodbye and she knew his extra nice goodbye came from his great relief that she was leaving.

All four of her sisters were standing with them, and were all crying. The four boys were standing a little away from the girls and were trying very hard not to cry. Mama had a river of tears running down her face. Sally had given her one last hug before getting in the wagon.

"Let's go, Jesse. Please, just go." And as he urged the horses on Sally turned and waved and yelled. "I love you all. I love you." And she waved and waved at her mama.

The wagon was light and Jesse had them moving as fast as he could without hurting the two horses. Sally looked back but it didn't take but a few minutes until the house was out of sight behind the trees. She leaned on Jesse and cried.

He gave her a few minutes then asked, "Have I ever told you I'd shore like to get you under the covers?"

Sally looked at him and said, "Yes, about every hour since the first time."

She laughed and wiped her tears away. "You're pretty good at this, you know."

"What I do to you under the covers?" He asked.

"No. Distracting crying women. That's what you did when you were with us on the way to La Grange that time too."

"So I'm pretty good at distracting crying women but not pretty good under the covers."

"Yes. I mean no. I mean you're good at both. Oh, just thank you." She said and leaned her head on his shoulder again.

"I love you." He said quietly.

And just as quietly she said, "I love you too."

CHAPTER 11

Sally and Jesse were living in Gonzales, and she'd never been so happy in her life. That seemed strange, because when Daddy died, she thought she'd never be happy again.

Jesse had stayed around long enough to help get a small cabin and adjoining corral built, and then he could no longer resist the need to ride off and see what was happening with the 'soldiering' occurring all around the Gonzales area.

The first evening he was gone was extremely long for Sally. She had a garden started so she worked in it until it was almost dark, then realizing it was not safe to be out, she hurriedly fed the few cows and two horses, and went inside the cabin. She hated to admit she was afraid, but she was.

Sally stood in the small house and felt very alone. She thought of Mama and her brothers and sisters and started to cry. That didn't last long before her practical nature took over. She fixed herself something to eat and then looked around for something to do.

After she'd eaten she got out the sewing she'd been working on, something Mama had given her, and sat by the lantern to work on it. That didn't last long either. She sighed, put the sewing away, thinking to herself, 'Sorry, Mama, but that's just not what I want to do.'

She looked around, straightened the few things that weren't perfectly straight, swept a floor that didn't need swept, and finally said out loud "Maybe I'll just sit here and go crazy"!

She sat down in front of the fireplace feeling kind of silly about talking to herself. Then as she looked to the left side of the fireplace, in the corner of the cabin, she noticed the old pair of leather pants that Jesse had discarded. Nothing was thrown away that might be used in some way, so the pants were in the corner until there was a place to stow things out of the way.

Sally got up, went and picked the pants up, held them up, and had an inspiration!

She'd always had a yearning to have a bullwhip. Not like the old whip they used when the oxen were pulling the wagon, but a heavier larger whip. As she looked at the old leather pants she thought, 'I can make a whip. At least it might keep me busy enough to not sit here and go crazy.'

She got the sharpest knife she had and started cutting long strips of leather from the pants. It was hard work, and when she nicked a small place on her finger, she put her finger in her mouth and realized how tired she was. She decided to call it a day.

She coiled the leather strips she'd cut, cleaned up her mess, and crawled into bed. As she went to sleep, she thought again of Jesse and how lonely she was without him. But she'd enjoyed her evening.

The next few days went by in much the same way and after working on cutting the leather strips each evening she finally finished. But her hands were scratched and sore so she put it aside to work on later.

Jesse had been gone almost a week and Sally was so lonely that she decided to ride over to see the woman that lived a mile further away from Gonzales. Sally had only met her once before, but she seemed like a friendly person and Sally thought she'd like her.

Her name was Mary. She was a frail woman with three small children, and her husband was also gone from home most of the time. When Sally rode up to her house, Mary was so glad to see her that Sally felt sorry for her.

After accepting a cup of coffee Sally talked her into allowing her to let her help with her chores. They chopped some wood, worked in the garden awhile, and Sally helped with a number of repairs. All the time they worked Mary talked. She was pleasant to listen to and she reminded Sally of her sisters.

Sally began to realize that at times Mary would talk less and less until she trailed off to nothing. Then Sally would know that she had to talk some to make Mary feel comfortable. So when Mary got quite Sally would ask her something about herself or her children and Mary would talk for another length of time.

Sally enjoyed the company and liked being able to help. She especially liked visiting with the children, a boy and two girls. She didn't have to worry about keeping them talking. They were full of energy and comfortable just doing and being.

Sally stayed most of the day with Mary and her children then went back home. As she left they were waving and telling her to come back soon. She hoped they'd be okay. It wasn't a very safe place to be and Mary didn't seem very strong.

It was almost dark when she got home and she was tired. The evening went fast and she had a good nights sleep. The next morning she decided she'd walk to the store and see what was happening with the militia. She finished the morning chores and was getting ready to leave the house, when she heard horses coming.

She picked up her rifle, went to the door, and waited. Into the yard rode Jesse and William. "Hello the house. Where's my sister?"

By the time he got off his horse Sally was out of the house and had grabbed him and was hanging on like a sticker burr. She was laughing and crying at the same time.

He laughed, hugged her in return, and gave her a long look. "You look real good, Sally. And it sure is good to see you."

Sally went and gave Jesse a hug and kiss too. But at the moment she was really more interested in William. She wanted to know when was the last time he'd seen Mama and the rest of the family? Had Mama had the new baby? Who else had had a baby? And what else was happening?

William said, "Slow down and I'll tell you what I know, which isn't very much." They talked for about an hour and then William said he had to get going.

"Oh, don't go yet." Sally didn't want him to leave.

"I'm sorry, Sally, but I need to get back to camp. I need to stay with the militia for another week at least. After that I'm going back to

Egypt and I wanted to see you before then. So I came over with Jesse for a short visit. And besides if I hadn't come over to see you before I get back home to see Mama I'd be in real serious trouble. She'd never forgive me if I didn't stop by to see how you're doing."

Sally said she understood but she didn't want him to go and it was hard telling him good-bye. She stood and watched him ride away. Her heart felt heavy and alone until she turned around toward the house.

Jesse was leaning against the door and was looking at her like she was something sweet to eat. They looked at each other for a long minute then Sally laughed and ran to him. She decided she didn't want to go to the store after all.

After making love for long enough that they were both drenched in sweat and exhausted, they stopped.

Jesse took a long breath and said. "You know you're going to kill me, woman!"

Sally just laughed.

"I'm serious." He said. "But I guess I'd rather die this way than being gut-shot by some Mexican or carved into strips of meat by an Indian."

"Don't talk about dying." She said.

"Well, now don't you think I should prefer you killing me instead of a Mex or an Indian?"

"Yes!" Sally said happily and got up and got some biscuits and coffee for them and they took it outside and sat on the bench with it.

After she finished her coffee she put the cup down and got as close to Jesse as she could. He pulled her even closer and they sat that way a long time.

She looked up at him and thought that she missed the relations they had as much as she missed him. She guessed that was normal, but she didn't know. And she didn't know a woman around here that she'd feel comfortable asking.

And she didn't really need to know if other women felt like she did. She knew how she felt. She remembered the old dog that'd go out in the sun, find a soft spot, circle three times, lay down in a coil, give a big sigh, and go to sleep with a smile on his face. Yes!

"What're you thinking about?" He asked.

"How much I love you." She said.

"I think you're thinking about how much you love how I make you feel, not how much you love me."

Sally smiled and kissed him and whispered. "Both. I love you. And how you make me feel."

Jesse was only home three days when some men rode up and told him they were heading back to the camp. He told them he wanted to finish the lean-to he was building so thought he wouldn't go with them just yet.

Sally was relieved. She was afraid he'd go and he'd just barely gotten home. But the relief didn't last long. He was more restless each day, and another three days was all he could stand.

She fixed him something to eat and got some food together for him to take with him, and he headed out the next morning. He kissed her long and hard, but she could tell his mind was on getting back to the camp.

Sally tried to be just lonely, which she was, but she was also angry. He didn't have to go. There was no fighting going on right now. It felt like she wasn't important enough to him for him to stay at home with her.

She worked on the lean-to all the rest of that day, and had it almost finished when it was time to get inside for the evening. She got out the leather strips and started working on the bullwhip again. It wasn't as smooth as she liked, so she undid it, and re-braided it.

It turned out to be a much longer whip than she'd thought it'd be. She thought about redoing it again and making it shorter, but that was a lot of work and would have to wait for the next day. Besides she wanted to try it at this length before making a change.

The next few days she spent working on the lean-to and trying out her bullwhip. After numerous bruises, burns, and even a few small cuts, she'd about quit hitting herself. She decided to leave it long; she could reach a long distance with it. Who knows? That could come in handy.

By the end of the fourth day she knocked a rock off a post at the outer reach of the bullwhip. Nice!

The next day, she went to the store to see what was going on. Once inside, she just walked around looking at things and listened to the talk. There was some talk about Indians, but mostly everyone was talking about the Mexicans.

A man called, "Howdy there, Miz Robinson. I got a letter here for you."

It was a letter for Mama and was Sally's very first letter! She was really excited but wanted to wait until she could get somewhere by herself to read it.

She knew that most people opened their mail in the store, read it, and then shared the news with whoever happened to be in the store at the time. But Sally couldn't do that. Not only did it seem like you were sharing something entirely private with a bunch of strangers, but also she was a terrible reader. She'd be embarrassed to try to read something out loud.

She rode to the river, tied her horse to a tree, and sat down to read her letter. She had to struggle with almost every word, but thankfully Mama knew what a hard time she had, so made it as simple as she could.

First thing Mama told her was that she had a new little sister, Ann Eliza. Mama said the birth was no problem at all, and the baby was good-natured, which was a blessing. All the rest of the family was doing well and everyone missed her. Thomas and Ali complained all the time about how much work there was, so they finally realized how much Sally had done to make life easier on them. Mama said they both said to tell Sally to come back home!

Sally stopped and thought about how much she missed them all and almost wished she could just go back home. She thought about the new little sister too. Mama had eleven children now although four of them were no longer living at home. Sally wondered if she'd feel the same about Ann Eliza as she did her own full brothers and sisters. She hoped so.

The rest of the letter was even harder to read but it helped that Sally had heard a lot of it before. Mama said the Texians decided to call for a convention to be held to prepare a petition asking the Mexican government for separation from Coahuila and full statehood for Texas.

She said Uncle Andrew was selected as a delegate, representing the District of Mina in Austin's colony. The Convention was held in San Felipe in April, just after Sally had gotten married there. And a man named Sam Houston was chosen to head a committee having the responsibility of writing a proposed constitution for the new state.

Uncle Andrew was made a member of Houston's group, and helped draft the final document. They didn't really expect Mexico to consider the proposal, but Uncle Andrew said that in the long run it wasn't going to matter!

It took Sally an hour to figure out all those words and she had to read it two or three times to make sense of it. She was proud of Uncle Andrew's part in it all. She wasn't sure how she felt about what was happening, but she thought everything would work out just fine if the Texians could just run things for themselves. She didn't know why it should be any other way.

The last paragraph in the letter brought tears to her eyes. Mama said things were about the same with Mr. Rose. Then she said, "Sally, you take good care of yourself, and stay safe. I wish you weren't so far away. I do miss you, Child. Love from your family. Your mother, Rachel."

Sally put the letter in her blouse, and went back home. She was lonely for her family. And she was sleepy and kind of tired, so spent the rest of the day just doing little things in the house.

The next morning she got up, ate breakfast as usual, headed outside to work and made it about three feet out into the yard and vomited.

'Great goodness!' She thought. 'What in the world did I eat? It must have been something bad.'

The rest of the day passed like most days go, and then the next morning went the same as the day before. She lost her breakfast again!

As she sat on the bench with a wet rag in her hand, she realized she'd been feeling kind of strange for awhile. She'd been around her mama, aunts, and older sisters all those years and she should've recognized the signs. She was going to have a baby!

Sally didn't know how to feel about this. Her spirits went up and down in a matter of minutes. Other than losing her breakfast every morning, regular as clockwork, she felt great. She did get sleepy more than normal and sometimes felt a little like crying for no apparent reason.

And she felt the strongest desire to share this with the two people that mattered so much, Jesse and Mama. She wished Jesse was at home and wished Mama wasn't so far away.

It seemed like a long time, but was only a few days after her discovery when Jesse came riding into the yard like he'd only been to town for awhile.

She ran to him, kissed him hello, started crying, got furious, and gave him what-for almost all at the same time.

He stood and held her while she went off into some place he didn't know anything about. She finally settled down, caught her breath, and realized that Jesse looked like he'd just experienced something foreign and was wishing strongly that he hadn't.

Sally took him by the hand, led him to the bench, and asked him sit down. He looked at her like maybe he half wished he was still at the camp, but he sat down.

She stood in front of him and as was her way, said, "I'm going to have a baby."

He looked at her again like she was speaking a foreign language. He sat there for the longest time, then jumped up, grabbed her and whirled her around, all the time yelling, "You are? You are?"

She told him to put her down and said, "Yes I Are"!

It was a wonderful sweet loving evening. Jesse was very thoughtful and worried about her condition. He told her over and over about how careful she had to be.

Sally knew all about childbirth. She also knew that many women, especially young ones, died in childbirth. And she knew that women had to worry and take care. But she was healthy and had never been sick, so she wasn't worried. She planned on having at least ten children.

Jesse stayed home for two full weeks! But too much was happening and there came the day that he rode off again. He was sweet and concerned, but he rode off and again she was alone.

Sally tried not to be disappointed that he was leaving, but she was. She just stayed busy so the time would pass faster. There was always so much to do just to have food to eat that it was no problem keeping busy. She got past the morning vomiting and nothing except the size of her stomach kept her from feeling and doing just like she always had.

She still went to see her neighbor Mary and her children, at least once a week. And she'd made friends with an older couple, Mr. & Mrs. Mason that lived not too far from the store. Mrs. Mason reminded Sally of a sweet grandmother-type just waiting to happen.

Sally decided to go pay a visit to Mrs. Mason. Then she'd go to the store and ask what was happening with the militia, and also mail the letter she'd written to Mama to tell her she was going to have another grandchild. Mama would worry about Sally not having any of the family around to help her, but another baby wouldn't be anything special. There were already so many in the family. Sally thought, 'but very special to me!'

Sally had mentioned in her letter to Mama that there was a very nice older lady here, a Mrs. Mason that'd help with the birth and the baby. That'd make Mama feel better. She thought of Mama so often and wished it could be her here when the baby came. She thought of her daddy, and grandma, and granddad, and wished they were still alive. She really wished her children could have known her daddy.

Thinking of her daddy made her do something she'd been thinking about for awhile. She went to the building where the county business was conducted and registered her daddy's cattle brand, JN, as her own. That particular brand hadn't been registered in Gonzales, so she could use it.

When she drew the two letters, JN, the clerk asked her name and she said Sarah Newman.

He wrote her name down, then asked, "Aren't you Mrs. Robinson?"

She blushed bright red and said yes she was.

He then added to the register, 'the wife of Jesse Robinson', and added the date, September 25, 1833.

She felt good about registering the brand. Then as she was leaving the building she heard someone call her.

"Miz Robinson. Hold on a minute."

Sally turned and saw the man she knew was the sheriff.

He took off his hat, lowered his voice, and said, "Excuse me ma'am, but could you tell me when you expect your husband back home?"

Sally didn't think it was anyone's business, but she just told him that she didn't know for sure.

The sheriff then said, "Well, ma'am, you need to tell Jesse that he needs to get that debt paid, before I have to auction off his land to pay it off. Tell him it's going to come to that."

Sally looked directly at him and in a quite, steady voice said, "You can tell him that yourself."

The sheriff looked at her strangely and said, "Ma'am, your husband has been told and warned several times about that debt. I guess he won't be told again."

He put his hat back on, said "Ma'am." And walked away.

Sally was disturbed because she hadn't known what the sheriff was talking about and also because she hadn't handled the situation well. Her directness offended most men and she knew she'd been too blunt with the sheriff. She'd try to undo the damage next time she saw him, but at this moment she was too angry.

She walked back to the house in such a hurry that it only took a few minutes to get there. Her mind was bubbling and boiling all these thoughts in her head. Not only had she not know about any debts Jesse owed, but she hadn't even known about the land he owned.

She guessed it was his land grant he'd gotten for coming to Texas, the one-quarter league of land each single man got. But he'd never mentioned it. Now she was not only angry with Jesse but with herself too. She should've thought to ask him about his land grant.

Sally had been raised with the thought that almost the only thing more important than land was your family and your honor. And now she'd discovered that Jesse didn't seem worried at all about the land. She was beginning to think all he really cared much about was fighting Indians and Mexicans.

She spent the next few days thinking about what was involved in a marriage, a family, and making a living. She had no idea what those things meant to Jesse so she thought it was time to discuss it with him. But when he rode up to the house a few days later she was so glad to see him that she decided to wait until the next day to approach the subject.

169

The next morning had a pleasant feel of fall in the air so after breakfast they took their coffee and went out and sat under one of the large oak trees.

"Jesse, the Sheriff told me they'll have to auction off your land to pay the debt you owe."

He jumped up and said, "What the hell are you talking about, woman? Here I was sitting easy and happy and all of a sudden you make me feel like a cannon just unexpectedly went off right next to me."

Sally was surprised at his anger. It was the first time he'd been mad at her, at least as far as she knew. She told him what the sheriff had said and asked him what it was all about.

"So are you mad at me or mad at the sheriff?' He asked.

"I'm not really mad at either one of you." As soon as she said it she knew it probably wasn't exactly true. She was a little mad at both of them.

"Well, it sounded like you were mad to me. You sounded just like an old-maid school-marm I had when I was a kid. 'Jesse, the Sheriff told me you didn't read your lesson for today and you're going to be punished.' Damn, I hated that sour-faced old woman."

"That's not fair, Jesse. I wasn't being mean about it. I just wanted to know about the land and the debt."

"The land was my quarter-acre and I bought five cows and calves to put on the land. I didn't have the money to pay for them so used the land as security for the cattle. I've been too busy with the militia to stay there to take care of them. There's been a judgement against me for what I owe on the cows since May of '31, so the sheriff has a right to do something about it. Now is that what you wanted to know?" He finished.

"A quarter league is over 1100 acres. If you've had that land and some cows all this time why aren't we living on our own land, instead of this little plot we're on now?" She asked him.

Jesse looked at her like she was a bit dense and said, "My land is too far from Gonzales and you wouldn't be safe there alone."

"It could be safe enough if you stayed home and we tried to make it a real farm." She knew how he'd take to that message. He wasn't going to stay home and be a farmer. He's a soldier; that's what he's good at and that's what he's going to be.

"Listen, Sally. This is an argument that's not worth having. There's millions of miles of land here, so why get all worked up over such a little amount. I'll talk to the Sheriff and tell him to do whatever he needs to do but not talk to you about it again. Your job is to take care of the baby." And he got his horse and rode to the store.

Sally thought about all they'd talked about and tried to get it settled in her mind. But it irritated her that Jesse didn't really care if his land was sold to pay his debts or not. It also irritated her how he'd turned the conversation around where she felt everything was her fault.

Jesse stayed gone most of the day and when he got home he was all stirred up by the talk of fighting Mexicans and the sharing of a jug.

Sally got them something to eat then afterwards said. "Jesse, I know I'm young but I'm not some weak woman that can't take care of herself. And I don't like being treated like that."

"Ah, come on, Sally. Let's don't argue. I'm not here often enough for that." Jesse said.

"You don't understand. I'm not arguing. I just want to tell you how I feel." She said.

"Alright. Then say it and get it over with so we can go to bed."

Sally barely kept from showing him how dense she thought he was for saying that, but she didn't. She just wanted to tell him what was important to her. "Jesse. After the baby is born I don't want to live on a piece of land that doesn't belong to us, especially a piece of land just barely big enough for a garden. Especially when the land I'm going to inherit from my daddy will just be sitting there not being used."

Sally didn't mean it as a threat to him but she saw that at first he took it that way. Then after a few minutes had gone by he said, "Its looking more and more like we're going to be fighting the Mexicans for our independence. We sat around all day at the store and talked about it. Gonzales is going to be less safe with the passing time.

"I guess maybe we should plan on settling on your daddy's land after the baby gets here. At least until I can get the rest of the league that'll be due me as a married man."

Instead of staying a few more days like he usually did, Jesse left the next morning to go back to the militia camp. Even though they kissed each other goodbye and told each other to be extra careful, there was a distance between them.

Sally knew that neither one wanted it that way, but she didn't know how to change it. She didn't feel in the wrong and maybe to be honest she thought neither did he. For the hundredth time she wished Mama were close enough so that she could ask her questions.

Then the thought of moving back close to Mama and the rest of the family brought a new excitement that made her forget her problems with Jesse. She already had big plans for her own place.

Sally was having a harder time getting out to shoot something to eat, and chopping wood was becoming harder as she got bigger. Jesse had started coming home more often and always tried to bring something, especially fresh meat. He was also doing more of the chores while he was there.

Sally had decided not to bring up any of their problems again, and they seemed to be getting along almost as well as in the beginning. Jesse told her that most of the men his age already had some almost grown children and he was getting anxious to have his child get here!

A letter came from Mama to wish them a good Christmas. It was full of news about the family and the happenings around home. She said a flood, above La Grange, had taken out Granddad's mill, but none of her brothers or their families were hurt. Sally loved getting letters from Mama, but this one just made her cry.

Jesse made sure he was home for Christmas, but it wasn't much fun for either one of them. Sally was so uncomfortable she couldn't do much and she missed her family more than ever. Jesse only stayed a couple of days then went back to camp so someone else could go home to be with his family awhile. Sally didn't even mind much. She thought they were just both glad when the season was over and it was a new year. Maybe 1834 would be a peaceful year and they could get a better start on their lives together.

A week later Jesse came home for another short visit. As he was getting ready to go back to the camp he said, "Are you sure you're going to be alright? I wish you'd let me take you over to Mrs. Mason's house."

"I'm fine. I'm just big as a barn and can't move. If I figured right it'll be another week at least before I have the baby. You can come home in three or four days and that should work out just right. Then you can take care of me and your baby." And she smiled as she patted her stomach.

"I think I ought to just stay here or go get Mrs. Mason to stay with you."

"Jesse. Mr. & Mrs. Mason come over every day to see about me. I'm fine.

And if you or Mrs. Mason were here all the time I'd just feel like I had to be doing things. This way I can just rest. Please don't worry."

Sally was relieved when Jesse finally left for the camp although she knew he probably wouldn't stay gone very long. She was so tired. She lay down on the bed and fell asleep for a short time but woke with a backache. She got up and walked around the room but nothing relieved the backache.

She ignored it as best she could, but finally couldn't do much except keep the fire going and hurt. By late afternoon she was miserable and thought she should get help. She was afraid to get on the horse and it didn't seem smart to try to walk to the store, so she got her gun and went to the door. She aimed at the sky in the direction of the store and fired the gun three times.

Sally wasn't scared yet but she thought, 'I'm getting close.'

She sat down in front of the fireplace and wished Jesse had stayed and hadn't listened to her. It seemed like a long time and the pain was getting really bad and she thought, 'I'm not getting close, I am scared. And I'm not sure what to do.'

There was a banging on the door and a man's voice called. "Mrs. Robinson. Are you in there? Are you alright?"

"I need help. Get Mrs. Mason. Please." And she heard horses and men in front of the house.

"Get out of the way here." She heard the Sheriff say and he opened the door and came inside.

Sally started crying when he came in. She looked up at him and said, "I'm so glad to see you."

"You just take it easy now." He said. Then he started barking orders almost as well as Mama did.

"You two get on over to the Mason house and get Mrs. Mason here as soon as you can. Didn't I see Jesse leave here just a few hours ago? Why don't you three men head toward the camp and see if you can find him. All he's talked about for months is this baby, so let's see if we can't get him here in time to be one of the first to see it.

"Here, you help me move her to the bed. Pull that quilt back there." And Sally was being picked up by the Sheriff and moved to the bed. Then someone took her shoes off her feet.

She felt a hard pain and tried not to groan but she couldn't help it. The sheriff acted like he hadn't heard a thing. She reached and caught his hand and he held hers without any hesitation.

"Do you mind if I have one of the men pull a chair up beside the bed? Just until Mrs. Mason gets here?" He asked.

"I'd really like that. Thank you." Sally said. She wondered if he knew how scared she was and how grateful she was for his presence.

She gritted her teeth as another pain came.

"You know what a mystery is, don't you?" The Sheriff asked.

"Yes sir." She answered.

"Well, I'll tell you. A few months ago I had a big mystery on my hands. I didn't know what I was running into so I didn't tell anyone. I was afraid it was something I was supposed to know all about and I was afraid I'd get embarrassed if I didn't figure it out. It seems as how there were strange marks all over things back in the woods and it just didn't make any sense."

He waited a minute until Sally was past the next pain then started talking again.

"I finally figured out what was making those marks, but then I had me another mystery. I couldn't understand why somebody that was that good at something wasn't going around showing off about it. So I just kind of hung around paying pretty close attention and finally one day I heard a snapping sound. So I just real quite like made my way close enough to see and there was my mystery person."

He stopped talking as another pain racked her. She was finally able to say, "My whip."

And he smiled and nodded his head. "I've never seen anyone any better with a whip. Especially one that large. Who taught you how to use it?"

"Taught myself." She gasped out. "And I need help."

"I heard the wagon coming a bit ago. You hang on. Mrs. Mason will be here in a minute."

Sally knew that the Sheriff was probably almost as glad as she was that Mrs. Mason would be there very soon.

In just a few more minutes Mr. & Mrs. Mason came in the door and Mrs. Mason took over. She was older than Mama, far past childbearing age, but she was the woman who helped when it was time for babies to be born. Sally liked her.

Mrs. Mason looked around, asked the sheriff to stay where he was, and then she ran all the other men outside.

"What about me?" The Sheriff asked almost in a panic.

"I can see that Sally feels safe with you. I may need some help so you just stay here until one of the other women gets here. One or two of them should be here anytime now." Mrs. Mason told him.

Sally kept hold of his hand and he started talking to her again. She wasn't sure what he was saying most of the time but she heard him talking about her uncle, Tommy Rabb. Seems the Sheriff thought he was someone special.

She knew the Sheriff was trying to distract her and it had worked for awhile. But now Sally was trying to decide if this was what any woman in her right mind would really want to do. The pain was so bad and they were coming so close together that all she could do was clinch her teeth to keep from crying out.

Another woman came into the house and the Sheriff immediately stood up. Sally managed to say, "Thank you very much." But by then he was just about through the door to join the other men.

Then in a matter of a few more minutes, half the people of Gonzales were at the little house. The women were inside helping with Sally and the men were outside visiting. Some one had started a large fire in the middle of the yard so they were all standing around that. Since Jesse wasn't there for them to tease and give encouragement to, they were just joking and having a good time.

Sally could hear them around the fire. She'd been at enough births to know that this is the way these things happened, but now she knew that it was no fun being the one doing all the hard work.

She heard something going on outside, and when the door opened she saw it was Jesse coming in. He walked over to the bed and the women made room for him. He leaned down and kissed Sally on the forehead and asked, "Are you alright?"

"Oh, Jesse. I'm so glad you're here." That was all she got said before two of the women ushered Jesse back outside.

The next thing she heard was Mrs. Mason saying "Here's your little girl, Jesse."

Sally wasn't sure she remembered anything between Jesse going back outside and Mrs. Mason telling him he had a little girl. She looked on very tiredly as Mrs. Mason placed the baby in his arms. He had the most beautiful smile she'd ever seen on his face as he looked at his newborn daughter.

Jesse held her for a few minutes then put her down next to Sally. He knelt next to the bed and said. "Thank you, Sally. She's beautiful like her mama."

He got all choked up and Sally's eyes filled with tears.

Finally he was able to talk. "Do you mind if we name her after my mother?"

"I wouldn't mind that at all." She said; and she thought 'It's the tenth of January of this year of 1834, and I have a baby girl.'

As she drifted off to sleep she heard her husband say. "I love you. I love you, little Nancy Robinson. Welcome to Texas!"

CHAPTER 12

The winter wasn't too harsh. And Jesse was coming home more often and staying longer periods. He didn't mind helping with Nancy at all.

Sally saw another side to him and it was a wonderful few months.

But the problems all around were getting worse. There was always the worry of Indian raids and the sentiment heard more than anything else was, 'You know, its just a matter of time until we have to fight the Mexicans'.

Sally didn't like for Jesse to leave her alone now. It hadn't seemed so bad when she just had to worry about herself. But now that she had Nancy she felt that every Indian that got close to the house was a threat.

She didn't waste ammunition, but she practiced for accuracy every time she went hunting. She knew that Uncle Tommy was right; she was a natural shot. She got to a point that she could hit just about anything she could see, from either side. It was a satisfying feeling, but she knew it wouldn't do any good and she wouldn't be able to protect Nancy if more than a few Indians or Mexicans came around.

With the whip she could snap off the top of a flower without leaving a mark on the flower stem. She smiled to herself about that. Now the Sheriff would very seldom see mystery marks.

Sally often took meat to the women that were located close to her. None of them hunted very much and they were all afraid to get very far from their houses. Almost all anyone talked about was the potential danger.

One summer day, when Sally went to the store to see if she had a letter, she ran into the Sheriff. He was pleased to see her and Nancy, and he wanted to know all about how they were doing.

"Do you need anything? Can I do anything for you?" He asked.

"No, sir. We're doing fine. Thank you very much."

He said, "I've been trying to run into Jesse. But every time I get around to looking him up, he's gone back to the camp."

"Do you need me to tell him something?" She was pretty sure what it was about and she didn't want the Sheriff to be uncomfortable about it with her.

"Well, I need to get word to him that I've been told to collect $38.00 for the debt he owes on those cows and calves."

Sally replied, "I'll tell him. Just as soon as he gets home."

She didn't have a letter, which was disappointing, but it was a nice day to be out. She visited with the few people in the store, asked about all the latest news, then left for home. All the rest of the day she thought about their own land and cows and having a house that'd belonged to them. By that night she'd decided what she wanted to do. All she now had to do was convince Jesse.

He came home a few days later. Sally waited until he'd had something to eat and had rested, then told him what the sheriff had told her.

He looked at her for a minute and just said, "Alright."

"Jesse, I'd like for us to move back to the Egypt area and start a farm. There are military units in that area that'll need your help." She expected him to get mad and argue with her but she got a surprise.

"I've been thinking about it too." He said. "I've nearly worried myself sick thinking about you and the baby being by yourselves so much. I'll go back to the camp, tell the men what I'm going to do, then I'll come back and help you get ready."

"Oh! That's wonderful." Sally wasn't sure she'd heard him right. It was just too easy. He must've really been worrying about them.

As soon as Jesse left for camp, Sally started getting as much ready as she could so that it wouldn't take as long to get on the way. She wanted to get moving before Jesse changed his mind.

However, it didn't go the way they'd talked about. A few days after Jesse had gone, a neighbor on his way home from the camp stopped by to see Sally. After exchanging pleasantries he cheerfully told her that Jesse had asked him to let her know that he'd be gone a little longer than he'd planned. But he'd get back as soon as possible.

Sally told the neighbor 'thank you' and to give his wife her regards and she bid him a pleasant goodbye. Then she allowed some pretty dark thoughts about her husband to stir around in her mind and she said a few choice words. Her anger and frustration lasted a large part of the evening, until she noticed the look on Nancy's face.

Sally had made a swing out of an old quilt so that she could hang it in a tree or on the porch or over a hook in the middle of the house and Nancy could sit in it. It kept her off the ground, safer and happier than having to lie on the quilt most of the time. She could also see Sally all the time which made her happy.

They were inside the house and Sally was getting something ready for them to eat when she looked at Nancy who was busy chewing on a toy. When she saw Sally look at her she wrinkled her forehead and made her face as mean looking as a fat happy six-months old baby could manage. Sally was so surprised that she walked over to the swing and stared at her. Nancy smiled sweetly, gurgled happily, then made the wrinkled, mean looking face again.

"Great goodness! Is that what I look like?" Sally stood there a minute shaking her head. Then she laughed and made a funny face at Nancy. The two played peek-a-boo for a few minutes, then Sally gave her a hug and kiss and went back to getting supper ready.

She looked at Nancy real often and didn't see the mean face again. She thought, "Who would've thought a baby so young could pick up how I look. And worse than that try to look like me. I guess my anger shows too much, and she's getting some good lessons in looking mean. I'm going to have to watch not only what I say but how I look.'

"I love you, beautiful child." Nancy laughed and gurgled and clapped her hands.

Sally thought, 'I can't do anything about the situation with your daddy but I can try to keep you from having to look at an angry mother all the time. But that's probably going to be the biggest job I ever took on.'

The time went by slowly and Sally got used to hearing about Jesse from someone stopping by to give her a message from him. She tried not to worry, but that was hard.

Sally got a letter from Mama telling her all the news from home, and at the end of the letter she'd written, 'I got a divorce from Mr. Rose. We just couldn't seem to see eye to eye on anything.'

Sally felt guilty because she thought it was such good news; she'd never liked that man. It would feel more like her old home again, if she ever got to go back.

It was late in the year when Jesse finally came home. First thing he said was "How'd you like to go see your mama and family for Christmas?"

Sally was so overjoyed with that thought that she decided not to be mad at him for being gone so long. It took very little time to have everything ready to go. They asked the neighbors to keep an eye on the house and started out. It was a long three days for Sally; she was so anxious to see the family. And at last, they were home.

Jesse was driving the wagon when they rolled into the yard, and Sally jumped down before they'd totally stopped. Mama ran to her and started crying. Sally was crying too and when Jesse got down with the baby, it was all to do over again.

Mama took Nancy, and Sally and Jesse traded hugs with Louisa, Elizabeth, and the four younger brothers. Then Sally got to meet Ann Eliza, her new baby sister for the first time. She was a pretty little girl and Sally felt kind of bad that she was so glad that Ann Eliza's father, Samuel Rose, wasn't there. She knew she could love Ann Eliza, but she couldn't even like Mr. Rose. Later on she'd have time to ask Mama about all that had happened this last year, but for now it was time to enjoy the family.

By the next day the entire clan was at Mama's house. Mary and her husband, Preston, and their two children; and Minerva, expecting her first child, and her husband David came over. William was serving in the local militia and was able to come by for awhile. They had a wonderful visit.

Very quickly Sally fell back into her old routines. Up early and outside doing the work she liked best. Louisa and Elizabeth both liked taking care of Ann Eliza and Nancy, so Sally got the younger boys to help her. The place had gotten kind of run-down, so Sally kept them all working until most things were looking good.

Jesse was spending a lot of time with William and the local militia, and occasionally Thomas, who was 13, went with them. Mama didn't like for Thomas to be gone, but there wasn't much she could do. He thought he was more than old enough.

Time passed so fast and all of a sudden it was Christmas Eve and the family was able to all be together again. After all the preparations were made, the tree decorated, and the toys ready for Christmas morning, someone suggested that they go tell Daddy Merry Christmas. So they wrapped up against the chilly night and took lanterns and trooped up to the cemetery. They stood around and talked a little, and then in her sweet voice Louisa started singing 'Silent Night'.

Jesse was holding Nancy and Sally had her arm through his and all her family was on this little hillside. It was a wondrous time and she wished it could last forever. As they walked back down toward the house more than just Sally was heard to whisper, "I love you, Daddy."

Christmas morning! There is just no other time like it when a house is full of love and children. And Mama's house was very full of both.

Sally couldn't decide who was happier with the little toys, Nancy or Jesse. She'd never seen him have so much fun. He was on the floor at least half the day with usually more than one little child on top of him.

The Christmas dinner was huge with all kinds of good food to eat and to top it off Mama had made a large blackberry cobbler.

Sally said, "Oh Mama. The memories are so strong that I can almost feel Grandma here."

"I feel her presence lots of times. But what are you thinking of?" Mama asked.

"That first blackberry cobbler we had at our first Christmas in Texas, on the Colorado. I think of that day often. What an amazing day that was." Sally said.

"Tell us about it." "Tell us, please." "I want to hear."

Mama laughed and said, "Well, Sally, I think you got the interest of all the little ones. You want to tell them about our first Christmas in Texas?"

"Oh no. Not by myself. But I bet all us older ones have some memories of that day. I'll tell about getting those first pair of pants you made me and then someone else can tell their memory." And Sally told her story.

The conversation went on for over an hour with stories about that day, questions from one person or the other, lots of laughter, and a few tears. Everyone joined in and Sally thought that Daddy, Granddad, Grandma, and Uncle Ulysses must be listening in heaven because they were so much a part of the stories.

Later in the afternoon Sally was putting a new pot of coffee on the stove when she felt someone pull on her skirt. It was Amanda, Mary's little girl.

"Hello, there." Sally said.

"Aunt Sally, I hope you're here again next Christmas so you can give us the same present then too."

Sally was puzzled because she'd only made some cookies for the little kids this year. "Do you mean the cookies, Amanda?"

"No. I like the cookies, but Gramma makes better ones. I mean the member day."

Sally laughed. "How old are you, Amanda?"

"I'm four years old." And she held up four fingers.

"Well, Child. We'll just see if we can't have a Remember Day every so often. And when you're a grown woman with your own children I hope you'll have a Remember Day for them. Maybe you can tell them about this day." And Sally gave her a long hug and kissed her on the cheek. As she watched the little girl run back into the other room she thought that a Remember Day wasn't a bad idea at all.

The children had a wonderful time and by evening were so tired that sleep came early. But it was obvious that now that Christmas was over there were other things on the minds of the adults.

It was as though storm clouds were constantly brewing and everyone was anxious about what the next day would bring. Anywhere a couple of adults got together the talk was about what was happening in Texas. Rumors were flying around about Mexican troops, and all sorts of reinforcement of the Mexican military detachments. Meetings of the Texian colonists were taking place with more frequency and everything seemed more intense.

And now, even after the past two days of fun with the children and the joy of the family being together, the evening talk had turned to the uneasy situation in Texas. They talked quietly about things as if they wished they could hold all the trouble off just this one more day.

"Excuse me." Mama said. "I'm sorry to interrupt, but I know William can't stay much longer. He wants to get back to camp and the evening is passing. There's something we need to talk about."

Very quietly, and with a slight quaver in her voice she said, "It's time we divided your daddy's land among you children."

No one said anything for a full minute and no one seemed to be looking directly at anyone else. Sally glanced up and happened to see Louisa and saw there were tears running down her checks. Sally was feeling the same sadness Louisa must be feeling, but she also had some other strong emotions. Breaking up their daddy's dream, the land that he'd worked so hard for seemed wrong. But a part of that land would be hers now and she was thrilled that she'd get to own a piece of land.

Then Mama brought up something that Sally hadn't even thought about. She told them she wanted the land divided between the children now so as not to have to worry about any future claim by Mr. Rose, although she didn't expect a claim from him. Sally hadn't even considered that he'd claim anything. She felt a little sick even thinking he might get some of daddy's land. She had to make herself pay attention to what Mama was saying.

"I want the land to be divided equally between you ten children. I won't take any part of it. That way no one can make a claim on my part."

William said, "I don't like that idea, Mama. It wasn't just Daddy's land. It belonged, it belongs to you too. You should have this piece, with the house and barns on it, just like Daddy wanted you too."

The other children voiced the same thing, but Mama quieted them down and said, "Let me explain how I think of it. It's not like I'm going to move away. It'll be a lot of years before all you children are grown and gone. I'll stay here in the house. And don't forget that I'm going to inherit a sizable amount of land from my daddy. That will be more than enough land for me."

No one said anything for awhile. Sally wondered if everyone's thoughts were like hers, sad and happy and strange.

Mama said. "There is one other part of all this that I need to talk about. I plan on giving Ann Eliza close to the same amount of acreage that the ten of you get, but it will come from my daddy's land." She held up her hand to quiet them and said. "I know none of you want to treat her any different than the rest of you and I thank you for that. And I also know that it wouldn't have mattered to Joseph for me to give my daughter an equal share. But I wouldn't feel right giving your daddy's land to her and I'm the person I have to feel comfortable with. Do you understand that?"

The all said. "Yes, Ma'am."

"We'll divide Joseph's land between the ten of you children and I'll give Ann Eliza a piece of land from my share of Rabb land. Then when I die the rest of the Rabb land will be divided between the eleven of you."

All the children accepted Mama's decisions, so they talked about what they'd need to do to get it changed legally. The decision was that after the first of the year, whichever man was free first would go with Mama and petition the government to settle the estate. In the meantime, Mama would write her brothers to let them know what she was doing, and see what they were planning to do about dividing the Rabb property.

It was a sad conversation and the next morning it seemed to Sally that all the children lingered a bit longer than planned. Each spent a few extra minutes at the cemetery. It seemed almost wrong to break up the league of land that they thought of as Daddy's land.

As it worked out, Jesse was the one able to go with Mama to get the paper work started. The two of them along with Sally, Louisa, and the younger children went to San Felipe. And on January 15, 1835, Mama renounced all her share of Joseph's land and gave it to her children.

They had to wait until the next day to do the other paper work, so they camped out on the southern edge of town that night. The next day they went back and Jesse petitioned for the division of the estate of Joseph Newman. Jesse signed the petition and F. W. Johnson, the Judge, made it official.

Judge Johnson told them that Mama and all the children would have to answer the petition and say they had no objections. So while Mama, Louisa, Sally, and the kids stayed again in San Felipe, Jesse, Thomas, and Ali went to get the others to come to town to get the paperwork done. By the nineteenth, everyone was there and they again went to the court and stated that there were no objections to the petition.

Uncle Andrew had come down to help Mama, and Uncle Tommy had also joined them. So it wasn't as hard a time for Mama as it might have been. A visit with her brothers was always a special time.

The next thing to do was divide the land by lots. So Mama and all her family, and the two uncles went to San Felipe to get this step done. Ten pieces of paper, with the numbers one though ten written on them, were placed in a hat. In front of Judge Johnson they drew their numbers. Mary drew lot number five, then William drew number three, Louisa drew number seven, and Minerva drew number six.

It was then Sally's turn and she felt a great excitement that she was going to own her very own piece of land. She reached in the hat and drew out a piece of paper. It had a nine on it. She didn't even know which piece that would be and it didn't really matter. She just knew that she now owned lot number nine, of league number seven, and she had 555 acres of Texas land.

Mama drew for the five younger children: lot number one for Elizabeth, number ten for Thomas, number two for Ali, number four for Joseph, and number eight for Andy.

It was April the 30th and so with the paperwork requiring the children's presence finished, most of the older ones headed back home. Jesse went back to Mama's house, but Sally and Louisa wanted to stay with Mama.

Mama was required to petition the court to be appointed as the administrator for her minor children. It was a requirement of the Mexican Government that a man must also be appointed, and that was one of the reasons why she'd asked Uncle Andrew to come.

Sally thought it was ridiculous for a mother to have to petition the court to be appointed as the person to take care of her own children but that was the requirement. So at the bottom of the petition to divide the land was the appointment of Rachel and her brother, Andrew Rabb, as administrators. Sally noticed that Mama signed the petition as Rachel Newman, not Rachel Rose. No one objected.

Uncle Andrew had been with them for more than a week and it'd been a great visit, but he left for home after the papers were signed. Uncle Tommy and his family were going with him to visit for awhile with the families in La Grange. Sally almost wished that Mama could go with them too. Maybe a visit with Uncle John and the rest of her family would help her forget the emotions of the last two weeks. But she had one more thing to do. The next day she went back to the court and gave 400 acres of the land she'd inherited from her daddy to Ann Eliza.

Then they headed for home. Mama was obviously exhausted from all the emotions and it was a quiet trip. When they finally arrived at the house, Mama got out of the wagon and walked to the cemetery. No one went with her. They could see her standing in front of daddy's grave; she stood that way a long while. When she came back to the house she seemed to be at peace with what she'd done about the land.

Sally could barely wait until the surveying was done and she could go and stand on her own land. Even though Jesse wanted to get back to Gonzales he seemed to know how important this time was to Sally so he spent most of his time with William and the local militia and let her stay for awhile longer.

But by early summer he couldn't stand it any longer; he was just too far from the action. So Sally loaded the wagon, got her and Nancy ready, and told Mama and the family a sad farewell. As they topped a small rise, Sally tried to see her land. She couldn't tell for sure where it was, but she promised herself that she'd be back and someday she'd live on that land.

The trip back to Gonzales went by quickly with no trouble. After greeting the friends in Gonzales, cleaning out the cabin, and getting a late garden started, Sally settled in to a fairly pleasant life. It was peaceful for a short time at least and Jesse stayed around some at first. But of course that didn't last long. He was soon back at the military camp more than at home.

The summer passed slowly, then a major change occurred. One September day was suddenly interrupted with shots and shouts coming from the store. Jesse was home at the time. He grabbed his gun and with hardly a look to Sally, said, "Stay inside and bolt the door." Then he ran toward the store.

Sally hesitated a moment, then said out loud, "I'll be damned if I'll stay here." She grabbed her gun, picked Nancy up, and followed Jesse.

By the time she got to the front of the store it seemed that everyone in the community was there. There was talking and shouting and an occasional shot fired in the sky. Everyone on the fringe of the crowd was asking what was happening. Sally backed away a little because the crowd was so unruly.

Two men that Sally didn't recognize came out on the store porch, followed by other men, and they were all trying to get the attention of the crowd. Sally saw Jesse among the men on the porch and noticed he looked so excited that he couldn't stand still. He was practically prancing. Dear God, what was happening?

One of the men on the porch grabbed a metal bucket and started banging on it with a wooden mallet. After much banging and shouting the crowd quieted down. Then the first words out of the mouth of one of the "visitors" caused the crowd to roar even louder than before.

All he had time to say was, "Stephen Austin is back home safe, and he says, 'Texas must be free from Mexico'!"

People were crying, stomping, shouting till they were hoarse, hugging each other, and acting like they'd already whipped Mexico. Sally had known and loved Mr. Austin for many years and she was crying mostly for his safe return.

She knew Mr. Austin had left for Mexico in the Spring of 1833, to try to win Mexican statehood for Texas. She also knew he'd spent a year in prison and even after being released wasn't allowed to leave Mexico City until the government had resolved his case. Now it seemed he was back. The rest of it hadn't sunk in yet.

Jesse had seen her at the edge of the crowd and made his way to her side. He pulled her and Nancy into his arms and laughed happily. Other men were laughing and it was contagious. It ended with a small street celebration that lasted until very late.

Sally bought something in the store for Nancy and her to eat. Jesse was sharing a jug with some of the men and didn't want to eat. Sally had never seen him like this and wondered if she was seeing the Jesse that was the fearless fighting man that everyone talked about.

There were a few of the men that all the others deferred to, and Jesse was one of those. She watched him awhile and didn't think he'd even notice if she left. She was tired, so she quietly made her way back home, put Nancy to bed, and wondered what this news would do to her plans to go back home.

When she got up the next morning, she already knew what would happen. For once she guessed she agreed that Jesse would have to go to the camp and find out what the military plans were going to be. She loved Texas as much as he did, and she wanted what was best for the country. She was just so very tired of always being alone.

Sally had some food and other things ready when Jesse came in. He looked absolutely awful and smelled worse. Sally told him so and asked, "Did you get any sleep?"

"No." He smiled sheepishly at her then said, "Sally, I know how bad you want to go home and I want to take you there too, but I have to go. I have to do this. Please try to understand and don't be mad at me."

"I'm not mad at you. I'm proud of you." She guessed she'd never voiced that before; she got a look full of love in return.

For a minute he even looked like he might like to show her how much he loved her, but he was too anxious to be on the road. He hugged and kissed her and Nancy, went to his horse, then came back and kissed her again. Then for about the tenth time he told her. "Now don't take any chances. If you feel in danger at all take Nancy and go stay at the store. You hear me?"

"Yes, Jesse. I'm always careful because of Nancy. You just please stay safe. And try to get some kind of word to me as often as you can."

She stood in the front yard holding Nancy and watched him ride away. This time just before he got out of sight he raised up in the saddle, turned, and waved his hat.

Sally waved back, and kept waving even when she knew he couldn't see her. Then loneliness took over, just as it always did, and she went looking for some hard work to do.

It was only a few days later, when Jesse came galloping into the yard at full speed. She got to the door about the same time he did. He was very agitated and told her to get some things together fast so he could take her and Nancy to the store where some of the older men were going to see that the women and children made it to a safer place for now.

As she was grabbing a few things he told her what was happening.

"A Mexican General, named Cos, has landed on the coast of Texas with over 500 men and is headed for San Antonio. But our immediate problem is that the Mexican Colonel in charge of Bexar, I can't even pronounce his name, has demanded we return their cannon. You know the little cannon next to the store?"

"Yes" she said.

"Well," he continued. "The Mexicans gave it to us a few years ago, and now this Colonel wants it back.

"I don't know if he's trying to impress this General Cos or what, but he sent a detachment of five men to get it. Can you believe that? I think the son-of-a-bitch really thought we'd just give it to them.

"Andrew Ponton refused to give it up, of course, and we're fortifying the town and getting ready for a battle. Words gone out to get the women and children out of the way, and messengers have been sent to the surrounding settlements to tell them to come a running."

He went and saddled her horse, then helped her load the things she'd gathered to take. He held Nancy as Sally bolted the door then with Jesse carrying Nancy they rode to the store.

They were there in minutes and Jesse handed Nancy to Sally then went in to check the situation at the store. It had all happened too fast. Sally was almost paralyzed with fear. She looked down at her daughter's face, and Nancy was looking at her with big scared eyes.

Sally made herself calm down and said, "I've been through tough things before. I can get through this too." She hoped she wasn't just whistling into the wind. She got down and was going to go into the store when Jesse came out.

He told her. "Hang onto your horse. He's your security right now. If the people in the store aren't ready to go in an hour or less I want you to go hide somewhere east of town. Alright?"

She just nodded and Jesse caught her by the arms and said, "Sally, listen to me. You have to take care of the two of you for me. I know I should've already moved you to your mama's. I can't tell you how much I regret that I didn't. And I know you wish I'd stay with you now, but you're better off if I'm with the men fighting to keep the Mexicans out of town. And that's where I have to be"

"Nancy and I'll be alright." Sally gave him a fierce hug and said. "Go on, Jesse. And don't let them have our cannon."

As he rode off she looked around and saw that Mr. & Mrs. Mason had just gotten to the store. They had their wagon and already had a woman and some kids in it. She also saw Mary and her three kids riding up with her husband. Mary's husband said hello and then left. Sally and Nancy joined Mary and her children, and they all went over and joined the Masons. It felt safer just being with neighbors.

Very soon most of women and children that lived close to the store were moving east to a safe place. At least they all hoped it'd be safe. They camped out in the woods not too far from Gonzales and waited. It wasn't but two days later until some of the Gonzales men came out to get them. The men were laughing and full of good news. They'd routed the Mexicans and kept the cannon.

Sally rode straight home and still had to wait a half a day longer before Jesse came home.

He was full of news about the confrontation. "The Colonel, whatever his fool name is, sent around eighty or so men to get the cannon. By the time the Mexicans got here, John Alley and some men from the Navidad and Lavaca rivers had joined us, and we just proceeded to whip their butts. We killed two of the Mexicans and the others hightailed it back to San Antonio to tell the Colonel we weren't going to let him have our cannon.

"But the best part, Sally, was that someone made a flag that we hung on the cannon. It said 'Come and Take It.' And they couldn't do it!"

Sally was amazed at how fired up he was and she was enjoying his enthusiasm, when he suddenly stopped and got serious.

"Oh damn, here I am going on and forgetting the most important thing. We got to get you and Nancy out of here. Real soon it's going to be even more dangerous. I've asked two of the men I know that have families east of here if they'd take you and Nancy and see you get to your mama's place."

As he talked she was beginning to shake her head. And before he could say anymore, she said, "Jesse. We're not going anywhere unless you take us."

He was immediately angry and said, "You'll do what you're told, woman. I'm not going to let you get killed by a bunch of Mexicans! And besides you've been after me to take you to your mama's house for a whole damn year."

"Jesse, please calm down and listen to me for a minute. I've been thinking about this ever since we had to hide out in the woods. I think Nancy and I'd be safer here in Gonzales than with two of those men somewhere between here and home. You know if it came down to them taking care of their families or us, their families would come first."

She stopped and took a deep breath and then went on. "And are you sure there aren't any Mexicans, or Indians, for that matter, between here and there? I'd be more afraid going without you than waiting here until you can take us. Please don't make us go."

She could see he was torn about what to do. She didn't even ask him why he didn't just take them and then come back and join the fighting. She had no doubt that he'd give his life, with no hesitation, to protect them, but to leave now when the enemy was almost within reach was an impossible thing to ask of him.

She waited silently for another few minutes while he paced the floor. Finally, he said, "Well, messengers have been sent all over Texas with the news of our contact with the Mexicans. I'm sure everyone that can come will head this way. So I think it probably would be safer if you stayed here. But just for now. Soon as I can get you to your mama's the better. Cause sooner or later there's going to be hell to pay."

They had a good evening and then an even better night. But the next morning Jesse had a fighting look in his eyes. Sally was beginning to see it more all the time. And not just in Jesse, but all the men around. And she saw a look in the women's eyes like she imagined was in hers, a tremendous fear for her husband and her children.

Jesse told her the camp was very close to town so he'd probably see her every day and if he were going anywhere he'd get word to her. He kissed her goodbye and gave Nancy a long hug then went to the door. At the door he turned and said, "Come here."

Sally walked over to him.

He said, "Stay alert and don't take any chances." Then he caught her by the arm so hard that she almost let out a cry of pain, and in a tone she hadn't heard before he said, "And, Sally, the next time I tell you what I want you to do, I'm not going to listen to an argument." He kissed her hard and left.

Sally walked to the store the next afternoon to see what was going on, and was surprised to see a number of men around, many of them she hadn't seen before. A long letter from home had come so she took Nancy and went and sat under a tree to read it.

Mama started it out by saying how worried she was about her and Nancy. She thought they were just too close to San Antonio and wished they'd moved home during the summer.

Mama went on, "You wouldn't believe the celebrations that took place when Stephen returned to Texas. It's said that he has united the different parties and even that young William Travis, the one so involved in the War party, has expressed the thought that only Stephen can guide the Republic through these perilous times.

"On my last trip to San Felipe, I saw Stephen briefly and was able to greet him and say a few short words. The poor man is kept constantly busy and he looks ill. He's moved into Sam William's vacant house, as his cabin is in such disrepair. That in itself is a disgrace. His cabin should've been kept in good repair in anticipation of his return. Ah well. Nothing to be done about that now."

Sally stopped reading for a few minutes and thought about all she'd just read. Mama had obviously been writing in haste and Sally was having a terrible time reading it. It helped some that she'd already heard much of it. It seemed that since Mr. Austin's return, and all the problems here in Gonzales, someone was traveling daily between here and San Felipe with the news.

The last part of Mama's letter was news about the family. Then she finished by saying, "Oh, my dear Child, I'm so concerned for you and Nancy, and all those I love and hold dear. We've already paid so steep a price for our love of this Texas. I can only pray that it doesn't cost us more than we can bear. Please be careful and make your way to us as soon as possible. Your loving and devoted mother, Rachel Newman."

Sally felt the worry and love that Mama had put in that letter and wished she could ease some of the worry. She got some paper from the store, went back out to the tree and wrote a short letter to her. She didn't know when Mama would hear about the happenings at Gonzales but it'd probably be soon. Sally tried to make it sound much better and safer here than it probably was. And she ended the letter by telling Mama that Jesse would get her and Nancy to Mama's house the minute he could and for her not to worry.

Sally went back in the store and posted the letter. She hoped that someone would be taking the mail to San Felipe the next day or so. As she walked back to the house she held both Nancy and Mama's letter close, and wished all the worries were for nothing.

The next few days were very exciting. Volunteers were flooding into Gonzales, including many of the people they knew from San Felipe and the Egypt area.

James Fannin and some other men sent a message to Stephen Austin requesting that he come immediately. And in less than a week, Austin and his nephew Moses Bryan rode into Gonzales. Sally saw Mr. Austin from a distance; there was no way to get anywhere close. She thought he looked terrible and was afraid for him. Could he live through all that was expected of him? All of Texas, including her, seemed to expect a miracle from him.

He was elected commander-in-chief of the Army of the People. It couldn't have been anyone else. And even though he'd always preferred to settle things through peaceful means, he didn't seem to hesitate now. He made the decision to immediately march toward San Antonio to remove General Cos from Texas.

Sally stood and watched the men heading out of town. She heard an older man in the crowd say something about 'a ragtag army heading toward an unknown fate'. She didn't know about that, she was just proud and afraid.

She'd been able to have Jesse at home for a few hours before he left, which she was thankful for. Jesse had told her that he thought both Uncle Tommy and William were somewhere close but he hadn't seen them yet.

Sally was terribly disappointed that they didn't get to stop by. She would've especially liked to see William for awhile. And to make matters even worse, she'd now have the two of them to worry about along with Jesse.

The days were so long and it seemed like forever that they didn't hear any real news, and the rumors were much worse than having no news at all. Finally, one cold day, early in November, someone rapped on the door.

The wind was blowing and Sally hadn't heard a horse come up. She looked out through the peephole and saw that it was their neighbor, Mary's husband. She hurriedly opened the door, got him to come in, and at the same time she was shutting the door she was asking about Jesse.

"Well, now Ma'am. Other than being cold, hungry, and missing you and your youngun of course, he's just fine as he can be. He asked me to come and tell you so and not to worry."

Sally had a dozen questions and was beginning to ask them when he said, "Listen, I got my Mary and my younguns in the wagon and we're going to the store for a spell. There's a number of us just come back from the war and we're going to pass the latest on to the rest of the citizens. You might want to join us."

"Oh, my word! You mean you have Mary and the kids out there in the cold? You go on to the store with them and I'll get Nancy ready and join you there in a few minutes."

Then she touched his arm and said, "Are you sure he's alright?"

The reply was, "Yes Ma'am. He's surely alright."

Sally was so excited she could hardly wait to get to the store to hear all the news. She bundled Nancy and herself up and decided to walk the distance to the store instead of taking the time to saddle the horse. Besides there was no sense in having the mare stand out in the cold when she could stay in the lean-to.

She hadn't counted on the trail being icy in spots. She had to walk carefully and slower than she wanted to. Well, if they were already telling the news they'd just have to repeat it.

The store was crowded and in an uproar. Seemed like everyone was talking at once. Sally pushed her way in and then tried to move away from the cold at the door, but there were too many people.

Mary's husband had been watching for her though, and when he spotted her he said real loud. "Listen up here, make way for Jesse Robinson's Missus. Come on up here by the stove, Ma'am, so you can hear everything. You can be almighty proud of your man and the way he fought them Mexicans."

Sally was helped to a chair by the stove and as she sat there holding Nancy, she was as anxious to hear the stories as they all were. At first people were yelling questions and two or three of the men who'd been there were all trying to answer at once and it wasn't making any sense.

Then at a point that the den lessened a bit, it was old Mr. Mason who got things settled down. He very calmly said, "Can I please make a suggestion? How about we have these men tell us all about what happened and then maybe they won't mind if we ask questions, one at time. That way we can all hear."

There was a chorus of. "Yes, Sir. That's a good idea." Then after another minute or so it actually worked like that.

Mary's husband, feeling kind of important for a change, got it started. "Well, you all know that we marched out of here ready for whatever was required of us."

He and three other men told the story of the last few weeks. The Texas army, led by Stephen Austin, left from Gonzales on October 12 and made it to Salada Creek, five miles east of San Antonio, a week later. General Cos had the town and the old Alamo mission well fortified. He had around twelve cannons. Austin offered to negotiate a peaceful settlement, but Cos refused. They both received reinforcements, bringing the totals to around six hundred men with Cos and more than four hundred with Austin. Two six-pound cannons were also added to the Texan arms.

One of the men said, "We was joined by Jim Bowie and Deaf Smith, who both live in San Antonio. Then just as important, Juan Seguin and 134 other Mexican Texians joined our side. You know a lot of them don't want Mexico telling us what to do either. And Seguin knows that part of Texas like the back of his hand. Him and them other Mexicans were able to find food for us."

Another man joined in. "Austin chose Bowie and James Fannin to look for a better site closer to San Antonio. I was with Bowie. And so was Jesse, Ma'am."

As he said this he looked at Sally, then started to continue. "It was our bunch that got in the fight and . . ."

"Hey." interrupted Mary's husband. "You're getting ahead of the story."

Sally wanted to hear about Jesse, but she didn't say anything. Better to let them do it this way, at least only one was speaking at a time, usually.

"About that same time, big ole Sam Houston came riding in and you can believe he caused a stir. He's a mighty impressive man, both size and appearance. Makes you kind of feel sorry for Austin, him being so ill and not really taken for a military type. He was somewhat at a disadvantage."

That statement caused a minute of silence; then he continued. "Meeting after meeting were held and all we wanted to do was get it over with. Strange to say, Austin wanted to go in and whip them and Houston was preaching caution. But anyway, Bowie is the one that got into a fight." He looked at the other man, and said, kind of reluctantly, "I guess you ought to take it from there."

The other man was primed and waiting and told his story. "Austin was waiting with the main part of the army and Bowie was going to report back about the best site. Well, it took us all day to find a good place, so Bowie sent word back to Austin that we was going to hold that place. As I understand it, Austin was pretty put out with Bowie for disobeying his orders, but there weren't nothing he could do about it then.

"Anyways, the next morning, Austin was headed our way, but ole Cos was getting there faster. Close to one of them missions, this one was called Concepcion or something, we had about four hundred of Cos's men attacking our one hundred men under Bowie and Fannin. Bowie had us well dug in by a sunken riverbank and for us riflemen, it was a good defensive position.

"You wouldn't believe how dumb their leaders were. They had all those men coming at us across a flat, open prairie. Guess they never knowd about boys raised in Kentucky and Tennessee. It was nearly sad cause we just sat there and picked them off like a turkey shoot at home. They said later that we killed around fifty of them and we lost only one man."

Questions were immediately yelled. "Who was it? Who was our man?"

He said, "No need for any of you to worry. It wasn't any one I ever seen before and I know most of the men from all the surrounding settlements."

"Anyways." He repeated. "Let me get on with the fight. I'll tell you, Miz Robinson, that man of yours is a caution. Why, Ma'am, I don't think he'd be afraid of the devil hisself. You outta see him fight."

He went on to tell about other men from Gonzales that were heroes, including himself, and Sally was only hearing parts of it as her thoughts were crying inside, 'Where are you Jesse? Why aren't you here?'

Her attention returned to the conversation when Mary's husband had recaptured the attention of the crowd by declaring loudly that Bowie and Fannin's men would've been in a real pickle if Austin and the rest of them hadn't gotten there when they did.

Sally listened closely as he said, "When we arrived it was in time to see Cos's men running back to San Antonio, but they might've whipped you men later if we hadn't showed up."

There was some argument about that but they finished by saying that Austin wanted to follow the Mexicans and run them out of San Antonio, but his officers disagreed. They thought that the town was too well fortified and the Texians would lose too many men. Austin and some of the men were disappointed, but since most of the officers were against an assault of the town it didn't occur. So now the Texians were holding the town, but a lot of the army had left for home. Houston had left for San Felipe.

Sally had heard all she wanted to hear, got up, said thank you, and made her way outside. As she walked home, among all the things she'd just heard, only two thoughts kept running through her mind, 'Where are you Jesse? Why aren't you here?'

It was late in November, a bitterly cold day, when he came riding into the yard. Sally had heard nothing about him since the get together at the store. She was torn between anger and relief and hugged him then hit him on the arm and then hugged him again.

He just grinned at her and sat down heavily in a chair. He was always thin, but now he looked terribly thin and tired.

She fed him hot stew and cornbread until she thought he'd explode, then she made him take off his filthy clothes and climb into bed. He was asleep almost by the time his head was on the pillow.

It was a dark dismal day. She turned the lamp low and kept Nancy busy with things so as not to disturb him. Of course the way he was snoring, she didn't think a musical band would bother him.

As night came on, she fed Nancy and herself some stew, got Nancy to sleep, then puttered around some. She kept stopping by the bed to check on Jesse once in a while, just to assure herself that he was really home.

She walked over again, looked down at him and saw he was watching her. She said, "How long you been awake? You want something to eat?"

He said, "Hush, woman."

He lifted the covers and said, "All I want is for you to take your clothes off and come to bed."

CHAPTER 13

They were moving. Sally had a hard time telling her friends good-bye, especially Mary and her children and Mr. and Mrs. Mason. The Masons thought of themselves as grandparents to Nancy so were particularly sad to see them go.

The parting was difficult, but by the time their wagon was on the eastern edge of Gonzales, Sally was so excited that she felt like she couldn't get enough air. She'd gotten a few letters from home, and William had come by once, but it'd been months since she'd seen the rest of the family. She thought the miles from Gonzales to Mama and home was an eternity long.

Jesse was feeling good about the move too. Even though he was being very careful and watchful he was also playful with Nancy and extra attentive and helpful to Sally.

They were barely out of sight of town before he was letting his hands sneak in a few pats here and there. That was more than all right with Sally but made the day even longer. It seemed like it would take forever to get Nancy to sleep. But they both decided it was worth the wait. The three nights on the trip were downright fiery. Sally could almost wish they could just go on like this forever.

But then they were at Mama's house and her urges turned in a different direction. After the greetings and a short visit with the family, Sally wanted to get a cabin built on her land; now, today. Everyone else thought that was a bad idea, that she should just live with Mama through the winter at least.

Sally just couldn't wait that long. She was standing in Mama's kitchen the third morning there and said. "I have something to say. I know how you all feel and I wish I could just do what makes you happy, but I can't. I have an overpowering need for a house of my own on my own land. And if I have to build it myself that's what I'll do. And that's what I'm going to start on this morning."

She waited for Jesse and Mama to protest but neither one did. But she could tell that Mama was worried and disappointed and that Jesse was angry. He stomped past her going outside, and didn't say but a few words to her all that day. But he did help load the wagon and then helped get the area cleared for the cabin.

And with lots of help from Thomas and Ali, and occasional help from Jesse and William, Sally got a small cabin built. It was only a few miles from Mama's house, so she could go visit often and feel fairly safe being this close.

Jesse seemed pretty content with the place and helped build a small barn, corral, and some other outbuildings. But he was also spending more and more time with the local militia. Sally didn't mind that too much. She was so busy and happy; she couldn't have been prouder of a big house and a whole league of land.

The cabin was nice and cozy by Christmas, but they spent that time at Mama's house. It was the favorite time of year for the family and with a war that always seemed to be just a few days away, all their time together was more precious.

The first of the year had come and gone and Sally began to notice restless signs in Jesse. He worked very hard around their place and spent all the day of January tenth, Nancy's second birthday, with Nancy and Sally. She tried to ignore the restlessness and to pay extra attention to him, but it did no good.

Right after Nancy's birthday, he said, "You know, I think I'll ride over to Gonzales and see what's happening."

Sally nearly exploded, "You're just going to take a small ride over to Gonzales are you?"

It was at that point that they had their first bad argument and went to bed without making up. When Jesse left the next morning, it was with a cool hug and a short kiss.

All day Sally wished she'd not been so mean, but she couldn't take it back now. Besides, she was still mad about him leaving. Two days later he came riding up and she just looked at him a minute before she ran and held on to him.

He grinned at her and said, "Well, I decided I maybe ought to help these fellows around here and let Gonzales take care of itself. So as of today, January 14, 1836, I'm on the muster roll, along with your brother, William. Your brothers-in-law, David and Preston, and Preston's brother, Jasper, are on the same roll. We're all members of Captain William Walker's Company."

Sally let him know how happy that made her.

A few days later when they were working on the corral, they heard horses coming and always careful, both picked up their rifles. It was Thomas and Ali.

Mama wanted to let them know that Uncle Thomas, Aunt Serena and their children were visiting and would like to see 'the children'. Sally was excited about seeing Uncle Tommy and his family; she hadn't seen them in over a year. She got Nancy ready and they were on their way.

Uncle Tommy was out in the yard when they arrived and helped her down from her horse. He gave her a squeeze, kissed Nancy, then whispered to Sally, "Damn, Tag-tail, you've turned into one fine-looking woman."

Sally blushed but said, "I'm so glad to see you. You look wonderful."

Tommy and Jesse kind of arm-wrestled a minute to cover up how glad they were to see each other and by then everyone had spilled out of the house. Aunt Serena, still small and pretty, came to greet Sally and they exchanged compliments about each other's children. Tommy and Serena had a boy and two girls. It was a little cool, but the day had turned out rather nice so the children could play outside. It was a good thing, because there were lots of little ones around.

The adults gathered in the kitchen with coffee as they usually did. And as it usually did, the talk turned to the gathering troubles. Jesse told them some about what had happened in Gonzales and San

Antonio and then Uncle Tommy told what he knew about the latest governmental activities.

"Early last month, Stephen was back in San Felipe and appeared before the Council. He strongly urged that they call a convention as soon as possible. With little urging they agreed to call for one in January. They also elected Stephen, along with two other men, to go to the United States to seek financial aid and any other help they can get for Texas. The three men left the day after Christmas.

"The Council elected Sam Houston, unanimously, to command our nonexistent regular army. Stephen has never claimed to be a military type, so I don't think he was displeased by the appointment of Houston. He seems to respect him.

"But he seemed deeply concerned by the actions of many of the delegates and feared they'd make poor decisions. I'm afraid he's right, because they've decided not to have the convention meet this month, but to wait until March."

Uncle Tommy stopped talking and was just sitting there in deep thought. No one else said anything for awhile, and then they started talking about other things. Sally wanted to know all about Uncle Andrew, Uncle John, and their families. They had a good visit and soon it was time for Uncle Tommy and Aunt Serena to leave.

After they'd said their farewells, Uncle Tommy was still standing with Mama, as if he didn't quite want to leave. Finally he said, "Rachel, I know I'll be away much of the time, even more than I have been, and so will all the other men." He looked around at all the family, then back to Mama. "I want to be sure you're aware of how bad things might get."

Mama said, "I know, Tommy. We'll take good care. And please take good care of yourself."

They all promised to get together again soon and Sally knew they all hoped it would be possible. She saw tears in Mama's eyes as she watched her brother and his family ride away. Sally thought, 'I guess you always miss your family and worry about them.'

The talk about a coming war was getting so strong it seemed to take on a life of its own. Jesse was hardly home, and when he did come home it was only for short visits. Sally not only got lonesome but doing all the work by herself was hard. One evening when he came home, she was really out of sorts. Jesse took one look at her and paid more attention to Nancy that evening.

The next morning after he left she decided her out of sorts state was due to being pregnant again. She'd been thinking that might be the case for the last week or so. She thought about the danger Jesse was going to be facing soon, and made the decision not to tell him about the new baby. She knew he'd be delighted; he wanted a dozen kids. But why give him something else to worry about when he was gone.

She also decided to be sweet to him. She laughed to herself and hoped she could actually learn to be a sweet person. Well, that wasn't totally fair to her; she was always sweet to children and old people. She stopped and thought about that for a minute. Maybe for now she could just pretend Jesse was a child or an old person and she could be sweet to him.

She laughed out loud at that thought and Nancy, who was a cheerful, energetic, two-year-old began laughing and clapping her hands. Sally danced around with her and felt better than she had in a few weeks. When Jesse came home the next evening, he was so surprised at the sweetness and attention he got that he kept looking at Sally to see if something was wrong with her. They had a wonderful evening and night. But underneath it all they both knew it was going to be short-lived.

Jesse was spending a lot of time in San Felipe with Houston's group of men. He came riding in one afternoon with the message that Sally had been dreading to hear. A large Mexican force under Santa Anna had invaded Texas and they were marching toward Bexar.

Jesse told her, "Your Uncle Tommy has been recruiting for the army. He's been made a captain in the First Regiment of the Texas Volunteer Army. He'll have Company F. I'm hoping both William and me can get in his company. Either way, I think we'll be heading toward Gonzales just as soon as the army can be ready to move."

For once Sally saw something more than just the excitement about a coming fight in his face. She said, "Jesse, how big a force does this Santa Anna have with him?"

He looked at her a long moment then said, "We've heard it could be as many as three or four thousand men."

"Oh my God." And she sat down heavily on the edge of the bed.

He sat down beside her and held her close. They sat that way for a long time and then he kissed her on the head and gently said, "I have to leave in the morning, and I have a lot of things I need to get done for you and to get myself ready."

She helped him and tried not to be sad and act like such a crybaby. But she was scared.

The parting the next morning was the hardest they'd ever gone through. Sally spent the early part of the morning just moping around feeling sorry for herself. Then she decided it would make her feel better if she actually got something accomplished, so she started moving some of the posts they'd cut over beside the corral. That way when some of the brothers came over to help her it wouldn't take so long; the corral was temporarily usable, but she wanted it finished.

She worked on it the rest of the day and started on it again the next day. By afternoon she was terribly tired and suddenly felt very weak. She got Nancy and her into the house, gave the little girl a biscuit and a cup of milk, and went and sat in the chair. She felt a terrible pain and gritted her teeth. She knew what was happening and knew it was her fault. She'd worked too hard all day.

She was really scared, but she knew she couldn't make it to Mama's so she had to get through it by herself. It was a terrible evening. Nancy cried and was scared and all Sally could do was talk to her and try to calm her down. Sally lost the baby, but finally the worst was over and she got herself to bed.

Early the next morning she heard Nancy calling her. When she roused herself and saw what she'd done she cried. Nancy had spilled milk and made a mess, but somehow she'd been able to set the table with their two plates, with a biscuit in each, and a glass of milk for the two of them. The little girl came over to the bed, caught Sally's hand, and said, "Come on, Mama, I'm hungry."

Sally gave her a tight hug and finally made it to the table. She spent most of the day in bed with Nancy trying to wait on her. And then with Nancy by her side she slept through the night.

She felt stronger the next morning, but thought she should go spend a few days with Mama. She got the saddle on her horse but was so tired she had to rest awhile. Finally she had the cabin door bolted and was ready to go. She put Nancy on the horse to ride in front of her and she stood on the porch to make it easier to get on the horse. Then after she had mounted she had to sit there a minute until she wasn't so weak.

As she rode slowly away she thought about the mess the cabin was in and hoped no one would see it like that. She thought that was a strange foolish thing to think of at a time like this. All she really wanted right now was to get Nancy safely to Mama.

Nancy busily chattered all the way, saying, "We're going to Grammas. We're gong to Grammas."

The short trip seemed long and Sally was miserable by the time she rode into the yard. She just sat on the horse with Nancy saying, "Get down, Mama, get down."

Thomas saw them and came running and yelled. "Mama. Come quick.

Something's wrong with Sally."

Mama, Louisa, and Elizabeth came out of the house and by then Joseph was there too. Louisa reached up and got Nancy and Mama told Thomas and Joseph to get Sally in the house. Sally knew she and Nancy were safe now and she just let go.

The next thing she felt was a small weight on the bed and little arms around her neck. The child smelled like blackberry jelly and Sally thought about her Grandma Rabb, then about how hungry she was.

She put her arms around Nancy, opened her eyes, and saw Mama sitting in a chair beside the bed, and all her sisters standing around it. They all looked anxious and concerned and then Mama lit into her.

"I told you it wasn't safe for you to be by yourself, and see you could've died from this. And then what would've happened to Nancy?" She went on for a bit more and the sisters were nodding and agreeing.

Finally, Sally raised up on her elbow and said, "Mama, don't scold me, and can I please have some blackberry jelly?"

Louisa laughed and went and got a plate she had ready. Two of the others helped Sally sit up in the bed, and as Louisa handed her the plate full of biscuits and blackberry jelly, she said, "I told Mama the best way to get you up was to let you smell the blackberries."

Louisa reached and touched Sally's face and Elizabeth sat down on the end of the bed and showed Sally the cup of coffee she had for her. Mama was patting her on the shoulder while trying to hide the tears in her eyes. Mary was straightening the cover while Minerva was trying to fluff the pillow. Sally knew they must all be here because of her. It made her feel good.

Then over by the table one of the boys asked, "Mama, is Sally going to be alright?"

And Sally answered him. "Yes. How could I not be alright when I'm here with all of you."

She finished one biscuit, drank some coffee, and then felt better than she had in days. Only one thing could have made it better. Jesse.

"Mama." She asked. "Does anyone know if the army has left San Felipe yet?"

Thomas answered instead. "They hadn't last I heard. You want me to go get Jesse?"

"No! I don't want him to know about this. I don't want him to leave worrying about me. I'll tell him about it when he gets back."

Mama said, "I thought that's the way you'd feel. But if I'd thought you wouldn't make it, I would've sent Thomas to get him."

Sally just nodded.

Everyone got busy doing various things and Sally was made to stay in bed. By mid-day she was so restless Mama let her get up and sit at the table and help by peeling some potatoes. They were all so relieved that she was going to be all right that they were laughing and talking and carrying on. But then Minerva walked over to the door and looked out and everyone got quiet. Sally thought, 'We're all thinking about the men we love and worried about our children and even ourselves.'

Sally stayed another few days then over many objections by Mama and her sisters she said she was going home. Mama was really upset about it and insisted that she take Thomas with her.

Sally said, "No. You need Thomas and Ali here with you. But how about I take Joseph and Andy with me if they want to go?"

As she asked she looked questioningly at the two younger boys and they were both nodding yes very vigorously.

Mama agreed easily, since she could see the boys wanted to go and she knew Sally would go one way or the other.

Nancy was delighted to have the two boys there and Sally loved it too. Joseph was nine, but large for his age so seemed older, and Andy was six. Sally didn't feel quite up to working on the corral yet, but there was always work to do.

She and Joseph worked on a number of things, while Andy kept Nancy busy. Then by the end of the week Sally couldn't stand not knowing what was happening with the army. So early the next morning she said. "Hey. You boys have done a great job this week. Joseph, what do you think about taking a break and let's go get a big turkey to take to Mama's tomorrow?"

Joseph couldn't hide his happiness about going hunting with her. They left Andy in charge of Nancy and without going too far from the house, they spent the entire morning hunting. Sally was pleased with how well Joseph handled his gun and found out very soon that he was good with it too. When she told him so all he could do was duck his head and grin.

"Well, I guess we'd better get serious and get us a turkey now." She told him.

They walked around quietly until they heard some turkeys, then stopped and waited for them to come into the clearing in front of them. It didn't take long and Sally gave the signal for Joseph to shoot.

He didn't hesitate; he shot one of the bigger hens. Sally gave him a nod of approval and he kind of strutted as he carried the heavy bird back to the house.

They visited with Mama and the family for a few days. The only real news that was known was that Santa Anna had taken over the town of Bexar and a small army of Texians were holed up in an old Mission. And Sam Houston had left San Felipe with the main army heading toward Gonzales.

They were all so worried about the men that it was a miserable time. Mama didn't want her to leave, but Sally wanted to be at home, working. Joseph wanted to go back with her and Mama agreed. Andy thought he'd stay home with Mama if that was alright with Sally.

And that's the way it went. Sally and Joseph worked well together and got a lot done. Then one windy day in March, when they were in the house getting something to eat, they heard a horse. Sally and Joseph both grabbed their guns and went to the door.

It was Thomas. Sally would've gotten after him severely about how he'd ridden his horse, but one look at his face and she knew something was wrong.

"The Mexicans are coming! Our Texians were slaughtered at a place in Bexar called the Alamo! Gonzales was burned! Sam Houston and the whole Texian army are retreating this way! The Mexicans are killing everyone in sight! We got to get out of here fast!"

Thomas was so excited the words were tumbling over each other.

Nancy started to cry and for a moment Sally could only think, 'Was Jesse at this place called the Alamo?'

She quickly got herself under control. "Is Mama all right?"

Thomas said, "Yes! She's getting as much together in the wagon as she can, and will wait on all of the family before she leaves. Ali and I started out, and stopped at Mary's house on the way. Preston is home right now, so he'll help Mary and their kids.

"I told Ali to stay and help Miranda, cause David isn't home. Andy can help Mama some, but we need to get back there soon as we can. Mama wants us all to be together. She said she wouldn't leave until she knows all her children are alright, except for William of course. When we leave she plans on going by to get Aunt Serena and her children."

Sally was already working before he'd finished talking. As soon as he did, she said, "Get you a drink, then hitch the wagon. Throw some hay in and get that bag of feed just inside the lean-to.

"Joseph, saddle your horse and mine and when the wagon is loaded tie my horse and the spotted milch cow to the back. One of you turn the rest of the cows out and that old mare too. They'll just have to make it on their own."

She had a pile of things ready to take to the wagon. As she was getting things from the kitchen area she thought of something else. She went to the door and yelled to Thomas. "Get that barrel of water and Joseph and I'll help you get it in the wagon. And keep your eyes open out there."

She thought to herself, 'What better time for the Indians to take advantage of the situation we're in.' With that thought she looked around and knew that probably nothing much would be left when they returned. As she loaded the last of the things from the house she prayed for all those men she loved.

She put a quilt and pillow on the wagon seat beside her, put Nancy in the middle of it and tied her in with a long cup-towel. With Thomas riding on one side of the wagon and Joseph on the other, Sally moved out at as fast a pace as she thought wise. She looked back once, thought of Jesse, then turned and faced what was to come.

When they got to Mama's house, everyone was there except Ali. Mama had sent him to see Aunt Serena to let her know they'd be coming by to get her.

Ali came back sooner than expected and had great news. He'd met Uncle Tommy on his way home. He told Ali he'd get Serena and the kids ready to go and would meet them sometime the next day at the place they usually camped just south of San Felipe.

Ali told them. "Uncle Tommy grabbed my arm hard and told me, 'You tell Rachel to get the family out of there and do it fast! Tell her to not worry about anything except something to eat for awhile. Tell her to hurry! It's gonna be bad for anyone caught by the Mexicans.'"

It was a terrible trip, they moved along all night. Everyone was afraid and tired, but they made it to the camping spot below San Felipe. By late afternoon that day Uncle Tommy and his family joined them.

The only thing Uncle Tommy knew about William, Jesse, and the other family members from this area was that they were with Sam Houston's army. Uncle Tommy said, "I stayed as long as I could but we just kept retreating. I told Houston that if he let the Mexicans cross the Colorado, I was going to go get my families out of harm's way. And the Mexican's are still coming."

Sally could see how worried Uncle Tommy was about Aunt Serena. She was pregnant again and didn't look too strong this time. This trip wasn't going to be good for her. Sally thought about the baby she'd lost and knew how hard that had been on her.

Mama and Uncle Tommy were also worried about Uncle Andrew, Uncle John and their families. None of them were as young as they once were.

More and more people had gathered in the camping area and a number of them came over to ask Uncle Tommy what was happening. He told them about being at Gonzales with Houston. He said most of the men, including himself, wanted to go to Bexar to fight, but that Houston didn't think that was the wise thing to do.

Tommy said that a Mexican Texian had arrived in Gonzales on March 11, to tell Houston that the Alamo fell to Santa Anna on March 6. "They slaughtered all those Texians, maybe two hundred men, while we sat at Gonzales."

Then he took off his hat and rubbed his forehead for a minute. The family and all the others just stood there in silence. When he continued he said, "I understand that Travis, Bowie, Davie Crockett and his men, and …"

He stopped again, then finally said. "All dead. They're all dead."

The women and children were crying and the men were trying not to. It was the first time he'd told any of this to the family too, so they were just as upset as the rest of the people.

Uncle Tommy got himself under control and said, "Everyone needs to get some rest. We have to get moving real soon."

A man came up to him and said he was from San Felipe, that he'd just ridden out to see if anyone knew what was going on for sure. He asked Uncle Tommy if he'd ride back to town with him so he could tell the people still there what was happening.

Uncle Tommy told Aunt Serena and Mama. "I'd like to see if anyone in San Felipe has heard anything about Andrew or John or anyone from the La Grange area. So I'll go with this man and then I'll be back soon. Rest as much as you can but stay ready to go."

There were now lots of other people around so Mama allowed Thomas and Ali to go with Uncle Tommy. Mary's husband, Preston, also went with the men.

The women fixed some food and tried to rest a little. They were all worried about Aunt Serena. Mama made her lie down and Louisa was taking care of her children. Sally walked outside their wagons and was looking around at all the other people. She decided that an awful lot of the other women hadn't taken time to pack much of anything. They must've just grabbed their children and a few things and ran. It'd be a miracle if half of them didn't die on the road. She hoped it didn't come down to a choice between feeding themselves or feeding all these other people.

As she was looking around she noticed two scruffy looking men nosing around the wagon next to hers. One of them saw her looking at them and nudged the other one. As they started toward her, she quietly called to Joseph, "Bring your gun and come over here by me."

He picked it up, walked over beside her, and cocked the gun. Sally had no time to look at him to see if he was alright but she knew he'd do what she told him to do.

The two men stopped a short distance from her and the tall one laughed and told the other, "Lookee here, Ben. We got us a pretty little gal with a big ole rifle. I wonder if she's a gonna take a shot at us?"

Before the other man could answer, Sally said, "Joseph, you aim at the top button on the short ugly one. You remember the signal we use to hunt turkeys?"

Joseph answered, "Yes Ma'am." And from the corner of her eye she could see that he'd aimed his gun where she'd told him too.

"Well, when I give you that signal, you shoot yours and I'm going to shoot the right eye out of that tall red-headed bastard with the big mouth."

"Hey, Red, I don't think she's bluffing. Maybe we outta find somewheres else to get what we need."

"Shut it up, Ben. I ain't never let no woman get the better of me and this one sure as hell ain't gonna. I don't like her mouth one little bit."

To Sally he said, "We got guns too, so what makes you think you can get the better of us?"

Sally said, "My brother and I are willing to die to keep you away from our family. And we'll be able to kill at least one of you, and probably both before you can kill us.

"And besides, by now my mama and a sister or two also have guns trained on you. And they can all hit what they aim at. Are you willing to die today, or do you want to walk away while you can?"

There was a little grumbling and bravado but the one called Ben didn't want any part of it and the big one knew it. He looked at Sally and said, "Don't sleep too hard, little missy, cause I'm gonna make you pay for insultin me. And you ain't gonna like what I do to you afore I kill you."

Sally didn't say anything and didn't move an inch. The men turned around and tried to swagger off. Sally watched them out of sight then looked at Joseph.

He was looking at her and actually had a grin on his face. "You would've shot him in the eye, wouldn't you." he stated.

"Yes. And you'd have shot the short one in the button, wouldn't you?"

He said, "Yes, ma'am. I was going to do just that."

Sally gave him a squeeze on the shoulder, then as she turned and went to where the others were waiting for them she thought, 'I hope it doesn't turn out that we should've done just that.'

Uncle Tommy and the others came back shortly and said they needed to get started again. He said the town of San Felipe was in a panic also, with everyone trying to get away. No one in town had heard anything about Uncle Andrew or Uncle John or anyone from the La Grange area. Uncle Tommy said it'd take them a while to get this far, so they'd put word out with everyone they met to let the Rabb brothers know where they were. They'd get with them sooner or later.

Aunt Serena told Uncle Tommy about the two men that had threatened them and he came over and gave Sally a hug. She saw him also give Joseph a pat on the back. Then a little later, during the early part of the night, he got Thomas to drive his wagon. As Sally watched him quietly ride away, she wished she could go with him.

He joined them about five hours later, as quietly as he'd left. Sally thought that a lot of the group wouldn't even know he'd been gone.

By the middle of the next morning they knew they had to rest the animals and themselves. Everyone was exhausted. They fed the livestock, but didn't unhitch the wagons. They just had no way of knowing how close the Mexican army was.

Sally didn't hear many sounds so she knew everyone was sleeping, even the babies and young children. She slept about an hour while holding Nancy next to her. She thought she'd just shut her eyes, when someone touched her shoulder and said her name. It was Uncle Tommy.

"Sally, we need to get on the road again."

She raised up to one elbow, and saw that Mama and some of the others were already up and getting ready to go.

Uncle Tommy gave her a hand up and said, "Don't worry about those two men. They've been taken care of."

"I know. Thanks, Uncle Tommy."

"I didn't have a chance to do anything." He said. "When I found them they'd bothered their last person. They tried something with another woman and her man shot them both." He kissed her on the forehead, went to his wagon, and they started east again.

It was like some horrible nightmare, each day worse than the last. Their family had four wagons and enough to eat if they could supplement it with some meat once in a while. But many families along the way had almost nothing. Within a few days their wagons were full of women and children that needed help.

Sally drove her wagon most of the time, always keeping Nancy beside her. Uncle Tommy wouldn't let them panic even when some fool would come through yelling some rumor or other. He told them constantly that they must take care of the animals and they must be alert at all times. They took turns on watch even during the day. Some of the people on the run were so afraid that they didn't have good sense. They were almost as dangerous as the Mexicans.

One evening Uncle Tommy decided to stop a little early to rest the animals. The women had some food about ready to eat when a man came riding through. He was looking for his family so was checking with each group of people as he passed by.

He stopped when he saw Uncle Tommy. "Howdy, Capt. Rabb. I heard tell you left to get your family to safety. Wish to hell I'd done that. I got me a bad broke leg and since I couldn't do much to help fight the Mexicans, I decided to come find my wife and children. Have any of you seen them?"

Uncle Tommy told him that he hadn't seen his family. Then he said. "Asa, you look bad. And you look like you could use a bite to eat and some rest. Why don't you stop a while and join us?"

The man hesitated a few minutes, but he was just about exhausted, so he accepted the invite. He allowed Uncle Tommy and Preston to help him off his horse.

While some of the women got him a plate of food, Mama took one look at his leg and told him it needed cleaned and redressed. She took care of that and tried to make him comfortable.

Uncle Tommy barely allowed him to eat a few bites before he was questioning him. "Asa, what do you know about what's happening behind us?"

"Well, first of all, I seen your brothers and their families two or three days back. They was all doing well." He had to stop because Mama and Uncle Tommy were both asking him questions. They laughed and gave each other a hug.

"They was both worried about you and their sister and your families. They asked me to keep an eye out for you. And your brother, Andrew, asked me to tell you not to wait on them, but to keep going and you could find each other when you had the families safe in the United States. But if I were you I'd just slow down a bit until they catch up to you in a few days. It's too hard on a person worrying all the time about your family. I know."

Sally saw Mama wipe her eyes with her apron. Ali picked up a stool and brought it over to Mama; she looked at him and smiled her thanks. Sally thought, 'Mama needs to sit down. She's been worried to death about William and Uncle Andrew and Uncle John. At least this much is a big relief for her.'

It hadn't taken long for word to get around that there was a man at the Rabb wagons that had some recent news. The group around the fire became large. Sally was surprised to see the Masons walking towards the gathering.

She stood up and called to them and they immediately came over to where she was standing. They were glad to see her and especially Nancy. They hadn't remembered that Sally was related to Capt. Rabb so hadn't known she was so close to where they had their wagon.

Sally was glad to see them and told them she wanted them to join their wagons the next day. They were pleased with that idea. Then

Sally realized that she'd interrupted Asa and apologized. He also knew the Masons and asked if they'd seen his family.

The answer was a sad "No, I'm sorry we haven't."

Then the Masons asked him about some of the other people they all knew. The answers were mostly that no one knew where their neighbors and friends were. Mrs. Mason started crying and told how hard it was when they had to burn their homes, as Houston had ordered so that the Mexicans wouldn't have the use of anything that might help them. And what sadness they felt when they looked back and saw all of Gonzales burning.

Sally asked, "Do you know where Mary, our neighbor in Gonzales, and her three children are?"

"No, we lost track of Mary and the children. We can only hope they're safe." Mr. Mason said.

"We think her husband is with her and not dead like all those other Gonzales men." Mrs. Mason added, and she started crying again.

Sally looked at Mr. Mason and asked, "What other Gonzales men?"

She and all the others were overwhelmed with hurt when Mr. Mason told them about the 32 men from Gonzales who'd passed through lines of Mexicans and made their way into the Alamo to help defend Texas. They'd all died with the rest.

Sally shed bitter tears as she heard Mr. Mason tell them the names of as many of the men as he could remember.

Albert Martin, who was a storeowner at Gonzales, was the Captain of the group. He'd been a part of the confrontation over the cannon and had participated in the other battles that Sally remembered hearing about. Isaac Baker, Moses Baker's son. George Cottle, James Curtis's son-in-law. She remembered that Curtis was another of Stephen Austin's colonists.

Claiborne Wright and George Tumlinson. Sally was thankful when Mr. Mason either couldn't remember any more names or just stopped out of pure sadness. She didn't want to hear anymore.

In a voice choked with emotion Uncle Tommy asked. "What about the rest of the army, Asa? Did Fannin and his men fall back and catch up with Houston?"

Asa just sat and looked at Uncle Tommy with a strange look on his face.

"Well, damn it, speak up, man."

In a sorrow filled voice Asa spoke directly to Uncle Tommy. "I didn't realize you hadn't heard. James Fannin and more than four hundred men were killed at Goliad. They surrendered. And were still murdered by the Mexicans."

A man sucked in a shuddering breath and a woman openly sobbed. Than another woman screamed, "We're going to all die right where we stand. We got to get out of here." She went running off and it took Uncle Tommy and the other men to get everyone else calmed down.

The crowd of people sat around for hours and talked. Sally stayed up for a while, then carried a sleeping Nancy up into the wagon and lay down with the child in her arms. She spent a long almost sleepless night thinking of all the men she'd known that were now dead, and their families homeless, or worse.

And as so many times in the past, she fell asleep with the thought going over and over in her mind. "Where are you, Jesse? Oh, Jesse. Where are you?"

The next day Uncle Tommy got their wagons started slowly forward while Preston, Thomas, Ali, and Joseph left to drift back along the wagons of people to see if they could find Uncle Andrew and Uncle John. Mama was worried about them going, but wanted to see her brothers.

It took a week but the day finally came when the Rabb families from La Grange and the Newman and Rabb families from Egypt, joined forces. When Uncle Andrew and Aunt Margaret and their five children, and Uncle John and Aunt Mary and their six joined the family and the others traveling with them, it made a very sizable group. It was almost like Christmas time. Everyone was so happy to see each other and they fell easily into the routine of being together.

But it was a strange mixture of emotions. The circumstances were terrible but made so much worse because Aunt Serena was getting weaker each day. And Aunt Mary and Uncle John's little boy, Lorenza, was sick. Everyone was worried and tired.

The days seemed endless and just repeated themselves. But finally came the day. "We've won! We've won! Texas is in-de-pen-dent!" Yelled a man as he came riding past the Rabb and Newman family wagons.

"We whupped the Mexicans and captured Santa Anna himself, at a place called San Jacinto!

"The wars over and us Texians is free. Texas is finally free!"

CHAPTER 14

Uncle Tommy hailed the man riding through broadcasting the news and he stopped. He got down and accepted some food and a drink. He was more than willing to share what he knew with the people gathered around the wagons, but it turned out he didn't know much more than what he'd been shouting. And now he was mostly just interested in finding his wife and children in the mass of people.

At least it was now known that on April 21, 1836, Sam Houston and his army had beaten Santa Anna at a place called San Jacinto. Houston had been wounded but no one was sure how badly. They were all happy with the news, but frustrated with not knowing more.

After resting a day, the families headed back toward home, or whatever was going to be left. Mama was worried more about William than she was the house and place. And Sally felt the same way about Jesse. They could always build a new house.

The trip back was slower than they wanted it to be but they took their time to make it easier on Aunt Serena and Lorenza. They were both sick and weak. Then in spite of everything anyone could do, Lorenza died. He was not even one year old.

Sally had been around more deaths than she wanted to remember, but she'd never been around when someone's child died. It was the worst thing she could imagine.

The pain of Aunt Mary and Uncle John and their other children was horrible. And then it was even worse when Aunt Mary realized they'd have to bury her little boy in the piney woods of that part of Texas and leave him by himself.

They stayed at that spot for three days until Uncle John said. "Come, Mary. God wants us to go home and take care of our family. He's already watching out for our Lorenza."

Finally, they arrived at Uncle Tommy's house. The house had been partially burned and lots of things were missing, but it wasn't as bad as it could've been. Uncle Andrew and Uncle John and their families were going to stay a few days to help Uncle Thomas get his house back in shape.

The brothers offered to come help Mama too, but she said no. She had all her children to help her and she knew everyone wanted to get to their homes as soon as possible. They all stayed together for the rest of that evening and that night. It was a strange visit, full of joy that they'd come through this alive, but terrible sorrow for Uncle John and Aunt Mary, and fear for the ones still unaccounted for.

Mama had decided to stay one more day with her brothers and their families. She told the older children that she and the younger ones would leave for home the following day. Mama wanted Sally to take Thomas with her until she found out what had happened at her place and Sally had agreed.

When morning came and it was time for part of the family to say goodbye, it was hard to do. Sally gave Uncle John a hug and just said, "I love you." And then did the same with Aunt Mary. She didn't know what else to say. When she got to Aunt Serena she gave her an extra hug and told her to take good care of herself. And then they rode away from Uncle Tommy's house.

Everyone was exhausted, including Sally, and she was trying not to think about her home or Jesse! Now that she was so close she had to fight to keep the panic from sweeping over her. Where was he, why wasn't he here? And is William all right?

Sally thought about driving her wagon by way of Mama's house, to see if William was home, but she didn't. She drove the straightest route she knew toward her own house. And it was very difficult not to drive the horses too fast.

When they were just a little way from the house, she saw Jesse riding toward them. She knew he must have heard the wagon. He didn't even get off the horse, but leaned down, grabbed Sally and pulled her up in front of him.

In a broken voice he asked, "Thomas, will you drive the wagon?"

Thomas said, "Sure, Jesse." And before he even had time to get off and tie his horse to the back of the wagon, Jesse had reached and picked up Nancy, put her in Sally's lap, and was walking the horse back home.

Sally was uncomfortable sitting where she was, but Jesse was holding her and Nancy so close that she couldn't move. She wanted to ask him a dozen questions but she was crying and realized by the shaking of his body, that he was crying too.

Sally held her daughter, leaned hard against this man and felt great relief and joy to be where she was. The questions could wait.

Jesse and William had come together and William was waiting at Mama's house. They'd been home a number of days, but Jesse said it'd seemed like weeks. He'd wanted to go look for them, but William had convinced him they wouldn't know where to look. The most important thing when they got home was the stock and anything that was salvageable so they'd helped each other round up what stock could be found, and had worked on the pens. The houses hadn't been burned, but were in bad condition. It was going to take a lot of work to get things back as they were.

After they got to their house, Thomas left almost immediately to go see William and tell him where they all were. Sally told Thomas to give William a hug for her and tell him to come see her when he could.

There were not many minutes throughout the rest of that day that there was more than a foot or two between Sally, Jesse, and Nancy. They talked long into the evening, sharing all they had gone through. Then when their little daughter fell asleep, the distance between Sally and Jesse disappeared for awhile. The next few days were filled with hard work and sweet togetherness.

But then they received very bad news; Aunt Serena and her newborn baby had died. They went immediately and joined the family.

At first Uncle Tommy was like a crazy man and none of them could help him. Then after the funeral he was just totally withdrawn from everyone. Some of Aunt Serena's family was staying awhile to take care of the three children, until Uncle Tommy could get himself together. Sally wished there was something she could do to help, but she didn't know how. So she just told him she loved him and left. It seemed so inadequate.

Finally, Sally, Jesse, and Nancy were back at their own home. The structures weren't in bad shape; at least they hadn't been burned. But almost everything that could be carried off had been. At times Sally wanted to cry, but lately she'd just shed too many tears.

And losing some belongings didn't seem very important when she thought about Uncle Tommy and those poor little motherless children, and Aunt Mary and Uncle John and their family. That was what could make her cry, so she shoved all those thoughts aside and got to work. Hard work had always been what got her through the problems of life.

The time went by in a pleasant way for Sally. Jesse was tired and was glad to stay at home with his two girls. There was so much work to do to get their place back in shape and Sally would hurry her chores inside the house to get outside to help Jesse.

She made a new carrier for Nancy and often as not, the little girl was on her Daddy's back as he worked. Sally was glad the two of them were so close and hoped that life could stay this way now.

They visited with Mama and the family about every month and would catch up on the rest of the families. Every so often two or three men would stop by to tell Jesse what was happening, and during the summer they loaded their wagon and went to San Felipe for a few days.

It wasn't long after that trip that Sally began to feel sick at her stomach. She immediately suspected that she was pregnant again and she wanted this baby so much that she told Jesse right away. He was delighted and told her to take it easy and he'd do all the heavy work.

Jesse was so good to her and took great care of Nancy too. He didn't seem to have a great desire to go off traveling, was only gone for short periods, and Sally thought that at last she could live the life she wanted. Together as a family, on their own land.

On September 5th, the Texans elected their first President. It was Sam Houston. When the family heard the results of the voting, they were all shocked. Mama especially had hoped that Stephen Austin would be the first president; she said she couldn't imagine anyone but him being in that position.

But she knew that even a number of the early colonists hadn't voted for him and the new settlers felt no loyalty to him. It was a sad situation and knowing how sick Austin was made it even sadder.

Christmas came and went and it seemed like the whole Texas countryside was at peace and trying to rebuild their homes and build this new country of Texas. It was an exciting time.

Then in late December, a neighbor came by and told them the shocking news that Stephen Austin had died! They knew he'd been sickly for quite some time but never thought he'd die so young. He was only forty-three years old. Sally knew Mama would be upset with this news as would many of the early settlers. She quickly got ready and they went to Mama's house. Sally had known Stephen Austin for most of her life, and couldn't think of Texas without also thinking of him.

William came to Mama's house that evening and said that Stephen's body was going to be taken by steamboat from Columbia Landing down the Brazos River to Peach Point. But he'd heard that the steamboat wasn't there yet so there'd be time to go to Columbia to pay their respects if Mama wanted to go.

She wanted to do that, and the rest of the family did too. So the next morning the women and children loaded into two wagons and the men rode their horses to make the trip to the landing. They planned to camp out that night and be there to see General Austin off for his final trip.

The area was already full of people when they arrived late that afternoon, but they found a spot for their families. It was almost a holiday atmosphere seeing so many old friends and meeting new people. Some friends and neighbors joined their family group and the time was spent talking mostly about Stephen Austin.

Someone said, "I heard that Stephen had Texas on his mind till the last moment of his life. Word is that he opened his eyes and said, 'The independence of Texas is recognized! Don't you see it in the papers? Doctor Archer told me so!' Then less than an hour later he was dead."

Everyone was silent for a while, then William asked, "Does anyone have a copy of the announcement by Sam Houston?"

A man said he had a copy but would like for someone else to read it.

None of the men offered to read it so after a few minutes of silence Mama said she'd read it. She took the announcement and started reading it to the group. "The Father of Texas is no more! The first pioneer of the wilderness has departed!"

After a short hesitation Mama read the rest of the announcement. "Mr. Houston has commanded all officers of the government to wear black arm bands for the next thirty days in respect to his high standing, undeviating moral rectitude, and as a mark of the nation's gratitude for his undying zeal, and invaluable service." "Houston has also ordered every military post to fire a twenty-three-gun salute – one volley for each of the republic's counties – and to have the garrison and regimental colors, hung black during the space of mourning for the illustrious deceased.'

"That's good and right." Jesse said. "Stephen deserves that and more."

That brought forth several "Amen."

"Mrs. Newman." A man said. "I've got a copy of the funeral notice and I'd really appreciate it if you'd read it out loud too."

"Well, the light is not very good, but I'll be glad to try." Mama said and she took the notice from him and got closer to the fire.

"It's a funeral announcement by Gail Borden. The title at the top says 'The Patriarch has Left Us.' 'We perform a most painful duty in announcing the death of General Stephen F. Austin, who departed his life, yesterday, at half-past 12 o'clock, P.M. at the house of judge McKinstry. His friends and relations have sustained an irreparable loss; his country, just merging into existence, the best and tenderest of fathers; the sons and daughters of Texas have now full cause for mourning, with one solitary consolation, that they will meet the just man above.'" Her voice broke at that point and she had to stop for a minute.

"The announcement says that 'His remains will leave for Peach Point, for interment, at twelve o'clock to-day.'" She looked up from the paper and said. "But we know his body wasn't moved today."

"The announcement goes on to say, 'Columbia, December 28, 1836'and there is a P.S. The P.S. says 'The steamboat having arrived, the remains of General Austin will be removed from Judge McKinstry's at eight o'clock to-morrow morning, to the steamboat, at Columbia Landing, and not to-day, as above stated.'"

Mama handed the announcement back to the man and said, "Thank you for bringing that. Now if you will all excuse me I'm going to retire for the night." She went to her wagon and went to bed and most of the rest of the group followed her example.

Early the next morning the family joined the people that were waiting for the body to be carried on to the steamboat for the trip down the Brazos River to Peach Point. They were pleased to see that Sam Houston and members of the Texas cabinet were there to accompany the body. There was also a military escort and of course Stephen's family and numerous friends.

There were tears shed by many people, both men and women, when his body was brought to the steamboat. Then with hats off they watched until the steamboat, named 'Yellowstone', was out of sight around a bend in the River.

As they loaded into the wagons to return home, Sally thought about the steamboat that was carrying that beloved man to his final resting place.

And she heard Mama whisper, "God bless you, Stephen Austin, and please God, bless Texas!"

Spring came early and it was a beautiful time. But Sally wasn't doing well. She was worried about it and told Mama. So during the last of her pregnancy, Mama had Louisa go to Sally's house to stay with her.

At first it was fun having Louisa there, but then Sally started having such a hard time, and nothing was fun anymore. She had to stay in bed more all the time and she would've hated the inactivity, but she felt so bad that she mostly just didn't care. Finally, one morning Sally heard Louisa tell Jesse that he should go get Mama.

Sally knew Jesse was scared. She tried to tell him not to worry but she just didn't have the energy to say much more than "Have Mama be careful."

She thought, 'He'll probably ride his horse to death getting to Mama's house, then he'll drag her over here with no preparation time at all.' But she was scared too and she wanted Mama here with her.

Sally was so weak and tired that she didn't realize any time had gone by when she felt Mama's hand on her forehead. "Mama? Where are the others?"

"William is home. Elizabeth will help him take care of the younger boys. Thomas and Ann Eliza came with me. Louisa said you haven't eaten in days. I want you to eat some soup and then rest."

Sally thought, 'Mama is here now so everything is going to be all right.'

But it wasn't all right and when she went into labor the next night the birth was very difficult. Sally was drifting in and out of consciousness and at one time she heard Mama tell Jesse and Louisa that she was very worried.

Sally wondered if she were going to die. She didn't think that'd be so bad but she didn't want the baby to die so she had to try to stay awake and help the baby live. Jesse was holding a wet cloth to her head and was talking but she couldn't quite tell what he was saying. She thought it was strange because he was dripping tears on her face.

She could hear Mama talking to Louisa and knew they were trying to get the baby. She kept drifting away and couldn't keep her mind on what was happening. Then she heard Mama say, "It's a boy, Jesse. And he looks perfect."

Sally thought, 'That's nice. Someone has a new little boy. What day is this? I know. It's May 28, 1837.'

Sally knew Mama had cleaned the baby and had handed him to Jesse. She saw Jesse look at him then at her. She couldn't keep her eyes open long enough to see the baby but she heard Jesse say, "Rachel, we're going to name him Alfred. Sally and I talked about it and she said it was all right with her. She said she wants to name the next boy Joseph, after her daddy, and then the next girl, Rachel, after you."

Sally drifted too far away to hear anymore and it was days later when Louisa told her what happened next.

'Mama took Alfred from Jesse and laid him down by you. Then she asked me to stay with you and she checked on Ann Eliza and Nancy. Thomas was asleep on a mat, with a little girl in each arm. We were all relieved that they were asleep; we knew it'd been a hard time on

225

everyone. I knew the two little girls would need some comforting the next day.

'Mama was exhausted, but she asked Jesse to come outside with her. I walked to the door to hear what she was going to say to him. They stood on the porch for a few minutes before she said anything. Then she said, 'Jesse, we came very close to losing Sally, and she's not out of the woods yet. I think it'd be a good idea to get the doctor from San Felipe to come see her.'

'Jesse looked like he'd faint, if men fainted, then he said, 'I'll leave right away.' He started off the porch so fast that Mama had to move quick to grab him by the arm.

'No, Jesse.' She told him. 'You need to stay here with Sally. I'm going to ask Thomas to go.'

'It's not safe for him to go by himself.' Jesse told her.

'And Mama said 'I know. But he's sixteen now, and he'll want to do it for Sally. Besides, we don't have a choice. I can't have Louisa go with him. I need her here to help. And you have to be here in case Sally…'

'And she just let it trail off unspoken and I got scared like I did when Daddy died.

'Jesse's voice was full of tears when he told her, 'I'll go get Thomas's horse ready.'

'Mama came back inside and went over to your bed. She put her hand on your head, re-wet the cloth in cool water, and washed your face with it. Then she put the cloth back on your forehead. I knew you must be running a fever.

'While Mama woke Thomas I heated the coffee and set out some cold biscuits. When Mama told him what she wanted him to do, he didn't hesitate. He walked over and looked down at you. I saw him reach and touch your hand and when you didn't stir at all he looked back at Mama with a question on his face. I knew what he was worried about. The same thing we were all worried about.

'Mama put her arm through Thomas's arm and walked him out on the porch. I got him a cup of coffee and a couple of biscuits, and kissed him on the cheek. Then of course I started crying. He probably didn't know it was fear for both you and him.

'By then Jesse was walking up to the porch leading the horse. Thomas asked, 'Mama, is Sally going to make it?'

'And Mama told him the truth. She said, 'I don't know son, it doesn't look good. When you find the doctor, you tell him that she's had one live child, and has lost at least two children early in carrying them. It's important that he know that or he may think since she had the first one all right that she'll probably be fine in a day or so. He needs to know that she's had troubles before.'

'Thomas was surprised but he just said, 'Yes, Ma'am.'

'Then Mama gave him a fierce hug and said, 'Thomas, please be careful. Don't take chances. I want you back here alive and well. Do you hear?'

'Thomas said yes he understood, then he went to get on his horse. Jesse gave him a few last instructions about the way to go, told him the rifle was loaded, then asked him to hurry as fast as he could.

'The next two days were terrible, and when the doctor and Thomas got here it wasn't much better for awhile.'

Louisa had filled in all the blank spaces that Sally hadn't known about. But Sally didn't have to ask her about what the doctor said before he left. She had heard the doctor tell Jesse and Mama that she would live but it was unlikely that she'd ever have any more children.

Thomas, Mama, and Ann Eliza went home after a few days. Louisa stayed another month to help Sally then she let Jesse take her back home too. Now it was just Sally and her family.

Sally was well physically, but not emotionally. She'd always loved having all her brothers and sisters and had planned on having a big family. She was depressed, moody, and just down right fussy. But as she gained her strength back she began to realize how blessed she was to have two healthy children, and fortunate enough to have both a daughter and a son. So once again as she so often had to do, she decided that it was time to quit letting her emotions rule her life.

The rest of the year went well. Jesse was around most of the time, and was so proud of his two children. Alfred was too young to appreciate Christmas, but Nancy thought it was so much fun that they should have it every week. They spent two days at Mama's house with the family.

At one point during the visit, Sally hugged Mama and told her. "You know, maybe it's not such a bad thing to have just two children."

Mama looked around at all the noisy excited little ones and said, "Yes, I know what you're saying." Then with misty eyes but a happy voice she added. "And aren't they all just wonderful."

In January of 1838, Jesse went to San Felipe and applied for his three-fourths league and one labor of land that was due him as a married man. He got Land Certificate No. 11. The land was located in Jackson County about thirty miles west of Gonzales. It was a little more than half way between Egypt and Gonzales.

William married Margaret Nelson in February and Mama was seeing a man named Nathaniel Barr. Sally liked Margaret but didn't care a lot for Mr. Barr. But she had so much going on in her own life, that she thought as long as Mama was happy, then she'd be too. At least William was happy. And with William married and making his own home, the younger boys needed a man around. Sally just hoped Mr. Barr could handle the strong personalities of Joseph and Andy.

Jesse was gone much of the time again and Sally had to do most of the work herself. Now that she had Nancy and the baby, she was so busy that she couldn't get as much work done. Jasper Gilbert, his wife, and family lived not too far from her and she knew that they had a young Negro girl that they thought wasn't quite right in the head and they didn't give her much to do. Sally had seen the girl with the Gilbert family a few times and thought there wasn't anything wrong with the girl; she was just putting on a good act.

Sally disliked Jasper and didn't like his wife any better, so she'd enjoyed watching the girl get away with fooling them. The last time she'd watched her the girl had smiled at her. Sally didn't hold with owning people, although some in her family did, but she thought it wouldn't hurt to ask the Gilberts if the girl could come stay with her awhile.

She gathered Nancy and Alfred up, put them in the light wagon and drove over to the Gilberts. After visiting for as short a time as she could politely get away with, she asked Jasper if she could borrow the girl. As she said it she watched the girl's face and saw a look in her eyes that she just barely concealed in time.

Jasper said he couldn't imagine why she'd want to put up with anyone as dumb as the girl but he guessed he didn't care if she kept her awhile. But not to think it was a permanent thing. He had money tied up in her. Sally said thank you and excused herself as soon as possible. When she asked the girl to come with her, she ran and grabbed an old cloth doll and jumped up in the back of the wagon.

Sally drove until she knew the Gilberts couldn't hear the wagon any longer and she stopped. She looked at the girl and smiled and got a shy smile in return. "What's your name, Child?"

"It's Blessy, Ma'am." She replied in a sweet voice.

"Well, Blessy, come up here and sit with us. There's room for all of us on the seat."

Sally noticed that when she came up to the seat she didn't bother to bring the rag doll that had occupied so much of her attention at the Gilberts.

Sally got more done the next few days than she had in months. Blessy not only kept the two children happy and well taken care of, but she was a big help to Sally too. The evenings were spent sewing and talking and playing with the children. Sally found out that Blessy was twelve years old, that she'd been born in someplace called Alabama, and that her mother had died when she was young. She didn't know who her father was.

One evening after the children were asleep Sally said, "Blessy, tell me about yourself. How did you get to be with the Gilberts?"

In a matter of fact voice, Blessy said, "My mother and her younger brother were bought by a family and allowed to stay together. It wasn't too bad for them for a long time. She had me when she was thirteen and she died when I was six. My uncle took care of me after that. His name was Charles. He was a very nice looking man and he was smart, so he was kept in the house and taught numbers and some letters. He wasn't supposed to but he taught me too."

She stopped talking and looked strangely at Sally. "Excuse me, Ma'am. Did I say something to offend you?"

"No. No. I've just never really thought about this from a … from your side of it. If you don't want to talk about it that's all right." Sally said.

"I don't mind, Ma'am. I'd like to tell you so you'd maybe remember me later on." And she told her all about the uncle she'd loved.

After they'd sat in silence for awhile Sally asked, "Blessy, what happened to your Uncle Charles?"

"Oh nothing that I know of, Ma'am. When I was ten the Master's wife said I was getting to be too pretty, so they sold me to a man that brought me and some others to Texas. Then I was sold to Mr. Gilbert not long after that." Blessy was looking into the fire while she talked and Sally was looking at her.

Sally couldn't say anything. She sat there thinking about her family and her life and she couldn't say anything.

"Is it time for bed yet, Ma'am? I guess I'm kind of tired."

"Yes. I believe it's time for bed." Sally got up and puttered around doing one thing or another instead of what she wanted to do. Finally she couldn't stand it any longer and she went and hugged the little girl.

Sally said, "I'm sorry, Blessy." And she cried.

"You don't have to be sorry, Ma'am. You're the first white person to ever treat me like a real person."

A few days later, early in the morning Jasper came over and said that his wife thought that a week was long enough to borrow the girl and that she wanted him to bring her back.

Sally took one look at Blessy's face and said, "No. I don't think I want her to go back right now. I tell you what, Jasper, I'll bring her back over in a few days."

He got huffy but left without saying anymore.

A little more than an hour after that Sally heard a horse being ridden hard. It was Jasper's wife and she was angry. She barely spoke to Sally just yelled at her. "Where's that girl. I want her to come with me right now."

Sally looked around and wasn't surprised that Blessy wasn't in sight. "I sent her into the woods to get some roots I want. It's real hard work and she probably won't be back for awhile. Do you want to get down and visit a spell?"

"Listen here you, you... I'm going to get the Sheriff after you for stealing my property." And she was so angry that she was practically spitting threats. She sat on her horse while Sally just stood and looked at her. Then she rode off at full-speed.

Sally went around the house and saw Blessy sitting on a tree stump petting one of the new puppies. She stood up and waited for Sally to walk over.

"I'm sorry, Ma'am. I should've gone back with Mr. Gilbert. I can walk on back over there now. I don't want to cause you any more problems."

"Don't worry about causing me problems. My only problem at the moment is that I didn't feel like I had the right to smash that biddy in the mouth. And I sure wanted too." Sally said. "Come on in the house. I'm going to try to think of something. I don't know what, but something."

Sally thought, 'Why am I talking like this. I know and Blessy knows that there's not one thing I can do to stop her going back.' But the next morning, Sally took Nancy and Alfred and went to Mama's house for a short visit. She told Blessy to stay out of sight until she got back. Mama said what Sally knew she would, that Sally shouldn't have gotten involved like she had and there wasn't anything she could do to change things.

On returning home that afternoon, just a short distance from her house, she met Virgilia Gilbert, another of Jasper's sisters. Sally stopped the horse and asked, "Virgilia, what are you doing here? Have you been to my house?"

"Yes I have. And you're hiding that girl out and I'm going to tell Jasper that you're causing trouble." She said.

Sally had Nancy in front of her and Alfred in the pack she had strapped on her back, so she was limited in what she could do. But her temper wasn't limited. "What have you got? That bag of cotton is mine, you little thief. What the hell are you up to?"

Virgilia looked scared and rode off, with Sally sitting there so angry she didn't know what to do. She wanted to go after her, but didn't want to endanger the kids, so she reluctantly went on toward home.

When she got there Blessy came out of the woods and told her that when she saw Virgilia coming she'd gone and hid in the woods.

Sally looked around the house and decided that a number of things were missing. She got even madder and the children started crying. She made herself calm down and fix them something to eat. She'd go see the Gilberts tomorrow and get her things back.

"Blessy, I'm sorry about all this. You'd be better off if I'd not ever brought you here." Sally said.

"Oh no, Ma'am. That's not true. I'm much better off for having these days."

About an hour later Ary Peratt, a friend of Jesse, stopped by to visit. Sally invited him to join them for supper.

All of a sudden, without even knocking, Jasper Gilbert came striding into the house. Sally was startled and that immediately turned into fury. She and Jasper both started talking at once. Sally said, "How dare you barge into my home like this."

And at the same time Jasper said to the girl, "Do you feel like walking home this evening?"

Sally looked from Jasper to Blessy and could tell that she was afraid of him. Blessy said, "Yes sir. I'm ready to go home."

Sally turned to Jasper and asked, "What kind of screws was your sister eating today? She came here, plundered my house and stole my cotton."

Jasper said, "If you say that again I'll break your mouth."

Sally was so angry that she would've said anything at that point, so she said the same thing again and added, "And you're a thief too."

Jasper said he was not a thief.

And Sally said, "If you don't steal you make your Negroes steal for you."

Jasper hit her with his fist. It knocked Sally down and not only her face hurt but so did her backsides. It seemed to Sally that everyone in the house was shocked. The children started crying; Nancy ran to her, and Blessy grabbed her things and went outside to wait for Jasper.

Ary was just standing by the table wondering what to do, and Jasper looked angry and maybe a little ashamed at the same time. Sally got up, went and sat Nancy in a chair, then turned to Jasper.

"Get the hell out of my house!" Sally's voice was quite and deadly.

Jasper said he'd stay until he was ready. But before Sally had to decide what she was going to do, he turned and went out.

Ary asked if he could do anything to help and Sally said, "Yes. I'm going to file charges against him and I'd appreciate you telling what happened here this evening."

"I'll do that." he said and then very quickly left.

Sally had a very bad night. She was so angry she couldn't sleep well, and she couldn't decide if she was most angry with Jasper Gilbert, Jesse for being gone all the time, or herself for not handling things better. By morning she still didn't know the answer to that, but she knew she was going to go file charges against Jasper, even if it was embarrassing.

She got the children up and fed, and took them to Mama's house. The second Mama saw the bruise on Sally's face she started asking all kinds of questions. After Sally told her what had happened, the whole family was ready to go get Jasper Gilbert, especially Thomas and Joseph.

Sally very quickly told them that she didn't want anyone to get involved, that she was going to take care of Jasper by herself. She did allow Mama to talk her into taking Thomas and Ali to town with her.

The District Court where she'd need to file a complaint was located at Columbus, which wasn't too far from Mama's house. She and her two brothers were there by noon and had to wait an hour until she could find the right person to talk to.

Thomas and Ali were thoroughly enjoying themselves. Not only did they have the rare treat of getting to wonder around the town, but they were getting a day away from work. Sally could tell they were feeding off her anger though, and both boys were almost looking for trouble. She tried to calm herself down and them at the same time, but it was hard to do. She knew herself pretty well by now, and knew her temper was always just below the surface.

At last she got to see Mr. Daniels, the Justice of the Peace, and the case was filed against Jasper Gilbert, for insulting and striking her in her own house. Ary Peratt would come in the next day or so and give his testimony, and they'd then do whatever they'd do to Jasper. It was a relief to Sally, but not very satisfying. She realized that what she really wanted to happen was for her to get to smash Jasper herself.

On the way back home she thought of Blessy and was sad and ashamed about what had happened to the young girl. She thought about the time Blessy had told Sally about being sold and taken away from her Uncle. It'd been Sally that had shed tears hearing that. Blessy hadn't shed any. Sally wondered about a life that is so bad that all the tears have been squeezed out of it.

Jesse returned a few days after her incident with Jasper and saw the bruise on her face. "I heard that something was going on with you and the Gilbert family. What in the world happened?"

Sally started telling him and he interrupted.

"What in hell were you keeping one of their Negroes for?"

She tried telling him about Blessy, but he just wanted to know what Jasper had said and done. His anger was about out of control anyway so when she told him his friend Ary saw Jasper hit her he exploded. "I'm going over there and beat the shit out of Jasper."

As he started out the door Sally said "No, Jesse. I don't want you to do anything."

He was surprised. "What do you mean you don't want me to do anything. You're my wife. What would people think if I didn't do anything?"

Sally took a deep breath and was just standing there looking at him.

He said, "What are you looking at me like that for?"

She said, "You haven't once asked me if he hurt me or not, or was it hard for me to go to Court, or anything about me personally. All you're worried about is what people will think about you."

Jesse threw his arms out and said, "I'm well aware that I'm not home enough for you and that you're usually a little mad at me anyway, but I thought you'd want me to go break Jasper's nose. Now I don't know what to say or do."

Probably the best thing for both of them was just to not say anything more at the moment. They were both too angry. Sally just stood there looking at him trying to decide what to say.

Jesse took his own deep breath then said, "Listen! I'll go over there and beat the hell out of him if it'll make you happy. Or I can just stay here and do nothing, but don't just stand there looking at me. I've never been able to read your mind and I sure can't right now."

He waited a minute for her to say something, then blurted out, "Well, what do you want me to do?"

She said, "Nothing." And she turned and walked away.

"Wait a minute." He almost yelled at her. "I feel like you're making this all my fault."

"Well, who is it that's never home. Maybe it is your fault." As she said it she knew she shouldn't have, but they seemed to be on the brink of arguing all the time lately.

Jesse was so angry he was red in the face. "You know, Sally, with the mouth and temper you've got, I can see how someone could get the desire to hit you."

That was just barely out of his mouth when he said. "Oh, hell. That was a dumb thing to say and I'd take it back if I could. But I can see by the look on your face that I'm going to pay for it anyway." He gave a big sigh and went outside.

Sally knew the thing that bothered him the most was her silence. And she was so angry with him that she didn't say another word to him for the rest of the day. He worked around outside some and talked and played with Nancy and Alfred.

She knew that at least half of the problems of the morning were her fault, so by evening time she was ready to make up. And Jesse was more than ready. The love making that night was better than good and they'd been a long time apart.

For the next few days Jesse worked hard around the place and got more done than he had for a long time. He did a number of extra things and Sally always appreciated hard work. Nancy and Alfred loved having their daddy around, so the home situation got back to at least a comfortable existence.

William stopped by one day and told them that they needed to go get married again so that Jesse could claim the other land due him for being one of the early colonists. Their earlier Mexican marriage, by contract, wasn't sufficient.

They talked awhile and he filled them in on the family news, including the fact that he thought Mama was thinking about marrying Nathaniel Barr. Sally hoped that would turn out to be a good decision.

It was strange and also seemed kind of silly to get married for a second time, but on March 31, 1838, they were officially married in Colorado County. A number of people they knew were in town to get married so they all made a big day of it. All the men were especially pleased because they could claim more land. Sally liked that idea too.

In April, Sally stopped by Mama's house to leave Nancy and Alfred, and to ask Thomas and Ali to go to Columbus with her. Jesse wasn't home. She wanted to be in town to see how her case against Jasper Gilbert turned out.

Jasper was fined $200.00 for striking her. That made her feel that it'd been worthwhile to go to court, but she felt even better when she talked to Jesse's friend, Ary Peratt. She'd stopped to talk to him to tell him she appreciated him testifying about what had happened at her house.

After talking a few minutes she said, "Wait a minute, Ary. I don't know what you're talking about now. You mean Jesse went and talked to Jasper?"

"Why, yes Ma'am. Didn't he tell you?"

Sally said. "No, he didn't. So you tell me, please."

"Well, Ma'am. Jesse came to see me and asked me to tell him exactly what had gone on between you and Jasper. And I told him. Then he asked me to go with him to see Jasper. And I did.

"When we got to Jasper's house I could tell how mad Jesse was. And I could tell how nervous Jasper was too. I wouldn't want Jesse Robinson mad at me like that."

Sally asked, "What'd Jesse say to him?"

Ary said, "Real polite like, Jesse said, 'Jasper, how bout you step out here a ways from your house so that we can talk and not disturb your family?'

"And Jasper said, 'Well, alright, Jesse, but I don't want no trouble now.'

"When we got over close to the barn, Jesse didn't even get off his horse.

He just looked down at Jasper and said, 'Jasper, I brought Ary over here with me for two reasons. One, I want you to know that I know everything that happened in my house. And two, maybe he can keep me from doing something you'd regret. Because right now I'd really enjoy beating the bloody hell out of you. But I'm not sure I'd stop with that and I don't want to cause your family all that grief.'

"Jesse sat there looking at Jasper for what seemed like a long few minutes." Ary continued. "And Jasper was white in the face and he told Jesse he guessed he'd just lost his temper and he sure was sorry.

"Then in a voice quiet as death, Jesse told him, 'If you ever lay a hand on Sally again I won't hesitate a minute. I'll kill you. That clear?'

"Jasper said as how that was real clear. Jesse rode real slow right out of the yard and I followed him. He didn't say a thing for a long time. And I didn't say a word cause I could tell how mad he was. But pretty soon he kind of relaxed and we talked about what's been happening around Texas lately and then I went back home.

"I just assumed that he'd told you all about it."

Sally said, "No, he didn't tell me anything about it. But, thank you very much for telling me."

As she, Thomas, and Ali rode back to Mama's house the two boys were all excited about how Jesse had told Jasper off. Sally felt a different kind of excitement; she hoped Jesse would be home when she got there. She knew a way to show her appreciation that they'd both enjoy.

She didn't stay long at Mama's, just gathered Nancy and Alfred and went home. 'Good fortune.' She thought, as they rode into the yard. Jesse was just coming out of the barn.

He helped the little ones down, then offered a hand to Sally. As she slid down against his body, he looked surprised then pleased.

"What's this?" he asked.

Sally laughed. Then she raised on her tiptoes and whispered in his ear. "If you can help me figure out some way to get these two to bed early, I'll meet you in the barn for an hour you won't forget."

Jesse said, "I'll take care of your horse if you want to go get some supper ready. She started off to the house with Nancy and Alfred, and when she looked back at him he was still standing in the same spot watching her.

She could see the evidence of what he was feeling. She laughed again and he just grinned.

Sally got supper ready as fast as she could and Jesse told the children stories and helped get them ready for bed. Alfred went to sleep easily but it seemed to take forever for Nancy.

Each time they got close to each other they couldn't keep from touching. Sally hadn't been so excited in a long time. She told Jesse that if he'd get a place ready in the barn she'd be there in just a few minutes. By this time his eyes were smoldering and she suspected hers looked the same to him.

She checked the children one more time, latched the door to the house, and went to the barn. Jesse had a lantern turned low and Sally could see that he'd spread some blankets in the wagon.

She walked slowly over to him and he said, "Sally, do you remember the first time we were in a wagon together? At your Mama's house?"

"Yes." she answered.

"Well, this time I'm going to do what I wanted to do then."

He picked her up, sat her on the end of the wagon and kissed her. Then for the next hour they behaved as two people who know what it takes to completely satisfy the other person.

In May, Mama let all the family know that she was marrying Nathaniel Barr. They had a big family get-together and had a good time together. Sally and the other older children talked about the marriage and hoped this match would be better than the last one.

Sally felt more comfortable with Mr. Barr than she ever could have with Samuel Rose. And now that Sally was older she'd begun to realize that a large part of her independent nature had come from Mama. If Mr. Barr learned real quick that Mama was not a woman that could be pushed around, they might make a go of it. Sally wasn't sure he was that smart though, so time would tell. She just wanted Mama to be happy.

Then in July, Mrs. Mary Milsap petitioned for an injunction to exclude Jesse from the land in Jackson County. She claimed it belonged to her; her husband had died in the battle at the Alamo. It was unpleasant to go against her, but Jesse felt strongly about that piece of land. He claimed the same land was given to him and he fought Mrs. Milsap in court.

Sally didn't want him to go to court over the land. She was against it because of Mrs. Milsap. But she was also against it because it was not all that close to home. She wanted him to trade his land grant for land that was closer but he didn't want to. The case was decided in favor of Jesse and Sally felt like not only Mrs. Milsap had lost but she had too.

He'd always favored the area around Gonzales and east of there, and she understood that. But she just didn't believe his promises that if she'd move there, he'd stay home. She knew he had good intentions and that he'd probably stay there more than he would here, but she'd still be alone most of the time.

Also she'd much rather be alone than put up with his friends. The last time she and the children had gone and stayed at the ranch with him she'd been very unhappy. She had no privacy and couldn't keep anything clean. She asked Jesse to tell his friends that when she was there they couldn't just come and go as they liked. He just thought she was being unreasonable and she felt the same way about him.

He'd seldom been home more than a few days every few weeks since they got married and the visits were getting farther and farther apart. One hot summer day they had a very heated argument about his absences from home and her unwillingness to move. Both expressed their anger that the other couldn't understand how they felt. That day she watched Jesse ride away and he didn't look back. And maybe for the first time, it didn't bother her.

She finished the chores in the house and then went outside. Around noontime, she decided to go in and get her and the children some food. She brought the biscuits and milk outside and they sat under a tree and ate. There was a nice breeze and it felt good.

She thought about Jesse and their life together. About how everything seemed to go from bad to worse with only brief spells of happiness. She admitted to herself that she was lonely, but didn't really mind him not being there; it was less trouble. And she'd decided months ago that she'd rather be by herself and close to her family, than by herself that far away.

'Here we are.' She thought. 'All the land we'll ever need, two beautiful children, and a fairly peaceful time for the first time in years. And if two people could be any more unhappy with each other, I don't want to know about it!'

CHAPTER 15

Sally was finishing the chores that needed done before they could go to Mama's house for the family gathering. It was May of 1840, and they were going to have a double wedding in the family. William was marrying Martha Ann Shedricks and Elizabeth was marrying Joseph Tumlinson.

Sally didn't know Martha Ann well at all but she was so glad she'd come along to help heal William's heart. Mama said he seemed really happy for the first time in months. Sally thought, 'It's been two years since poor Margaret's death; time for him to have some happiness.'

William's first wife, Margaret, had borne a son a year after they were married and the baby lived less than a year. Two years after that she had another son and he too lived less than a year. And then to add to the terrible tragedy, Margaret couldn't recover from the last birth and died less than a month later. It'd been a terrible time for William.

Sally had known Joe Tumlinson since she was a little girl. His father, John Tumlinson, had been riding with her daddy, Joseph Newman, when the Indians had pulled him off his horse and killed him. Sally's daddy had barely escaped with his life. That was in 1823 when Joe was twelve years old. There were a number of Tumlinson sons and cousins, and they were all fighters. Joe Tumlinson was said to have become a fierce fighter and hater of all Indians because of the death of his father.

Sally thought he should fit right in with her family. Jesse, Uncle Tommy, and some of her brothers fit the fierce fighter category too.

And probably if you asked Jesse he'd add her name to the list. Oh well, she didn't want to think about that.

Joe was about nine years older than Elizabeth and had been married before. His first wife had died early. He didn't have any children. Sally hoped the difference in age wouldn't be a problem for the two of them and she hoped both marriages would last a long time and be happy ones for both couples.

'Well.' She thought. 'Shows you what a fool I can be, wishing someone a happy marriage. What the hell would I know about that?'

She stopped what she was doing for a few minutes and felt bad about thinking about marriage in such a bad light. But other than her two children, all she could think about her marriage with Jesse was anger and sadness. And of course, Jesse was gone.

Sally didn't know where he was, but figured he was somewhere close to Gonzales, maybe at his place not far from there. For the last two years she and the children had lived mostly on her land, but had gone to his place four different times and stayed for awhile. It hadn't made any difference. Either place they lived, Jesse was mostly gone.

And when he was there some of his friends were always hanging around too. Sally wouldn't have minded that so much if they helped with the work. But they spent their time drinking, horsing around, and telling tall tales. And most of them were so dirty the hogs wouldn't stay around them. So Sally had decided to stay on her own place and let him do whatever it was he wanted to do.

She'd given up depending on him, and had started hiring some work done. Just last week she had a man from San Felipe, a George Scull, come out and put shoes on their horses. She could do it but it was hard and took her a lot of time.

George had helped with some other things while he was out and had visited awhile. He'd come to Texas a few years before the independence and had served with Captain Posey's Company in 1836. He'd been very proud of the fact that in October of 1839, he got the one third of a league of land that each single man received for volunteer services in the Texian military.

He was an easy-going person and she enjoyed his company. She hadn't realized how lonely she was and how much she missed having a man around until the visit with George. She had a few troubling thoughts about that for the next few days, but decided she probably needed to keep those kinds of thoughts out of her mind, if she could.

Sally, Nancy, and Alfred had a wonderful time at Mama's house. All the families were there and they had a celebration for the two new married couples. Of course, the two new couples couldn't wait to get off by themselves, but the rest of the family had fun being together.

Mama told them that she and Mr. Barr had bought a town lot in Matagorda and were going to build a house there. None of the children liked that idea much, but they didn't say anything negative to Mama. Sally hoped that maybe nothing would come of it. She didn't like the thought of Mama moving to Matagorda; and she couldn't imagine Mama being away from her family.

The hot summer days dragged by. Jesse came home, stayed about two weeks, and was gone again.

Then one day in the fall, Sally got word to come to Mama's house for a visit, that they had news about a big Indian fight. Sally wasn't told it was bad news, so wasn't worried much, and she always liked visiting with Mama and the family.

She hadn't been there long, when Minerva's husband, David, asked her if she'd heard from Jesse lately. Seems this big Indian battle happened near Gonzales, around the first part of August, and they assumed Jesse would've been in it.

He went on. "The Indians killed a man named Foley, and a large group of men went after the savages. Don't think they killed but one Indian then and our people weren't armed very well, so they had to withdraw. But real soon they were joined by others and the combined Texan forces overtook the Indians and defeated them soundly."

Thomas joined in. "Yes Sir. I heard that one of Colonel Henry Moore's Ranger Companies was led by Captain Thomas J. Rabb. And that as usual he acquitted himself very well, thank you."

Preston, Mary's husband, said, "They say that ought to be the end of any real trouble with the Comanches. I understand that just about anybody that had a horse and a gun went along." He turned to Sally and said, "I was told that Jesse was right in the thick of it and not hurt at all. Have you heard from him yet?"

That was the second time she was asked so she had to say something. She just said, "No, I haven't heard from Jesse lately." No one else said anything for a few minutes, then the talk started again about the Indian battle.

Sally visited for awhile longer with Mama and her sisters, but as soon as she could, she told Mama she thought she'd get on back home.

Mama followed her out to the wagon. "Sally, do you need someone to go home with you for awhile?"

"No, Mama." She stood silent for a moment then said. "I seldom know where Jesse is, let alone if he's alright. The saddest thing about it is that lately I'm more embarrassed that people feel sorry for me. I should be more worried about him, don't you think?"

Mama looked sadly at her but didn't answer that.

Sally called Nancy and Alfred and told them it was time to go. The family was saying goodbye and passing messages along and Sally just wanted to leave.

Mama gave her one more hug and said, "Child, I'm here if you need me."

"I know Mama, thank you. I'll see you soon."

She managed well enough until she was out of sight, then she had to wipe tears from her eyes. Nancy and Alfred were on a quilt in the wagon, playing with some toys, and Sally didn't think they'd even noticed how upset she was. Was it fear for Jesse or embarrassment? She didn't know and there weren't many tears this time. Her anger took over too soon. She was beginning to find that anger was kind of a comfort.

One day in September, Jesse came riding into the yard. Nancy and Alfred were happy to see him and he was happy to be with them, and Sally admitted to herself that she was glad to see him too. She knew he was keeping a sharp eye on her and she hoped she could keep her temper under control.

It was a pleasant enough evening and by the time the children were in bed she and Jesse were both somewhat relaxed. They took a cup of coffee out to the porch and sat down to talk. He told her the place looked real good. She told him about what had been going on and about all her family.

Then she asked about what he'd been doing, and what was happening in the Gonzales area.

Jesse told her about some of the people they knew, about the latest news, and just touched on a small Indian skirmish the first part of the previous month.

Sally said, "Oh? Well, it seems like I heard about a big Indian battle close to Gonzales. Is that battle and the skirmish you're talking about the same fight?"

Jesse said, "Sally, let's don't fight; not tonight. I've missed you terrible, and I have a terrific longing for you."

Sally felt her temper warring with her longing for him. She thought the temper would win. But the feelings in her body that always got stirred up when he was around were too strong. She got up, reached for his hand, and led him into their bedroom.

When she woke early the next morning Jesse was lying on his side looking at her. She smiled at him and asked him. "What are you doing?"

"I was trying to store up the memory."

"What memory?" She asked.

He answered so quietly that she had to strain to hear. "The memory of loving you and the good thing we have in bed."

She put her arms around him and they held each other for a few minutes.

Sally made herself stay away from any conversation that would cause her to lose her temper. She suggested that they go to Mama's for a visit, and they spent two days there and had a great time.

Jesse settled in, they worked hard on the place, and they got along better than they had in a long time. Sally was pleased and almost content but she reminded herself to stay ready. Because one of these days, Jesse would leave!

The fall turned out to be nice and cool, and Christmas was just right. Alfred was three and a half and Nancy was almost seven. Both Jesse and Sally made them some toys and things, and it was great fun watching them enjoy the day. During the holiday time, the families all spent some time together at Mama's house. It was the best Christmas in many years.

January 10, 1841, was Nancy's seventh birthday. Sally baked a cake, an unusual happening, and the day went well. When the children were in bed, and Jesse and Sally were having a last cup of coffee, Sally brought up some of the work she'd like to get done the next few days.

Jesse didn't answer right away, and Sally stopped in the middle of raising her cup and looked at him. She got up, walked to the sink and rinsed her cup. Jesse hadn't moved, he was just watching her.

"You're leaving, aren't you?" she asked.

Jesse answered, "I want to go see how things are at the ranch. And I've been here a long time. Why don't you and the children go with me. We could stay there maybe a month and then come back here if you want."

She said, "I'd rather be alone here than alone there." She gave him a cold look and went to the bedroom.

For awhile Jesse stayed where he was. Finally he got up, blew out the lamp, and went and stretched out on the cot in the corner. Sally heard him give a long sigh.

As for her, she sat on the edge of the bed for awhile, wishing she could go back to Jesse and hold him and be held in return. But she could feel the loneliness of all the days to come and her resentment built until her anger took over. At that point, she stretched out on the bed and finally drifted off to sleep. She wasn't even surprised that this time she didn't even feel like crying.

Early the next morning, after telling Nancy and Alfred goodbye, Jesse looked at Sally for a long moment, then slowly rode away.

On the eighteenth of February, Thomas and Ali came over to tell Sally that a new nephew had just made his entrance into the world.

"Is Martha Ann doing okay?" She asked. "How big is the baby? Who does he look like? What's his name? Oh, and how is William?"

Both Thomas and Ali laughed and Thomas said, "My gosh, you women are all so strange about new babies. Let's see. Martha Ann is doing great. He's a nice size boy according to Mama. He looks just like all babies to me, face all round and red and with squenched-up eyes. And what else did she ask?" He took a breath and looked at Ali.

Usually Ali was quiet and let Thomas do all the talking, but this time he said, "I don't think I ever saw William as happy as he is right now. And Sally, they named the baby Joseph Austin Newman. After Daddy."

The three of them were quite for a moment, then Sally told them to make themselves comfortable until she could get ready to leave. "I want to go see William and his new son."

The days and weeks ran together and each time Jesse came home was worse than the last. Sometimes they had harsh words for each other, but as often as not, they were both quiet and didn't have much to say.

Sally was glad that Nancy and Alfred were able to see their father once-in-a-while, although they didn't show as much emotion as they had earlier. She knew that bothered Jesse, but as far as she was concerned it was his fault. He wasn't around enough for them to feel close to.

The only thing she and Jesse still enjoyed about each other was their private relationship and that was becoming less pleasurable and less often too. It wasn't easy when you were mad all the time. And Sally was honest enough to know that it worked both directions.

Sally was relieved that Jesse happened to be there when they got word that Mary's husband, Preston, had died. All the Newmans and Gilberts got together, and Uncle Tommy was there too. It was one of the saddest days Sally had gone through for a long time. It reminded her too much of when Daddy died. Mary was hurting so badly and so were the three children. Death was so cruel when it took a young person, and there was nothing to do to ease the pain of the ones it left lonely and hurt.

Sally hugged her sister tight and told her she loved her and did the same with the three children. Amanda, Mary's oldest, was eleven now and was always the one that wanted to hear 'a remember day.' She said, "Oh, Aunt Sally. I don't want this to be one of the days I remember."

Sally gave her an extra hug. "No, Amanda. Remember days are only the days that are happy." 'But,' she thought, 'The day you bury your daddy will always be a day you remember.'

It was a terrible time for the families, and for once Sally was glad to load her two children up and go back home. And it was a comfort having Jesse there—at least for a time. But it wasn't long until he was gone again.

During the summer, Sally allowed a man named Brown to stay in a small rundown shed in exchange for help with the heavy work. He wasn't a great worker but was a pleasant fellow. In the evenings Sally and the children stayed on the porch where it was cooler and Brown would come over most evenings and sit and visit. He'd done lots of traveling and was good at spinning stories. Sally figured most of it was exaggeration, but it was entertaining.

Late in the summer Jesse served with Captain J. B. P. January's Company; January also lived in Jackson County. There'd been strong fears of the Mexicans invading again so Jesse had spent time with January's Company. He came home right after he was through with that service. Knowing that all the military doings that involved the Mexicans was big news in Texas, he told Sally all about his part in this latest one.

She realized that a large part of her interest now was how the events affected the Republic of Texas. She wasn't very concerned for his safety any more. He'd lived through more battles than she could remember.

He talked a lot during the visit about what they were hearing about the Mexicans. The Mexican government had never given up on getting Texas back and constantly threatened to invade. But they had so many internal revolutions by one factor or another that it kept them too busy to do much of anything about Texas. He said that the Texans needed to be ready, because it was only a matter of time before they had to fight them again.

Sally enjoyed the conversations and had enjoyed him being there. She'd benefited from his company a few nights. She no longer spent any time dreading that he'd soon leave; that was just a part of their life. She could wish the situation was more conventional but she realized that she'd begun to look at his leaving as the time she could get back to a regular routine.

The morning arrived when it was obvious that Jesse was getting ready to leave. And he started the morning conversation with a surprise.

"I don't like Brown hanging around. It doesn't look good, so I'm going to run him off." And he walked outside.

Sally immediately lost her temper. She followed him out. "It doesn't look good? Now just what the hell does that mean? And if so why didn't you run him off the minute you got here? Was it just a little too convenient to have him do the chores while you were here? Didn't leave much that you had to get up and do, did it?"

"You'd better watch how you talk, woman. I'll do what I feel is the right thing to do." He said. And he went and mounted his horse.

"The right thing to do? The right thing to do would be to stay home and help with the work and then I wouldn't have to hire someone to help around the place. You just leave and mind your own damn business." And she boldly stepped in front of his horse before he could ride down to Brown's shack.

"Get out of my way. Now!"

Sally moved and stood just below the porch and watched him ride to the shack. She couldn't hear what was said, but it was obvious that Brown was getting his stuff together to leave. She felt angry and helpless and wanted to hit something, and she preferred it to be Jesse.

He stayed long enough to see Brown ride away, then rode back to the house. He got off his horse and very roughly grabbed Sally by the arms. He lifted her almost off the ground and got right in her face and said. "You better real quick learn how to behave like a wife's supposed to or you're going to be very sorry. You understand me?"

Sally saw that her anger and dislike of him was mirrored in his eyes, and she thought, 'I don't think Jesse likes me any better than I like him.' She didn't give the nasty answer she wanted to because she thought she'd have to pick herself up off the ground if she did. But she wasn't going to be cowed either.

"Yes, Jesse. I think I understand what we're both feeling."

He looked at her a long moment and finally decided to leave it at that. He put her down, got back on his horse, and said. "I'll see Nancy and Alfred in a week or so. I'd appreciate it if you'd tell them goodbye for me." And he rode away without looking back.

She was glad he was gone but frustrated with unshed anger. And her arms hurt where he'd grabbed her. She ended up spending the rest of the morning working on a fence that needed repaired. Hitting something with a hammer was at least somewhat satisfying.

Joe Brown came back the next day to pick up a few things he'd left. He tried to act like he hadn't caved in to Jesse but it didn't matter to Sally. She didn't want Jesse to think that he could tell her what to do. So even knowing it was probably a mistake, she told Brown he could stay.

The weeks went by much as always. More and more often Sally went through days without even thinking about Jesse. She knew he'd probably be there close to Christmas time, because that's always when he showed up. He then stayed until after Nancy's birthday, which made a two-week stay. That seemed to be about his limit.

Not wanting to have any trouble at Christmas time, she planned to ask Brown to leave before then. But things don't always go according to plans.

She was unpleasantly surprised when only a week into December, Jesse came riding into the yard. And if she was surprised to see him, she was even more surprised by his actions. There he was! Like an irritated bear! Throwing a tantrum!

At first Sally wasn't even sure what was going on. But when Jesse started for Brown she knew. She told Nancy to take Alfred and stay in the house until she told them to come out. The poor children were so familiar with two parents that were almost always at war that they usually started toward the house before they were told.

Sally had a moment to feel bad about that. Then she went toward the shed to see what was going on.

Jesse was throwing things around, kicking things in, and making a shambles of everything in his path while he was trying to get to Brown. In the meantime, Brown was grabbing what he could of his belongings and working mightily at staying out of the grasp of Jesse. It seemed terribly funny to Sally until she saw Jesse draw his gun.

She jumped toward him, grabbed his arm, and yelled. "Jesse, what in hell's name are you doing?"

He turned on her, shook her off his arm so forcefully that she fell down. He practically growled as he told her. "I wanted nothing more today than to be able to beat him to death, but since he doesn't seem to want to face that like a man then I'm going to shoot him three or four times."

Sally stood up, dusted off her backside, and looked at Jesse in astonishment. "Why?"

He got right in her face and said, "You know why, you bitch!"

At the same time Sally was trying to make sense out of all the thoughts tumbling through her head, Brown was smart enough to quietly make his way to the opposite side of the shed and make an unmanly-like run for cover.

Husband and wife stood looking at each other for a few more minutes and for once Sally realized that if she let her temper control her now she might end up dead. She instinctively knew that Jesse was very close to having no control over himself.

She didn't move backwards like she'd like to, but instead looked toward the shed. She'd heard Brown go, but didn't know if Jesse had or not.

He hadn't, because when he looked that way and didn't see him, he said, "Oh, shit!" And walked quickly around the shed.

Sally wasn't sure what to do. She wanted to stand her ground, but she'd never seen Jesse like this and it scared her. She had time to think, 'Alright, this is the "fighting Jesse" and I can see why he scares his enemies so bad.' By then he was almost back to her and she quickly said, "Jesse, it's cold out here, lets go to the barn so we can talk, and so Nancy and Alfred won't see us fighting."

She brought the children up on purpose, and it worked. She could see him trying to calm himself down a little and when he looked toward the house he lifted his shoulders and let them fall, and took a deep breath.

Then all he said was "Alright." And he walked to the barn.

Sally followed him, trying very hard to think of how to handle this. She knew what he was thinking about her and Brown and at this moment could even imagine how it would look to him. Her feelings were so intense, and so mixed up, that she couldn't seem to sort through them and get her mind to stop jumping from one thought to the other. And she knew she needed to be in control when she walked into that barn.

She hesitated outside the door, glanced once toward the house, then stepped into the barn. She thought that he'd be standing just inside waiting on her, but he wasn't. When her eyes adjusted to the dimness inside the barn, she could see him, pacing back and forth.

When he stopped and looked at her it was with anger and hurt all mixed together. And Sally realized that was what she was feeling too–angry and hurt!

She said. "So, do you want to talk about this, or do you want to beat me to death or just shoot me three or four times?" As she said it she knew it could provoke an action dangerous for her, but she didn't want to be in the position of the weak opponent.

Jesse took a step or two closer and said, "I'm not sure that I want to shoot you, but yes, I'd sure like to beat the hell out of you."

Then he asked. "Sally, how could you do such a thing? Right here with the children and all?"

She answered with a question of her own. "Just what are you accusing me of doing?"

He just looked at her and didn't answer.

"Let me tell you something." She said. "Brown showed up here with nothing but a broken-down old horse and the clothes he had on his back. And as far as I can tell he doesn't have any ambition to better himself. He's a pleasant enough fellow, can do some average chores, but close to totally useless as far as I'm concerned. You've seldom seen me that I wasn't working. Do you really think he's a man I'd pay any mind to at all?"

She was getting madder by the minute. "And now that I've been forced to think about what you're suggesting has been happening, I can tell you that you're full of horse-shit and ought to be ashamed of yourself. Do you really think I'd sleep with a man like Brown?"

By now Sally no longer cared if she ended up on the ground or not. She interrupted whatever he was starting to say by asking another question. "You're gone most all the time, Jesse. Are you able to tell me that you haven't had relations with anyone but me since we got married?"

Jesse was caught unawares by the rapid change in the direction of the conversation. It took him a moment but then he said. "Don't change the subject. You're the guilty party here, not me. You're the woman taking care of the children and you should behave like a decent wife and mother."

They yelled at each other for a long time. Each one bringing up all the things that they disliked about the other.

"It'd be so easy to hate women, especially a spiteful little witch like you."

Sally let his statement hang in the air. She thought. 'We do hate each other. How can you love and hate someone at the same time.'

In a tired voice she said. "This isn't settling anything, and I know the children are worried to death about us. "Jesse, I haven't slept with Brown. But if any woman had a right to find someone else it'd be me. You haven't been around but for short periods for years. You never do your share of the work or even see to your own children."

She waited a moment then finished. "And you sure haven't been around to take care of my needs!"

Jesse looked at her like he was seeing her in a whole new way. "This is over! Whether you slept with this Brown guy or not, everyone around thinks you have. I can't put up with that." And he headed toward the house.

Sally quickly followed him. She didn't know what he was going to do and she was too exhausted to think straight.

Jesse went in, gave Nancy and Alfred a hug and said he'd see them Christmas day. Then he left without even looking Sally's direction.

Sally didn't hear anything from him the next day so she assumed he'd gone back to his ranch and would come back for Christmas like he usually did.

But a week later he came riding into the yard.

He grabbed Nancy and Alfred, hugged them, and told them he sure was glad to see them. Then he said a polite hello to Sally.

She answered him in the same polite, cool manner and then excused herself. She went in the house and worked but she'd go to the window occasionally to watch them. He played catch with Alfred for a few minutes, then swung Nancy up in the air a few times all the time talking to them. That wasn't so unusual but something about it made Sally stop puttering around and stay at the window to watch.

He was doing lots of talking to them and twice Nancy had looked toward the house with a strange look on her face. It was beginning to make Sally nervous so she decided she'd rather know what he was talking about, even if it meant getting into a squabble.

She went out on the porch and Nancy and Alfred came that way immediately. Jesse joined them. Sally stayed quiet and let him visit. He was talking mostly about how great it was on his ranch in Jackson County. Sally noticed a difference in him this time.

He seldom looked at her but when he did it was as if there was a long distance between them. She guessed she didn't care and that to be honest she felt about that same way. She waited as long as she could but he didn't say he was leaving and it was past suppertime. She didn't want him to stay, but even a husband you couldn't stand couldn't be sent away hungry.

She invited him to have supper with them and was surprised when he accepted. After they'd eaten and Sally had cleaned up, Jesse then told the children that he'd be going. Alfred started to cry and said, "But you only got here today, and you didn't stay last time either."

So Sally said, "Why don't you stay the night? You can sleep on the cot and be here to visit with them in the morning." And at the same time she was saying to herself. 'Please go away. I don't want you here.'

Nancy was strangely silent, but Alfred was saying. "Please, Daddy!"

So he agreed. Sally thought it hadn't taken much to talk him into staying, but she wasn't sure what that meant.

They all sat on the porch throughout the evening, and the children finally went to sleep. Sally carried Alfred and Jesse took Nancy and they put them in their beds. Sally could sense strong feelings of some kind in Jesse, she wasn't sure what, so she walked back out to the porch and sat in one of the chairs. Jesse followed her and sat down on the porch step and leaned against the post.

They were quiet for a long time then Jesse said, "I guess I should've sent word to the children about that last Mexican scare."

Sally noticed he said to the children and not to her.

"But I wasn't directly involved, and by the time I got around to thinking about maybe they'd worry I figured it was better if I just stayed still about it."

Sally didn't say anything for a few minutes then said. "Yes, it would've been nice for them to have heard about it from you."

He mumbled something that sounded a little like, "Yes, I'm sorry."

After another quiet time she said. "Listen, Jesse. I'm tired and about ready to go to bed, but you seem to have something more on your mind. Do you have something you want to say to me?"

She could see him looking at her but it was too dark to really tell what he was thinking. She'd wondered all evening why he was being so polite.

He said, "I got some bad news and I guess I'm having a hard time with it. Some guilt I guess." He waited a minute then continued. "I got a letter from home that my daddy is not doing too well. I haven't seen him or my mama in years. I've thought a lot about going to Tennessee to see them, but I don't see how I can leave right now with our country being threatened.

"You know the Mexicans are constantly making noises about reclaiming Texas and we'll eventually have to fight them again."

Sally looked at him and thought. 'Everyone says that all the time. God forbid that Jesse Robinson is gone at the wrong time and misses a good fight.'

She knew that was unfair of her because she loved Texas as much as Jesse did. But her family was so important to her that she couldn't imagine not being with them at a time like this. She thought of her daddy being sick and dying.

Jesse seemed to really feel bad and her heart softened. She went and sat on the porch beside him. He looked down at her for a moment, then looked out at the stars.

Sally wasn't sure why she did it, but she reached and put her hand on his hand and he grabbed her like a drowning person holding on to a rope. They held each other for a few minutes and the heat in their bodies rose so quickly that there wasn't a stopping point. They got up, went in the house and went to bed, together.

Sally woke up first and lay there without moving. She thought, 'That was almost a violence we committed on each other last night, and was amazingly good. But now I just wish he wasn't here.'

After they got up Sally could tell that Jesse was just as uncomfortable as she was, maybe more. He didn't ever really look at her.

He went and woke the children and visited with them while Sally got breakfast ready. He was nervous and watchful while they were eating and then he wanted them to go outside with him while their mama cleaned up.

Alfred was acting excited and Nancy kept looking at Sally with an uneasy look. Sally felt like something was wrong, so she stopped what she was doing and went outside on the porch. Jesse had his horse saddled and tied over by the barn, and the children were standing there beside him.

Sally was watching them when she heard the wagon coming. And the minute she heard it she saw Jesse look her way.

"What's going on, Jesse?" She called. "Who's in the wagon?"

Nancy started to walk toward Sally and Jesse stopped her.

A full jolt of fear hit Sally and she started to go in the house for her gun but was afraid to let the children out of her sight. At the same time a small wagon was coming fast into the yard. One of Jesse's friends was driving it.

Jesse handed Nancy then Alfred up to him and told him to get going that he'd follow him.

Before Sally could get to the kids, Jesse caught her and took her back to the porch. In a quite voice he said, "Sally, I've told the kids that we've agreed for them to come visit me at the ranch. If you interfere I'm going to tie you to a chair. So you can make it easy or hard on them. Either way they're going with me."

Sally was having a hard time getting her breath. She couldn't even think right. She heard the wagon moving and at the same time heard Nancy calling her. She felt light-headed and couldn't stand up.

Jesse held her up and she saw something like sympathy in his eyes. She managed to say, "You bastard! You bastard! You planned this all along. You had him waiting with the wagon."

Jesse said. "You brought this on yourself. Do I have to tie you down?"

Sally was still dizzy and unsure of what to do. Then they both heard yelling and looked toward the wagon. Nancy had gotten loose from the man and had jumped off the wagon.

She'd fallen hard, but got up and was running toward the house. The man had stopped the wagon and was holding Alfred on the seat.

Sally jerked away from Jesse and started running toward Nancy. Jesse wasn't as quick as her, but had almost caught up when she reached Nancy. Sally fell on her knees and grabbed the little girl.

Jesse stood and looked down at the two of them and the pain he was feeling showed in his face. Both Sally and Nancy were crying.

Jesse squatted down and reached for Nancy, "Come on, Honey, you need to go with me. Your mama can't take care of you proper. You'll like it at the ranch."

"No Daddy. I love you but I don't want to leave Mama. I want to stay with her. You can come see us more often. I'd like that."

Then as Jesse kept reaching for her and telling her that she had to go with him, Nancy said, "If you make me go I'll run away. And I'll keep running away. And if an Indian or a Mexican kills me I won't care."

Sally was sitting on the ground with her arms and legs wrapped around Nancy. She finally found her voice. "Jesse. I won't let her go. You'll have to hurt me to get her and then you'll have lost her for good. She won't forgive you."

Jesse looked from Nancy and Sally to Alfred on the wagon and back. "Nancy, honey, I want you to go with me. I didn't want to tell you this, but your mama is not a good woman, and she can't raise you right. You need to come with me."

There was pleading in his voice now and Sally had the desperate thought that maybe she could keep Nancy and not lose both children. She could barely see Alfred through her tears and she wondered how she could think of not having them both.

Her mind was swimming around in a black pool of water and it seemed that she'd drown there. She forced herself to concentrate on what was happening.

Nancy said, "No, Daddy."

And she turned her face from him and buried it in her mother's blouse.

Jesse looked like he wanted to cry. "This is all your fault, Sally. This should've never happened."

Sally tore her eyes away from Alfred and the wagon and really looked at Jesse. "What was last night about?"

He looked flustered for a minute then said, "I guess I was weak. And I guess I wanted to prove that you like it too much. You don't behave like a good woman ought to behave. And you won't ever be able to. And I don't want my daughter raised like that."

Sally looked down, put her hand over Nancy's ear, and quietly said, "Jesse, you've cost yourself this marriage by never being home. And your jealousy is pitiful. So from now on every time you have a woman I want you to think about me.

"Because, you son-of-a-bitch, you're never going to have another one that makes you feel as good."

He surprised her by saying, "You're probably right."

He reached over gently and touched Nancy's hair. "Let me tell her good-bye."

Sally moved her hand off her daughter's ear, thinking that she'd probably heard most of the conversation anyway.

Jesse said, "I love you honey. And I want you to think about coming to live with me." Nancy didn't say anything and didn't look at him either.

Jesse touched her hair again and then touched Sally's face lightly. Then he stood up and walked quickly over to his horse and the wagon.

Sally tried to get up while still holding fast to Nancy and started yelling, "Don't take him, Jesse. He's just four years old. Please don't take him."

As the wagon started moving she yelled. "Alfred. I love you Alfred."

And the little boy answered. "I love you too, Mama. I'll bring my pony back so you can see him."

By this time, Sally had Nancy by the hand and was running after the wagon. The last she heard was Alfred yelling, "Bye, Nancy. Bye, Mama."

And the last she saw was Jesse. This time he looked back before he got out of sight.

Sally ran and ran and realized she was saying over and over. "Don't take him. Don't take him."

When Nancy stumbled and fell, Sally stopped. "I can't run anymore, Mama. I'm too tired."

Sally sat down in the middle of the road with Nancy in her lap. She sat and rocked back and forth with her for a long time, until she knew she wasn't going to drown in the black pool.

A part of her heart turned hard as an anvil, and she embraced it. Finally she got up, brushed herself off, then Nancy, and said. "Come on, Child. I'm thirsty. Let's go home and get something cool to drink."

Instead of an extra hard job as was her usual way, she sat all the rest of the day teaching Nancy how to sew. They made a dress and apron for Nancy's oldest doll. Sally was quiet and just allowed Nancy to talk about whatever she wanted to, neither one of them mentioned Alfred or Jesse. It could've been a very pleasant day except for their heartache.

Early the next afternoon Sally heard horses coming. She got her gun and stood at the open door until her two youngest brothers, Joseph and Andy, came riding into the yard.

Joseph was almost 15 now and was already the biggest of all the brothers. Both he and twelve-year-old Andy were a handful for Mama. Both were headstrong and independent; life had made them tough.

They got off their horses and Sally went out and gave them a hug. Joseph wasted no time. "Sally, a neighbor came and told us what Jesse did. Mama sent us over to tell you she wants you to come to the house. But before that, do you want me to go get Alfred?"

"No, Joseph. But thank you." Sally told him. "And I don't want to go to Mama's and have everyone mind my business; she'll just have to wait until I'm ready for a visit. I'm surprised she didn't come over here herself."

Andy chimed in. "Ali's not doing well again and Mamas worried about him. It'd be good if you'd come home, Sally. It'd make Ali feel better to see that you're alright."

Sally looked at him and grinned. "That was really good, Andy. Did Mama tell you to play that card if I didn't agree to come over?"

Andy laughed and Joseph said, "Well, it's working, isn't it?"

And Sally said, "Yes, it worked. Help me with a few chores and we'll go."

When they were ready to go and Nancy was in the wagon, Sally said she'd forgotten something and would be right back. She went back into the house and picked up one of Alfred's toys and held it close.

Joseph didn't wait outside, but walked into the house and came over and stood beside her. Then he did a strange thing for a young man; he reached over and took her hand.

She looked at him and said. "I've got the tightest grip on my emotions that I can muster, Joseph, and I'm afraid I'll lose it at any minute."

"Sally, you're the strongest person I've ever known. You ain't going to let him beat you."

She put the toy down and walked outside with him. "It's my heart that's beating me, Joseph. It's this big hole in my heart."

The visit with Mama and the family was short; Sally didn't like knowing that they were all feeling sorry for her. She was embarrassed thinking about what people were saying about her and she blamed Jesse for that. And she was so lonely for Alfred that she felt as though her body was sick.

She didn't know what to do to get their lives to some sort of normal place. She decided that she and Nancy would go back home and hope that Jesse would bring Alfred back. Sally couldn't imagine that he wouldn't bring him back for Christmas.

But he didn't bring him back for Christmas. Instead he sent a man out with a present for Nancy and no word at all about Alfred. It was the most miserable time in Sally's life. She knew it was unfair for Nancy but they spent the day with Sally crying and going from the chair to the window and back again. They didn't put up a tree, had no special food for a Christmas dinner, and went to bed extra early.

Sally lay in her bed for an hour with a heart so heavy she wanted to die, and then she heard Nancy. She was crying as quietly as she could. Sally thought that the poor little girl probably thought her mama was asleep and she was trying not to upset her. Sally started to get up and go to her but maybe it was better not too. She couldn't handle her own emotions and would just end up crying with her. She lay there silently cursing Jesse for what he'd done and how he'd made their lives so miserable.

Suddenly some unbidden thoughts made it to the surface and she had to look at them. 'It wasn't Jesse that didn't put up a tree, or cook a meal, or show a little girl that you loved her and was glad she was here. Oh, God. What have I done? How did I make such a mess of things? And even more important, how do I quit feeling sorry for myself and do something about changing what I can?'

Sally got up and said. "Nancy, get up. We're going to cook some flour cookies. And we're going to decorate a tree and have a Christmas celebration. Come on, Child, hurry up. Time's a wasting."

As she got out of bed Nancy asked, "What're you talking about, Mama?

Are you all right? Have you taken leave of your mind?" "Your senses. And no I haven't, but I was getting close."

"I don't know what you're talking about, Mama."

Sally had turned up the lamp and was raking the coals around in the fireplace and she turned to her and said. "You've heard your gramma say that. But its have you taken leave of your senses, not your mind."

She went and hugged Nancy and said. "I'm so sorry about today. But the day is not over yet and we can still have a Christmas celebration." And she watched as Nancy's face brightened and she asked what they were going to do.

Sally made some dough, patted it out, put sugar on it and then put it in the pot to bake. While it was cooking she looked through the wood box, next to the fireplace, until she found the longest log. She took it out, stood it on its end in front of the fireplace and said. "Here's our tree! Now what are we going to decorate it with?"

Nancy laughed; and clapped her hands.

Sally got a quilt and their pillows and put them on the floor in front of the fireplace. They spent the next hour decorating a log and eating half-done sugary tasting dough and sitting on the quilt with a bunch of dolls. They had a wonderful time.

She was going to put Nancy in bed but was just too tired to move her. She got another quilt and covered her up. She lay back down beside her and whispered, "Tomorrow you can talk to me about Alfred. I promise."

"I love you, Mama."

"I'm sorry. I thought you were asleep."

"Mama. I heard you tell Joseph about the hole in your heart. I guess I have one too."

"I know, Nancy. I'm sorry."

"I wanted to tell you what I'm doing with mine and maybe you can do the same thing with yours."

"I'm not sure what you're talking about, Honey." Sally said.

"I thought about having a big hole in my heart and I thought about what you do when there's a hole somewhere that you don't want. You fill it up. So I decided that every time I feel sad about Alfred, I'll think about pouring love in that hole. That way I can just think about Alfred staying in there with all that love until he can come back and be with us."

"I think maybe that's the wisest thing anyone ever told me. Thank you." And Sally thought about the picture that was in her head now instead of the awful one that'd been there a few minutes earlier and she was grateful.

She kissed her on the forehead and said, "I love you too, Child." But this time Nancy was asleep.

Nancy's eighth birthday was in January and Sally counted on getting to see Alfred then. Surely Jesse would bring him to see her then. But again he just sent a friend with a present for Nancy.

Sally thought it was so strange how the mind could work. As long as you kept all the awful loneliness and sadness locked away in that hole filled with love you could manage the days in an almost natural way. It was the nights when you got pretty close to giving in to total despair.

She'd discovered that for a mother the constant thoughts through the nighttime, and sometimes not to be held off in the daytime, was 'What is Alfred doing? Is he thinking about me? Does he blame me for not being there? Is he all right? Oh, please. Is he all right?'

Sally had wanted to ask Thomas and Ali to go see if they could find out about Alfred, but Ali had been feeling kind of poorly and she wanted to wait until he was better. She knew Thomas wouldn't want to go without him.

It was William that went to see Jesse to see how Alfred was doing. Then he came to the house to tell her.

All she got out of what William told her was clouds of horrible thoughts bumping each other around. 'They're at the ranch, but not all the time.' 'Alfred looks fine, but kind of sad.' 'Jesse wants Nancy to come live with him.' 'Probably won't see Alfred on his birthday in May.' 'Won't consider any kind of compromise.'

Sally had thought her heart couldn't get any harder toward Jesse, but she was wrong.

Most all anyone could talk about was war with the Mexicans again. Sally tried not to worry about it but not knowing where and how Alfred was, made the fear all the more terrible. It was hard not to think about the time in '36 when they'd all had to run away from the Mexicans. She'd heard people refer to it as 'the runaway scrape' and she guessed that was a good description.

One day George Scull came by for a visit. Sally was surprised to see him, but not displeased. She hadn't seen anyone in a week or so and was wondering what was happening.

Almost without a pause for proper greetings, he asked. "Have you heard about the big Mexican force that's taken over San Antonio and some other places?"

Sally said. "No, I haven't heard any news in a while, but give me a minute to get us some coffee. I'd like to hear everything you know about it."

They sat on the porch and George started telling her what he knew. "Best we could find out, was that early this very month of March, a Mexican force under a General Vasquez appeared at San Antonio and with hardly any problem at all took over the town.

"And to make it even more serious, at that same time, some other Mexican forces seized Goliad and Refugio. That whole part of western Texas took up arms while their womenfolk got ready to run for it again. But that wasn't necessary this time, cause a citizen army mobilized real quick and entered San Antonio on March fifth with good results.

"The Mexican forces high-tailed it back to the Rio Grande. Our people didn't follow them, but a company or two of men have remained on duty to guard the country from anymore invasions from the Mexicans."

He finished with the usual thought. "I reckon it'll happen again until we finally put a stop to them thinking they can have Texas back."

Sally had listened without interrupting him. When he didn't seem to have anything else to add, she asked, "Was any of our people hurt? Did you hear anything about any of my kinfolk being involved?"

She wanted to know if Jesse had been involved but she didn't want to ask. She couldn't allow herself to think that he'd go off for days or even a week or more to fight the Mexicans and not bring Alfred home.

She realized that George was answering her questions. "No, ma'am. I don't think anyone was hurt, and I didn't hear any particular mention of your kinfolk. Or your husband."

They talked for a while more then he said. "Well, I guess I'd better be getting on back to town."

Sally thanked him for coming by, then noticed that he didn't have his horseshoeing equipment with him. "Mr. Scull, did you come all this way just to tell me about the Mexican troubles?"

"Well, Ma'am, everyone knows that you're pretty much by yourself. I mean that your husband is not . . . I mean . . . I realize that some of your brothers are over here real often, but I mean . . . ." He looked very uncomfortable and finally let the statement kind of drift off.

Sally was thinking about all that he'd said and hadn't said and she remained silent.

The silence was too hard on him and he said. "Truth is Miss Sally, I worry some about you, and just wanted to see that you was doing alright."

He tipped his hat and now totally uncomfortable, climbed on his horse.

Sally said, "Mr. Scull, I take it from what you just said and didn't say, that people seem to think that my life is somehow some of their business."

She stopped. Here he'd come out to be nice and he probably wished he were anywhere else right now. "I'm sorry I said that, George. I do appreciate you coming out."

He said goodbye and left as fast as he could. Sally watched him go without really seeing him. Her thoughts were in turmoil. As she so often did, she went and found the hardest job she could and worked on it until time to fix supper for her and Nancy.

Alfred's fifth birthday was on May 28, and the day passed without a word about him. Sally hadn't seen him in almost six months. She missed him only a little more than she despised his father.

One hot muggy day in early July, after Nancy had helped Sally pull the last of the weeds out of the garden plot, she made a plea. "Mama, I'm so hot and sticky and I've got dirt all over me, even in my hair. Can we go to the river and cool off. Can we? Please?"

"Its still two hours away from supper time, Child. We can get a lot of work done in that time." And as she saw the look of sad resignation on Nancy's face Sally thought. 'Now what difference would missing an hour or two of work mean if it'd make her happy for awhile.'

"Alright. Let's go wash up. I bet I can get there first." And Nancy's happiness made her heart feel a little lighter. Sally got her gun and they both ran toward the place that they called their bath place. It was a wonderful spot under a big cottonwood tree that hung almost across the river; it was always cool there.

By the time Sally had checked everything out and put her gun in a handy spot, Nancy was already laughing and yelling, "I beat you. I got here first."

They took their dresses off and their shoes and Sally told Nancy to go ahead and get in while she shook the dirt out of their dresses. Sally watched as Nancy giggled and splashed her way into the water and then as happened almost all the time a memory of Alfred got in front and she had to gently push it back and think of Nancy.

She shook the dirt out as best she could and hung the dresses on a low branch of the tree. Then she got in the water and turned over on her back to float. It wasn't that easy with the heavy underclothes and she wished it were dark so that she could take some of them off but of course she couldn't.

Nancy cavorted around, splashing water on her, and generally having a great time. Sally admitted that it felt wonderful and she wondered why she didn't do it more often. But usually once a week was the only time they took the time for it. She got the soap they kept in a crevice of the tree and washed Nancy's hair and then her own. And they cleaned their bodies as well as possible with the underclothes in the way.

Sally was a good swimmer; after the big flood they went through her daddy had taught all the children to swim. And Sally had taught Nancy. They swam and floated and played until Nancy ran out of ways to distract her mama from the inevitable, "Alright, little girl, it's time for you and me to get busy. Time's a wasting."

"Do we have to, Mama?" Nancy asked with a long drawn-out sigh, but she followed her out of the water.

It was then that Sally noticed that a man was walking away from the river. She felt a bit of shock but before she could really be afraid she realized it was George Scull. She stopped and said, "Mr. Scull. Is that you?"

"Yes Ma'am. I'm real sorry. I heard the two of you and thought you were just having fun but then wondered if maybe you were having troubles."

"No, we weren't having troubles. If you'd wait over there a few minutes I'd appreciate it." She said. And she wondered at why she wasn't angry that maybe he'd been watching them.

"I haven't been here but just a minute or two. I called but you were splashing and talking and you didn't seem to hear me." He kept explaining himself and Sally could hear something in his voice that created some heat that she hadn't allowed herself to feel in awhile. And into her mind, unbidden, came the image of her standing in the water with Jesse waiting for her on the bank. And she thought of the pleasure she'd experienced after that.

She shook her head to rid herself of those thoughts and Nancy said, "Mama. You're getting water all over me from your hair."

Sally thought, 'Oh, hell. If I were a man I wouldn't dare go where anyone could see me cause they'd know what I was thinking.'

"Mr. Scull. Would you mind going to some spot where you can't see us for a few minutes? I'd rather not put these dirty dresses back on over our wet undergarments. We'll go to the house and make ourselves decent and then you might join us for a bite to eat if you'd like." And Sally thought, 'That probably sounded too familiar. I should've asked him to come out some other time.' But she didn't want him to leave.

He said. "Yes Ma'am. Of course." And she could tell he was already walking away.

She grabbed her gun and the dresses and she and Nancy went quickly to the house. She changed out of the wet things, dried off, and dressed in the new dress she'd made for all the weddings she'd had to go to lately. As she helped Nancy dress she was asked. "You look pretty, Mama. What are you wearing that for? Are we going somewhere?"

"No, Honey. It's just cooler than the other one." She tried to tell herself that she was wearing it only because the everyday dress she'd been wearing was too dirty to put back on and her other everyday dress was getting old and needed replaced. Besides she'd made this dress with the replacement of the old everyday dress in mind; it wasn't a really fancy dress. It was a lighter fabric and cooler and very practical.

'Oh, hell. It fits my body real well and I look good in it; that's the reason I'm wearing it. I'm not fooling myself at all. Thank goodness I can fool Nancy.' She thought.

She went out to the porch and saw that George was standing over in the shade of the barn playing with one of the dogs. She called to him and he came over.

They sat and talked about various things but Sally couldn't keep her mind on any one thing for very long. And George seemed to be the same way. Nancy was busy talking to and playing with her dolls and wasn't paying any attention to them.

"Mr. Scull. George. Would you like to stay for supper?" Sally asked.

"Thank you. I'd like that." He answered.

"It won't take long. I'll just make some cornbread and heat the soup."

"Could I help you with anything?" And as she stood up he did too.

She stopped beside him for a moment. "I need to think about it. Excuse me."

She knew he had feelings for her and she didn't want to hurt him. He was a nice person and she did like him, but she didn't feel love for him. And weren't you supposed to love someone if you did what she was wanting to do? Oh hell. She had such a need. Do other women ever feel this way? None of the women she knew ever said so and she could never ask; it didn't seem to be the proper thing to talk about.

Well, I've always done things the direct way, and that's the only way I know to do this. So we'll just see what Mr. Scull's real feelings are and what the evening has to offer.

After they ate supper and Sally cleaned up, they went out on the porch. George seemed reluctant to take his leave and Sally was glad. She assumed that he wanted something else too. He told them about Louisiana, where he came from, and some about his family, and he asked about where she was born. Nancy was interested in what both of them had to say and stayed up and listened until she got sleepy and sat in Sally's lap. She fell asleep a short time later.

"George, would you mind carrying Nancy in for me? She's getting to be a bit heavy lately."

"I wouldn't mind at all." He said and when he leaned down to pick Nancy up he was just inches away from Sally. He leaned in and kissed her lightly on the mouth and she kissed back.

Sally opened the door and led him to Nancy's bed and he put her down. Sally took Nancy's shoes off but it was warm in the house so she left the cover off. Then she turned and saw that George was standing just inside the door. She walked over and looked at the folded quilt at the end of her bed. She knew if she picked that quilt up she was making a decision and he'd know too. She picked it up and walked outside.

She took the quilt and spread it out on the end of the porch farthest away from where Nancy slept. She slipped her shoes off and sat down on the quilt.

George was still standing a few feet away. "I didn't tell the whole truth today, Sally. I was at the river for more than just a few minutes and I watched you while you bathed."

It was so dark that she couldn't see his expression but she didn't have to. "Sit down, George." The excitement level was very high and it took only a minute before they were engaged. A lot of energy was used and they were both happy with the results. A bit later she said. "I need to go back inside. I don't want Nancy to wake up and I'm not there.

You can sleep in the barn if you'd like. There's a comfortable place in there for guests."

"Alright. I'll do that. And I'll leave early in the morning so you don't have to think about explaining to Nancy why I'm still here." Then he said. "Sally, I don't know if you know it but my feelings for you are terribly strong. I've been in love with you for a long time."

"Good night, George. It was a very nice evening."

She walked in the house and tried to feel like she was a bad person but she couldn't. She felt good. As she climbed in bed she thought of the satisfied old dog that made his three circles then curled up and went happily to sleep. "Not as good as blackberry cobbler, and not as good as you, you bastard, but damn good." She whispered. She lay there only a few minutes before falling asleep.

On September 20, Sally went to Mama's house for Mary's marriage to a man named, George W. Cotrell. Mary's husband, Preston, had been dead for over a year, and she needed a husband and a father for her kids.

None of the family was very sure about Cotrell; Sally thought he was just too slick. But Mary seemed taken with him, so Sally was happy for her.

She'd been going over to visit with the family more often lately. It was good for her and for Nancy. Louisa, Ali, Joseph, Andy, and Ann Eliza were always there, and as often as not one or two of the others would show up at the same time for a visit. And on this visit all her brothers and sisters were there.

For the entire week before, there'd been a lot of news about the latest problems with the Mexicans, but they'd not gotten many details. Two of Cotrell's friends were there for the wedding, and one of them had just gotten back from the San Antonio area. Everyone was anxious to hear from him and he was only too happy to tell all he knew.

"Fact is" he said with a great deal of self-importance, "When word got around that I was heading back to Columbus, both Capt. Thomas Rabb and Jesse Robinson asked that if I ran into some of their families to kindly tell them that they were well and healthy."

He looked toward Mama when he mentioned Capt. Rabb and toward Sally when he mentioned Jesse. Mama asked him for more information about Uncle Tommy. When he'd supplied all he knew about him he turned to Sally.

But all she said was "Thank you."

He looked surprised that she didn't question him, but Sally was thinking, 'That means the son-of-a-bitch isn't with Alfred! And he has this stranger tell us that he's doing fine. Damn, I hate him.'

Even though she was terribly upset and worried about Alfred, she was never the less still interested in the news about the Mexicans. So she listened closely as the man told about this latest incident.

On September 11, a Mexican army, under a General named Adrian Woll, had captured San Antonio. Some Texans had escaped and carried the news to the surrounding towns. A citizen army gathered and headed for San Antonio. Uncle Tommy was a Captain under Colonel Henry Moore, of Fayette County, and Jesse and other men from Jackson County had joined that group. A second company under Colonel Moore was led by Captain Nicholas Dawson, also of Fayette County.

On their way to join the Texas forces, Captain Dawson and 53 volunteers were surrounded by Mexican cavalry and all were killed. This was in a place called Salado Creek near San Antonio.

At this time in the man's story, Sally got up and excused herself and walked outside. She already knew that General Woll had retreated back into Mexico and that for the time Texas was still in the hands of Texans. They also knew that the danger with the Mexicans was still just a few days march away. But that was the small part of her personal worries.

Mama and Louisa came out and joined her.

"Mama." Sally said. "I think I'll take Nancy and go on back home."

"I'm sorry, Sally. Hearing about all that is unpleasant." Mama said.

Sally looked at her a minute and then exploded. "Oh, Mama. We both know what's bothering me and I might as well say it. I don't know where Alfred is.

"I don't know where my son is or who he's with. He could be at the ranch in Jackson County, or in Gonzales, or even in San Felipe for all I know. And is he with some of Jesse's no-good friends, some Negro woman, or maybe some whore?"

Mama frowned and said, "Now, Sally, I can't think that Jesse would have a woman like that keeping Alfred."

"Oh no? Well, I've tried to make myself think that he wouldn't leave him with a stranger, that it'd be important to him to stay home with his son. But he's off to war and Alfred is not with his mother or his daddy. Oh damn, I hate his miserable guts. I'd really, really, really like to kill the bastard."

"Sally, don't talk like that! I don't want you to think like that either. You've got too bad a temper to be harboring such bad thoughts. You just remember that you don't want your children having to do without both parents. Now why don't you come on back in and visit a while longer?" Mama said.

"No. I don't want to hear any more about all those men dying either. All I can see is all those wives, children, mothers, and sisters that are now alone and hurting. Sometimes life can just be a dismal lonely thing to be endured."

After assuring Mama and Louisa that she indeed would be alright and not to worry about her, she got Nancy, and the two of them told everyone goodbye, and left for home.

She was extra glad to get to her own place. At least there she could stay busy and not dwell on all the trouble and strife of this Country they'd chosen to live in. And at least part of the time she could push the thoughts about Alfred back into that little hole in her heart.

CHAPTER 16

Sally was afraid she wouldn't even get to see Alfred at Christmas time. She'd counted on Jesse wanting to see Nancy enough so that he'd allow Sally to see Alfred. But she was trying not to get her hopes up.

About a week before Christmas, around noontime, a well-dressed man she didn't know rode into the yard. Sally was at the door with her gun when he got stopped. He introduced himself, said he was from Columbus, was Jesse Robinson's attorney, and he had a message for her.

She was so fearful that it'd be something bad about Alfred. She was shaking as she put the gun down and invited him in. It was cool out and she asked if he'd like a cup of coffee and a bite to eat.

He seemed surprised by her appearance, and was obviously curious. As Sally put out the biscuits and sausage left over from breakfast, and poured some coffee, she could see him studying her and Nancy and also looking the house over. The house was in perfect order, as it always was, and so was Nancy. The child could wear an old feed sack and still look beautiful, and Sally was aware that the good looks had come from her.

She couldn't get but a bite or two down because she was afraid of what was coming. But she tried to be patient as the man passed on the latest news of Columbus. She half listened to him and with the other part of her was thinking, 'From the way he looked so surprised I guess

Jesse has told him what an awful woman I am. Maybe he expected two or three men around and a drunken party going on.'

She knew she had to stop thinking like that or she'd get angry and she couldn't allow herself to do that. Seeing Alfred was the most important thing in her world right now.

When he was through with the food, she refilled their coffee cups, stacked the few dishes in the wash tub and returned to the table. Ever since the man had said 'attorney for Jesse Robinson', Nancy had been like a little sticker burr at her side. She didn't know what the man would make of that and she wasn't going to say anything to Nancy. She'd been this way since the day Jesse had taken Alfred away. Other than at Mama's house, if someone else was around, Nancy was as close to Sally as she could get.

Sally sat down, caught Nancy's hand and pulled her over to sit beside her. It was crowded, but it made them both feel better. "Now, please tell me what your message is." She said.

"Mr. Robinson would like to see his daughter, Nancy, and he said that he thought you'd probably like to see the boy, Alfred."

He'd barely gotten the words out when Sally said, "My son, Alfred."

"Yes ma'am, your son. Mr. Robinson has authorized me to tell you that he'll meet you in my offices at noon on the day after tomorrow. You can visit with your son while he visits with your daughter."

Nancy got up and walked behind the chair. She leaned close and whispered in Sally's ear, "Let's don't do it, Mama. He might try to take me away again. Please."

Sally got up, reached for Nancy and pulled her close. As she held the child, she said, "I would do anything in the world to see my son, save one. I won't upset my daughter by putting her in a position of feeling unsafe. You go back and tell Jesse that the only way I'll agree for him to see Nancy is for us to meet at my mama's house.

"That way I'll have my brothers there to see that Nancy is allowed to do what she chooses to do, either go with him or stay with me. And he can have you and anyone else he wants with him to see that Alfred is allowed the same choice."

The man started to offer a protest and Sally cut him off. In the voice of cold steel that was becoming more a part of her all the time she said. "That's the deal. I'll be at my mama's house at noon, day after tomorrow. Thank you for coming." And she walked over and opened the door for him.

The next afternoon Sally and Nancy went to Mama's house. She was glad that mama's husband, Mr. Barr, was in Matagorda for a few days; she was so nervous that it was easier without him being there. She thought the evening would never end. It reminded her of all the long dreadful evenings she'd spent by herself when she and Jesse were first married.

By mid-morning the next day, all five of her brothers were there, all with guns. Three of them were waiting outside and the other two were always just a step or two away from her and Nancy. Everyone was on edge. Sally thought this was probably a case of too much protection, but she didn't want to change it. She was nearly sick at her stomach from wanting to see Alfred and being afraid of losing Nancy.

Just at noon, Jesse, with Alfred riding on the horse behind him, the attorney that'd come to see Sally, and two other men came riding into the yard. It was cool, but not unpleasant, so Sally, Nancy, and the rest of the family trooped outside.

Nancy was clinging to Sally, but all Sally could see was Alfred peeking at them from behind Jesse. She wanted to run and get him but she knew she couldn't. It seemed like hours that they all just stood there, but she knew it wasn't but a minute.

William pointedly leaned his rifle against the wall and walked off the porch toward Jesse. The other brothers were all in plain view and in four different locations. If that surprised any of the men with Jesse, it just meant they hadn't grown up in a world where you were either alert for trouble or dead. Sally was sure it didn't surprise Jesse.

After talking to William for a few minutes, Jesse got off his horse and lifted Alfred down. The other three men rode over to the trough in front of the barn to let their horses get a drink. William, Jesse, and Alfred walked toward the porch. Suddenly Alfred broke free from Jesse and came running toward the porch.

Instead of running to Sally, he ran to Nancy. Sally was hurt at first, but as she watched the two children hug each other she was glad for them. It made her think of her love for her brothers and sisters.

Jesse was at the porch steps, but Sally didn't even look at him. She was just watching Alfred. He was standing about halfway behind Nancy and was looking at Sally. Sally took a step closer, reached out and touched his hair. All of a sudden she was holding him and trying not to cry. She sat down in a chair with him on her lap. She leaned back and looked at him and tried to talk, but couldn't. He shyly kissed her on the cheek.

She looked at Nancy and saw her look at her then at her daddy. Sally looked at William and nodded her head toward Nancy. He walked over and caught Nancy by the hand and led her over to Jesse. Jesse picked her up and held her close and she was hugging him too. Sally watched as he took her to the other end of the porch and sat down with her.

She didn't have to look to know that her brothers were watching every movement also.

Mama came over and gave Alfred a hug and then Louisa did too. But soft-hearted Louisa broke down. She was crying so hard that Mama took her back in the house. Sally was able to keep herself together only because she didn't want Alfred to remember her like that. She wanted him to think of her and Nancy and want to be with them. But that wasn't to be.

About an hour after they'd gotten there, Jesse got up and came around to the front of the porch. He was holding Nancy's hand, but she wanted him to let her go and he did. She went immediately to Sally.

Alfred had both arms around Sally's neck and was kissing her on the cheek. Sally was trying to memorize every inch of him. She was cooing to him and hadn't even realized it. In a cold voice Jesse said, "Sally, I've asked Nancy again to come live with me, but she's declined. I'm going to keep trying until she agrees. Come on Alfred, its time to go home."

Alfred held on fast for another minute, again kissed Sally on the cheek, then wiggled away from her and went to his daddy. Sally jumped up and was at the porch steps when William reached out and caught her.

He moved her in front of him and put both arms around her waist and held her. She stood there with her back to her brother and her daughter hanging on to her side and watched Jesse get on his horse, reach down and flip Alfred up behind him.

It came out like a croak, but Sally was able to say, "I love you, Alfred."

In return she heard "I love you too, Mama. Bye, Nancy. Bye, Mama." And they rode away.

Nancy was crying and Sally couldn't keep her tears in any longer. She cried in William's arms and then in her mama's arms. Mama led her inside and wanted her to lie down awhile. But then loud angry voices were heard on the porch and Sally and Mama went back out.

All five brothers were on the porch, all talking at the same time. When Sally came out the door they all got quiet.

She asked, "What's the matter? What's going on?"

None of them said anything. She looked quickly at all of them and then to William. "Well?"

"Well." he answered. "Your little big brother" and he looked at Joseph "wants to go kill those four men and get Alfred back for you. To quote him, 'especially your son-of-a-bitch husband'. Pardon the language, Mama. And us other four are trying real hard to let him talk us into it."

"Sally, as impossibly hard as this had to be on you and Nancy, it was almost as hard on the rest of us. The emotions here are running pretty high. While Andy and I go whip Thomas and Ali at horseshoes, why don't you go for a walk with Joseph."

Sally immediately said. "That's a good idea. But first you guys need to line up and let me give each of you a hug. And I'm not going to cry."

And as she gave each one a fierce hug she was able to keep from crying but not by much. By the time she got to the last brother, they'd already started to drift off the porch. Joseph was standing in the middle of the yard gazing down the road.

William yelled at the other three. "You guys get the horseshoes warmed up. Cause I need to get back home and before that your old brother is going to whip your butts. I may just take all three of you on."

Then in a totally different voice he said. "Sally, I'm sorry you're hurting. But right now you need to help Joseph. He has a short fuse, like you. And he just worships you. We don't want him thinking it'd be better for you if Jesse was dead, because that's not true. Alright?"

"You're right." She said. Then she raised on her tiptoes and whispered in his ear, "Thank you, William. You are so very special." And before he could answer she went out and joined Joseph.

She and Joseph talked about all kinds of things but not about Jesse. There'd be time for that later. In the background they could hear the clank of horseshoes and the noise of the four brothers enjoying themselves.

Before they went back to the house she asked Joseph if he'd come stay with her and Nancy for awhile and he said he'd really like that. Sally hoped that with a brother around to do things with maybe it'd help keep her mind off Alfred. Maybe, but probably not.

Joseph stayed with her until Christmas Eve when they went to Mama's house for a few days. Then he and Andy both stayed with her for the month of January. It was a hard time, but they stayed busy and time passed.

The second week of February, William came to the house. Sally was glad to see him, until she saw his face. After finding out that all was well with Mama and the family, she asked William what was going on.

"Sally, on the first of the month, Jesse went to court and petitioned for a divorce. He's asking for custody of both children."

William hesitated for a moment then added, "Because I'm a county commissioner I was allowed to bring the papers to you instead of you being served by the Sheriff. I'll go outside and visit with Nancy while you read it. And Sally, it's pretty bad."

She just looked at him for a few seconds, then took the papers. When she looked she saw that it was two long pages of writing. "William, read it to me, please." And her hand was shaking as she tried to hand it back to him.

He had a miserable look on his face and in a broken voice he said, "I don't want to read it out loud to you. You can read it. Take all the time you need." And he took Nancy and went outside.

It took Sally almost an hour to make it out and she wasn't sure of some of the words. But she got the meaning of all Jesse had said about her. And she was torn between a dozen different emotions, not the least of which was the strongest anger and embarrassment she'd ever felt.

She got two cups of coffee and went out to the front porch. William came over and joined her. She had to work to compose herself and William just waited quietly. At last she said, "Well, I'm a little surprised, but I guess I've been expecting it. I'm not sure what I should do."

William said, "Well, I've learned a little about things such as this. You need to hire an attorney to go to court and state your side of things. And you'll have to try real hard to get the children."

"He can't take Nancy away from me too. He can't, can he?" she asked.

And William's reply filled her with the worst fear she'd ever felt. "I don't know, Sally. Jesse is looked at as someone special. His service in the military and his attitude kind of set him apart. I don't think the men around here would go against him."

He waited a minute and then added in a sad gentle voice. "And a lot of people believe you haven't been a faithful wife."

Sally just sat in the chair looking at him with a haunted look in her eyes. She thought about George Scull and the times they'd been together recently and knew she could no longer say she was a faithful wife. But that had nothing to do with what Jesse had done and what he was trying to do now.

After a few minutes of silence, William said, "Sally. Do you realize how you intimidate people?"

"I guess I do." she said.

William said, "Any jury selected to hear the divorce petition will include a few men that will feel intimated by you. And they'll go against you because of that. And then some of the other men will believe you were an unfaithful wife and they too will go against you.

"And no man can tolerate the thought that a woman, especially a young good-looking one, could feel like his equal. So you have to guard how you act when you go to town. Do you understand what I'm saying?"

"Yes." Sally answered in a tired voice. "But I'm not sure I can act different enough to make a difference. Why can't I just be who I am?"

William had no answer for her. They visited for awhile longer, then he told her that when it was time he would go with her to Columbus, and he left.

George came out the next day. He said he'd heard about the divorce petition and was worried about her.

"George, I don't want to hurt you but I can't see you again. I mean not like we've been seeing each other. I've got to go to court and try to get my children, at least keep Nancy, and no one can know about you and me. You haven't said anything to anyone, have you?"

"I haven't said anything to anyone. I wouldn't disrespect you like that, Sally." She could tell that he was hurt but she didn't know how she could do anything else.

"I thought maybe you might want me to go with you for support." He said.

"Oh, George. I'm sorry. That would make it really bad for me. Please. I just can't see you. Not now." She felt really guilty about how she was treating him. He stood by his horse for a few minutes and she knew he was hoping she'd say something more, but she didn't.

"If you need me you can always get word to me." He said.

"Thank you, George. I appreciate that." And she turned and walked in the house. A few minutes later she heard him ride slowly out of the yard and she said to herself. 'You're a heartless woman, Sally. A really heartless woman.'

William had told her that the Court would meet on March 8 and that she had to see an attorney before then. So on March 6, she took Nancy and went to Mama's house. She even dreaded being with Mama and the family; she knew she was facing a terribly trying next few days.

The visit with Mama was about as bad as she'd expected. Mama was depressed about what was happening and she gave the impression that she thought all was hopeless. Nancy didn't want Sally to leave her so she clung to Sally and cried. Sally thought she'd never make it to a place in life where people around her weren't always crying and upset. She managed to leave Nancy with Mama and she went to Columbus by herself. She wouldn't allow anyone to go with her; it was going to be embarrassing enough without more witnesses.

William was waiting in town for her, just as he'd said he'd be. "Sally, I wish you'd come in before now. Court is in session tomorrow."

"I know. I'm sorry. I just couldn't face all these people so I put it off. What do I do?"

"I suggest you go to Menefee & Fields Law Firm. I've talked to Menefee and he'll meet with you right away."

Sally only nodded, so William led the way. She didn't know what to expect, but was greeted politely by a male clerk, and she and William were escorted into Mr. Menefee's office.

They were asked to sit down and he began immediately. "I don't want to appear impolite, but time is of the essence here. I'll get all the information, have my clerk write it up, and you can come back this afternoon to make sure it's correct. It'll have to be ready for submission by first thing in the morning. So let's begin by reading the petition."

It couldn't have started out in a worse way for Sally. She hadn't thought about having to hear Jesse's petition read out loud.

"Republic of Texas, County of Colorado, To the Honorable William J. Jones, Judge of the second judicial district. The Petition of Jesse Robinson." Mr. Menefee's strong voice seemed to echo in Sally's head. "Humbly complaining herewith unto your Honour that for a long space of time Sarah alias Sally his wife, treated your petitioner in a most cruel and unkind manner. That she was a great scold and termigant. That she treated and used him in the most ill and unnatural manner."

Sally wasn't sure what termigant meant and she was sure Jesse didn't either. She had no idea what Jesse had meant by her treating him in an unnatural manner but she sure wasn't going to ask anyone.

The attorney was still reading and she made herself pay attention. "… conducted herself toward other men with the most unjustifiable familiarity and especially one Joseph E. Brown with whom her conduct was in such open violation of decency and decorum as to scandalize your petitioner and his family. That her familiarity with said Brown was too notorious…"

Sally was having to work very hard to control her emotions and she knew that the next part of the petition was going to be the most humiliating.

"Your petitioner first hand knoweth that the said Sarah did commit adultery with said Brown and divers other men" Menefee glanced up from the page and looked at her strangely.

She was so embarrassed that she didn't react more than to turn redder in the face, but the attorney got a scorching glare from William. He very quickly looked back at the papers and continued reading.

"And on or about the fourteenth day of December AD 1841 she abandoned your petitioner and has succeeded in getting the custody of one of the children."

Sally thought about Alfred and again had to make herself listen to the attorney.

"That the said Sarah is a woman of ill fame, and therefore unfit to superintend the raising of said children. Your petitioner further showeth that he is poor and has but a small amount of property. Wherefore he prays to be Divorced."

Sally knew the last part was Jesse not only asking for custody of the kids, but also for all the property of his, and even for her to be ordered to pay all the Court cost for the divorce. She began to hear the words again as the attorney finished reading.

"A. M. Lewis Attorney. Case Number 220, filed February 1, 1843."

Menefee leaned back in his chair, removed his spectacles and wiped them off. As he put them back on he said, "Well, now lets see."

Sally could feel the redness in her face, and she wasn't sure her voice wouldn't break when she talked. The temper that always hovered so close now seemed to have abandoned her. She realized that was a very strange thought for a person that had fought all her life to control that temper.

The attorney waited a few minutes then cleared his throat and asked, "Well, Mrs. Robinson, I've already talked some to William about this and I think I know what you want to do. But you need to tell us how you want to pursue it."

Sally noticed that he was looking somewhere just beyond her shoulder. She took a breath, and William reached over and touched her arm. Just for a brief moment. Sally no longer worried about her voice breaking and knew that wasn't what was worrying William either.

So she sat up even straighter and cleared her own throat. Attorney or not he was going to look at her when they talked. She was looking directly at him and when he made eye contact he turned slightly red in the face.

Sally thought, 'Damnation. He believes everything in those papers.'

"Mr. Menefee, I don't want to offend you because I need your help. But if you're going to be my attorney you need to know that I'm a direct person." She said.

He waited a second to see if she was through speaking then replied. "Yes, William told me that you're not only direct but a somewhat forceful woman. That's just fine. So if you will, why don't you tell me how you feel about what has been said in these papers." And this time he was looking directly at her.

"Thank you." She said, and then it just boiled out. "Almost the only truthful statement in all of that is that we have two children. Nancy turned nine in January and Alfred will be six in May. Jesse and I were married by bond, in 1833. We lived together as man and wife until the middle of December of 1841.

"At least we lived together the few times he was at home. The separation was brought about by his roughness and cruelty, not only the physical, but all the things he constantly accused me of.

"For a long time before the separation he didn't provide any financial help to me or the children. I've had to make a living and take care of all our needs, including doing most all the work. Most of the times he was at home I had to put up with his loud, foul-talking, drunken friends dropping by. And that's more than any woman should have to take.

"And the property involved, and him being poor. . . ." She stopped talking. She was so upset and angry that she didn't think she could sit in the chair any longer.

"I'll tell you what." Menefee said. "Let's take a break from this and have a cup of coffee, although by now it's probably strong enough to bite us.

William, you want to give me a hand? It's in the other room. Maybe Sarah would like to have a minute to herself."

They all stood up and William squeezed her arm before he left the room. She walked over to the one little window in the room and gazed out at the back area behind the building. There was nothing to see, but she wasn't really looking at anything anyway. Her mind's eye was seeing a slew of rushing memory pieces, all sorts of bits and pieces that her talking had brought up.

There had to be some good things to remember, but at this moment they were all ugly. The thought that she was caught in a nightmare that would never end was interrupted by the two men returning to the room.

William gave her a sweet smile and handed her a cup of coffee. She took a small sip and nearly made a face. It was strong, bitter, and tasted burned but it'd keep her alert. They all took their seats again and the attorney started in right away. "I didn't ask, but it is alright if I call you Sarah?"

She nodded a quick yes.

"Well, Sarah. I need to ask you a few things of a personal nature and I'd like you to answer all you're comfortable with. Then we'll get to the property and finances of the two of you." He looked at her with a questioning look and she again nodded yes.

William said. "Sally, would you rather I stepped out for a few minutes?"

"No. I'd like you to stay here." She answered.

Menefee said. "To begin with I should've told you right at first that I know Jesse. I think everyone around does. That's going to be one of your problems. But we'll get to that later."

He then asked. "Sarah, how old are you?"

"I'm 25."

"And how old is Jesse?"

"He's 43."

"How old were the two of you when you got married?"

"He was 33 and I was 15. Close to 16." She quickly added.

"When was the first time that Jesse let you know he was interested in you? I mean like a woman and a man interest?"

Sally thought about that for a minute then asked. "Why does any of this matter?"

"It may not matter. But I need anything and everything I can get that might help you."

"I guess I knew what he was thinking right after my daddy died. And I'd just turned 13 then."

She felt William looking at her and hoped he didn't think badly of her. That thought was immediately followed by, 'Now why the hell do I feel guilty?'

She was glad when Mr. Menefee said, "Alright, Sarah. Just a few more questions and we'll get to the property part."

"About how often was Jesse gone from home?"

"It'd be a lot easier to tell you about how often he was home. Christmas through Nancy's birthday usually. That's about two weeks. Then usually a couple of weeks around Alfred's birthday in May. And maybe two or three other short visits during the year.

"All you have to do is make a list of every time something was going on in Texas and you can pretty much know that he was right in the middle of it. Probably before, during, and after."

"And now, Sarah. Did you abandon your husband and your children?"

"I did not! The kids and I were living on my property then. In December of year before last he came by and outsmarted me and took Alfred."

This was the first time that her voice broke. He gave her time to get her composure and in a moment she was able to continue. "Nancy wouldn't go with him. She's at my mama's house right now."

Menefee asked more questions about all that had happened when Alfred was taken. Then he said, "The most unpleasant thing I have to ask now is about the accusation of adultery." Sally noticed that his voice got quieter when he said 'adultery'. Like even the word was dirty.

She thought about George but very quickly pushed that thought away. There'd been nothing between her and Jesse when she got with George. "I didn't sleep with Joe Brown. He was a hired hand, nothing else. And I sure didn't have relations with "divers" other men, whatever the hell that's supposed to mean."

Menefee looked a touch startled when she said hell.

Sally said, "I'm sorry for the oath, sir. It's just hard not to get extremely angry over all this. I feel like I've already been convicted and sentenced without a hearing."

"Let's talk about the property now. I know some about your circumstances of course. I know the Newmans and Rabbs came in with Stephen Austin. God rest his soul. And that your mother, and you children, inherited a sizable amount of land.

"And let me say right now that I'm sorry I didn't have the privilege of knowing your father. I know all your mother's brothers, and a finer, more decent lot of men you just aren't going to meet. They're all three of absolutely sterling quality. I especially think highly of Judge Andrew Rabb."

Both Sally and William murmured the appropriate thanks you.

"To continue. I need to know all the information you can supply about your property and the property acquired or disposed of during the marriage between you and Jesse."

Sally answered all his questions and gave him as much information as she knew. When he was through with those questions, he asked them to please sit quietly for a few minutes while he finished his notes. They did.

"Sarah, I always endeavor to be totally honest with my clients." Menefee paused, then reading her direct look as a desire for just that, he continued.

"I'm going to try with everything at my disposal to win this for you. And you don't have to doubt that because I don't like to lose." He hesitated, looked down at the papers on his desk, and seemed to make up his mind about something.

"I don't think we have a good chance at all. I'm terribly sorry to tell you that, but I'd like you to be prepared. I think there is a chance we can keep the property you inherited from your family, but maybe not much else." He looked at her this time with sincere sympathy in his eyes. It could've been a comfort, but wasn't.

Every muscle felt like she'd been holding them tight for hours. She could only say the two words that had been running over and over in her mind. "My children?"

He almost shrugged, but didn't. "I'm just not sure. I'm sorry."

Sally could no longer control her expression, so walked around his desk and stood looking out the window.

"William, why don't you get a room at the hotel for Sarah. When the papers are ready, I'll get word to you and the two of you can come back and make sure everything is complete. It won't take too long.

Sally was so relieved to get out of that room. She was in such a state that William was leading her into a small room in the hotel and she didn't remember anything in between.

He said, "Sally, you need to eat something. I'll go to the store and get a few things. Alright?"

"I couldn't eat anything. I'm not hungry." Then large tears started running down her face.

"Sally, I'm hungry, so I'm going to go get me something to eat. I'll come back and check on you in a little while."

She didn't answer so he said, "I bet you haven't slept in days. Come lock the door behind me and lay down and get a little sleep. Please."

"I can't sleep," she said, but she followed him to the door.

He walked out in the hall and she shut the door. She knew he'd stand there until he heard her put the latch in. She walked over and lay down on the bed and the bedsprings made a loud squeak. Then she heard William walk slowly down the hall. Being raised with so many sisters, William was used to their tears, but she knew it still hurt him. She wished she wasn't putting him through this but she didn't know how she'd make it without him.

Sally stretched out on the uncomfortable bed and was asleep in less than a minute. Then she heard the strangest sound and thought it was Alfred playing with the little blocks he liked. But then she was awake and knew it wasn't Alfred, but someone quietly knocking on the door.

She went to the door and let William in. "I see you did sleep some." He said.

"Like a log, I guess." She answered. "What time is it?"

"It's almost five o'clock. We need to get over to Menefee's office. He has the papers ready."

"Alright. I need to comb my hair and straighten my clothes. And I'll need to go out back." She said.

"I'll meet you in the lobby."

It was only a few minutes until she joined William in the lobby. He was sitting on an old overstuffed settee and he motioned for her to join him. She was good at reading his face, so with dread she sat beside him and waited to hear his bad news.

"Jesse is in town."

"Is Alfred with him?" She asked.

"No. I spoke to him only briefly, but I did ask him where Alfred was. He said he thought it best he keep that to himself." She could see how agitated William was, so didn't say anything.

"You know, Sally, I've known Jesse Robinson more years than I can remember. Fought side by side with him many, many times. I've slept beside him, drank with him, and gotten into all kinds of scrapes with him, and now I just want to beat the hell out of him. It's hard. But you know all that, don't you?"

He stood up and said. "There's lots of people out at this time of day. Take my arm and let's go see Mr. Menefee. And Sally, you just be you." He got a grateful look from Sally.

Menefee read the papers he had prepared for her. She listened closely and made sure she heard the words, "it is intently out of her power to live longer with her said husband, and she prays the court to grant her a divorce . . . also prays the court to grant her the guardianship of her said children."

All the information about the property was there, including the land she'd inherited, the twenty-eight head of cattle she'd owned when they married, and the other property items that were hers. She was trying to follow along with the copy she was given, but it was close to impossible for her, so she was just listening.

"...alleges that since the marriage a tract of three quarters of a League and one labor, of land since acquired by her husband, was a grant from the Government to him as his head right which is a part of the gains of matrimony, situated in the County of Jackson and upon which the plaintiff now resides. She prays for a partition of the said land . . . And for all other relief. She prays for judgement for costs, etc. Menefee & Fields, Attorney for Defendant."

Mr. Menefee looked at Sally and said. "Now, is that acceptable to you?"

"Yes, sir. It is. Thank you."

"Good then. Now you must meet me here a bit before nine o'clock in the morning because Court will commence at nine. I've got us scheduled first thing. I have only a few suggestions. Don't say anything unless you are asked a question. Glance at the jurors occasionally so that they'll see that you're paying attention, but please don't make eye contact with anyone. Your direct gaze tends to be somewhat disconcerting. Just try to remain calm. All right?"

"What is dis-con-certing?" Sally asked quietly. "Like intimidating?"

"That's close enough," he said. Then he got up, came around the desk, and reached for her hand.

She stood up and he took her right hand in both of his.

"I wish we could make you look a bit plain, frumpy, and helpless, but I don't think that's possible. We'll just pray for results tomorrow. Try to get some rest tonight and I'll see you in the morning."

Sally said "Thank you. Very much." And really meant it. She'd noticed that he'd talked to her this evening and not to her through William.

It was almost dark outside as she and William crossed over to the hotel. When they entered the lobby, Sally saw her four other brothers waiting for them. She started toward the settee where they were gathered and then felt herself slipping into that black pool of water. She couldn't understand what was happening, tried to fight, but lost.

She woke up about half way up the stairs. Joseph was carrying her and the other four were all getting in the way. William got the door of her room open. She was trying to get Joseph to put her down, and was being ignored. He kind of dumped her on the bed and all five were standing around the bed looking awkward.

Sally raised up on an elbow and said, "You know if this hadn't been one of the worst days of my life, this would be one of the funniest things that's happened to me. What are you boys doing here?"

They all started to talk at once and Sally raised her hand. "Wait! Thomas, you're the oldest of the youngers, so what's going on?"

"No, wait a minute." Joseph interrupted. "What's wrong with you? Are you sick or hurt?"

"She fainted. That's all." William said. "She hasn't eaten hardly anything for days and with all the emotions this cursed day has brought about its not a bit surprising."

Before anyone else could say anything more, Sally said. "As soon as you tell me what's going on, then I'll let you feed me. Alright?"

Thomas told her what she wanted to hear. "Nancy is fine. Mama was worried about you and would of come to be with you, but she thought Nancy needed her more than you do. She asked Ali and me to come see if you and William needed anything. And of course there was no getting away without Joseph and Andy. So here we all are."

"The whole family is thinking about you, Sally." Added Ali.

"And this part of the family could eat a hog. Uncooked. Have you heard enough? Now can we get something to eat?" Joseph asked in a teasing manner.

Sally smiled at him and asked. "William, do you think we'd get in trouble if we brought some food up to the room? I don't think I want to look at anyone else tonight. Just the beautiful faces of my brothers."

William said, "I'm sure it's done all the time. I'll go over to the store and get some things."

"I'll go, William. You look nearly as tired as Sally. I can tell it hasn't been a day either one of you want to do again." And Thomas motioned to Andy and they left the room.

Joseph looked like he wanted to go too, but he didn't insist. Sally was sitting at the top of the bed leaning against a pillow, and Ali was sitting at the end of the bed.

"William, come sit here on the bed." And she patted the place beside her. "Thomas is right. You look tired."

William didn't object. He groaned when he sat down and they all laughed.

There was one straight-backed chair in the room and Joseph moved it over beside Sally, turned it backward, and sat straddling it. Sally reached down and patted him on the knee, then reached and patted Ali on the leg. He gave her a smile and then said something to William.

She really looked at Ali for a moment. 'Oh, dear God. He's gotten so thin. He's just nineteen. And he looks exhausted. I've done nothing but feel sorry for myself for months and haven't noticed Ali. Poor Mama. She must be scared to death about him.'

She felt Joseph looking at her. When she looked his way, he just barely nodded his head from side to side. She understood. Ali wouldn't want her worrying about him when he was here to support her. He'd never liked anyone making him feel different from his brothers.

It was a struggle not to start crying, but she was able to think of all the love being sent her way this evening and it gave her strength. Now if she could call on that tomorrow.

About that time Thomas and Andy came back. They had all kinds of food and Andy was excited about getting to go to the store. He'd talked Thomas into getting a piece of candy for each of them.

When they noticed the candy, Thomas explained, "Well, I thought maybe we deserved a treat for a change, and besides, I charged it all to Mama's account."

That got a laugh from everyone and they dug into the food. Sally ate more than she'd eaten in days, and they all laughed at the amount of food both Joseph and Andy consumed. They sat and talked for an hour or so until one of them noticed that both William and Ali had fallen asleep.

Sally said. "Let's just let them sleep. William's bedroll is over there and I'll use it. I see all of your bedrolls are here too so why don't we all find a spot on the floor.

Thomas said. "We ought to go out to the place we usually camp. That way you could have the room and not be so crowded."

"I've never slept in a hotel before." Joseph said.

"Me neither." Added Andy.

"Then that settles it." Sally said. "Besides, I'd really like to have all my brothers here tonight."

By eight thirty the next morning they were all at the attorney's office. William introduced the two youngest boys to Mr. Menefee. He already knew Thomas and Ali.

William said. "We want to know what you think is going to happen today and if there's anything any of us can do to help Sally."

Mr. Menefee called to his clerk to bring in some more chairs and in the meantime led Sally to the seat in front of his desk.

He said. "You look like you slept some last night. And perhaps ate a bite or two?"

Sally nodded yes to both statements. Right now she didn't even want to think about food. She was so nervous that she was afraid she'd get sick at her stomach.

As soon as they were all seated, he began. "Men that are potential jurors shouldn't go around saying what they think about a case that's scheduled to come up in court, but the truth is they do. It would be inappropriate for me to be soliciting that kind of information, but I've had my clerk and a couple of friends 'listening'."

He hesitated for a long minute, then looked directly at Sally and said, "There is a special regard shown to the early settlers that paid such a price for the rest of us. So around here the Newman family and the Rabb family are thought of with respect. Your mother, Rachel, is held in high regard. And there's some sympathy toward you, Sarah."

Sally spoke for the first time. "But, Jesse Robinson was an early settler too. He fought in almost every battle for independence. Was even one of the heroes at San Jacinto. And he's a man, so he's going to win. Twelve men that know nothing about my children are going to take them away from me and give them to a father that is never home."

"That can't happen, can it?" "That's not right." Came from two of the boys.

Before the attorney could answer, Sally asked. "When will he get to take them?"

"His attorney has talked to me, and in the event that Jesse wins custody of the children, they will pick them up tomorrow. Jesse is willing to allow you this evening with your daughter. But it is to be a supervised visit at your mother's house. It wouldn't surprise me if two or three deputized men aren't already there to be sure your daughter is not gone when Jesse arrives." Menefee told her.

Sally thought she was going to faint again and grabbed on to the arms of the chair. Menefee got up quickly and went around his desk to her chair. He called to his clerk to bring a glass of water. All the brothers were standing close by and the anger and frustration was like a live being in the room. Both Thomas and Joseph were angrily pacing the floor.

"It's almost time to get over to the court. You don't have to be there, Sarah. You can wait here in the office and we'll return as soon as a verdict is in. I promise I'll do everything I can to win this for you." And he patted her on the arm.

Then Menefee said. "William, it won't help Sarah now or in the next few days if your brothers lose their tempers."

William asked. "Sally?"

"I want to stay here." She said.

"None of us will make trouble. Sally is what's important here." And William looked around at his brothers.

Sally said. "Please." They all nodded agreement, but it was hard for Thomas and Joseph to do.

"I'll stay with Sally." Ali said.

Each of the other four managed to touch her someway–a squeeze on the shoulder or a touch on the arm–and then they filed out after the attorney.

Ali talked for a long time about the things he remembered as a little boy. Sally knew he was trying to keep her mind occupied, and she tried to join him in some of the memories. She tried to concentrate on what he was saying but found it too difficult to do. Eventually they both sat in silence, with Ali holding her hand.

Around noontime she heard a number of voices outside the building and knew that the court was probably in recess. She stood up and Ali stood beside her. She heard a deep sigh from him. Then the attorney and William walked into the room.

Sally looked at them closely and still couldn't tell the outcome.

Mr. Menefee asked her to please sit down again, and she did. He started in immediately with the news. "Well, Sarah, we have news that is not good, but could be much worse. Not to keep you waiting, I will tell you the findings of the jury. We won't get the paperwork until later today."

Sally wanted to scream 'What about my children?' But she just watched his mouth moving in slow motion. It was all right though because that was the speed her mind was moving in too. Like trying to think in molasses.

He was referring to some notes and said, "The final papers will read. 'We, the jury find for the Plaintiff a divorce on the grounds of excessive and cruel treatment on the part of the Defendant and that all the property, real and personal, be equally divided between the parties after the payment of all debts, now existing against them'.

"You realize that means the jury granted Jesse a divorce and its not very complimentary to you. But we were able to get the property divided between the two of you. And also to keep your name from being besmirched further in open court.

"But of course of primary concern to you, the jury did not grant custody of the children to either one of you."

Sally and Ali both let out a pent up breath and she asked. "What does that mean. Then who has custody?"

"Well, because they found for Jesse as to the divorce, his lawyer is saying that means they gave him custody of the children. But that isn't the case. I believe it just means that those twelve good men just didn't want to decide for or against either one of you.

"I'm not sure how you should handle it. I could advise you to go back to court in a short time and seek full custody, but that might be a dangerous thing to do. They could still go against you. I think the prudent thing to do is to go home and take good care of your daughter."

He stood up, walked around the desk, and took her hand. "I have another matter scheduled for this afternoon and I need to find time for a bite to eat. So, I will tell you goodbye for now. If you'll ask someone to come by later this evening or tomorrow, I'll have those papers ready. They can be picked up from my clerk."

Sally stood and shook his hand. "Thank you, Mr. Menefee. Thank you very much."

"You are more than welcome. I wish the outcome could've been better for you." Menefee said goodbye to William and Ali, then turned back to Sally.

As he showed them to the door he said. "You're divorced now, Sarah. Good luck to you."

Sally was in a daze and allowed Ali to lead her out the front door. The other three boys had the horses ready and the six immediately mounted and rode out of town. Sally was aware of numerous people staring at her as she rode away.

They were out of town but hadn't reached the river crossing when she had to stop. She lost what little breakfast she'd eaten. Dismounting, she went over to the river, leaned down and scooped up a handful of water and rinsed her mouth. Then she wet her kerchief and wiped her face with it.

When she looked, her brothers were all looking at her like this was something she could just handle by herself. She almost laughed. "You'd have fought that whole damn town, but you sure as hell don't want to clean me up when I'm puking."

She got a few grins. Then Joseph rode over and reached down for her horse's bridle. As he led her horse away, he said. "Come over here. Away from what you just did and let's have something to eat. I'm starving."

"You're always starving." Thomas said. But they all joined Joseph.

"We need to talk anyway." William said.

"Yes, I know." Sally agreed. But they were quiet while they ate some biscuits and dried meat.

Sally ate only a part of a biscuit then said. "I can't tell you what it meant to me to have you all there. I don't think I could've gotten through these last two days without you."

She waited a minute to get her voice under control then went on. "Now I want to tell you what I'd like for you to do. I don't trust Jesse any farther than I can spit, so I'd like for Thomas and Ali to go right on to Mama's house and make sure Nancy is there when I get there.

"And since I know you guys won't agree to let me go off by myself, I'd like for Joseph and Andy to stay with me." She looked at the two of them and said. "I just need you to give me a little room for an hour or so and then we can head for home too." They both nodded.

William said. "I'm staying with you too, Sally. Until I see you safe at Mama's house. You can have whatever time you need."

"No, William. You're not going to do that. I've kept you away from your wife and baby long enough. I know you have all kinds of work waiting on you and you're tired. This has been almost as hard on you as it's been on me. Please just go home and tell Martha Ann how much I appreciate you being with me."

He started to protest so she walked over to him and said. "William. You know what wonderful brothers Mama has?" And she waited until he nodded yes then continued. "Well, you're a match for all of them. You've been there for me all my life. And after Daddy died, you took on the roll of father to all of us and we love you for it."

She stood on tiptoe and kissed him on the cheek, and saw that his eyes were full of tears. He got on his horse, started to say something, then just waved to them all and rode off toward his home.

"I don't need any arguments from the rest of you. I've had all the emotions I can stand today and I need to get myself together before I get to Mama's house. I just need a little time to myself. Besides I'm the oldest here now so that ought to mean something."

Thomas said, "Ali and I'll head on home. Mama won't let Nancy out of her sight, but we'll make sure." He went and gave her a hug then got on his horse.

Sally went over to where Ali was leaning against his horse. She hugged him and then touched him on the face. "Thank you for being there for me. I love you, Ali."

"I love you too, Sally." It took two tries before he was able to pull himself up on his horse. Sally wanted to help him but she did just what Thomas and the other two boys did. She acted like she didn't notice.

She was still watching the two ride away when Joseph asked. "What do you want us to do, Sally?"

"Just ride down the river toward the crossing. Stay where you can see me if that'll make you feel better, but I don't want you close enough that you can hear me. And please hurry, because I can't hold this together any longer."

She didn't look at them, just listened as they mounted their horses and rode off. Her chest felt as if there was a weight on it so heavy that it made it hard to breath. She was filled with sadness and an almost overpowering fear. A fear that she might never get Alfred back and might lose Nancy too. She walked over to one of the big cottonwood trees and sat down with her back to it and she wept so loudly that she was afraid the boys would hear her.

But there was no way to be quiet when she hurt this much. Finally she stopped crying. She got up and dusted herself off and went and got on her horse. She rode over to the river and stopped to let the horse drink. As she sat looking at the Colorado River slowly flowing along, she shuddered. The horse raised his head and moved nervously as if to see what had frightened his rider. Sally automatically soothed the horse, then wished she could sooth herself as easily.

She heard again the words Mr. Menefee had said to her. 'You're divorced now, Sarah. Good luck to you.'

"Right. Good luck to me. If two people that love each other can turn that love into hate what chance do they have with anyone else? I'm going to need a lot more than good luck."

She looked again at the Colorado River, really seeing it this time. And she thought about how her life seemed to be moving along like that river and she didn't have any control over either one.

CHAPTER 17

"Sally"!

Startled, Sally turned around and faced her mother. "Mama, what are you doing here?"

At the same time Nancy jumped up from what she was doing and ran toward Mama yelling, "Gramma."

"Well, I'm here because you don't seem to realize that I worry about you when I don't hear from you for so long." She hugged Nancy and added, "Hello, sweet child."

It was obvious that Mama was pretty agitated, so Sally knew she needed to make extra efforts to calm the situation down. She put down the hoe she'd been weeding with, wiped her hands on a rag, and went and gave Mama a long hug. She thought, 'Interesting the difference in the voice used when she talked to me and the one when she said hello to Nancy.'

Joseph and Andy came over and also got hugs, but they immediately made some excuse about needing to take care of the horses. Joseph picked up Nancy and the three of them made a fast retreat. Sally knew from their actions and quietness that they were more than willing to let her deal with Mama.

"I'm glad to see you, Mama. Let's go have a cup of coffee and you can tell me how everyone is doing and what's been going on."

She could see that Mama had a lot to say, but she caught her by the arm and led her over to the house. She was hoping she could put any conversation about herself off at least for awhile. She'd try to get Mama to talk about the other families first.

But before they even got to the porch Mama started in on her. "Sally, you're thin as a rail, and I can't believe we rode right up to the house and you didn't even notice we were anywhere close until I spoke. That's just not like you."

Sally didn't even make an attempt to answer because she knew Mama had a lot more to say. She poured them both a cup of coffee and got ready for the rest of it.

"So where is Mr. Scull today?" Mama asked.

'Damn.' Sally thought. 'Just as I think she'll chew on me awhile she asks a question so that I'll have to answer her.'

But before she had time to answer Mama gave her a sad little smile and said, "Sit down, Child, and lets talk."

Sally put the coffee pot back on the stove then sat down at the table. "First, tell me how Ali is doing?"

"He's not doing well, but I'll tell you all about the family later. Right now I want to hear about you."

"George is over close to Egypt, shoeing some horses for a man. He'll be back this evening."

Sally thought about how shocked Mama and the rest of the family had been when she married George Scull on March twentieth, just two weeks after the divorce. She dragged her thinking back to what Mama had said. "I'm a bit thinner than usual cause it's been so hot this summer. You're awful thin too, Mama. Are you feeling alright?"

"You're just determined not to talk about yourself, aren't you?" Mama said. "But, I'm not going to let you get away with it this time. Have you heard anything more about when you'll get to see Alfred again?"

Sally answered, "Jesse has agreed to let Alfred spend next month with Nancy and me, and then Nancy and Alfred will spend the next one with him. We've done it once since the divorce and it worked out pretty well. It sure helps to be able to meet at your house to make the exchange. I know it's hard on all of you but I'm sure thankful we can do it that way."

"I'm glad the two of you meet at my house. That way I get to see Alfred too." Mama said.

They were both silent for a time. Then Sally broke the silence and talked about George and her, and how surprisingly pleasant it was when Nancy and Alfred were with them. She finished with. "George is a nice man."

She saw Mama look at her with as close to no expression as she could manage, and Sally thought, 'That's probably a really lame thing to say about your new husband.'

Mama changed the subject by telling about some of what was happening with the family and the neighbors. She'd heard from Uncle John recently and all the Rabb families seemed to be doing alright.

Sally knew they were both putting it off, but at a pause in the conversation she said. "Mama, please tell me about Ali."

"He's getting weaker all the time." Mama said quietly. "He doesn't have enough energy to help with even the light work now and that really disturbs him. The doctor told me there wasn't anything he could do for him, so for us to just keep him as comfortable as we can.

"I think it's almost harder on Thomas than it is on me. You know how close he and Ali have always been. Sometimes in the middle of the night, when I go to see about Ali, I find Thomas sitting on the side of the bed, holding his hand. Lately Thomas works on whatever will keep him close to the house and Joseph and Andy have taken on more of the work so that Thomas can be with Ali."

Sally thought about Ali and about how often they'd lost someone they loved. As bad as the thought of losing her brother was, she couldn't even imagine the pain it must be causing Mama. She got up and went and put her arms around her.

Mama let her hug her only a moment, then got up from the chair and said, "I need to get back to the house. Louisa and Thomas are watching out for Ann Eliza and Ali and they'll all be worrying about the boys and me."

"I'd ask you to stay longer, but I know you need to get home." Sally said, and when they walked out on the porch, she saw that Joseph and Andy were both sitting on the porch with Nancy, ready to go. She suddenly realized how quiet they'd been.

"Mama, Nancy and I'll come over tomorrow for a few days. It's time for a visit. Tell Ali I'll bring some of my dried blackberries and we'll have a big cobbler."

"That's a good idea. Ali will be pleased to see you."

Sally and Nancy gave all three of them a hug, got hugs in return, then stood and watched them leave. Instead of going back to work Sally sat down in a rocking chair on the porch. She sat there for a long time thinking of Ali and her family. When her thoughts drifted in the direction of Alfred she got up and went back to work hoeing weeds out of the garden.

Later as she was getting supper started she also got things ready for a few days at Mama's house. George wouldn't mind taking care of things here.

Sally allowed her thoughts to turn to her husband. 'He is a nice man and he tries hard to make me happy, and I am happier than I've been in awhile. But getting married for the reason I did wasn't very smart. It isn't going to help me get Alfred back. In fact it just looks worse because I married George so soon after the divorce. I can't seem to do anything right.'

She'd arrived back at Mama's house the day of the divorce and allowed Mama to talk her into staying one night with the family. But by early the next morning she and Nancy went back home. Sally was surprised that Jesse gave her no problems about Nancy. She'd expected trouble.

When George came over a few days after she got home she told him she wanted to talk to him about a very personal matter. That's when she told him she thought it would look better if she were married in case Jesse went to court to try to get the children. And she wondered if he would consider marrying her. She could see by the look on his face that she'd hurt him. She was sorry for that but it was too late by then.

He said he'd have to think about it and left. When he came back a day later she knew what he'd decided. "Sally, I never told you how I feel about you because you were a married woman. So I guess I can't fault you for not knowing how deep my feelings are. Lord help me, I care so much for you that I'm agreeable to marrying even under these circumstances. I'd just appreciate it if you'd keep the reason we're getting married just between us."

Sally had taken Nancy to Mama's house to stay for a few days and she and George had gotten married on the twentieth of March, just ten days after the divorce. She ignored the looks she got from the Clerk and the Judge but it was harder to ignore the looks that Mama and Louisa couldn't hide.

George seemed to be happy and he tried to make her happy, which was different than when she'd been with Jesse. At first she thought that maybe this wasn't a bad decision and that she could learn to love him and make this a good marriage. But she was beginning to wonder.

And she still wasn't really sure why she'd done what she did. Was it actually because she thought it'd look better if she were married? Or was it to spite Jesse? She thought it might just be more of the latter.

Sally brought her mind back to the present and looked at Nancy who was happily playing with her doll. She watched her a few minutes then went to the window and looked in the direction Mama and the boys had gone. She wished she'd gone with them.

'So am I regretting that I married George? It's a little late for that and a silly thought to have. Besides the lovemaking is fine and his work around the place is fine. He gets along fine with my family too. And maybe that's what's wrong. Everything is just fine. Hell, nice weather is fine.'

She turned back from looking out the window and said, "Well, little Miss Nancy, let's get supper on the table. Too much thinking is going to make me crazy."

It was almost Christmas time again and Sally was hoping she'd get to have some time with Alfred. She and Jesse had managed to be civil enough the two times they'd met. She'd gotten to have Alfred twice during the year and she'd let Jesse have Nancy two times also. But it was very difficult for both of them because neither one trusted the other.

Sally had thought often of taking both children and leaving the country. But when she tried to actually plan for that she knew she couldn't leave her family. She worried that Jesse might be thinking of the same possibilities. And she knew that the only reason Jesse had brought Nancy back the times he'd kept her was because of Nancy herself. But what if someday he decided that he wouldn't bring her back no matter if that's what she wanted or not. Sally worried about it each time, but when Christmas time came they again shared the time with the two children.

It was obvious to everyone that Ali was not going to live much longer. He coughed more and more and he was too weak to get out of bed but for very short periods. By the end of January all of the family was visiting Mama's house almost daily. After a visit in early February, Sally told George that she was going to stay at Mama's house to help out. She knew it couldn't be long.

And during the night, in the middle of February 1844, Ali died. Mama and all the sisters and brothers were by his bed to tell him goodbye. Ali was the first child in their family to die, and he'd lived almost twenty-one years, far longer than they'd thought possible. Most of the people they knew had lost a brother or a sister and some had lost more than just one or two. They knew they'd been fortunate. The world they lived in was a hard one.

They buried Ali in the Newman Cemetery beside Daddy, and that evening wasn't just about tears and heartache. They talked and reminisced about this beloved brother and all the good things they'd remember about him. Sally thought to herself, 'The only things I remember about him are good. I don't think there were any bad things. But the Ali I'll remember best is the one that held my hand in that lawyer's office, when I needed someone so much.'

William talked Thomas into going with him for a week to help with some major fence work he had planned. Sally thought it was something William had been waiting to do until this time because he was worried about how Thomas would handle Ali's death. She thought that Thomas was aware of that too but was probably relieved to have some hard work to do.

Jesse had come to Ali's funeral, which didn't surprise Sally. He'd known Ali since he was born. Against her better judgement and against Nancy's wishes, Sally let Jesse take Nancy back to the ranch with him. She thought she should stay at Mama's house a few days to help; Louisa was too broken up to be of any help. As soon as she went back home she could send word to Jesse that she wanted Nancy back home with her.

Sally stayed a week then went home. She sent a message to Jesse and waited for a week, which was more than enough time for him to get a reply to her. She sent a second more direct message and still didn't hear. By this time she was not only worried, but also very angry.

George didn't want to, but she insisted they go get the children. She knew the set-up of the ranch and the best way to get there without being detected and they went without telling anyone what they were going to do. They sat beneath some trees for a day and a half before they got the opportunity to get the children. Jesse and two men rode off during the second morning and Sally waited until they were out of sight then got on her horse and rode straight up to the ranch house. She'd told George to wait under the trees for her; she thought that'd be safer for all of them, especially George.

She didn't want George or her to run into Jesse in a situation like this. She'd seen the two men exchange some dirty looks at Ali's funeral. Sally couldn't tell George, but she hoped he was aware that he couldn't win if he took Jesse on.

She tied her horse to the porch rail and went in through the kitchen door. A Negro woman of about fifty was stirring something in a frying pan and nearly dropped the spoon she was stirring with. She didn't say anything just stared at Sally.

Nancy jumped up from the table and ran to her. Sally held her next to her and looked at Alfred. He stood up but didn't move her direction and it was like a knife twisting inside her. Sally thought, 'I've lost him to Jesse.'

"Alfred. I'm taking Nancy home with me and I wish you'd go with us." She said.

Tears welled up in his eyes. "I want to stay with Daddy. He needs one of us."

As Sally fought with her own tears she thought, 'He didn't say "I should stay or I guess I'll stay." He said, "I want to stay with Daddy."'

She said to Nancy, "Go get your stuff, Honey."

The Negro woman had barely moved a muscle but at this point she said, "Miss Nancy. I don't think Mr. Jesse would like you leaving."

Nancy never even slowed down.

Sally said, "I don't want to hurt anyone, but I will if it's necessary. And the gun I'm wearing isn't for show. I can shoot a hole in the spoon you're holding before you can move your hand."

The woman looked down at the spoon and didn't say anything else.

Sally said, "Alfred, I won't force you to do anything you don't want to do. But I would really like to hug you if it's alright."

He came to her and she picked him up and hugged him tightly. "I love you more than you'll probably ever know, Alfred. Will you remember that?"

"Yes. I love you too, Mama."

Then she and Nancy were on the horse and riding out of the yard with Alfred standing at the kitchen door watching them.

For the next few months Sally stayed constantly on guard and usually managed to know when Jesse was in the area. At those times she'd take Nancy and be away from the house when he came by. She'd heard that he was furious about her taking Nancy.

Alfred's seventh birthday was on May 28 and Sally had made him a quirt. She knew she couldn't go see him, but she asked Joseph and Andy if they'd take her gift and one from Nancy to him. When they returned they had the quirt with them. Jesse had let them leave the gift from Nancy but sent Sally's gift back to her.

She asked Joseph how Alfred looked and he said, "Well, he's grown a bit and he looked healthy. But he's so quiet you don't know what he's thinking. And he doesn't smile much."

The rest of the summer went by about like the spring had. Jesse was so busy with his ranch and the military situations that he didn't try to visit. Sally hoped he'd finally gotten to the point that he'd realize he couldn't live the life he was accustomed to and also take care of a daughter. But she didn't let her guard down.

During the early fall, Jesse got word to Sally, through William, that he planned on seeing Nancy at Christmas time and was willing to visit with her at the Newman house. But he didn't want to see Sally or her husband. And he wanted it to be clear that if it didn't turn out that way, his next step would be with the sheriff, to get his daughter.

Sally wanted to see Alfred so bad it hurt, but she didn't think that was going to be possible. She'd known when she took Nancy and Alfred chose not to go with her that she was ruining her chances of getting to visit with him. Even though she hadn't wanted it to be that way, she'd felt like she had no other choice. And because of what she'd done she now couldn't trust Jesse. If he ever got Nancy she'd never get her back.

Earlier in the year George had made a suggestion that was very unsettling to her, but she thought about it now. He'd said, "Sally, you could take Nancy to Louisiana and hide her in a convent until she's older and can make her own choice as to where she wants to live."

"A convent. That's awful. We aren't even Catholic."

"That don't matter. The nuns take real good care of children. And Nancy would get a better education than she'd get anywhere around here." George answered.

Sally remembered that conversation but again put it out of her mind. Until one beautiful November day when Mama, Joseph, Andy, and Ann Eliza came over for a visit. Sally was always glad to see them, but knew that it wasn't good news by the look on Mama's face.

After finding out that the rest of the family was fine for now, Sally heated the coffee. It was such a nice day, that they all sat on the front porch and talked for awhile. Then Mama asked Joseph and Andy to take Nancy and Ann Eliza to play with the new colt.

Sally thought 'Now I'll find out what brought them over; I wish someday it'd be just for a pleasant visit.'

"William saw Jesse in Columbus and he said he's going to go to court to get custody of the children, then he's going to keep them permanently." Mama said.

"He's been threatening to do that for months. Does William think he's serious this time?"

"He told William that just this last month his family finally settled his father's estate in Tennessee. He said there wasn't any great amount of money or land, but it made him think about his father and his family. So now he wants both his children, all the time." Mama answered.

By this time Sally was pacing back and forth on the front porch. She stopped and said, "He's already got Alfred to a point where he barely knows I'm his mother. And he knows that Nancy wants to live with me. He's not satisfied to keep me from seeing my son; he wants to keep me from seeing either one of them. Well, he's not getting Nancy away from me."

Mama said, "Jesse told William that he didn't have any desire to make it any worse for you so he'd rather work it out where you could bring Nancy to my house for him to pick her up. He'd even let you see Alfred while he gets Nancy."

"Oh, Mama! You know he'd love to make me as unhappy as possible."

"He told William that if he had to he'd definitely be coming out with the Sheriff, even if he had to camp out in your front yard until he can get Nancy. I agreed to give you this message and I'll take your reply back for William to pass on to him." Mama stopped and waited on Sally to say something.

Sally was standing looking at the children playing with the little colt and didn't answer.

"I don't like being any part of this because the children belong to both of you. But I can't see Nancy not living with you. A daughter should be with her mother. What will you do?" Mama asked.

Sally said. "First of all you couldn't take the message back that I have for Jesse Robinson. The words wouldn't fit in your mouth." Then she turned to face her and said, "I'm sorry, Mama. I'm sorry you and William and all the family have had to be involved in all of this. It's not only hurtful it's embarrassing."

Sally paced back and forth for a few minutes then sat down beside Mama and blurted out, "George said I could take Nancy to Louisiana and hide her in a convent until she's old enough to make her own choice as to where she wants to live."

Mama jerked and was practically sputtering as she said, "What? A convent! Sally, what in the world are you thinking of? Oh dear God."

Sally immediately regretted telling Mama and said, "Mama, I shouldn't have told you that, and you must not tell anyone, not anyone. Please! Do you understand?"

"Of course I understand that. But why couldn't you just move somewhere with Nancy where he couldn't find you? Why would you have to leave her in a convent? I don't like that idea at all."

In a quiet desperate voice Sally said, "I can't move away and never see you and my family again. I've thought about it for a long time and I just can't give my family up.

"I hoped Jesse would just keep on the go, and leave Nancy with me. He can take a boy like Alfred with him some of the time, but not a little girl. He's never home, so who'd be raising her? And when he is home he has those rough rowdy men around all the time. I'm just not going to let him take her. I don't like the idea of a convent either, Mama, but I think it'd be best for Nancy until I can figure out how to do something different. At least in a convent she'd be taken care of."

After Mama had gone, Sally said, "Nancy, lets make you a dress with that fabric we got last week." And as she looked at Nancy she knew she'd made an awful decision.

That night after Nancy had fallen asleep, Sally said, "George, we need to talk. Come out on the porch with me so that Nancy won't hear us." Then Sally discussed not only the decision to take Nancy to a convent, but her decision to sell some of her land to have enough money to do what she needed to do.

"We can sell my land, Sally. I know how much your daddy's land means to you." George said.

"Thank you, George. I mean that." Sally said. "But as important as this land is to me and as much as I hate to break it up, it's just a material thing.

I'm about to break two hearts, Nancy's and mine.

"It's not like I'm the first one to sell Daddy's land either. My sister, Mary, sold her land three years ago, and Thomas sold a hundred acres of his the next year. William sold his last year and Mama sold Ali's land in July. I won't sell all my land, only a hundred acres or so. I need the money."

Sally thought, 'Convincing George is easy, it's me I'm still having to work on. So it's time to make a move.'

"George, will you go to town tomorrow and ask around quietly to see who might want to buy some of my land? I don't want to leave Nancy with anyone right now and I don't want to take her where I might run into Jesse."

The deal was struck a few days later and Sally ended up selling two hundred and twenty nine acres of her land to Charles Worland. She, Nancy, and George rode to town and signed the papers on November 13. The nine hundred dollars she got made the pain of selling her land much easier to handle. And she consoled herself with the knowledge that she still had over three hundred acres left.

She also knew that word would soon get to Jesse that she'd sold a piece of her land. He knew what that land meant to her so he'd immediately know that she was up to something. It was getting close to the time to make the next painful move.

Sally spent the next month thinking that every day might be the day that Jesse would come for Nancy. It was a terrible time. So a week before Christmas she decided they'd go stay at George's cabin until after Nancy's birthday in January and hope to avoid Jesse that way. She still hadn't heard any more about a custody suit so she had hopes that he wouldn't follow through with it. But she knew Jesse would come to her house and then to Mama's house at Christmas time to get Nancy. So that meant not spending Christmas with the family, another thing to add to the list of why she disliked Jesse so much.

She took Nancy and they went and spent a day with Mama and the family. Privately, Sally let Mama know what she was planning to do and told her not to worry if she didn't see her for awhile.

Then she got Joseph aside. "I'm going to be gone for a few weeks. Will you take care of my animals for awhile? Without letting anyone know what's going on?"

"Sure. By anyone I'd guess you mean Jesse?" He asked.

"Yes. He's threatening to take Nancy again, and I'm not going to let him. So we're going to get lost for awhile. Until he gets tired of looking."

"You want me to do anything else to help?" He asked.

Sally wasn't sure what he meant and she didn't ask. She just said. "No."

"It could be that I bring the animals over here and have Andy take over checking on your house and buildings. That is if this war with Mexico actually takes place. Cause I'll go join up." He said.

Sally found herself looking at Joseph from a different view. He was her little brother, but now she could see a tall, strong young man of seventeen. She couldn't imagine him going to war and hoped he'd never have too. She gave him a hug and wondered where all the years had gone. The rest of the day was colored by Mama acting miserable and sad and Sally thinking about how her family was getting older. Finally the day was just no fun so she got Nancy and left.

The next day she packed all the things that meant anything to her and all of Nancy's things and was ready to go. Her explanation to Nancy was that they were going to go stay at George's cabin for awhile and she might need some of the things. They'd stayed at George's place a few times before, but the cabin was small and rough so she got some long questioning looks from Nancy.

They stayed at the cabin through Christmas and the rest of the month of December. Then a few days into January, Joseph and Andy came to see them. They had some gifts for Nancy from Jesse and Alfred. They'd been left at Mama's house.

Sally asked Nancy to show Andy all the improvements they'd made to George's cabin. Then she told George she was going to go outside with Joseph. She knew he felt left out but this was her business and she was going to handle it.

She put on her coat and joined Joseph outside. "What's happening at home. Is everyone alright?"

"Everyone's just fine and your place is just fine too. We came so I could tell you that Jesse filed a paper asking for full and permanent custody of Nancy. I got a copy of it for you." And he handed her the papers.

"Thank you. I'll read it later." She walked over to the shed out of the wind and Joseph followed. "Damn him. I'd hoped he'd leave it alone."

"Sally. Ever since we were at your house that time Mama's acted different. She's always worrying about us, but she seems to be especially worried about you right now. What's going on with you?"

Sally looked at him thinking of whether to tell him the truth or not.

He said, "It's not fair for Mama to have to carry a heavy load all by herself. If I can help you know I will."

So she told him about taking Nancy to a convent and asked him not to let anyone except Mama know what she'd told him.

"Damn, Sally. That sounds like an awful thing to do to a little girl."

"I know that." She growled. "I'm sorry, Joseph. The truth is I don't know what else to do. I'm not going to let Jesse have her."

They all visited through the evening and then the boys left the next morning. Sally told George what Jesse had done and that it probably wouldn't be many days before he or someone from the Sheriff's office came to George's place to get Nancy. Sally told him she was ready to go to Louisiana, so they packed what they needed for a long trip and left the next day.

Sally knew Nancy was wondering what was going on but she didn't want her to know the truth yet. She didn't know how in the world she was going to tell her what she was going to do. So she told her she thought it'd be nice to see some country they hadn't seen before. George started telling them all about the country they were traveling through and what Louisiana and the people there were like. Sally barely listened to him, but was grateful that he was keeping Nancy somewhat occupied. To Sally it was a horrible trip.

They took two weeks to get to Louisiana and then spent another month traveling through that state. They were all fascinated with New Orleans and the ocean. They were told it wasn't an ocean, it was the gulf. But to Sally and Nancy it looked like an ocean. It could have been a wonderfully fun time but Sally could tell that even Nancy was watching and waiting.

On the trip to Louisiana, Sally had done everything she could think of to throw Jesse off their trail. She didn't think he'd ever guess where to look so she no longer worried about that. Now her problem was leaving Nancy.

They drifted slowly back to the western part of Louisiana and camped a little way away from the convent that George had suggested. Very early one morning Sally left before Nancy was awake, leaving George to take care of her. She went to the convent and made the arrangements necessary to leave Nancy. She wouldn't have to become a Catholic but they told Sally truthfully that they would teach her how

309

to be one. Nancy would get the best education they had to offer. Sally paid them a small fee and also gave them a large donation. She told them she didn't want Nancy to lack for anything.

Even as she said that she knew that Nancy would rather do without everything to be able to stay with her, or Jesse. But Sally had convinced herself that this was the best thing for Nancy. So she told the Mother Superior that she'd bring Nancy sometime later that day. Then she left and went back to the campsite.

Sally knew she had to do this thing immediately or she wouldn't be able to do it. Every other thought was 'You can't do this'.

It was almost the middle of the day, and Nancy hadn't been awake too long. George said he'd just let her sleep. Sally went to her and held her close; she could tell that Nancy was uneasy.

"Mama, what are we doing here? Where have you been? And why are you looking at me like that?" She asked. "You look like you did when Uncle Ali died." And she started crying.

Sally quickly told her everything and ended by saying that as soon as she could get legal custody she'd come back to get her.

Nancy had stopped crying and was looking at her in disbelief. "You can't leave me. I won't stay here."

Sally loaded the things on the packhorse as George saddled his and Nancy's horses. "Please, Nancy. Try to understand. This isn't something I want to do. I just don't see another choice. I've told you all that." And she tried to reach for her.

Nancy moved away from her but George caught her before she ran. "Please, Nancy. Don't make this so hard." And Sally saw that even George had tears on his face.

George held Nancy on the horse with him and Sally got on hers and led the other two. And they went to the convent. The gate was open enough that they could ride through and they rode up to the living quarters that Sally had been shown. There was a young nun standing there waiting on them.

"Hello, Nancy. I'm Sister Kate." She said.

Sally got down and went and took Nancy as George handed her down to her. "You're a witch. That's what you are." Nancy yelled at her and she hit her in the face.

Sally was so surprised that it was a minute before she realized how hard she'd hit her and how much it hurt. Then Sally busted out crying, not for her physical pain but for the pain she was causing Nancy. And Nancy was crying and saying, "I'm sorry, Mama. I didn't mean to do that."

"It's alright, Nancy. It doesn't hurt. I love you, Child." And she looked at the young nun, then turned and got on her horse.

"Mama. Don't leave me." Nancy called, and the nun had her around the waist and another nun had joined them. Nancy was standing there looking at Sally with total disbelief, as if she were in a nightmare. And that's the way Sally felt, like she was in a nightmare.

She rode away with two nuns holding Nancy and the last thing she heard was Nancy crying, "Mama. Don't leave me here. Please. Don't leave me."

Sally rode through the gate, stopped just outside and watched as they shut the gate. Then she got off her horse, sat down and leaned against a tree looking at the gate. All this time the only thing George had said was 'Goodbye, Nancy. We'll see you in a few months.' Now he looked at Sally and didn't know what to say, so he got off his horse and quietly sat down beside her.

They sat that way for over an hour before he finally said, "Sally. What are you going to do now?"

"I'm going to sit here until I decide if I can think of anything more awful that I could do today."

"Sally, you've thought this over a hundred times. Do you have a better choice?" George asked.

"Well, first I could kill myself. It couldn't hurt any more." She said.

"Don't talk like that. I don't like you saying things like that." He said.

She was still looking at the gate of the convent. "The way I see it is I only have the three choices. Leave her at this awful convent. Take her with me and leave my family, including ever hearing anything about Alfred. Or let Jesse have her."

She was quite for a few more minutes then she said. "I won't leave her with Jesse. And I can't leave my family."

George said, "You can come see her every few months and it won't be forever. And it's not an awful convent. She'll be treated real well, and she'd get a real good education. I don't think it's a bad choice at all."

"Nancy will see it as an awful choice. She'll always remember that I couldn't leave my family but I could leave her, my own eleven-year-old daughter. Oh, Damn. I'm an awful person, and a worse mother."

"You're not a bad person, Sally. You've just had some bad luck and some bad things happen to you. Come away now. Let's go back to Texas."

As Sally got on her horse she looked at the convent and wondered if Nancy was trying to fill another hole in her heart with love, or would this new hole have a little hate in it too. Sally rode away saying over and over to herself, 'I'll be back, Nancy. I promise. I'll be back.'

CHAPTER 18

It was early summer and already very hot. Sally was slowly moving a small herd of cows toward the pens by the barn when she saw someone leaning against the corral. She had a pistol stuck in her waistband, but she got her rifle out of the scabbard and laid it across her lap. As she got near enough, Jesse opened the gate and she drove the cows in the pen.

She sat on the horse as he closed the gate. Then when he turned to face her she asked. "Were you waiting for me?"

"I've always been waiting for you." He said and laughed.

"I think you should leave, Jesse. You're drunk."

"No I'm not. I'm almost drunk. There's a difference. You can still do all kinds of things when you're just almost drunk." And he laughed again.

He'd moved toward her horse and she'd backed the horse up slowly. She moved the rifle to a better position and said, "Come on, Jesse. Don't be an ass. What do you want."

"What if I wanted you?" He asked.

And in spite of everything she would have thought possible, she got a feeling she thought was long gone. She wondered if the thought had shown in her face and then he laughed again and she knew it had.

She rode over to the water trough, put her rifle in the scabbard, and dropped the reins for the horse to drink. She pumped some fresh water, cupped her hands for a drink, wet her kerchief and wiped her face. Then she turned around and saw that he was sitting on the porch as if he belonged there.

She walked over and stopped a few feet in front of him and asked. "What the hell do you want, Jesse. Are you just here to plague me?"

"You know you're still the prettiest woman in the territory." He said. Then he made a motion with his hand as if it were a gun and asked, "Are you as good with that thing as I hear?"

"Better." She said.

"Really. As good as me?"

"Better." She said again.

"Would you use it on me?" He asked.

"I've thought about it." She said.

He laughed again and said, "Me too."

Sally looked at his long lean frame leaned back comfortably on the porch steps and she felt a stirring of the strangest mix of feelings she could remember. She walked over and sat in the straight-backed chair in a position that she could stand and get to her gun quickly. Jesse turned slightly so that he was facing her.

He grinned and in spite of herself she did too. "Where's Alfred? Is he doing alright?" She asked.

"He's doing real good. He's with my brother and his wife right now."

She wondered. 'What was he doing? He was acting so comfortable. Like a cat playing with a mouse. She needed to be careful but she didn't feel like she was in any physical danger, except for the strange way she was feeling.'

"So George is away for a day or two shoeing horses, huh?" He said.

She didn't say anything just looked at him.

He laughed.

"You want to tell me what you're so happy about? Maybe I can have a laugh too." She said. She was getting really aggravated and a little uneasy too. He was definitely playing with her.

"Well, first of all it gives me a deep down good feeling that I can still get a reaction other than hate out of you. You want us to do something to satisfy that reaction?"

Again she didn't say anything, just looked at him. She hoped he couldn't tell that she was thinking about his question.

"Suit yourself. It's your lose." He said, and he got up and stretched.

She stood also and before she knew what was happening he'd reached and grabbed her by the arm and pulled her off balance. She tried to get her gun out but he had her pinned to him. She quit struggling and looked up at him. She didn't feel good about being caught like this, but she hadn't expected it from him.

He leaned down and kissed her gently on the mouth and she kissed him back. She could smell the liquor. Then he held her close for a minute and kissed her ear like he'd done so many times.

She held him briefly with her arms but held her body back. She knew he was playing with her in some way.

He turned her loose and walked away. After he got on his horse he looked at her and said, "Hell of a shame, ain't it? We could've made sweet music together. I'll think about it tonight." He laughed and said. "And so will you."

He turned his horse around and then turned back around to face her. "Oh, by-the-way, Sally. I've been thinking about all this talk about fighting the Mexicans again and I want to go see what's going on. I may be gone a few weeks or more. If you'd like to have Alfred for awhile I'll bring him over next week."

"Of course I'd like to have him." Sally said. She couldn't understand what was happening.

"Good, that's good then." He had a big smile on his face.

"Jesse. What are you doing?" She asked.

"Well, I'll bring Alfred over next week and then when I come back to pick him up, I might tell you where Nancy is." And the smile was gone from his face.

"You bastard. What have you done?" And she pulled her gun and pointed it at him.

"No more than you did. I just moved her to a convent that I liked better." He said.

Sally's thoughts couldn't get any more mixed up if she worked at it, so she took a deep breath then put her gun back in her waistband so she wouldn't be so tempted to use it. As far as she'd known only she, Mama, Joseph, and George knew that Nancy was in Louisiana in a convent.

"How did you find her?" She asked.

"I got friends all around here. It's not too hard for one of them to buy a man a drink or two and ask him how his trip was. It's awful hard not to talk about such an interesting place as New Orleans, and everyone knows that's in Louisiana. You don't have relatives there and where else would you leave a little girl?" He said. "Why didn't you bring her back with you?"

"I was going to." He looked off into the distance for a minute then continued. "I figured leaving her there was probably pretty hard for you to do so I gave it a lot of thought. I thought maybe it's not a bad thing for now, and when all this new fighting is over I'll go get her and I'll keep her."

Sally didn't say anything. She was too angry.

"I'll bring Alfred over next week. I think he's looking forward to a visit." And he rode out of the yard without looking back.

Sally stood and watched until she couldn't see him anymore. Then she went in the house and tried to sort through all her feelings. That didn't work so she went outside and wasted some energy with the whip, knocking over almost everything in sight. That felt a lot better.

It took her all evening, but Sally wrote a short letter to Nancy and also one to the convent where she'd left her. She asked if Nancy's father had been there and if so what had taken place. She hoped they would write back and tell her where Jesse had taken Nancy; if they knew.

She'd ride to Columbus the next day and post the letters; she could stop by and see Mama on the way back home.

The week passed slowly for Sally because her fear was that Jesse was not only playing with her about Nancy's whereabouts but also about bringing Alfred to stay with her. Even though she was worried and angry about the situation with Nancy she wasn't concerned about her physical well being. She knew Jesse would never put Nancy in a bad place.

One week after he'd been there, Jesse and Alfred rode into the yard. Sally hadn't seen Alfred for over a year so she had to really guard her emotions. George ignored Jesse, told Alfred he was glad to see him, and then told Sally he'd let them have a few minutes. He went to the blacksmith shed and left them alone.

Sally was watching Alfred and didn't look at George. He'd been embarrassed and apologetic about talking too much and giving away where Nancy was. After being initially very angry with him she'd told him that because Jesse felt as though he had leverage she was going to get to spend some time with Alfred and that was what was important to her now. Later on she'd figure something out about Nancy.

For a moment she felt a slight sympathy for George but it was fleeting. She only wanted to see Alfred. He seemed kind of shy but Sally thought he wasn't displeased to be here. She noticed he did keep looking at Jesse; she wondered if Alfred was wondering like her if this was really going to happen or not.

But after a few minutes, Jesse said, "Take the horses and let 'em get a good drink. Your mama can tell you where to put your pony and your gear later."

Alfred looked at Sally and she smiled at him; her heart was doing handstands. When she turned to look at Jesse he was looking at her instead of Alfred.

"He's a good boy, but real quiet." He said.

"Yes, he is a good boy. You've done a good job." And as hard as it was for her to say that, she realized she meant it.

He looked at her for a minute then said, "I'd kill to get him back."

"I know that." She said.

They stood silent, watching Alfred until he brought Jesse's horse back over to him.

"Hey, Bud. You be good and mind your mama." Jesse said and he thumped Alfred lightly on the head.

Alfred looked up at him a minute then wrapped his arms around Jesse and hugged him. Jesse hugged him in return. Sally looked at Jesse and saw that he was looking at her.

"Strange that those two feelings can live together in one person, ain't it?" Jesse asked.

"Yes it is." She thought about the love and hate doing war inside her and was surprised that he'd admit to having the same feelings. But she had no doubt which one was the strongest for both of them, and it wasn't love.

She looked at Alfred and said. "Thank you, Jesse." Then grudgingly said, "Be careful."

"I'll do that." He got on his horse and said to Alfred, "Bye, Bud. I'll see you soon." And he rode out of the yard. When he got to the edge of the clearing he turned around and waved and Alfred waved back.

The next few days were so wonderful with Alfred that Sally had only short periods when she felt guilty about Nancy. She took Alfred to Mama's house, and William's house, and she took him hunting, and they rode for miles and miles together. He was a good rider but he'd probably never be a natural with a gun like she was or her brother, Joseph.

But she reminded herself that he'd just turned seven in May. He was so quiet and serious that he seemed much older than he was. That's what people said about her when she was young. They'd also said she was a tough little person and maybe Alfred seemed that way too. She wasn't sure yet.

She could manage to give him a very brief hug when he went to bed at night, but that was all. That was the way her brothers had been at that age too, so maybe it wasn't that he was uncomfortable with her.

Sally began to notice that George was being what Mama always called pouty when someone was feeling sorry for himself. She guessed she wasn't paying him enough attention, but she only wanted to spend her time with Alfred. And in a way, she didn't care enough how George was feeling. He started making more trips to his cabin and staying longer periods and she was pleased that he was gone so much.

But she also felt guilty about him; he was good to her and Alfred. So one evening after Alfred was asleep she picked up the old quilt and took it out to the porch. George was sitting in the rocking chair and saw her bring it out. She could tell he was paying close attention.

She spread the quilt out on the far side of the porch and sat down on it. He came over and joined her and they took a long time making each other feel good. "That was really good. The best time we've had together." Sally told him. And she stretched and felt good all over.

"You sure like it for a woman." He said.

Coldness crept into the edge of her feelings and she raised up on an elbow and looked at him.

"Was it as good as it was with Jesse?" He asked.

"Oh hell, George. That's not something we need to talk about."

"I saw the way you both looked at each other when he was here the other day." There was a hurt sound in his voice.

Sally wasn't sure she wanted to fix this. But he did deserve some consideration so she said. "George, you just misread the looks, you know we hate each other. Tonight was really good, let's don't ruin it."

She got up and went in to bed and he came in right afterwards and was asleep almost immediately. Before she went to sleep she thought about 'you sure like it for a woman' and she wondered why there should be such a difference. Fact is she'd always wondered why everything was so different between men and women. Well she hoped someone a whole lot smarter was working on that problem. She thought she'd just sleep on it.

Sally and Alfred were making a small whip for him. They worked on it a few hours a day; it gave him something special to look forward to. Unless someone else was with them, they mostly sat quietly together without talking. Sally would smile at him every so often and he'd smile back. They both seemed very comfortable with the silence.

One of the days when they were on the porch working on the whip, Alfred said, "Nancy hoped you'd know she was alright where she is. She didn't want you to worry."

Sally almost didn't keep from sucking her breath in with surprise. She waited a minute then asked, "Does she like the new convent as well as she liked the other one?"

"She said she missed Sister Katy that was at the old place. But there are two girls close to her age at the place she is now and she's glad about that."

"I'm pleased the two of you got to see each other. I didn't know you were with your daddy on that trip."

"I told Daddy I wanted to see her real much, to see if she was alright way over there. And he finally said I could go."

"I know she must have been really pleased to see you." Sally said.

"Yes, she was. But I think she thought Daddy would take her with us and he didn't. I don't know why not." And he looked at Sally.

Sally didn't say, 'I sure don't know why he didn't either.' She asked, "Did she look alright?"

Alfred said, "She's pretty like you. And she's getting pretty tall too, like you."

"Thank you. That's a nice thing to say. And I guess I am taller than most of the women you know." Then she tried to sound casual as she asked, "I don't guess you'd know the name of the place she's at now?"

He looked at her with a very serious face and shook his head in a negative gesture. "Daddy told me not to tell anyone about the place or where it is."

"That's alright. Don't feel bad about that. You should do what your daddy says to do." But she was really disappointed.

They'd almost finished the whip and Alfred was getting excited about learning to use it. "I hope I can be as good as you are someday."

"No reason you can't be. I'll teach you all my tricks." And she finished the whip and popped it lightly once, just as Alfred said something.

"What'd you say, honey?"

"Nancy taught me how to spell a word." And he spelled a word and pronounced it.

Sally said. "That's a pretty sounding word. What's it mean?"

"I'm not sure what it means. It's just the name of a little town." And he looked at her with a totally straight face.

'My goodness.' She thought. 'What did Granddad Rabb say? "Quiet waters run deep?" or was it still waters?'

"Let's go try this whip out. I hope you don't get all the bruises I got when I first was learning." She squeezed his shoulder as he passed her and he looked at her and smiled. He'd managed to help his sister without disobeying his daddy.

That evening after Alfred was asleep Sally asked George if he knew of a town in Louisiana with the name Alfred had spelled for her. He said he did and that there was indeed a convent there. Fact is it was a very nice one. She asked him not to mention to anyone that she now knew where Nancy was.

The next evening she wrote another letter to Nancy at the new convent. Nancy would not only know that her mama knew where she was but that Alfred had been able to pass on a message. Sally wanted to leave immediately and go see Nancy, but she knew she couldn't. She couldn't do anything to mess up her chance to get to visit with Alfred in the future.

The summer was hot, humid, and uncomfortable but it was passing too quickly for Sally. Each day she worried that Jesse might ride into the yard with no notice at all and take Alfred away. She had to push those thoughts into the back of her mind.

One hot day during the late summer, it was Joseph and Andy that came riding into the yard. They had terribly long faces and Sally knew something was not good. She didn't even let them off the horses before she asked, "Is Mama alright?"

"It's Ann Eliza. She's bad sick." Andy said. "She's got a fever and Mama didn't want us in the house."

Joseph added. "We stopped by and told William and Thomas. He's working at William's place right now. They said they'd get word to the other girls."

"Oh, dear God." Sally said. A fever was everyone's worst nightmare, especially with a child or an old person. You really had no control; the person lived through it or died.

"I should go see if I can help. You boys can watch Alfred for a few days."

"No." Joseph said. "Mama said you'd say that and I was to tell you that if you come over she won't let you in the house. She expects you to take care of Alfred and us boys. She's got Louisa to help her and in a day or so we can ride over and see how things are going."

"Hells bells, she's a bossy woman." Sally said and was kind of surprised when Joseph and Andy laughed and Alfred joined them.

"Alright, alright. That's enough fun out of one statement." She said. "Am I really as bossy as Mama?"

"You're not quite as good, yet." Joseph said.

Sally hit him lightly on the arm then found some work for all of them to do. Later on she'd need to find something else to occupy their time. It wasn't going to be easy to keep them all from worrying about their littlest sister.

Alfred was pleased to have Joseph and Andy around and he tried to work as hard as they did. Sally eased off her usual ways and suggested some fun things to do. They had a few horse races, some sling shot contests, and a contest to see who was the best with the whip. Sally won that hands down, but she was pleased to see how good Alfred had gotten with his small whip. They ended up both the days with a long swim in the river.

It was around midmorning the third day of the visit when William and Thomas came riding into the yard. Sally didn't have to ask anything, she could tell what the news was going to be. And so could the boys.

Looking at Joseph and Andy, William said, "I'm sorry. Ann Eliza…"

And that's as far as he got. Andy yelled, "Don't you say it. You go to hell. I don't want you to say it." And he ran off toward the river.

It was so unexpected that Sally didn't know what to say or do, except to cry. It was Joseph that went after Andy.

William and Thomas gave Sally and Alfred hugs and then sat down on the porch. William did the talking. "She died last night. Nothing they did helped. We didn't know it. We just decided to go over to see about them this morning." He stopped for a few minutes then continued. "Mama asked us to come here first. She said Andy would have a hard time."

They all looked toward the river. They could see Joseph and Andy squatting side by side looking at the river.

"He'll be alright. It'll hurt like hell, but he's got the family to help." Thomas said. He got up and as he passed William he touched him on the shoulder.

Sally watched as Thomas walked slowly to the other two boys and saw Andy get up and hug Thomas. Thomas was standing there holding his youngest brother and probably both were crying.

"I guess the hardest part is that every time someone you love dies, it reminds you of all the other people you loved that died." William said.

"Yes, and there's been so many. What did Mama say for us to do?" Sally asked as she tried to wipe away all the tears.

"She talked to us through a closed door. She didn't want any of us in the house until she and Louisa get it cleaned and aired out. She said she didn't think it was one of those bad fevers that are so contagious, said it didn't seem like the ones she'd been told about. She doesn't know what caused the sickness so she still wants to be real careful."

He looked toward the boys by the river and added. "She said we'd have the funeral in the morning, real early."

Sally tried to keep the thought out of her mind but she couldn't. It was the worst part of the hot summer and they'd have to bury her very soon. It was hard to think of that when you could only see a lively happy eleven-year- old girl. And that made her think of Nancy and of how hurt she'd be when she heard. The two girls were almost the same age and like sisters.

Then she noticed Alfred sitting on the porch with his knees pulled up to his chest and tears running down his face. Sally went and sat down beside him and he allowed her to pull him close and hold him.

The next day was one of those days that Sally had begun to think of as a 'bad remember day.' It wasn't at all like a day you wanted to remember it was just going to be one of those days you couldn't get your mind to forget. All the family was there except for William's wife. She'd just had a baby and they'd named him Ali Freeman Newman, after their brother Ali. Sally wondered who'd be the first to name a child after poor little Ann Eliza.

Both Mama and Louisa were almost inconsolable. Sally thought that Louisa didn't look well; she looked much older than she should. And as she stood around visiting with her family she knew that they were all getting older and many of them had troubles.

Mama was fifty-five now, apparently in good health, but she'd just ended her marriage with Nathan Barr. That marriage had only lasted a few years and had been a disaster from the beginning. He'd spent most of his time in their house in Matagorda and Mama had stayed here at the ranch. Sally thought that's what Mama preferred.

Mary was thirty-eight and had five children from Preston Gilbert. She still looked healthy but was in a terrible marriage with George Cotrell. He was an even worse cad than they'd imagined. Some woman had just recently filed a suit against him and was taking him to court on a bigamy charge. He couldn't keep his pants on it seemed.

Sally looked over at him and wished looks could kill. He didn't make eye contact with her. He was trying to look like he was being kind and helpful to Mary. Sally thought, 'What a sneaky, no good, son-of-a-bitch. Mary sure deserved a lot better than you.'

"I haven't thought of a bad enough name for him yet."

Sally looked behind her and saw Amanda, Mary's oldest daughter. She put her arm around her and said, "I was doing a good job in my head but I'd rather you didn't use those words. How are you?"

They talked for awhile and Sally had to shake her head when she realized Amanda was now fifteen years old. The child was already talking about a young man she was interested in.

After Amanda walked off, Sally kind of went through the rest of the family. 'William looks wonderful for his thirty-five years. Thank the Lord for Martha Ann and his two little boys. Everything seems great for William except for him having to play father to all the rest of us so often.'

'Louisa works too hard and looks older than her thirty-three years and she'll probably never marry. She's too devoted to Mama to ever leave her now. And Minerva looks good at thirty, especially after having the three little girls so quick. And she and David seem happy.'

'Then there's me at twenty-eight. So how am I doing? Well, I know I look good, but I also know I'm the worst messed up person here so I probably win the prize.'

Sally looked around the room to see where Elizabeth was and she saw her with her little girl, Ann, in her arms. She was standing beside her husband, Joe, and they were both staring at Sally. When Sally saw them looking at her she also saw Elizabeth elbow Joe and they both smiled. Sally walked over to them and asked, "Alright, what's funny?"

Elizabeth said, "I noticed you looking around at the others and I told Joe that it looked like you were reminiscing about all of us by order of birth. So we made a bet on it and I won. That's what you were doing wasn't it?"

"Yes. I'm guilty. But I didn't have enough time to give Joe a grade. So I may never know if he deserves you or not." Sally said.

"No man could deserve my Elizabeth." He drawled and he looked at Elizabeth with absolute adoration. Sally felt a little envy but if anyone deserved to be loved like that it was this sister, so she was just glad for her.

"Nothing is ever all blackberry cobbler, Sally." Elizabeth said with a smile.

"Well, I don't want to hear that. I thought I was the perfect catch." Joe said. "You girls can just carry on without me." He picked up little Ann and went outside.

"Now I want to hear everything you thought as you were running down the list of children. Or did you start with Mama? Of course you did. So tell me." Elizabeth said.

Sally laughed and told her all her thoughts. Elizabeth was nodding agreement with everything and when Sally got to the part about George Cotrell he got another dirty look, this time from Elizabeth.

They finished off the three younger brothers by saying that twenty-four year old Thomas seemed better now that he was seeing a young woman. He'd had a terrible time getting over Ali's death. Joseph was almost eighteen, kind of wild but good-natured and every young girl in the area had an eye on him. And fourteen-year old Andy was a nice-looking boy and a handful for Mama.

"We could start on the grandchildren, but I guess we'd better pay attention to Mama for awhile. First though, where's George? I thought he'd be with you." Elizabeth said.

"He's working over at his place for a few days. He doesn't know anything about what happened yet. It isn't his fault he's not here with me, but I'll still have to go through him feeling guilty about it." Sally said.

Elizabeth kissed her on the check and they walked over to where Mama and Louisa were sitting. After visiting for awhile longer Sally told them all goodbye.

She and Alfred got on their horses and Sally decided she wanted to go by the cemetery one last time. They rode up the little hill, got off and tied their horses to the fence, and went in through the gate. The small grave with the fresh dirt was on the other side of Ali's grave. His grave was beside Daddy's.

"The space on this side of Granddad Newman is being saved for Gramma." Alfred said.

"That's right, but who told you that?" Sally asked.

"I heard Gramma tell Aunt Louisa this morning at the funeral. She said she wished she was already there." He said and his eyes filled with tears.

"She didn't mean that, honey. She's just all torn up from losing Ann Eliza. Gramma's strong as she can be. We're going to have her with us for a long, long time.

"Did I ever tell you about how your Granddad and my Uncle John saved us all from the flood?" And in her heart she said, 'I love you, Daddy and Ali. And you too, little Ann Eliza. I love you all.'

As she ushered Alfred out through the gate and put her hands together to give him a boost up on his horse, she was telling him about the flood and getting his mind off death and pain. "You should've seen all that water. You wouldn't believe it in a hundred years."

Alfred was looking at her instead of the cemetery. "It's been a long time since you told me that story. Did Granddad really have to move the whole house?"

Three weeks after the funeral Sally was working outside when she heard a large group of horses coming. That many riders at once was so unusual that she got her rifle and she and Alfred moved to the side of the barn. Then before anyone came into sight the horses came to a stop and a voice yelled. "Hello the house! Sally! Don't shoot us. It's me and Andy and we got company." It was Joseph.

"Come on in." She yelled back and wondered who in the world it could be. It sounded like a small army. Joseph, Andy, and seven other young men came riding into the yard and they were all in a boisterous mood. Sally couldn't put names to many of them but from their looks she knew they were her cousins.

Joseph reintroduced them. "These three here are Uncle Andrew's boys. Course you remember William and John, and that giant there is Thomas called 'Tom'; he's the youngest of their family.

You remember Uncle John's two older boys, Gum and George, and the younger there is John Wesley.

And this one over here is Ulysses, Uncle Thomas's boy." By then they were all off their horses, with their hats in their hands, greeting Sally and Alfred. "Goodness gracious. This is great. You boys look wonderful." Sally went around and gave each one a hug. "Four of you are almost as old as me. Why aren't you married with a lot of children? Are have you just hidden them?"

She got various answers from them all and it seemed none of them were married yet. She particularly noticed Uncle Andrew's middle son, John; she always did. He didn't look exactly like Granddad Rabb but for some reason he reminded her of him. She wouldn't make it obvious now, but she hoped she'd get to know this John Rabb better.

"Alright enough of this. What's going on? Who's at Mama's house? And did she faint when everyone arrived?"

"She was still hugging everyone and crying when we left." Joseph said.

Andy said, "There are so many people at the house, Sally. It looks like a small town. I think the only ones not there are Uncle Tommy's wife and his daughters."

Sally turned to Ulysses and asked, "Is someone sick or is there a new baby in the family?"

"A new baby. She was just born a couple of weeks ago. Daddy's only going to stay and visit for a few days then he's going to go back home, but he's going to let me stay and ride back with one of my Uncles." Ulysses said.

Sally knew the family was here because of the death of Ann Eliza. Mama would have written to tell them. "What orders did Mama give you? We'll be a mob to feed so maybe I can take some food."

Joseph said, "You're right about the orders; even crying didn't slow her down much. She said for us to tell all the children to just load up and come over. We'll worry about the food later. And from the looks of the wagonload of things Uncle Andrew and Uncle John brought with them we won't need much anyway.

"And thinking about Mama giving orders makes me think we need to get going. We still have to go to Mary's house and Elizabeth's. Do you need some help? You want a couple of cousins to stay and help?" Joseph asked.

"I don't really need help but I wouldn't mind the company." Sally said. "Some of you boys want to stay and ride over with me?"

And she was amazed when every boy said. "I'll stay."

Joseph looked at her and laughed. "Well, hell Sally. It's your own fault for being so interesting to be around. It was you that told me to shoot the button off that vest, with the man in it. And the whole family knows the story. Being tough has a price, I guess."

"Three of you stay and help me. I'll take the youngest boy from each family. And the rest of you get out of here." And she wrinkled her nose at Joseph and then gave the rest of them one of her sweetest smiles.

She could tell the three boys, Tom, John Wesley, and Ulysses, were pleased to be staying. It was flattering and kind of uncomfortable too. She felt like they were watching every move to see if she'd shoot something or at least act tough in some way.

She couldn't wait to see the family so was ready in no time. She left a note on the table for George to join them when he could but she didn't know if he'd be home tonight or not. He didn't spend but two or three nights a week at home now and she guessed that probably suited them both.

"Before we go, can I ask a favor of you?" Ulysses asked.

"I hope so. What can I do for you?" Sally asked.

"We were all hoping you'd take that extra long bullwhip of yours so we can watch you use it. And maybe you'd give us some pointers too?"

Sally looked at the other two boys and they were looking hopeful too. "I guess I can do that, but we'll have to get a distance away from your Aunt Rachel's house when we use it. She doesn't like the popping sound."

The ride to Mama's house was an adventure. All three boys and Alfred tried to ride beside her and act like they weren't trying to at the same time. She hoped this wasn't a sign of the week to come.

Seeing all the family in Mama's yard was like looking at a small village of people and all of them were relatives. What a family! Sally jumped down and held her hands for Alfred but he ignored her and rode over to the shed and managed to get off by himself. It was going to be a 'keep up with the older boys week too'. She remembered those times so she led her horse over to Alfred tossed him the reins and said, "You'll take care of our horses, right?"

Alfred stood real straight and said, "Yes, Ma'am. I can do that." And she smiled as he led the horses to the pen.

Then it was like taking a bath in hugs and kisses and lots of love. She greeted Aunt Mary and Aunt Margaret and their daughters and younger children, and then she was able to go where she really wanted to go, to where the three uncles were standing. As she got closer to them they all three looked her way and Uncle Andrew was the first to greet her. "So here's our Sally." He gave her a big hug then it was Uncle John's turn, then Uncle Tommy.

"You three men are just nearly the best-looking men I know." Sally told them.

"Well, now I'd like to know who the best-looking men are if we're the just nearly." Uncle John said.

"And it's not fair to say your daddy. Every girl's daddy is the best-looking." Uncle Tommy added.

"I'm sorry. But your daddy with that head of white hair wins every time." Sally said. And they all three nodded and said they agreed. Then other people walked over to join them and Sally moved to the side.

"You're still the prettiest girl around." Uncle Tommy said.

"Just wait until my sister, Elizabeth, gets here. You might change your mind." Sally said. But she was pleased with the compliment.

Sally asked Uncle Tommy about his wife, Barthenia, and his other children. She could tell he was happy with life and she was pleased; he was still one of her favorite relatives. But then so were the other two uncles. Grandma and Granddad sure had done something right.

"Sally, you do look wonderful, but are you doing alright?" Uncle Tommy asked.

"Now how do I answer that?"

"Truthfully I hope. I'm really interested in how you're doing." He said.

"I have troubles, much of it my own doing. But other than where it affects my children and me, I'm not really unhappy. You know if I have work to do, and horses to ride and take care of, and . . . Well, I'm doing alright. Thank you for caring." She said.

"I don't think I've met your husband, but Rachel tells me he's a good man and good to the children. I hope he'll come over before I leave so I can meet him. His name is George?"

"Yes, George Scull. He came to Texas around 1835 or so." Sally said.

"Scull. George Scull. No I don't think I ever met him." Uncle Tommy said. "Say. That makes you Sally Scull. I like that name. Sally Scull. Seems to fit you somehow."

Sally didn't say anything. But she did like the name when Uncle Tommy said it.

"You can tell me to mind my own business if you want. But do you hear from Jesse? Is he still chasing around trying to find a fight or has he realized like me that we're too old for that now?"

"I saw him a few weeks ago. We don't get along very well so I can't answer for him except to say that the reason I'm getting to keep Alfred for awhile is because Jesse wanted to go see about this coming fight with the Mexicans. I think he was going to ride down to Victoria and then a place named Corpus Christi or something. He seems to be doing pretty good." She said.

"It sure looks like we're going to go to war with Mexico again." Uncle Tommy said. And as he talked about that the other men around gradually joined the conversation and Sally made a quiet exit without being noticed. She went over to visit with Mama and the aunts. She sure didn't want to listen to war talk on a day like today.

All Sally's brothers and sisters and families were there by that afternoon, and George came over the next day. Then the day after that Uncle Tommy said his good-byes and went back home. The week went by too fast but it always does when you're happy with the people you're with.

Sally had a loyal following of all the young men in the family. She'd shown them all how to use the various sizes of whips, and at Joseph's prompting had even shown them her prowess with the rifle and pistol. She'd always been able to use either hand equally well and that fascinated them.

Along with horse races and swimming, they had shooting practice and whip practice and contests every afternoon. Sally was sending all the boys in the family home with numerous bruises on arms, legs, a face or two, and a few places that no one had owned up to. She thought that one or two of the boys could be very good with a whip if they chose to be.

Both Uncle Andrew and Uncle John had come to her by the end of the week and told her how much they appreciated her keeping all the boys busy. They had worried that the older ones would be so restless as to be an aggravating lot to put up with. She'd been able to tell them honestly that she'd had a wonderful time and they could all be proud of such a great bunch of boys.

The time for everyone to leave for home was approaching, so the evening prior to the departure day Sally and her brothers and sisters decided to go to their homes and let Mama have the evening with the uncles and aunts.

Sally invited her brother, Andy, and the same three younger boys to go home with her for the evening. And this time she asked if Uncle John's son, Virgil, who was only six years old could go too, and got approval. Alfred and Virgil had become fast friends during the week so the two boys were happy.

William, Thomas, and Joseph took the older four boys to William's house, and the two teenaged girls went home with Mary and her daughters. Mary's husband had been absent for the last few days, so Sally thought at least the girls could have fun and not have to be around him.

That left only one little one at Mama's house and that was Aunt Mary's two-year-old Mary, and she was a quiet little thing. Mama would have the evening to enjoy her two brothers and their wives and it would be a wonderful time for the five of them. But Sally knew it would be a bittersweet visit since this was the evening that would bring their time together to an end.

Sally took her leave, again with many hugs and kisses, and please come see us. And much later, after a long fun-filled evening with the boys that had come home with Alfred and her, she finally got to bed.

She lay there and thought about Nancy, wished she too had been a part of the past week, and hoped she could make it up to her someday.

It had been a wonderful week. She knew she hadn't done anything to merit it, but she was very thankful that she'd had the good fortune of being given a most tremendous gift. This good loving family.

CHAPTER 19

It happened too soon for Sally but anytime would have been too soon. Jesse came back and took Alfred.

Sally didn't know which one of them it was the most difficult for. Alfred was glad to see his daddy but obviously unhappy to leave her. Jesse was very glad to see Alfred but not happy to see how much it bothered Alfred to leave Sally. And Sally was not pleased at all to see Jesse or to have to give Alfred up again.

But as she watched Alfred ride away with Jesse she had something new to make her feel better. She and Alfred had a new foundation that maybe would carry them through the next few years, and she knew where Nancy was. That was where she was going to go as soon as she could get things together.

Mama had sold the balance of her land in Matagorda in August, and had taken back the Newman name. All the friends and neighbors called her by that name anyway, so it just made sense. Besides Sally knew that was the way Mama thought of herself, as Rachel Newman. And that pleased all the children.

Sally told George that she wanted to go see Nancy and he said that was fine with him. He would enjoy some time in Louisiana again. So Sally went and spent a few days with Mama and the family. It seemed strange that it was only Mama, Louisa, Joseph, and Andy in that big old house; they were the only ones still at home. But when one of the older ones came home for a few days it wasn't unusual for the word to get around and all or most of the others would come over for at least a day. This was what happened when Sally went to visit.

And the big news was that Elizabeth and Joe were planning on moving to Joe's land in the DeWitt Colony. It was around fifty miles west of the Egypt area and about thirty miles south of Gonzales. Most of Joe's family lived there and he and Elizabeth had been dividing their time between the two places ever since they were married.

When Joe didn't do much to improve the place they lived in on Elizabeth's land, Sally knew that his heart was in his DeWitt land. Sally had visited them there once and knew why they liked the area so well. She liked it too. Best of all she knew that Elizabeth liked it there and was not going to object to moving there permanently.

Sally knew that Elizabeth would miss the family as much as any of them would, but she also knew that Elizabeth wasn't as tied to the Newman land as Sally was. The fact was that Sally didn't think any of them were, except her, Mama, and Louisa. And Elizabeth was totally tied to Joe and would always go where he wanted to go.

Sally was pleased they were happy about their moving plans but she would miss having Elizabeth close enough to visit when she felt like it. Elizabeth's answer to that was, "Come live there, Sally. It's wonderful land and you'd like it."

"I may actually give that some thought. I did like it there." Sally told her. Then she told the family that she would be going to see Nancy and would be gone for some weeks. The thought of Elizabeth moving had been hard enough on Mama and now Sally had made her plans known and the rest of the visit was kind of sad.

Sally made arrangements with Joseph and Andy to take care of her stock and the place and took her leave of the family. She always worried about all of them, especially Mama, but she was so happy about going to see Nancy that she had to work to not seem too happy. 'My that's a new feeling,' she thought.

As they were getting everything ready for a long trip and absence from home, she and George talked about the situation in Texas. She wasn't too worried about this looming battle with Mexico affecting her land and possessions although she did worry about some of her family getting involved if the country actually went to war.

She just hoped Jesse would stay at home and take care of Alfred. From the look of him when he returned from his trip to Victoria and Corpus Christi, she thought that he might now decide to leave the hard fighting to the younger men. Jesse had looked tired and older to her.

Sally became more impatient with each mile as she and George rode toward Louisiana, and Nancy. It had turned cooler during the week as it should in December and the weather was pleasant. She and George enjoyed their evenings together and except that he talked more than she liked in the daytime, it was a good time. And at last they were outside the convent.

Sally could hardly wait to see Nancy but was also uneasy. She hadn't seen her in almost six months and she didn't know what the reception would be. She had faithfully written to Nancy once a month, but had gotten only one very short, almost cold letter in return. And to make matters worse, if Nancy still wanted to go home with her, she couldn't make that commitment yet. Nothing in the situation between her and Jesse had been settled and she still wasn't ready to let Nancy go live with him.

She decided not to just barge right in to the convent, but to take the rest of the day to clean up and calm down some. She didn't get much sleep that night and was up early. She waited until mid-morning and then she and George rode into the convent grounds. He waited with the horses while she went to the church office.

A short pudgy nun was making some notations in a large ledger as Sally walked into the room. She looked up and broke out in a large smile. In a strange accent, she said, "I don't have to ask who you are. Our Nancy has your same looks. Welcome, welcome." And she got up and took Sally's hand in both of hers talking all the while. Sally couldn't help but like the woman and especially when in-between sentences she sent another younger nun to inform the Mother Superior that Nancy's mother was here.

Sally didn't like the fact that she couldn't just immediately see Nancy, but she knew this was how it worked, so she was prepared. And if she hadn't been so nervous about Nancy it would have been amusing to listen to Sister Francis. The accent itself was interesting, but the almost nonstop happy chatter reminded Sally of young girls playing. Then she was just as amazed when the chatter stopped as if a hand was placed against the mouth.

Sally turned and saw a small thin nun entering the room from an inner door. Small or not, she was obviously the one in charge. She introduced herself as Sister Mary Margaret, and Sally thought that would be easy to remember; she'd just think of the two aunts.

Sally waited patiently through the greetings, polite small talk, and even more polite but slightly probing questions. She wasn't surprised but was actually pleased that they would be careful about who came to visit the young girls at the convent. And with her and Jesse to deal with, well they had plenty to think about.

After assuring Sister Mary Margaret that she was indeed Nancy's mother, and she wasn't here to cause a riot, or run off with the buried treasure, the young nun was sent to get Nancy.

Sally was so anxious that she had to watch her breathing. Either she was breathing too fast or not breathing enough, she didn't know which. And she suddenly thought, 'They can't get many visitors, so I bet word gets around quick that someone different is here. Nancy probably already knows its George and me. So what is she thinking?'

And then Nancy was standing in the inner doorway. She stood there looking at Sally and Sally's eyes filled with tears; this was no longer a little girl looking at her. Nancy didn't move until Sally did and then they were holding on to each other. Nancy was guarding her emotions, so Sally got control of hers, but it was hard not to cry.

The nuns excused themselves and left Sally and Nancy in the room together. They said little silly things to each other, like 'How are you?' 'I'm fine. How are you?' 'I'm fine too.' 'You look real good.' 'Thank you. You do too.' And then they had run out of anything safe to say.

After a few minutes of uncomfortable silence, Sally said, "George is with me and he's been waiting a long time. Do you mind going out with me to say hello to him and let him know what's happening?"

"No, I don't mind at all. It'll be nice to see him." Nancy said.

When they arrived in the little patio area where George was, Nancy went directly to him and gave him a hug. He was pleased to see her and let her see his feelings by having to wipe a tear or two out of his eyes. "I swear Nancy. You're just as pretty as your mother, and almost as tall." He said.

Then the three of them sat on some benches and talked about the weather, and the pretty flowers, and the church, and the weather, and the beautiful trees, and the garden on the other side of the church, and the weather. George and Nancy were doing most of the talking, as Sally sat there wondering what to say and how to say it.

After a short silence, Nancy said. "If you don't have any other plans for the evening, I can tell Sister Maria that you're both going to join us for dinner. Guests are welcome, but I'll need to let her know fairly soon."

"George, would you mind giving us a few minutes by ourselves?" Sally asked.

"Course not. I'll go look at the garden. I haven't seen one that looked that healthy since I lived in Louisiana." He said.

Sally stood up and turned to face Nancy, took a deep breath and said, "The only way I know to deal with life is head on. So that's what I'm going to do now. I'm uncomfortable and I don't know what to say to you, except that I love you."

Nancy got up from the bench and looked at Sally. She was silent for so long that Sally was beginning to think she wasn't going to answer her, but she finally said. "You should be uncomfortable. I haven't seen you for six months."

"I know. I'm sorry." Sally answered.

"You should be." Nancy said.

They were both just looking at each other when Nancy said. "You know, I am almost as tall as you." She stood as tall as she could and added, "And I plan on being both taller and prettier than you."

"You're already the most beautiful person I know." Sally told her. "I love you, Child."

Nancy stood there for another minute then hugged Sally and this time it seemed to be without reservation.

They sat side by side, holding hands for what seemed to Sally like too short a time to memorize the feelings. Then it was Nancy that broke the silence.

"The thing that bothers me the most is not knowing what is going on. Please tell me what your plans are. And please be truthful and tell me all your plans. I would rather know and be sad than be surprised. Bad surprises are horrible to get past."

"Alright. That's the way I would feel about things too." Sally said. "So the first thing to tell you is that I'm not going to be able to take you home yet."

Sally stopped and waited to see if Nancy would say anything, but she didn't. So Sally continued. "I want to take you out of the convent to stay with me for the next few weeks. I want us to spend Christmas and your birthday together. We can go to New Orleans if you'd like. Would you want to do that?"

"I'd like that, although I'd rather just go home with you." When Sally didn't say anything Nancy asked. "When will we go to New Orleans?"

"Right now." Sally said.

Nancy laughed. "But we'll have to get approval from Sister Mary Margaret for me to be gone for that long. Usually the children are only gone for the week of Christmas so as not to miss too many prayers and lessons."

"The only approval I need is yours." Sally said. "I don't need some nuns approval to take my own daughter with me."

Nancy laughed again and it was like bright sunshine on a dark day. "What?" Sally asked.

"You sounded like you were ready to go to war and I was thinking about you pulling your gun on the poor nuns. They'd never recover." Nancy said. "It will be easy to get her approval and it's the right thing to do."

"I know it is. Let's go do it." Sally said.

There were a few horses kept at the convent and Sally was allowed to rent one for Nancy to ride. Sally picked the best horse they had which in her mind wasn't worth the feed they were letting it eat. But that didn't matter because two hours later, with George following along behind, and Nancy by her side, Sally was happy to ride away from the convent.

A year later Sally was sitting in a large comfortable chair, on the second floor porch of a hotel in New Orleans. She was watching but not really paying attention to a noisy group of people enjoying the French Quarter. She had a cool drink in her hand, both a little too strong and a little too sweet for her taste. She looked at it for the second or third time and wondered why she was even trying to drink it.

George had gotten it for her probably hoping it was strong enough and sweet enough to get her in a better mood. Not much chance of improving her mood or the drink as far as she was concerned. She guessed that was the same conclusion George had come to since he had left in a huff a few minutes ago.

Sally knew she'd been worse than unkind to him. 'Thanks for the drink, but I'd just soon be by myself right now.' She'd said to him.

'Well, the way you been lately, that suits me too. I'll go see Jake and his family. I may be back tomorrow. That is if you care at all.' And he had stomped off.

She put the drink aside and tried to feel something about George. They spent more time apart than together recently and it didn't seem to matter much right now, so she put him aside too. Then she allowed her mind to concentrate on what she had been trying to avoid, Nancy and that blasted convent.

Sally thought about she and George riding out of the convent with Nancy. A full year and a few weeks had passed since the time she was thinking about. She sat still and let her mind drift through the past year.

That visit with Nancy had been wonderful but the three weeks had gone by so fast. All of a sudden it was January the tenth and they were celebrating Nancy's birthday. Sally had tried not to think about how it was almost time to take Nancy back to the convent, but of course Nancy was thinking about it too. Taking her back and leaving her was absolutely awful. Sally felt like the worst mother alive and she thought that was pretty close to what Nancy felt too.

It wasn't long after Sally returned home that Elizabeth and Joe had made a permanent move to their ranch in DeWitt County. By the middle part of April they were gone.

Then in June, Joseph had gone into Columbus and was mustered into federal service as a Texas volunteer in the war with Mexico. He'd been gone until October, fighting in a number of places in Mexico. A number of the Rabb cousins had gone too. The war hadn't been the terrible impact that the previous one had been, and they had the feeling they wouldn't have to fight Mexico again. At least the impact didn't seem so bad once all their family members had returned safely.

Then it was fall, and October and November brought so much pain and sorrow that each day seemed too long to bear. In late October, Mary and her two youngest children, Mary and Louisa, died. Within a few days they received word that Uncle Tommy had died. And only days later, in early November, Minerva's husband, David, died. It seemed that every family for miles around were touched by the death of someone close.

Those memories were too recent and still hurt too bad. She tried not to think about how Mama was still grieving. Mama had lost a daughter, two granddaughters, a brother, and a son-in-law in just a few short weeks. Mary's older children were now without their mother and their father, who had died a number of years ago. And poor Minerva had lost her husband and the father of her three girls.

In December, Joseph and Andy had taken Mama to La Grange to visit her brothers, Andrew and John and all those families. Sally left home about the same time and so hadn't seen Mama since then. She hoped the visit went well and Mama and the boys were back home safe.

Sally shook her head and tried to think of something pleasant to take her mind off her family. And she settled on her perfect image of Alfred. She had been able to see him a few times during the year, for short periods. But she hadn't seen him for a few months now. During the fall months, when all the sickness started, she'd gotten word to Jesse that he should stay home with Alfred and keep him away from the towns and people.

She reached for her drink, took a sip and almost spit it out. Damn, that was a sorry tasting drink. She got up and poured the rest of it into a planter hoping it wouldn't kill the plant. Then she went downstairs to the eating place beside the hotel. She ordered a plate of food, ate it without much appetite, then with a cup of coffee returned to the porch and the chair. The coffee was stronger than the drink she'd had earlier, but much more to her liking.

It wasn't long until the darkness claimed everything but the few lights that could be seen along the street below. She felt like her thoughts were just as dark.

And she thought of another day, a very cool, but beautiful sunny day. It was a little more than a month ago, the week before she left for Louisiana to see Nancy. She'd gone by herself to Elizabeth's house, close to the town of Clinton, spent a day and night, than rode north of there to where Jesse and Alfred lived. Jesse's place was about twelve miles above Hallettsville. It was about forty miles from Elizabeth's house to Jesse's house, a little less than a day and a half ride.

She stopped on a hillside overlooking Jesse's place. She had no idea if he was home or not and it didn't really matter. She ground-tied her horse so that it could graze and squatted down beside a tree. It was about mid-morning. She'd been there about 15 minutes when she saw Jesse, Alfred, and two men come out of the barn. They had some fencing materials that they loaded into a wagon.

She had stopped on this hillside a number of times before just to get a glimpse of Alfred. She was always glad to see him, even from a distance, but the guilt and sadness it caused her was heavy. This particular day was even more distressing to her. She knew she had to do something about the situation Nancy was in.

The last visit to see Nancy, during the summer, was very uncomfortable and disturbing. Nancy treated her almost like a stranger as if she didn't really care if she came to visit her or not. Sally was proud of how smart Nancy was and how well behaved, but it bothered her that she was beginning to sound and even act like the nuns. Nancy was more attached to the nuns than she was to Sally now. And Sally didn't like that.

So here she was on this hillside trying to decide what to do.

The emotions she felt when she saw Alfred were strong and full of love. The feelings for Jesse were just as strong. They just weren't feelings of love. But she'd always been honest with herself and had finally made herself accept at least half of the blame for her situation. Even the lose of her children.

This time there was an added element and her emotions were fighting inside her as she watched Jesse. She glanced around to see where her horse was and her eyes fell on her rifle. She looked at it, then back at Jesse. It wasn't even a real thought, to shoot him, but she wished he knew how easy it would be. Then she chastised herself for even letting a thought like that in her mind.

She watched Jesse and Alfred until the wagon was out of sight, then got up and went to her horse. She leaned heavily against the mare, then mounted and rode towards home. She knew what she had to do. She had to go bring Nancy home to Texas.

She went straight back to her home and then she and George started for Louisiana. They had gone to the convent and taken Nancy with them for the three-week visit in New Orleans, just as they had the year before. But this time was different. This time Nancy was cool and seemed not to care whether she went with them or not. It seemed as if she would rather have Christmas with the nuns and her friends. So Sally delayed acting on the decision she thought she'd already made.

Nancy spent the three weeks with her and George then seemed relieved when they left her at the convent. As Sally rode through the gate she turned around to wave goodbye to her, but Nancy had already gone inside. That hurt.

Now two days later Sally sat in a hotel chair looking at the empty coffee cup she still held in her hand. She wondered why she hadn't already taken Nancy back to Texas. Or why she'd taken her back to the convent again, without telling her what she was thinking of doing.

Was she afraid that Nancy wouldn't want to go with her?

No. It still had to do with her not wanting to let Jesse have Nancy. And that was no longer acceptable. Sally knew she couldn't go home this time without Nancy.

The decision was made. So she went in and went to bed.

She slept fitfully and got up early. She'd long ago made preparations for what would be needed, so when she got to the hotel stable it didn't take long. She loaded her things on the packhorse, and saddled the other two horses, both hers and the one she'd bought for Nancy.

She stopped back at the hotel and paid to have someone take a message to George. He could catch up with her on the trail. She got a bite to eat, paid her bill at the hotel and left for the convent.

Sally leaned over and opened the gate and let it swing open. She rode through with the two horses trailing behind her. By the time she got to the front of the building, two of the Nuns were waiting outside the office door. 'They must have a pretty good watchman.' she thought.

Sally sat on her horse and waited. It didn't take but a moment until Sister Mary Margaret arrived and asked her if she could help her.

"I don't think so. I'm just here for my daughter."

The Sister was saying something but Sally wasn't listening to her. She was watching Nancy.

Nancy had come out through a side door and Sally could see that she was surprised to see her. Sally saw some guarded excitement in her eyes but she was also nervous. Sally realized that she was afraid to believe what might be happening.

The nuns didn't want to let Nancy go, and it seemed that a lot of people were all talking at once.

"Do you have anything you want to take with you?" Sally asked Nancy.

"Yes, Ma'am." And she turned and walked back into the building.

Sally was ignoring Sister Mary Margaret, but she'd heard the threat she made of a guard with a gun. Unless someone shot her with no warning, which was not likely here, she didn't feel as though she was in any danger. She was aware of what was happening around her though, she had spent most of her life that way.

Only moments after going into the building, Nancy was coming out of the door carrying a small bag. Sally had time to realize that the bag was probably kept packed just for a time such as this. That was another black mark to put beside her name. How many times had Nancy had to look at that bag after her mama or daddy rode off again without her.

There were now some children and a few more nuns in front of the building. Nancy ran to one of the girls and gave her a hug then the heavyset nun called Sister Francis got the other hug. There were some tears, but Sally saw that Nancy was handling her emotions well.

Nancy tied her bag to the back of the saddle, climbed up on the horse and looked at Sally. She reminded Sally so much of herself, and Sally was so relieved to see her on her horse, that she almost laughed.

But she knew that would be misunderstood and not a response Nancy would like.

Sally looked at all the nuns, but settled her look on Sister Francis and said, "Thank you very much for how you've taken care of Nancy. I will always be grateful."

While still hearing protests from Sister Mary Margaret, Sally with Nancy following her, turned and rode out through the convent gate. Once through Nancy reached down and closed and latched the gate behind her.

As they rode away, Sally wondered if there was a guard with a gun. If so they sure needed a new one. She looked over at Nancy but no look was returned. Nancy had a determined look that again reminded Sally of herself. 'I suspect getting Nancy back into that convent would be pretty hard to do.'

Nancy looked back at the convent once, just before the trees cut off the view. She looked a little sad but then that determined look was back. They rode for over an hour without saying a word to each other. Sally was trying to think of what to say and just decided to let Nancy say the first words. Of course she knew that was taking the cowards route.

After another hour of silent riding, Sally thought it was probably going to be left up to her to say the first words. She looked at Nancy and got an unreadable look in return. "There's a nice stream just up ahead. We can stop and get a drink."

Nancy didn't say anything.

When they got to the stream, Sally let the horses drink then sat down on a log under a tree. Nancy stood beside her horse and looked at Sally.

"We don't have to be in a hurry. I left word for George to join us at a lodge we know of. It's only a few hours ride from here. You and I will have to stay there until he can join us. It's not safe for the two of us to travel alone." Sally said.

Nancy was watching her and listening, but she didn't say anything in return.

"Why don't you sit down for a few minutes." Sally said. "Do you want something to eat?"

"No, thank you." Nancy said.

'Well, at least she can still talk.' Sally thought. She was surprised at how nervous she herself felt.

Nancy was now sitting on a log silently waiting for what she had to say and Sally didn't know how to start. So she just started talking.

"I saw Alfred before I came here. Well, not exactly. I mean I saw him but he didn't see me.

"You remember your Aunt Elizabeth and Uncle Joe Tumlinson? Well, they're living on their ranch in DeWitt County now. Lately I've been spending a lot of time in a small house next to Elizabeth's house. I work horses for Joe T to pay for my room and board."

Sally stopped for a minute and tried to settle herself down. "I'm not sure that George will go with me, but I'm thinking about moving to DeWitt County. I've sold part of the land I got from my daddy. And I plan on selling the rest of it so I can buy land in DeWitt County."

That finally caused a change of expression on Nancy's face, a look of surprise. But she still didn't say anything.

Sally talked more about where she was living, about working with Joe T, about the fun she had with Aunt Elizabeth and her children, and about how many horses and cows she now had. She told her she was pretty sure that Mama and all the family would eventually end up in DeWitt County.

Then she told her about Jesse's place and how pretty it was there and how close it was to the house next to Aunt Elizabeth's house. And then she couldn't think of another thing to say.

Nancy was not a child; she was an old thirteen. She'd been watching and listening closely. She made Sally sit through a few more silent uncomfortable minutes. Then she said. "Mama, you've talked about everything except what you plan to do with me."

Sally thought, 'That's straight forward and what needs to be asked.' But she found she couldn't just answer it that easily. So she began by saying how sorry she was for putting her in the convent, that it was probably a mistake, and that she had finally decided it was time to take her back to Texas to live with Jesse. And with Sally living next to Elizabeth she'd be close enough to Nancy and Alfred so that she could visit them more often. When she'd blurted all this out she stopped and waited on Nancy to say something.

Nancy had gotten up and was standing there looking at her.

Sally waited another minute or two then asked, "Well, what do you think? Do you want to do that?"

Then she answered her. "What do you mean, 'what do I think?' and 'do I want to do that?' When did you ever ask me those things? When did you or Daddy ever ask me what I wanted?

"To get back at Daddy, you took me away from my home, my family, even the culture I was used to, and just dropped me off in a convent in another country!

"And to get back at you, Daddy came and moved me to a different convent where I again didn't know anyone.

"Do you have any idea what that was like for an eleven-year old girl? Do you know what the discipline was like because I didn't know how to be Catholic? Do you know what it's like to hear children cry at night, all alone, and know you are just like them, all alone?

"Where were you? Where were you, Mama?"

Nancy was almost yelling at this point. She stopped and then in a much quieter voice said, "You have no idea what it has been like for me. You came to see me for a few days, maybe twice a year, and each time I'd pray that this would be the time you'd take me home.

"Then you'd just ride away again. When I'd see you cry as you rode away, I'd wonder how long you cried, because I knew I'd cry everyday. At least at first.

"And now you ask me what I want. Of course I want to go home. I want to see Alfred and Daddy, and Gramma and the family. I want to be in Texas again. I'd almost given up on getting out of the convent; I thought I'd have to become a nun.

"I have two questions for you, Mama." she continued. "Does Daddy know you're bringing me to his house? And if you're willing to let him have me now, why in God's name did you leave me in a convent for almost two years?"

Nancy stood with her arms crossed in front of her, looking down at Sally. And Sally felt like the weight of the world was on her. She didn't think she could move and barely could breath. She didn't have an answer to that last question. She just sat there, with tears running down her face, and looked at her daughter.

It wasn't Sally that made a move—it was Nancy. She walked over to her mother, offered her kerchief, then laid her hand on her shoulder. Sally took the kerchief, then tried to see Nancy's face through her tears.

Sally put her face in her lap and wept bitter tears. She cried so hard that she could barely get her breath. Then Nancy sat down beside her and held her close. They stayed that way until Nancy asked if they shouldn't start for the lodge before it got any later in the afternoon.

They rode in silence again until they arrived at the lodge. It was Nancy that made the arrangements for a room and some food for them. It was Nancy that insisted that Sally eat supper and then Nancy that helped Sally into bed and lay down beside her.

As Sally drifted off into a troubled sleep, she felt a hand on her shoulder. She reached and touched Nancy's face and felt tears. As her own tears rolled off the side of her face, she prayed this child could someday forgive her.

It seemed strange to Sally, but the next day was wonderful. They got up early. Nancy was excited about getting to go home, and about being away from the convent and all the rules they had. She wanted to know about each family member and the news of Texas and even about the latest war with Mexico.

They sat on the lodge porch, walked along the river, brushed the horses, and talked like two adults. The day went by too quickly for Sally.

She didn't think the convent could get a message to Jesse in less than two to three weeks. So when George arrived the next day, she decided they would take their time and go slowly back home. They could enjoy their time together and she could still have Nancy at Jesse's house before he got the notification. She didn't like being concerned with what he thought, but she didn't want problems with him either. She thought maybe they could work out a deal where she could have the kids visit her once-in-a-while.

The trip took three weeks instead of one. They stopped by Wharton County so that Nancy could visit with Gramma and the family. There was much sadness for all of them when they went to the Newman cemetery and saw all the new graves. Nancy cried the most when she stood over Ann Eliza's grave.

But the excitement of being home in Texas was too much to keep her sad for long. After a few days visit with Mama and that part of the family, they went to DeWitt County to the Tumlinson place. They stayed in the house Sally was beginning to think of as her own and spent a day or two visiting with Elizabeth and her family.

Much of this time Sally just stood aside and watched her lovely daughter. She was so happy and full of life. Then the time came to take her to Jesse's place.

It was mid-morning when she and Nancy got to the place on the hill overlooking Jesse's ranch house. They got off their horses and stood in the same spot Sally had stood just a few weeks before.

"Oh, look, Mama. There's Alfred, and Daddy." Nancy said.

Sally didn't answer she just looked at Nancy then back at Alfred and Jesse.

Nancy moved over and put her arm through Sally's arm. "Thank you for bringing me here. Now that I know where you'll be living I'll be fine living with Daddy and Alfred. You won't be so far away and I can see you real often."

"If Jesse will allow you to." Sally said almost to herself.

As Nancy looked at the ranch house below she said, "He will have no choice. I'm not going to give either one of you up again."

Sally looked at her daughter and thought, 'She sounded just like Jesse!' Then the next thought was, 'Or was it me she sounded like? 'God help her if it's a combination of both.'

"It's time to go, Nancy." Sally said.

"I know." she replied, but she stood without moving.

"I love you, Child. More than anyone in the world."

"I know, Mama. I love you that way too." Then she gave her mother a quick hug and went and got on her horse.

They rode slowly down the hill, side by side. When they got to the edge of the clearing, Sally saw Alfred standing beside the corral watching them. She thought, 'Hells bells! I have to be more nervous than Nancy!'

Just then Jesse came walking out of the shed and saw them. He stopped suddenly and put his hand up to shade his eyes. Then he walked to where Alfred was standing and waited beside him.

Sally had seen the look of utter surprise on Jesse's face and then all the other emotions that filled him. They were probably about the same ones she was feeling.

She and Nancy rode right up to the two of them and stopped. No one said anything for a long few minutes then Nancy got off her horse and went quickly to Alfred. She gave him a tight little hug. Then she turned to Jesse.

"Hello, Daddy!"

Sally didn't think Jesse was able to say anything clearly. He caught Nancy in his arms and held her close while tears ran down his face.

Sally looked from the two of them back to Alfred and saw him staring at her.

Then she heard Nancy say, "Daddy!"

"Oh, I'm sorry." he said. "Get down, Sally. Tell your mother hello, Alfred."

Sally wasn't sure what to do so she would let Alfred do what he felt like. He came over and took off his hat and held out his hand toward her. She caught his hand and held it a moment. Then she touched his shoulder lightly before he moved back a step. She wanted to hold him forever but instead she smiled at him. He smiled back.

At least that's something she thought.

And just then Nancy had Alfred by the hand and was saying, "Show me the house since I guess I'm going to be living with you." Then with Nancy chattering away, the two of them went toward the house.

Sally watched them walk into the house then looked at Jesse.

His eyes were red and he was putting his kerchief back in his pocket, and he too had been watching the children.

"You brought her to live with Alfred and me?"

"Isn't that what you want?" she answered.

"Sure it is. But I'm surprised that you . . ." and he didn't finish his thought.

"Nancy needs to be with her family. I'd rather have them both live with me, but that's not going to happen. So here she is." Sally said.

By then they were both leaning on the fence and neither said anything for awhile. Then Jesse said, "Why don't you come up to the house for a bit and we'll see what those two are getting into."

Sally just said, "Thank you." And she meant it.

When they got to the porch, Nancy and Alfred came out and Sally was almost overwhelmed with emotion. She made herself get control and then said she needed to get going.

Nancy would have none of that and Jesse immediately said, "Why don't you stay for supper at least."

Sally knew it was a toss-up as to which one of them would least like to be around the other. And she knew the invitation from Jesse was only because he was afraid that Nancy wouldn't stay if she left. But she also knew this was hard on the two children and maybe it would be a good idea to stay for awhile.

It was one of the strangest evenings she could remember. The four of them went all around the house and outbuildings with Alfred shyly showing Nancy and her the place.

Nancy would hold Alfred's hand for awhile, then hold Sally's or Jesse's. Sally noticed the softness in Jesse when Nancy walked by his side holding his hand. She noticed him reach for his kerchief more than once when he thought no one was looking. Jesse looks older than she'd been able to see from a distance; he'd be around **[add in Jesse's age]** now.

Sally had also been aware of how often Alfred was watching her and Jesse. She could only imagine what he was thinking. As usual she hoped he didn't think too badly of her.

After they had eaten supper Sally again said it was time for her to leave.

"I'll go with you, Mama!" Nancy said quickly.

Just as quickly Jesse said, "Why don't you stay the night, Sally. You can bed down in the house and I'll sleep in the barn." And he looked at her with a pleading look.

Sally almost felt sorry for him; but not quite. She did know that the situation was upsetting for Nancy, so she said, "I'll stay the night, but I'll sleep in the barn. The three of you need to get used to your house."

She said to Nancy, "I'm leaving first thing in the morning. That's what we decided was best. Remember?"

"Yes ma'am."

They sat on the front porch and talked about horses, cows, ranching, the Newman and Rabb families, dogs, chickens, crops, the Robinson family, rain, weather, and of course Texas. But they didn't talk about anything personal.

Finally Nancy yawned and said she was really tired. Sally was so glad. It had been an uncomfortable evening and she was ready for it to be over.

She gave Nancy a hug and told her goodnight, then told Alfred goodnight. She wanted to hug him too, but he kept a small distance between them. He wasn't very comfortable showing any feelings toward her when Jesse was around.

Then Jesse did an unexpected thing. He said, "Alfred, why don't you go with your mama and make sure she's got everything she needs. Goodnight, Sally."

"Goodnight, Jesse."

Sally and Alfred went to the barn, and after spreading some extra hay and putting a horse blanket on it, Alfred asked, "Do you need anything else?"

"That's going to be real comfortable. Thank you very much."

She stood and watched him walk to the barn door. He looked outside, then ran back and gave her a hug. It happened so quickly that she wasn't sure she had really hugged him back. But it had happened.

She lay down on the blanket and knew this was one of those nights she wouldn't get much sleep.

An hour passed and she'd almost decided to give up and just get up and be on her way. It would be easier on everyone concerned if they didn't have to say goodbye in the morning.

But then the door squeaked slightly and Sally saw a figure slip inside the barn. She always had her gun close by, but she didn't reach for it. The figure she had seen was a small one. At first she thought it was Nancy, but then realized that it had to be Alfred.

She lay very still and quiet and waited to see what he would do. He made his way quietly across to where she was and lay down almost right beside her. She didn't move a muscle; she was afraid he might not stay if she touched him.

In a few minutes he had inched over until he was almost touching her. Then he put his hand on her arm.

Sally could stand it no longer. She reached and pulled him close to her and instead of pulling away he snuggled up beside her. She cupped her body around his, kissed him on the top of the head, and held him tight. He made a quite sighing sound and in minutes was sound asleep.

She lay awake for hours just holding him close and trying to memorize the feelings she had. He was nine years old, almost ten, and had grown a few inches taller. It wouldn't be long until he'd be a grown man. She whispered, "I love you, son." And hoped he knew that. Sometime early in the morning she dozed off, then just before dawn, she felt him stir. He raised up and looked at the morning sky through the slit in the door. Then he turned toward her and gave her a hug.

She hugged him in return, and felt him kiss her on the cheek, and then he left just as he had come, almost silently.

She lay there in wonder for a few minutes then got up and saddled her horse. She led him out of the yard and then turned back to look at the house. She raised her arm just in case Alfred was watching.

Nancy would be temporarily unhappy with her for not waiting until she got up to tell her goodbye. Jesse would be almighty relieved. It was definitely easier on herself to not have to go through any more emotions. She wasn't sure about Alfred but suspected it would be easier on him too. She did know that it was time for all four of them to get started on this next stage of their lives.

As she rode toward home the loneliness she had felt for so long didn't seem quite so unmanageable. Guess she had some blessings to count.

CHAPTER 20

She was sitting on the back porch of a small café in Corpus Christi, drinking coffee. The porch had a railing around it and she had pulled a chair over close enough to rest her boots on the bottom rung. The café was almost at the edge of the Bay and the water was lapping lazily beneath the porch. It was early morning so not many people were around and it was almost too peaceful for Sally.

So many things had happened the last few years; some good but too many bad. She got up and went to the old coffee pot sitting on a table near the back door and poured herself another cup. As she sat back down, leaned back and got comfortable, she let her mind drift back to the day five years ago when she took Nancy to Jesse's place.

Sally shook her head again. Thoughts and memories swam around in her head like the fish she was watching. And problems and worries seem always as close as the gulls gracefully diving in to eat those same fish.

Nancy had married Benjamin Barber, a man twelve years older than her. Sally was thankful that he seemed like a good man and she thought it wasn't such a bad thing for Nancy. Besides, Nancy was 18, a hell of a lot older than Sally had been when she first got married. At least she'd be away from Jesse and the recent mess he'd made of his life. Damn, she disliked that man. Oh well; don't want to spend the morning thinking about him.

She picked up the copy of the Corpus Christi paper that was on the chair beside her. She had already tried to read the news in it, had muddled through the big print, and then had thrown it aside. She still had problems reading and writing. It was a paper from last month, some time in June of this year. Hard to believe it was already 1852. Time goes too fast. Oh well – again. Sally got up, took the paper to the table, topped her coffee off and let her thoughts drift where she knew they would.

Nancy told her about her dad's situation. He had met a woman that had some kids, maybe was separated from her husband or maybe divorced, and got involved with her. They had married and seemed to have problems immediately.

Jesse's problems had worked out to Sally's advantage; Nancy and Alfred spent much more time with her than they would have been able to otherwise.

Corpus Christi appealed to Sally; she thought it was a pretty and peaceful town right on the water. Sally walked the length and breadth of it before going to find something to eat and drink. She found a little café/saloon and went inside. Mostly, it seemed it was a better place to drink than eat, but she was able to get a steak, a chunk of bread, and a beer. When she came in, she noticed there were only two other women, who were overdone and old. She got looks from some men who, having been met with the look she gave when she didn't want to mess with anyone, didn't dare to look again.

When she finished eating as she please, she asked for another beer and lit a cigar. Even though she might have felt uncomfortable lighting up in front of people, she was never uncomfortable for long. She sat back, relaxed, and enjoyed looking at the bay and the goings-on of the town.

As evening approached, she though it was time to get her horse and find a safe place to camp for the night. As she left the café, she heard music and suddenly remembered it was Saturday. They were probably getting ready for a fandango. She loved to dance and she was lonesome. She walked to the entrance, asked a man who stood there it there was a dance, and when the answer was yes, she thought, "Great! Move over people, Sally's dancing!"

353

She didn't have money to waste, but she wasn't starving, so she decided to treat herself. She retrieved her horse, went to the little hotel on the corner, and rented a room. The hotel provided accommodations for horses, so she put her horse away for the night, took her bag, and went to her room. She had a light blue shirt, a along dark blue skirt, and a dark blue ribbon in her traveling bag.

Having cleaned up, put on clean clothing, and tying her long brown hair back with the blue ribbon, she stood and looked at herself in the dresser mirror. She looked good, compared to most women, she thought. Then she laughed quietly to herself and said aloud, "Well, Sally girl, you may turn heads because of how you look, but once a man gets to known he just wants a homely little housewife that will treat him like the lord and master. And you don't fit there!"

Se turned from the mirror, looked at the bed, and thought of having a man there, just for aa little while. She wished life was less unfair. A man had needs, and he was able to satisfy them without being judged poorly whatsoever, but a woman with the same needs was shunned and looked down upon. "Oh, hell!" She shook off the feeling to the best of her ability and went to the dance.

Sally had a great time. She danced her with many men, the most notable of which was John Doyle. He was about her age and somewhat attractive. Every time she turned around, he was right beside her. She laughed, danced, drank beer, and danced some more until she the music ended. She was sorry it had to end.

John Doyle asked if he could walk her back home. She said he could only walk her to the hotel, but no further. He said all the right things and was nothing but polite after he saw she was safely in the hotel lobby. She thanked him and walked away. As she shut the door, she wondered if she would have said no if he had insisted. She hoped she would because she certainly didn't want people to think she was no better than a whore who brought men to a room.

Sally had drunk so much that she slept better and longer than usual. When she woke up, the sun was already in the sky, and she felt guilty for the wasted time. She got up to go and decided she as really hungry, so she wanted to go to the little café before she left. When she walked out of the hotel, a man who sat in a chair quickly stood up and walked toward her. Sally put her hand inside her jacket to get her pistol, but then she saw the man was John Doyle.

She knew that he hadn't even noticed that she had reached for a gun. She assumed that meant he was unaware that there were women who could be as dangerous as men. He went somewhat in her estimation, but she smiled at him regardless. He was a nice-looking man and he was apparently taken with her. He asked if he could take her out to eat and she said yes. Instead of the safe she had gone to the day before, they went to a nice, clean, café on the next block. Sally was able to have eggs and bacon, and she thoroughly enjoyed it.

While finishing her coffee, Sally was watching him watch her. He was talkative but he hadn't said anything substantive yet. She waiting until he got to a stopping place and then asked, "What do you do for a living, Mr. Doyle?"

He said, "Well, mostly I've worked within my father on his place. But I plan on buying my owl land son." He went on about his family and such while Sally half-listened and half-thought about him in other ways. She nearly laughed at one point when she wondered what he would think if he knew when she was really thinking about.

She got restless sitting around, even if it was on a Sunday. And she made a decision that she was afraid she would later regret. She asked him, "Mr. Doyle, I'm to ride out and take a look at some land that I may want to lease. Would you like to ride with me?"

You would have thought she had given him a prize horse or something. He just beamed and said, "Oh, I would like that very much. And please call me John." They got their horses and rode away from town and Jahn talked the whole time.

Sally spent two days riding around the area she was interested in. She decided she liked where it was located and would go see the land owner about a lease. But she didn't want to go while John Doyle was around. She told him it was time to head back to town, and that's what they did. They spent two nights camped out and he hadn't attempted any advances. She almost hoped he would; it had been a long time since she had enjoyed the company of a man.

As they rode along, she thought it more and more until she was squirming in the saddle. They had crossed a creek the day before and she had noticed a really nice camping spot, but it was too early to stop. It was a bit early, but not by much, and she figured they would need to camp one more night anyway. She thought she was fighting this battle for too long, and she was losing.

She said, "John, I noticed that creek we crossed yesterday had a really nice-looking pool of water right beside a good place to camp. It being such a warm day, I think maybe it would be good to take a swim." She looked at him and actually laughed aloud because it took him a minute or so to grasp that she was actually talking about getting into the water.

The water was almost to cool for comfort, but it felt wonderful very soon. Sally had stripped down to her underwear and swam around as if she were a fish. John simply sat on a log and gawked at her. They had unsaddled the horses before she got into the water and Sally had put a piece of soap on her saddle.

She asked, "John, would you throw me that soap?"

He said, "Sure," and went and got it.

She swam closer to the edge of the pool so he could toss it to her. When she stood up, the look on his face made her look down at her body. He clothes were clinging to her and she could see everything through the cloth. She said, "Never mind the soap, John," and went to him.

They spread the saddle blankets side-by-side and never got around to supper. The first time was too wild and fast, but the second was much better. When they woke up early the next morning, they were both starving, but food would have to wait. This time, the sex was really good. John was exhausted but Sally felt it safe as if she were a new women. She stretched and almost purred as if she were a cat. When she got up, she said, "John, I'm going back into that pool of water and this time I'm actually going to take the soap with me. You want to take a bath?" He groaned and she laughed. She then gasped at the cold water and laughed some more.

When they got back to Corpus Christi, she told John she had things to do and she would probably see him later. He was hurt and she felt sorry. She also felt a twinge of guilt, but she quickly put that out of her mind; she had too much to do.

It was time to go for supplies, which Sally dreaded. She usually liked people and catching up on the latest happenings, but she wasn't happy John stayed nearby. He was so insecure that she was afraid they would have an argument that might end in a fight, which Sally knew she would win. She did not want to be embarrassed, and she knew she had to make some decisions regarding her situation immediately.

Sally made a number of stops in Corpus before she went to the general store. As was always the case, a hush fell on the crown in the store when she walked in. Sally knew that she should have left her guns in the wagon, but she wore than soften that she had simply forgotten. She was aware of how odd a woman with a pistol o each hip seemed. She talked for awhile to the men gathered around the domino table before she went and selected the items she wanted to purchase. Afterwards, she went to the counter to settle up. Ed the store owner was waiting on her and sked, "Anything else, Miz Scull?"

As Sally answered, "No thanks, Ed," John suddenly yelled, "The name is Doyle, dammit!"

Both Ed and Sally looked at him with different thoughts. Ed just said, "Yesser," and then to Sally, "Have a good day ma'am. Thanks for coming in."

A young man moved up beside Sally, and he was waiting to say something to her, but she suddenly turned around to leave. Sally bumped into him and a small package was knocked out of her hand. The young man quickly bent over to pick it up all smiles and apologies, and just stood and looked at her as he held the package. He then tried to tip his hat, which was hanging on the wall. He turned beet-red and became so flustered that he couldn't think of anything to say. Sally looked at him for a while, reached and gently took the package from his hand, and then gave him a beautiful smile. As she left the building, he heard a delighted musical chuckle.

Ed let out a repressed breath and said, "Well, I'll be damned. Son, I wasn't sure at all of what you were going to be the recipient of, but I sure didn't think it would be anything like that." Ed just stood and shook his head.

Ed laughed and answered, "Yeah, Jeff, that's really the famous Sally Scull."

'Oh no," Jeff said. "I've been waiting here for her over a month to interview some famous person and I made a fool of myself in front of the one I would like to write about her the most. You know people back East love hearing about Belle Starr? The public is fascinated by women that make a name for themselves. They would really love hearing about Sally Scull! Do you think if I followed her, she would talk to me?" Ed told him he thought he should wait for a better time.

One of the men at the domino table spoke up. "You know, that's the first time I've seen Sally Scull. I guess I thought maybe she was just one of those legend-things. She ain't as rough-looking as what you would think from her reputation. I figured she'd look meaner than a tree-wild cat. Hell, she's a damn fine-looking woman." He then looked at Ed and said, "Is that he latest husband? What's his name?"

"Yeah, that's number three. I think his name is John and I guess his last name is Doyle—dammit." Ed paused for effect and waited.

Jeff asked, "I've never heard of a name like that. Are you sure that's right?"

Ed made sure everyone was listening and then said, "Well, reckon it is, cause very time I call her Miz Scull, he bobs up and shots, "The name's Doyle, dammit!" They al laughed, two or three of the men started talking simultaneously, and one of them claimed their attention.

He said, "Well, I can tell you a true story about meeting up with Miz Scull. She don't remember me. And I'm not goin' remind her. But I was with my Pa once when we drove our herd of horses through her property. Now mind you, she weren't never dishonest with my Pa or anyone else that I knowed of, but it happened to be a day that Pa and I were out riding and Pa just thought he'd save Miz Scull some time later. Once in a while, when she drove her herd through our property, one or two of our horses would get mixed in with her herd. Miz Scull would always see that they got back to us.

"Pa got down from his horse, took off his hat, and said, 'Howdy, Miz Scull.' She nodded to him, and Pa went on, 'thought I'd just go through your herd and get out any horses that got mixed in with it.' She didn't say a word, just stood there straight and hard as an arrow. Pa moved a step or two closer, and said a little louder, 'I thought I'd just get my horses out of your herd Ma'am.'

"She still did not move an inch, just said real quiet-like, 'I heard you the first time.' Pa looked kind of uncomfortable, then turned around and climbed back on his horse and gave me a motion with his head. He moved back once and saw all the men followed him as we headed toward home. I looked back once and saw all the men sitting back down and no sign of Miz Scull. I asked my Pa what had happened back there. I said, 'I didn't hear her say anything hardly. How come you left like that? My Pa looked right at me and said, 'Well, son, when I looked into her eyes, all I could see was to tombstones."

CHAPTER 21

The Civil War was underway, and although folks along the Gulf Coast were seldom directly affected by the fighting per se, many contributed in their own way. Sally operated a freight business that hauled goods from Mexico to Louisiana and returned each time with cotton, used for the Confederacy. On one occasion she met a young Lieutenant, named Daniel Peabody of Alabama; they became friends and Daniel provided considerable help with the business.

Daniel said, "Sally, if I didn't have the prettiest wife and two kids east of the Mississippi River, I'd make a run for you." Sally responded: "Daniel, if I wasn't twice you age, and you didn't have that wife, you wouldn't have to run about two steps."

About two months later, Sally stopped by with a Mexican shirt and a Mexican dress for Daniel's kids. She learned that Daniel had been killed in a battle. So his friends told Sally they knew Daniel's wife and they would send the clothes to the kids. Sally sent also twenty one-dollar gold pieces wrapped in the clothes.

On another occasion, while resting in Corpus Christi, between trips, the topic of slavery was introduced within a small party. Sally commented that "she had never had a slave, and surely wouldn't want to; it reminds me too much of being married to a bad husband."

"If you don't want a slave, then why are you helping the Confederacy?"

"Men are marching or riding down from the north with the intent on killing any man standing in the way of what they think they should do. Whether you think slavery if right, good, or bad, if any army was threatening my family, home, and the way you are making a living, what would you do? Stand and let them flatten it all, or fight?"

Sally began to long for home and to see her family. So it wasn't long before she found someone to run her freighting business and rode west. She spent several days in Warton County and then rode on to DeWitt County. Joseph had recently moved to DeWitt County, where most of the family had already settled. Finally, after a long time, they were all together.

Sally was helping to build a barn. The sides of the barn had been put together on the ground. All the men, boys, and Sally, had just pulled the sides upright so that they could be joined to form the sides of the barn. William had been telling them 'alright now, altogether, pull' when a small grandchild of his had decided to run up and hug him. Not being prepared for the little onslaught, and slightly off-balance to begin with, William ended up on his butt with the grandchild sitting happily in his lap.

With laughter coming from all sides William said. "Well, from my angle it looks high, but very good."

Mama happened to be the one closest to William so she came over and claimed the little grandchild. "Don't let them bother you, William. They're just envious that you're in charge." And she laughed as she walked off.

William smiled at her and got up and dusted his bottom off. "So what are you waiting on? Have you got those sides fastened together yet?"

As she supported the part she was holding, Sally watched William. In a minute he looked her way and smiled. She smiled back and thought about what a great person he was and what a wonderful thing it was to have so many of the family together.

It wasn't long until the sides of the barn had been either fastened together or at least propped in place until they could be. Sally stood there for a minute and rubbed her arms, her muscles were tired from the weight of the boards she'd held. She looked around and saw that she wasn't the only one feeling tired.

"I think it's time for some food and a little rest." Mama said. And not one person objected. They had started working that morning and it was now mid-afternoon and no one had rested in between.

Some of the young girls had brought water from the creek and Sally headed that direction. She washed her face and hands and then dried them on the tail of her shirt. She walked over to the house and sat down on the porch. Elizabeth walked over and handed her a cup of cool water. "You look tired, Sally. Are you feeling alright?"

"Thanks for the drink. I feel fine, I just realized I'm not as young as I once was." She said.

Joseph sat down beside her. "Well, at least you're not so old that you can't pick the place to sit your butt down on." He raised his arm and deflected a small clod of dirt thrown at him by William.

"Foods ready. Gather round and someone can ask the blessing." Mama said.

'This whole day is a blessing.' Sally thought. She'd finished her food and was leaning back on the porch listening to her family and watching the little people playing in the yard.

CHAPTER 22

It was warm for late November, but there was a breeze, and it felt good. The horses were milling around and kicking up dust. It was good to get the branding done and at least a few of the horses green-broke. They wouldn't be easy to handle yet, but at least some of them could be ridden, so they could be sold as riding stock. There were a lot of horses that needed breaking and an extra cowboy or two sure would come in handy right now.

A horse whinnied, causing her to put her hand on her gun, and look around. Shouldn't be day-dreaming, should be on her toes. She chuckled to herself and relaxed. She knew she would never be able to be just a regular person, not be always cautious and aware of her surroundings. Too many years of that kind of living to change now. Besides, there was always the possibility that her past wouldn't stay buried.

Buried? That brought a smile to her face. Don't know who was buried with that little boot sticking up, but if people thought it was old Sally Scull, then it meant she might be left alone awhile. Sally nudged her horse and trotted over to the corral. Juan's boy looked like he needed a hand with the dun, and everyone else was occupied. It was coming on supper time and she was tired and knew the hands were too. She told them to finish up the ones that they were working with, and then call it a day. They had been at it since daybreak, so they were more than ready to quit.

Sally unsaddled her horse, rubbed him down and fed him. Then she went to the side of the old house and brushed off her clothes and washed her face and hands. Rosy wouldn't tolerate even her tracking in a lot of dust and grime. Rosy held the kitchen door open for her, fussing at her for working too long and too hard. She always sprinkled her lectures with a lot of Irish words thrown in, and when she really got carried away, her Irish brogue would get so thick you could hardly understand her. Mary Elizabeth Courtney, called Rosy for some unknown reason, wasn't but a few years older than Sally, but she was the motherly type. It didn't bother Sally, she found it kind of comforting and homey.

Rosy had worked for the Bakers for almost twenty years, and when old Mrs. Baker died, the old man had gone to live with his daughter in Corpus. He couldn't bring himself to sell the ranch, so Rosy had asked him if she could stay as caretaker of the house. He had a foreman and a couple of men and their families that took care of what little stock he still had. Sally had been acquainted with the Bakers for many years and had stopped there to water her stock on most of her drives. She had always repaid them in one way or the other and had become a trusted friend. She had been asked many times to stay at the ranch however long she wanted to and even to make it her headquarters. She had taken to staying longer and longer periods, but declined to take up permanent residence. But when Mrs. Baker died and Mr. Baker moved to Corpus, he told her he would take it as a personal favor if she would make it her home at least for the time being. Sally had taken him up on it and sometimes stayed for months between trips to buy or sell horses. She felt at home on the ranch and hoped someday in the future to buy it from Baker.

Sally had also become fast friends with Rosy. Soon after they had met, Rosy had told her that she had never had any children, that her husband had gone off and left her, and she needed to earn a living for herself, being as how she was Catholic and would not take another man for a husband. Sally knew Rosy was aware of what kind of life she had led as far as men were concerned, but the two of them never discussed those things again. Sally had spent so many of her years with cowboys and seldom with another female, so she enjoyed the company and wouldn't want to think of Rosy not being at the ranch.

She sat down at the heavy old wooden table in the kitchen and in a minute Rosy was setting a bowl of hot stew in front of her. Next came the end piece, her favorite part, of a fresh- baked loaf of bread, butter, and a cup of coffee. Rosy got her own bowl and joined her. t was quiet for a few minutes as they just enjoyed the wonderful taste of the stew and the bread. Rosy knew that Sally didn't like constant talking, so she usually tried to let her set the pace.

The old house was big and comfortable and Sally felt content with life at the moment. They weren't too far from Corpus, she wasn't too far from where Alfred lived, and she truly liked the area. It was home now, and it felt good not to be on the road all the time. She sat back, and asked Rosy, "what type sweet did you bake today? Do I smell apples"? But before Rosy could answer, Sally held up her hand for quiet. They both stopped and listened. She was right. She had heard a horse, and it was coming fast. It sounded like a horse that was laboring; the pace wasn't even. "I sure as hell hope the person riding that horse has a good reason for what he's doing, or he'll sure as shooting get a piece of my mind!" As far as she was concerned there were few or no excuses for ill-treating a horse.

She got up, went to the back door and got her pistol out of the holster, shoved it in her waist band, and went back through the kitchen to the front door, and out on to the porch. Juan was coming toward her, and she noticed that at least three of her men were in three different locations. She knew that others would be watching in case they were needed. Juan joined her on the porch and they watched as the horse and rider came through the gate, the man leaned down and shut it behind him. The way he sat on the horse reminded Sally of her youngest brother, Andrew, but that wasn't him. Then she saw that it was one of Andrew's sons. Probably the one called Ellie. There was an immediate surge of pleasure at seeing one of her family, followed just as quickly by fear. Who was it this time? Mama?

Mama had been living with Andrew and his family for the last year or so, and Sally tried to get up to see her at least every few months. She had been so busy with the new horses and hadn't gotten loose to go anywhere, so it had been awhile since she had seen her. The last time she had gone to visit she had noticed that Mama was getting more frail all the time. Sally had been planning on going to see her about two weeks before Christmas, and then come home by way of Lagarto to see Alfred and her grandkids at Christmas time. Damn, she wished she hadn't waited.

Sally was down off the porch and beside the hitch by the time Ellie rode up and slipped out of the saddle. He was so tired that he was a little wobbly for a moment, but righted himself, and grinned at his Aunt Sally. All the nephews and nieces were in awe of her. She was already a legend, and to them was not just an aunt, but was Sally Scull.

She grabbed him and gave him a hug, then said "Come on in the house before you fall down." She looked at Juan, he nodded, and went to tell one of the hands to get Ellie's horse taken care of. Sally called to him and said, "Juan, come back up to the house." He nodded again.

The minute they were inside the house, he said, "Aunt Sally, I've got some real bad news." Sally was thinking of her mama and asked, "Is she gone"? Ellie just looked at her like he didn't understand and in two strides she was beside him, gripping him by the arm, which hurt, saying, "Come on boy, speak up!" He gulped hard, and told her, "Uncle Joseph is dead." She seemed to stagger back a step, said "What? Who? Oh no." She turned, walked to the door of the kitchen and stopped. Ellie could only see her from the back, and he thought she took two or three deep breaths. Then she turned around and even though she had tears in her eyes, when she spoke, he couldn't hear any emotion. Sally said, "Ok, boy, come over here and sit down and tell me what happened."

By this time Juan had come into the front room and Rosy went and got them all a cup of coffee. Sally pulled a chair up in front of Ellie so she could watch him as he told her what had happened. She had to stop him once to concentrate on what he was saying. She found that memories of Joseph were running loose in her head like a remuda of horses turned loose after a spring rain. Ellie told her what his father had heard about how their brother had died. There were many stories, but it seemed that Joseph had been gambling with some guys and one got angry at him for winning a pot and they got in a fracas. When it looked like Joseph was getting the upper hand, one of the other guy's friends came up from behind and hit Joseph in the head.

No one knew how bad he was hurt at that time. Some of his friends got him to his house and by the next day, Elizabeth knew he was in a very bad way. The doctor at Clinton told them there wasn't anything he could do, but if they could get him to San Antonio he might could be helped. There was a German doctor there now that was doing all kinds of operations. They loaded him in the wagon and Elizabeth and some of the younger kids took him to San Antonio. The doctor, a Dr. Ferdinand Herff, did operate, but Joseph died.

Sally was just quietly listening to every word he said, and at this time in the telling, she lowered her head so low that Ellie couldn't see any part of her face. He stopped for a few minutes, then added a bit more. "Uncle Joseph's boy, Joseph Sylvester, told Daddy that when they had Uncle Joseph in the wagon that he could still talk. He said Uncle Joseph said to him, "Son, I'm going to San Antonio to see if they can do something for me, but I'm not going to see you again. I want you to promise me that you'll take care of your mama and the kids."

Ellie stopped again and looked at Sally. At this time she was staring right at him but still not saying a word. He got so uncomfortable; looked down at his feet, then back up at her, then totally embarrassed himself by blurting out, "Aunt Sally, I sure am hungry." He hadn't meant to say a word about not eating since the day before, and as soon as he said it, he wished he could take it back. But Sally immediately said, "I'm sorry. I'm sorry. I don't know where my manners are. I'll get you something to eat."

The four of them went into the kitchen, and Sally filled a bowl with stew while Rosy sliced off a large piece of bread and asked him if he would like some butter on it. Ellie said, "Yes Ma'am! I'd like that." Without asking Sally got him some milk to drink. She, Juan, and Rosy got another cup of coffee and sat at the table with Ellie. Sally was always amazed at how much food young men could put away and the lack of time it took to do it. When he had sopped up the last bite of stew, she asked, "Can I get you some more?" And he said, "No ma'am that's okay." And Sally said, "Yeah, I think we'd better." She filled the bowl a second time, and he gobbled it and some more bread and milk down about as fast as he had the first. She looked at him and gave him a questioning look. He turned a little red, and said, "That sure was good. Thank you." In the meantime, Rosy had cut a fourth of a pie and set it in front of Ellie. Sally could smell the apples and cinnamon, and it made her mouth water. She started to go and join him, but her stomach protested; she was too full of tears and uneasy fear.

She noticed he now looked as fresh as a new born calf, as if he hadn't been riding for two or three days. She liked the looks of this kid. She knew how most of the kids were afraid of her because of her reputation, deserved or not. And even though he was a bit nervous around her, he looked her in the eye when he talked to her. She had no use for anybody that didn't! Sally sat there thinking about her brother, Joseph, when he was this kids age, and she felt an overwhelming sorrow. She finally looked at her nephew again, and realized he was watching her as were Rosy and Juan. She decided she liked him even better because he wasn't one of those people that had to fill all the blank times with words.

She wasn't quite ready to face the other part of what she knew was coming, so she asked him, "I can't remember what your Christian name is. What's Ellie short for?" He answered, "Ellie, it's short for Riley Elwood." "Well, no wonder they call you Ellie. Must have come from your mama's side. I haven't ever run into a Newman with that name. Till now." She paused a minute, then got up and stood behind the chair with her hands on the back of it. She tried to get prepared for the answer she was going to get, but she didn't know how to. So, she took another one of those ragged breaths that seem to take forever to fill the lungs.

"Ellie," she finally said, "you didn't nearly kill a horse and wear yourself out to find me to tell me my brother died a week ago. How's my mama?" He was looking sadly at her, and said, "Not good, ma'am. Daddy told me to tell you to get there as soon as you can cause he doesn't think she will live much longer. Her losing another one of her kids seems to have taken away her strength."

"Okay!" She said. "You go in the little room off the kitchen, it'll be quieter there. Stretch out on the cot and get some sleep." Ellie had thought she would break down and cry or something, but she wasn't showing any emotion he could see. He said, "Oh, I don't need to, Ma'am." And before he could say more, Sally snapped, "Just do what

I say. We're going to ride straight through, but I've got a few things to see to first." He said, "Yes, Ma'am," and went into the room, laid down on the cot, and although he was the last one that would have thought he could have, he was almost instantly asleep.

Sally didn't look at Juan or Rosy, but spoke to the room, "I need a few minutes." She walked out to the corral and when her mare came over to her, she leaned on her and wept. She stayed that way for a few minutes, but two other horses were trying to get her attention, and the mare was aggravated with them and beginning to move around. She patted the mare, rubbed the noses of both other horses and then ignored them all.

She saw Juan and Manuel unloading the fencing material from the wagon and she walked over to where they were. She valued both these men and was very grateful to them, especially this evening. She would hate to be facing all this alone. "I'll get my things together to be taken in the wagon. Send two men with it, and start them out early in the morning. I'll try to get a few hours sleep, and then the boy and I'll head out around midnight,"

Sally told Juan. She anticipated his concern, and continued. "The road is good enough for the first miles so traveling at night won't be a problem. By the time we have to be on the watch, it'll be daylight." There were places to stop for fresh horses if they needed to, but they would each take a spare with them for trading off on. It would slow them down some, but would pay off in the long run. Juan said, "I'll go with you." She told him no. He bowed-up and started to insist, and she quickly said, "Juan, I need you to take care of the stock cause its all I've got now. And I have no idea when I'll get back home. Besides, remember I'm heading north, not south. I promised you I wouldn't go south again without taking plenty of protection with me, and I've kept my promise." This was not a situation that was going to be especially dangerous. He began to relax a little, so she knew he agreed.

Sally went back to the house and joined Rosy in the kitchen. Rosy handed her a cup of coffee and said, "I've fixed some food for you and the boy to take." "Thanks" said Sally, "I appreciate that very much. I don't want to stop more than we have to. It's a three-day ride but we're going to make it in less time than that."

She started for the room she stayed in to get some things, then stopped and said out-loud. "Oh hell, I've forgotten Alfred." Rosy said from the kitchen doorway, "Can I do something?" Sally answered her, "No. Thanks. Juan will be back to the house in a bit to help load the wagon, and I'll tell him to send one of my hands to Alfred's place with word about his gramma and my intentions. I hate to ride right past his house, but it will take him awhile to arrange things, and I don't want to be held up. He'll understand." She didn't want to use any time not totally necessary. She might not have time to get there as it is, and she wanted to be able to be with Mama before she died. Alfred had always been especially fond of his Gramma Rachel, so if he could get away to join them, he would.

Sally had all kinds of things made and half-made for Christmas presents. Just in case she didn't get home before Christmas, she tossed all the things she was working on in sacks and a box or two to send in the wagon. She would have plenty of time to work on them while she was at Andrew's. She could always send someone to the ranch to get the other things she was leaving, if she needed too. Rosy would know what to send. Sally also had a number of things she had been planning on taking to Alfred's bunch and Andrew's family when she went, so she added them to the things to be loaded in the wagon. She was always collecting things here and there, and had jars of jellies and other things she and Rosy had put up, to take along on her next visit. She liked doing things for people, especially for Andrew's wife, Molly, because she was so good to Mama.

Juan had come into the front room to talk to her while she got the last of her things together. She made one last look around and reminded Juan of a few things. He already had one of the men headed for Alfred's place, and others loading and getting the wagon ready to go. Sally had known while she was getting things together that she was not going to be able to sleep, even though that was the sensible thing to do. She could tell by the way Juan and Rosy were getting things done, that they knew she wouldn't wait, and would leave right away. So, she went in, shook Ellie, and said, "Can you ride some more, or would you rather sleep awhile and start out in the morning?" His answer was, "Aunt Sally, I feel great, and I wanna go with you." Okay, they would head out now. They could stop anytime they got really tired and catch a short rest. Besides, even after him just riding for three days, she knew it would be her that needed the rest before he did. It was nearly disgusting to be that young.

Juan and Ellie followed her outside and had to move to keep up with her as she headed for the corral. While Juan helped Ellie pick out a fresh horse, Sally whistled to the little paint she liked to ride when a trip would be long but not necessarily fast. The paint had great endurance. She had always saddled her own horse, so she was doing that now, while running over in her mind all the other things she should be thinking about. Juan had been with her for over fifteen years, and after Carlos died, he had been like her right hand. He was about ten years her senior, and not as fast as he once was, but she could trust him with her life, and had many times. He was her foreman and her best friend, and she could depend on him to take care of her stock and equipment as well as she would. She knew all this worry and activity was what she wanted, because once she got on her horse and started for Andrew's, she would have too much time to think. When her mama was gone, a link in life would go, and it was a strange discomforting thought.

Juan asked her what other horse she wanted to take as a spare. She wished she hadn't ridden the roan today, so she could have taken him, but too late for that. She said, "I'll take the black mare. She needs some work, she's getting fat." The three of them led the two saddled horses, and the two spares back up to the house, tied them at the hitch next to the wagon, and went back inside. Sally went to her room and got a heavier coat to take along just in case. You couldn't trust the weather at this time of year. When she came back into the living room, Rosy walked over and gave her a big hug, and told her, "Tell your mother hello for me." Mama had stayed here with Sally for a while last year, and Rosy had treated her like a queen. Mama and Rosy had both enjoyed it. "I'll tell her," Sally said. Rosy had tears in her eyes, wiped them away with her apron, and got flour on her face. It made Ellie laugh, and all of a sudden all four of them laughed. Sally had noticed so many times before, that when you were hurting the worst, the strangest little things could make you laugh. Juan and Ellie picked up the last things Sally had ready, Sally got her Winchester, and they all walked out on the porch.

Sally had about eight men working for her at this time and about half of them had their wives and kids with them while they stayed at the old ranch. Now all the men and the wives and some of the older kids were standing out in the front yard. The men all had their hats in their hands and were looking uncomfortable. Sally noticed Pete's wife, Mary, was crying. Mary had lost her mother not long ago, and the loss was too recent. Sally smiled at her to show her she understood.

Sally was well-known for barking orders right and left, and at those times everyone and everything came to a standstill to see what she wanted done. There wasn't a hand that had ever worked for Sally that didn't know what her displeasure meant. She could be as evil-tempered, and dangerous as a lightning and thunder storm if aroused, but was fair and loyal, and could be downright generous if she thought you deserved it. Her hands all knew which way they preferred her to be, thus they listened, and reacted as quickly as possible. Most of these men had been with her a lot of years, and knew and respected her.

As Sally stood there trying very hard to keep her composure, and knowing she wouldn't be able to for long, she tried to think of what to say. But she couldn't handle all these heavy feelings inside herself or from these people in the yard, so instead of saying anything at all, she quickly walked over, put her gun in the scabbard, got on her horse, and just nodded at them. Juan did something he rarely did. He put his hand on her leg, just above the boot, and left it there only a second or two, and very quietly said, "Viya con Dios, picita Mustanya! [Look Up.] Sally knew the love that was in that touch, and those words. If she had a father figure in her life, it was this man. She looked at him and hoped he knew how she felt. She should tell him but it would jut embarrass both of them. Besides, he knew. He handed her the lead rope of the mare and she tied it to a strap at the rear of the saddle. Sally reached down, touched Juan on the shoulder, then turned and rode out of the yard. Ellie, with his extra horse, was right behind her.

After going through the gate, they rode at a lope for about thirty minutes and neither one said a word. Sally knew horses and traveling long distances about as well as anyone. She knew that by trading mounts every two or so hours, the horses would do well for days. She also knew if they allowed some slow periods periodically it would help the horses and the riders. So, even though she didn't want to waste any time, she slowed her horse to a walk, and Ellie rode up beside her on her left side. She turned to look at him. He rode a horse well. His daddy said he was a natural and was making a good hand at breaking and training horses. He was so young, he would improve more as he got older, and just might make a fine horseman.

"How old are you?" she asked him. "I turned thirteen in September," he said. She mused aloud, "That's about the age I was when my daddy died." Ellie waited a few minutes but she didn't say anything else, so he said, "Gramma has been talking a lot about Granddad lately. My daddy was only a few months old then, so didn't ever know him. What was he like?" Sally thought about her daddy, mama, grandparents, uncles and their families during those early days. She realized all those early memories were about being surrounded by lots of people that loved her. In her line of work, riding a horse, or sitting and driving a wagon, its mostly just you and your thinking. Sally had long ago learned to push most memories back into a corner and not be forever dredging things up. But, to be honest, she realized she would like to tell this young man about their family.

She finally looked over at him again, and said, "You know, Ellie, it seems like a dozen lifetimes ago since that time." She was quiet for another moment or two, then started telling him about when the Newmans and Rabbs first came to Texas.

They rode hard, rested little, and made it to Andrew's house in just over two long hard days. The closer they had gotten the harder Sally had pushed the horses, but once they were in sight of the house, she slowed down to a walk. Ellie looked at her like he didn't understand, but he fell in beside her at her pace. Now that she was so close, the dread of what might be facing her was almost overpowering. She could see that half the world seemed to be on Andrew's front porch watching them ride up. And then the keen eyesight she had been blessed with paid off. She saw Mama's old rocking chair on the porch, and Mama was in it!

Sally rode right up to the porch, got off her horse, and handed the reins to Ellie. With barely a glance at the others, she walked to the rocking chair, got down on her knees and put her head in her mama's lap. Rachel put one hand on Sally's shoulder and with the other she stroked her hair. Sally finally raised her head and tearfully said, "Hi, Mama", and was answered with a kiss on the cheek and a "Hello, Sally girl."

Dear God! I love this woman, Sally thought, and she noticed how frail and weak Mama was. But, like she had always done, Rachel gathered her strength and turned the attention from herself. She told Sally, "Get up and tell your sister and brothers hello."

Sally did as she was told and was mobbed by her family. Elizabeth grabbed her and held her tight for a minute, then Sally shook hands with Captain Joe. Andrew and Molly were standing to her other side and she turned and gave them both a hug. She looked around and took a few steps to where William was standing. She hugged his wife, Martha, then hugged William, stepped back a bit and said, "William, you're getting old!"

"Well, so I am. But what about you, Sally?"

"Well, hell, brother. I've been old all my life!" They all laughed. Then she was introduced and reintroduced to all the nieces and nephews and their spouses and kids, and Sally laughed again and said, "There ain't no way I'm going to remember all these names, you know."

Elizabeth laughed with her and said, "Well, it's your own fault for not visiting often enough."

They finished supper and sat on the porch while two of the younger women sat in Rachel's room. For awhile someone played a guitar softly and it was a good night to visit.

Then. one by one the family started going to bed, until only Sally, Elizabeth, Andrew, and William were still there. They had been quiet for a few minutes, and Sally said, "Why don't you all get some sleep. I'm not too tired so I'll sit in Mama's room tonight."

William said, "Get me up about midnight and I'll sit the rest of the night. You don't need to stay up all night."

Andrew said to him, "Get me up too and I'll sit with you."

They all said goodnight and the two men went inside. Elizabeth looked at Sally and said, "You know she can't make it much longer. I'll sit up with you." Sally had known she would and that's how she wanted it, so the two of them went to Mama's room and told the girls to go to bed.

Sally and Elizabeth stood by the bed a minute, smoothed the cover that was already totally smooth, both gave Rachel a kiss on the cheek, and then neither one remarked on the fact that during all that Rachel had never stirred.

Elizabeth turned the table lamp down low, and the two of them moved two of the chairs away from the bed so that they could talk. They talked quietly off and on until suddenly they got quiet. It was around two o'clock and they seemed to feel rather than hear Rachel's last breaths. They got up quickly, went over and looked at her and knew. Sally put her arms around Elizabeth and they cried together for a minute.

Then Sally said she would wake William and Elizabeth went to wake Andrew. There were people bedded down everywhere, but Sally made her way to where William and Martha were. She put her hand on his shoulder and he was immediately awake. She didn't know if he could tell the difference in her or what, but instead of asking if it was midnight, he asked, "Is she gone?" She told him yes, then went back to Mama's room. Elizabeth was waiting at the door and the two of them went in together but waited just inside the door. William and Andrew came in just a few minutes and both went over to Rachel's bed. After another minute or so, the girls joined their brothers and the four got down on their knees beside their mama and told her goodbye.

Other people were coming into the room so the four of them moved to one side. William reached and gave Elizabeth a hug and then hugged Sally. Andrew hugged each of them too and then the two brothers gave each other a hug. By then their wives had joined William and Andrew, and Capt. Joe was holding Elizabeth. Sally could hear people in the kitchen and could smell the coffee. She took one last look at Rachel and walked out to the porch. She suddenly realized it was a time for a celebration. How else could you face the loss without thinking about what a fantastic woman their mother had been?

They went back to William's house in Riddleville for the night of the funeral, and Sally would leave early the next morning That morning, there are people standing around everywhere. How am I ever going to tell them goodbye?, she thought. I hate goodbyes. She had gotten everything ready to go the night before so that all she would have to do was saddle her horse. At Elizabeth's urging she had one last cup of coffee with them, then said she had to go get her horse. Andrew said he didn't think she had to worry about that and as they walked out on the front porch she saw why. Ellie, with a big grin on his face, was in the front yard with his horse and hers already saddled and with the two extra horses ready to go. She would have to tell him later that she didn't allow anyone to saddle her horse for her, but maybe she wouldn't do that for a while. Right now, she was just very thankful that she could leave and not drag this out any more than necessary.

She said a fast goodbye to everyone except for her sister and brothers. She gave Andrew a long hug, then Elizabeth. After she hugged William, she touched him lightly on the cheek and said, "I love you, old brother."

Ellie has already saddled her horse. Sally got on, looked around to see that everything was in order, then rode out of the yard and headed south. She rode slowly for awhile; it was a beautiful day and she felt good. As she so often did, she thought of Nancy, Alfred, and Mama.

She didn't hear the shot or even feel the bullet when it hit. And she would've been more than surprised to know that the woman named Sally Scull rode right on into Texas history!

AFTERWORD

Nothing is known for sure about Sally's demise. Records show that she still alive and active as of 1869. Some folks claim that she was shot from horseback because she always carried gold coins. Others claim she moved to New Mexico to join relatives who lived near Silver City.

WORKS CITED

Atwood, E. Bagby. 1962. *The Regional Vocabulary of Texas*. Austin: University of Texas Press.
Baker, D. W. C. 1991. *A Texas Scrap Book*. Austin: Texas State Historical Association.
Centennial History of Madison County, Illinois and Its People 1812 to 1912, Volume 1, ed. W. T. Norton. 1912. The Lewis Publishing Co., Chicago and New York.
Chronicles of Oklahoma. 1926, published by The Oklahoma Historical Society, Oklahoma City.
Fehrenbach, T. R. 1968. *Lone Star: A History of Texas and the Texans*. New York: Wings Books.
Gracy, David B. II. 1987. *Moses Austin: His Life*. San Antonio: Trinity University Press.
Keating, Bern. 1975. *An Illustrative History of The Texas Rangers*. Chicago: Rand McNally & Company.
Newman, Coleman C., and Annabel Newman. 1989. *From The Monongahela To the Colorado*. Granbury, Texas. Coleman C. Newman.
Rabb, Mary Crownover. 1962. *Travels and Adventures in Texas in the 1820's. Being the Reminiscences of Mary Crownover Rabb*. Waco, Texas: W. M. Morrison.
Ray, Worth S. 1970. *Austin Colony Pioneers*. Austin, Texas: The Pemerton Press.

Sinks, Julia Lee. 1975. *Chronicles of Fayette: The Reminiscences of Julia Lee Sinks.* Edited by Walter P. Freytag. La Grange, Texas: Bicentennial Commission.

Wegenhoft. Victor C. 1995. *The Rabb Odyssey.* Manuscript, pp. 85.

Weynd, Leonie Rummel, and Houston Wade. 1936. *An Early History of Fayette County.* Burnet, Texas: Eakin Press.

www.ingramcontent.com/pod-product-compliance
Lightning Source LLC
LaVergne TN
LVHW091700070526
838199LV00050B/2226